GMAT®

7th Edition with Online Practice

by Lisa Zimmer Hatch, MA, and Scott A. Hatch, JD

GMAT® For Dummies®, 7th Edition with Online Practice

Published by: **John Wiley & Sons, Inc.,** 111 River Street, Hoboken, NJ 07030-5774, www.wiley.com

Copyright © 2018 by John Wiley & Sons, Inc., Hoboken, New Jersey

Published simultaneously in Canada

For general information on our other products and services, please contact our Customer Care Department within the U.S. at 877-762-2974, outside the U.S. at 317-572-3993, or fax 317-572-4002. For technical support, please visit https://hub.wiley.com/community/support/dummies.

Wiley publishes in a variety of print and electronic formats and by print-on-demand. Some material included with standard print versions of this book may not be included in e-books or in print-on-demand. If this book refers to media such as a CD or DVD that is not included in the version you purchased, you may download this material at http://booksupport.wiley.com. For more information about Wiley products, visit www.wiley.com.

Library of Congress Control Number: 2017952681

ISBN 978-1-119-37414-5 (pbk); ISBN 978-1-119-37410-7 (ebk); ISBN 978-1-119-37408-4 (ebk)

Manufactured in the United States of America

10 9 8 7 6 5 4 3 2 1

Contents at a Glance

Table of Contents

Introduction

You're merrily skimming through the admissions requirements for your favorite MBA programs when all of a sudden, you're dealt a shocking blow. Your absolute top choice program — you'll die if you don't get in — requires that you take the Graduate Management Admission Test (GMAT). And you thought your days of speed-reading passages and solving for x were over.

Many MBA programs include the GMAT as an admissions requirement, so you'll be in good company. But how do you prepare for such a comprehensive test? What are you going to do? Get out your spiral notebooks from undergraduate courses and sift through years' worth of doodles? Many years may have gone by since you encountered a geometry problem, and we bet your grammar skills have gotten a little rusty since English 101.

Clearly, you need a readable, concisely structured resource. Well, you've come to the right place. *GMAT For Dummies*, 7th Edition with Online Practice, puts at your fingertips everything you need to know to conquer the GMAT. We give you complete math and grammar reviews and provide insights into how to avoid the pitfalls that the GMAT creators want you to fall into. We also try to make this book as enjoyable as a book that devotes itself to setting up equations and critiquing arguments can be.

About This Book

We suspect that you aren't eagerly anticipating sitting through the GMAT, and you're probably not looking forward to studying for it, either. Therefore, we've attempted to make the study process as painless as possible by giving you clearly written advice in a casual tone. We realize you have a bunch of things you'd rather be doing, so we've broken down the information into easily digested bites. If you have an extra hour before work or Pilates class, you can devour a chapter or even a particular section within a chapter. (If these eating metaphors are making you hungry, feel free to take a snack break.)

In this book, you can find

>> Plenty of sample questions so you can see just how the GMAT tests a particular concept. Our sample questions read like the actual test questions, so you can get comfortable with the way the GMAT phrases questions and expresses answer choices.

>> Detailed explanations of the strategies for mastering all four sections of the GMAT. Enjoy a grammar review for the verbal-reasoning section, an extensive math lesson to help you with the quantitative-reasoning section, a summary of good writing practices for the analytical writing assessment, and a how-to on reading all kinds of charts and graphs for the integrated-reasoning section.

>> Six practice tests. One appears in this book in Chapter 21, and you'll find that one plus five others online. Ultimately, the best way to prepare for any standardized test is to practice on lots of test questions, and this book, along with the accompanying online test bank, has more than 600 of them.

» Time-tested techniques for improving your score. We show you how to quickly eliminate incorrect answer choices and make educated guesses.

» Tips on how to manage your time wisely.

» Suggestions for creating a relaxation routine to employ if you start to panic during the test.

We've included all kinds of information to help you do your best on the GMAT!

You should find this book easily accessible, but a few things may require explanation. A few of the chapters may contain sidebars (a paragraph or two in a shaded box) with quirky bits of information that we think may interest you but aren't essential to your performance on the GMAT. If you're trying to save time, you can skip the sidebars.

Foolish Assumptions

Although we guess it's possible that you picked up this book just because you have an insatiable love for math, grammar, and argument analysis, we're betting it's more likely that you're reading this book particularly because you've been told you need to take the GMAT. (We have been praised for our startling ability to recognize the obvious!) And because we're pretty astute, we've figured that this means that you intend to apply to MBA programs and probably are considering working toward a masters of business administration.

Generally, MBA programs are pretty selective, so we're thinking that you're a pretty motivated student. Some of you are fresh out of college and may have more recent experience with math and grammar. Others of you probably haven't stepped into a classroom in over a decade but possess work skills and life experience that will help you maximize your GMAT score despite the time that's passed since college.

If math and grammar are fresh in your mind and you just need to know what to expect when you arrive at the test site, this book has that information for you. If you've been out of school for a while, this book provides you with all the basics as well as advanced concepts to give you everything you need to know to excel on the GMAT.

Icons Used in This Book

One exciting feature of this book is the icons that highlight especially significant portions of the text. These little pictures in the margins alert you to areas where you should pay particularly close attention.

This icon highlights really important information that you should remember even after you close the book.

REMEMBER

Throughout the book, we give you insights into how you can enhance your performance on the GMAT. The tips give you juicy timesavers and point out especially relevant concepts to keep in mind for the test.

TIP

WARNING

Your world won't fall apart if you ignore our warnings, but your score may suffer. Heed these cautionary pointers to avoid making careless mistakes that can cost you points.

EXAMPLE

Whenever you see this icon in the text, you know you're going to get to practice the particular area of instruction covered in that section with a question like one you may see on the test. Our examples include detailed explanations of how to most efficiently answer GMAT questions and avoid common pitfalls.

Beyond the Book

Be sure to check out the free Cheat Sheet for a handy guide that covers tips and tricks for answering questions in each section of the GMAT. To get this Cheat Sheet, simply go to www.dummies.com and enter "GMAT For Dummies Cheat Sheet" in the Search box.

The online practice that comes free with this book contains six full-length practice tests, so that you can really hone your GMAT skills! To gain access to the online practice, all you have to do is register. Just follow these simple steps:

1. **Find your PIN access code located on the inside front cover of this book.**
2. **Go to Dummies.com and click** Activate Now.
3. **Find your product (*GMAT For Dummies*, 7th Edition with Online Practice) and then follow the on-screen prompts to activate your PIN.**

Now you're ready to go! You can go back to the program at testbanks.wiley.com as often as you want — simply log on with the username and password you created during your initial login. No need to enter the access code a second time.

Tip: If you have trouble with your PIN or can't find it, contact Wiley Product Technical Support at 877-762-2974 or go to support.wiley.com.

Where to Go from Here

We know that everyone who uses this book has different strengths and weaknesses, so this book is designed for you to read in the way that best suits you. If you're a math whiz and need to brush up only on your verbal skills, you can skim Part 4 and focus on Parts 1, 2, and 3. If you've been writing proposals every day for the last ten years, you can probably scan Part 3 and focus your attention on the math review in Part 4. Because the integrated-reasoning section differs so significantly from other standardized test questions, you'll benefit from reading Part 5 regardless of your math prowess or verbal genius.

We suggest that you take a more thorough approach, however. Familiarize yourself with the general test-taking process in the first two chapters and then go through the complete GMAT review, starting with the verbal section and working your way through the analytical-writing, math, and integrated-reasoning sections. You can skim through information that you know more about by just reading the Tips and Warnings and working through the examples in those sections.

Some of our students like to take a diagnostic test before they study. This is a fancy way of saying that they take one of the full-length practice tests before they read the rest of the book. Taking a preview test shows you which questions you seem to cruise through and which areas need more work. After you've taken a practice exam, you can focus your study time on the question types that gave you the most trouble during the exam. Then, when you've finished reading through the rest of the book (Parts 1, 2, 3, 4, and 5), you can take another practice test and compare your score to the one you got on the first test. This way, you can see just how much you improve with practice.

This book provides you with a bunch of practice tests, but you can never get enough practice. So, if after taking all the practice tests provided at dummies.com, you still crave more, visit the official GMAT website at www.mba.com and download the free GMATPrep software there. This software mimics the computerized format of the test and gives you practice on the types of mouse-clicking and eye-straining skills you need to succeed on the exam. That way, you can experience using the same software you'll see on the exam.

We're confident that if you devote a few hours a week for at least six weeks to practicing the skills and tips we provide for you in this book, you'll do the best you can when you sit in front of that computer on GMAT test day. We wish you our best for your ultimate GMAT score!

1

Getting Started with the GMAT

IN THIS PART . . .

Familiarize yourself with the format of the test.

Find out how to maximize your score by organizing your time and streamlining your approach.

Discover what you can and should do to gain admission to the business school of your choice.

IN THIS CHAPTER

» Finding out how MBA programs use your GMAT score

» Deciding when to take the GMAT and knowing what to bring

» Figuring out the format of the GMAT

» Understanding how the GMAT is scored

» Considering whether you should retake the GMAT

Chapter **1**

Getting the Lowdown on the GMAT

Congratulations on deciding to take a significant step in your business career! More than 100 countries offer the Graduate Management Admission Test (GMAT), and according to the Graduate Management Admission Council, 2,100 universities and organizations in 114 countries use GMAT to make admissions decisions. That said, you're probably not taking the GMAT because you want to. In fact, you may not be looking forward to the experience at all!

The GMAT need not be a daunting ordeal. A little knowledge can help calm your nerves, so this chapter shows you how admissions programs use your test score and addresses the concerns you may have about the GMAT's format and testing and scoring procedures.

Knowing Why the GMAT Is Important

If you're reading this book, you're probably thinking about applying to an MBA program. And if you're applying to an MBA program, you probably need to take the GMAT. Many MBA programs require that you submit a GMAT score for the admissions process. (Some may require other tests or no test at all, so make sure you check each program's admissions checklist.)

Your GMAT score gives the admissions committee another tool to use to assess your skills and compare you with other applicants. But if you're seeking a career in business, you're probably resigned to being continually assessed and compared. The GMAT doesn't attempt to evaluate any particular subject area that you may have studied, but instead it gives admissions officers a reliable idea of how you'll likely perform in the classes that make up a graduate business curriculum. Although the GMAT doesn't rate your experience or motivation, it does provide an estimate of your academic preparation for graduate business studies.

REMEMBER

Not every MBA applicant has the same undergraduate experience, but most applicants take a standardized test. Other admissions factors, like college grades, work experience, the admissions essay or essays, and a personal interview are important, but the GMAT is an admissions tool that admissions committees can use to directly compare you with other applicants.

The most selective schools primarily admit candidates with solid GMAT scores, and good scores will certainly strengthen your application to any program, but you shouldn't feel discouraged if your practice tests don't put you in the 90th percentile. Very few students achieve anything near a perfect score on the GMAT. Even if you don't score as high as you want to, you undoubtedly have other strengths in your admissions profile, such as work experience, leadership ability, good college grades, motivation, and people skills. You may want to contact the admissions offices of the schools you're interested in to see how much they emphasize the GMAT. That said, the GMAT is a very important factor in admissions, and because you're required to take the test anyway, you should do everything you can to perform your best!

Timing It Perfectly: When to Take the GMAT (And What to Bring)

Which MBA programs to apply to isn't the only decision you have to make. After you've figured out where you want to go, you have to make plans for the GMAT. You need to determine the best time to take the test and what to bring with you when you do. The following sections can help you out.

When to register for and take the GMAT

When is the best time to take the GMAT? With the computerized testing procedures, this question has become more interesting than it was in the days of paper-based tests. When the exam was a paper-and-pencil format with a test booklet and an answer sheet full of bubbles, you had a limited choice of possible test dates — about one every two months. Now you've got much more flexibility when choosing the date and time for taking the test. You can pick just about any time to sit down and click answer choices with your mouse.

Registering when you're ready

The first step in the GMAT registration process is scheduling an appointment, but don't put off making this appointment the way you'd put off calling the dentist (even though you'd probably like to avoid both!). Depending on the time of year, appointment times can go quickly. Usually, you have to wait at least a month for an open time. To determine what's available, you can go to the official GMAT website at www.mba.com. From there, you can choose a testing location and find out what dates and times are available at that location. When you find a date and time you like, you can register online, over the phone, or by mail or fax.

The best time to take the GMAT is after you've had about four to six weeks of quality study time and during a period when you don't have a lot of other things going on to distract you. Of course, if your MBA program application is due in four weeks, put this book down and schedule an appointment right away! Be sure to come right back, though. You need to start studying — and now! If you have more flexibility, you should still plan to take the GMAT as soon as you think you've studied sufficiently. All the following circumstances warrant taking the GMAT as soon as you can:

>> **You want to start your MBA program right away.** If you're confident that you'd like to begin business school within the next few semesters, you should consider taking the GMAT in the

near future. After you know your score, you'll be better able to narrow down the business schools you want to apply to. Then you can focus on the other parts of your application, and you won't have to worry about having an application due in four weeks and no GMAT score.

>> **You're considering attending business school.** Maybe you don't know whether you want to pursue an MBA. Even so, now's a good time to take the GMAT. Your GMAT score may help you decide that you have the skills to succeed academically in graduate business school. You may think that you don't have what it takes, but your performance on the GMAT may surprise you! If you do decide to apply to an MBA program, you'll already have one key component of the application under wraps.

>> **You're about to earn (or have just earned) your bachelor's degree.** If you're nearing graduation or have just graduated from college and you think you may want to get an MBA, it's better to take the GMAT now than wait until later. You're used to studying. You're used to tests. And math and grammar concepts are probably as fresh on your mind as they'll ever be.

You don't have to start an MBA program right away. Your GMAT scores are generally valid for up to five years, so you can take the test now and take advantage of your current skills as a student to get you into a great graduate program later.

Giving yourself about four to six weeks to study provides you with enough time to master the GMAT concepts but not so much time that you forget what you've studied by the time you sit for the test.

Scheduling for success

Whenever you register, you want to consider your own schedule when picking a test date and time. Take advantage of the flexibility allowed by the computer format. The GMAT is no longer just an 8 a.m. Saturday morning option. You can take the test every day of the week except Sunday, and, depending on the test center, you may be able to start at a variety of times. Many centers offer 8 a.m. testing times, but some have other options, even 6:30 at night — great for those night owls who consider 8 a.m. a good bedtime rather than a good exam time. You have a little bit of control over making the test fit into your life instead of having to make your life fit the test!

If you're not a morning person, don't schedule an early test if you can help it. If you're better able to handle a nonstop, two-and-a-half-hour barrage of questions — not to mention the analytical essay — after the sun hits its highest point in the sky, schedule your test for the afternoon or evening. By choosing the time that works for you, you'll be able to comfortably approach the test instead of worrying whether you set your alarm. We're guessing that you have enough to worry about in life as it is without the added stress of an inconvenient test time.

Check the GMAT website for the available testing times at the test centers near you. Then study for the test at the different available times of the day to see when you're at your best. Schedule your test session for that time. Even if you have to take a few hours away from work or classes, being able to take the test at a time that's best for you is worth it. And you may end up picking a test center based on its available times rather than its proximity to you.

While you're thinking about the time that's best for the test, you should think about days of the week as well. For some people, Saturday may be a good day for a test. For others, the weekend is the wrong time for that type of concentrated academic activity. If you're used to taking the weekends off, scheduling the test during the week may make more sense for you.

Choosing the time and day to take the GMAT is primarily up to you. Be honest with yourself about your habits, preferences, and schedule, and pick a time and day when you'll excel.

Things to take to the GMAT (and things to leave at home)

The most important thing you can bring to the GMAT is a positive attitude and a willingness to succeed. However, if you forget your admission voucher or your photo ID, you won't get the chance to apply those qualities! In addition to the voucher and ID, you may bring a list of five schools where you'd like to have your scores sent. You can send your scores to up to five schools for free if you select those schools when entering your pretest information at the test site. (You can skip this step at the testing center if you provide your school information when you register online.) You can, of course, list fewer than five schools, but if you decide to send your scores to additional schools later, you'll have to pay. If you can come up with five schools you'd like to apply to, you may as well send your scores for free.

TIP

Because you can take two optional eight-minute breaks, we recommend you bring along a quick snack, like a granola bar, and perhaps a bottle of water. You can't take food or drink with you to the testing area, but you're given a little locker that you can access during a break.

That's really all you need to bring. You can't use a calculator, and the test center provides a booklet of five noteboards and a special black pen (but no eraser), which you're required to use instead of pencil and paper. You can ask for another booklet if you fill yours up.

Forming First Impressions: The Format of the GMAT

The GMAT is a standardized test, and by now in your academic career, you're probably familiar with what that means: lots of questions to answer in a short period of time, no way to cram for or memorize answers, and very little chance of scoring 100 percent. The skills tested on the GMAT are those that leading business schools have decided are important for MBA students: analytical writing, integrated reasoning, quantitative reasoning, and verbal reasoning.

The GMAT allows you to choose the order in which you take the four sections:

>> The original order of analytical writing assessment, integrated reasoning, quantitative, and verbal

>> Quantitative, verbal, analytical writing assessment, and integrated reasoning

>> Verbal, quantitative, analytical writing assessment, and integrated reasoning

Pick the order that's most comfortable for you. If you're unsure, we suggest leaving the less important writing and integrated reasoning sections for the end when you're more fatigued. Whether you take the quantitative or verbal first depends on which section is easier for you. You may want to lead with your strength or get the section you like least out of the way in the beginning.

Getting familiar with what the GMAT tests

Standardized tests are supposed to test your academic potential, not your knowledge of specific subjects. The GMAT focuses on the areas that admissions committees have found to be relevant to MBA programs. The sections that follow are an introduction to the four GMAT sections. We devote the majority of the rest of this book to telling you exactly how to approach each one.

Demonstrating your writing ability

You type an original analytical writing sample during the GMAT. The test gives you 30 minutes to compose and type an essay that analyzes an argument. You're expected to write this essay in standard written English. Although you won't know exactly the nature of the argument you'll get on test day, examining previous essay prompts gives you adequate preparation for the type of task you're bound to see.

REMEMBER

The readers of your GMAT essay score you based on the overall quality of your ideas and your ability to organize, develop, express, and support those ideas.

Integrating your reasoning skills

The second GMAT section is a 30-minute integrated-reasoning test that examines your ability to read and evaluate charts, graphs, and other forms of presenting data. You'll examine a variety of data representation and answer 12 questions based on the information.

The GMAT categorizes the four basic question types in this section as graphics interpretation, two-part analysis, table analysis, and multi-source reasoning. Graphics interpretation and table analysis questions are self-explanatory: You interpret graphs and analyze tables — simple enough, right? The two-part analysis questions present a problem and related data provided in two columns. You choose a piece of information from each column to solve the problem. Multi-source reasoning questions provide you with a bunch of information from which you have to decide what piece or pieces of data actually give you what you need to know to solve the problem.

Quizzing your quantitative skills

The quantitative section is pretty similar to most standardized math sections except that it presents you with a different question format and tests your knowledge of statistics and probability. In the 37-question section, the GMAT tests your knowledge of arithmetic, algebra, geometry, and data interpretation with standard problem-solving questions. You'll have to solve problems and choose the correct answer from five possible choices.

Additionally, GMAT data sufficiency questions present you with two statements and ask you to decide whether the problem can be solved by using the information provided by the first statement only, the second statement only, both statements, or neither statement. We show you exactly how to tackle these unusual math questions in Chapter 15.

Validating your verbal skills

The GMAT verbal section consists of 41 questions of three general types: the ubiquitous reading-comprehension problems, sentence-correction questions, and critical-reasoning questions. Reading comprehension requires you to answer questions about written passages on a number of different subjects. Sentence-correction questions test your ability to spot and correct writing errors. Critical-reasoning questions require you to analyze logical arguments and understand how to strengthen or weaken those arguments.

Understanding the computerized format

The quantitative-reasoning and verbal-reasoning sections on the computerized GMAT can be taken only in *computer-adaptive test* (CAT) format. The CAT adapts to your ability level by presenting you with questions of various difficulty, depending on how you answer previous questions. If you're answering many questions correctly, the computer gives you harder questions as it seeks to find the limits of your impressive intellect. If you're having a tough day and many of your answers are wrong, the computer will present you with easier questions as it seeks to find the correct level of difficulty for you.

With the CAT format, your score isn't based solely on how many questions you get right and wrong but rather on the average difficulty of the questions you answer correctly. Theoretically, you could miss several questions and still get a very high score, so long as the questions you missed were among the most difficult available in the bank of questions. At the end of each section, the computer scores you based on your level of ability.

Answering in an orderly fashion

With the CAT format, the question order in the verbal and quantitative sections is different from the order on paper exams that have a test booklet and answer sheet. On the CAT, the first ten questions of the test are preselected for you, and the order of subsequent questions depends on how well you've answered the previous questions. So if you do well on the first ten questions, Question 11 will reflect your success by being more challenging. If you do poorly on the initial questions, you'll get an easier Question 11. The program continues to take all previous questions into account as it feeds you question after question.

WARNING

Perhaps the most important difference of the CAT format is that because each question is based on your answers to previous questions, you can't go back to any question. You must answer each question as it comes. After you confirm your answer, it's final. If you realize three questions later that you made a mistake, try not to worry about it. After all, your score is based on not only your number of right and wrong answers but also the difficulty of the questions.

We're guessing you've figured out that the analytical writing assessment isn't in CAT format because it's not a multiple-choice test. But you may not know that the integrated-reasoning section also isn't a CAT section. You receive questions in a preordained order and that order doesn't change based on your answer selections. Like the CAT sections, though, after you've submitted an answer to a question, you can't change your answer.

Observing time limits

Both the verbal and quantitative sections have a 75-minute time limit. Because the quantitative section has 37 questions, you have about two minutes to master each question. The verbal section has 41 questions, so you have a little less time to ponder those, about a minute and three-quarters per question. The integrated-reasoning section is shorter; you have 30 minutes to answer 12 questions, or about two and a half minutes per question. You don't have unlimited time in the analytical writing section, either; you have to write the essay within 30 minutes.

TIP

These time limits have important implications for your test strategy on the quantitative and verbal sections. As we discuss later in this chapter, your GMAT score for these two sections depends on the number of questions you're able to answer. If you run out of time and leave questions unanswered at the end of a section, you'll essentially reduce your score by the number of questions you don't answer. In Chapter 2, we present you with an efficient, workable strategy for managing your time and maximizing your score.

Honing your computer skills for the GMAT

Technically challenged, take heart! You need to have only minimal computer skills to take the computerized GMAT. In fact, the skills you need for the test are far less than those you'll need while pursuing an MBA! Because you have to type your essays, you need basic word-processing skills. For the multiple-choice sections, you need to know how to select answers by using either the mouse or the keyboard.

Knowing Where You Stand: Scoring Considerations

Okay, you know the GMAT's format and how many questions it has and so on. But what about what's really important to you, the crucial final score? Probably very few people take standardized tests for fun, so we give you the lowdown on scoring in the following sections.

How the GMAT testers figure your score

REMEMBER

Because the GMAT is a computer-adaptive test, your verbal and quantitative scores aren't based just on the number of questions you get right. The scores you earn are based on three factors:

>> **The difficulty of the questions you answer:** The questions become more difficult as you continue to answer correctly, so getting tough questions means you're doing well on the test.

>> **The number of questions you answer:** If you don't get to all the questions in the verbal and quantitative sections, your score is reduced by the proportion of questions you didn't answer. So if you fail to answer 5 of the 37 quantitative questions, for example, your raw score would be reduced by 13 percent: after converting the raw score to the scaled measure, this loss may decrease your percentile rank from the 90th percentile to the 75th percentile.

>> **The number of questions you answer correctly:** In addition to scoring based on how difficult the questions are, the GMAT score also reflects your ability to answer those questions correctly.

GMAT essay readers determine your analytical writing assessment (AWA) score. College and university faculty members from different disciplines read your response to the essay prompt. However, one of your readers may be an automated essay-scoring machine programmed to evaluate the important elements of your essay. Two independent readers separately score your writing assignment on a scale from 0 to 6, with 6 being the top score. Your final score is the average of the scores from each of the readers.

If the two readers assigned to your writing task give you scores that differ by more than one point, a third reader is assigned to adjudicate. For example, if one reader gives you a 6 and the other gives you a 4, a third reader will also review your essay.

Your integrated-reasoning score ranges in whole numbers from 1 to 8, with 8 being the highest. Scores of 1 and 2 are rare and unusually low, and very few GMAT-takers score as high as 7 or 8. Generally, if you receive a score of 4, 5, or 6, you've done a respectable job answering the integrated-reasoning questions.

How the GMAT testers report your score

Your final GMAT score consists of separate verbal-reasoning, quantitative-reasoning, integrated-reasoning, and analytical writing assessment scores and a combined verbal and quantitative score. When you're finished with the test — or when your time is up — the computer immediately calculates your verbal, quantitative, and integrated-reasoning scores and provides them to you in an unofficial score report. You'll have a separate scaled score from 0 to 60 for the verbal and quantitative sections. The two scores are added together and converted to a scaled score ranging between 200 and 800. The mean total score falls slightly above 500.

You won't see your analytical writing assessment scores immediately after the test. These scores are included in the official score report that's either mailed to you or made available online about 20 days after you take the exam. So although you'll be able to view your verbal, quantitative, integrated-reasoning, and total scores immediately after the test, you'll need to wait three weeks to see how well you did on the AWA section.

When you do get your official score, the AWA score appears as a number between 0 and 6. This number is a scaled score that's the average of the scores for all the readings of your response. The final score is rounded to the nearest half point, so a 4.8 average is reported as 5. The integrated-reasoning scaled score ranges between 1 and 8. Neither the AWA nor the integrated-reasoning score affect your total GMAT score in any way. Both scores are reported separately, and each MBA program decides how to use them in their admissions decisions.

Official scores, including the verbal-reasoning, quantitative-reasoning, total, integrated-reasoning, and AWA scores, are sent to the schools that you've requested receive them. The score reports they receive include all your scores, as well as a table showing the percentage of test-takers who scored below you. (For example, if your total score is 670, then about 89 percent of test-takers have a score lower than yours.) You don't have to pay for the five schools you select before you take the test to receive your scores, and for a fee, you can request your scores be sent to any other school at any time up to five years after the test.

Why you should (almost) never cancel your GMAT score

Immediately after you conclude the GMAT and before the computer displays your scores, you're given the option of canceling your scores. You may see this as a blessing if you've had a rough day at the computer. You may jump at the chance to get rid of all evidence of your verbal, quantitative, and writing struggles.

WARNING

Canceling your scores is almost always a bad idea for several reasons:

>> **People routinely overestimate or underestimate their performance on standardized tests.** The GMAT isn't a test on state capitals or chemical symbols, so knowing how well you did isn't always easy. As long as you answer most of the questions and are able to focus reasonably well during the test, you'll probably earn scores that aren't too different from the average scores you'd get if you took the test repeatedly. People who retake the GMAT and other standardized tests rarely see their scores change significantly unless they're initially unprepared to take the exam and later attempt it with significant preparation. You're reading this book, so you don't fall into that category of test-taker.

>> **You may not have time to reschedule.** It may take a while to reschedule the test. If your applications are due right away, you could miss an application deadline because you don't have GMAT scores to submit.

>> **You'll never know how you did.** If you cancel your scores, you'll never know how you did or what areas you need to work on to improve your score if you decide to retake the test later.

A few circumstances exist in which you should consider canceling your scores. These situations aren't based on your estimation of how you did, which may be inaccurate, but on extenuating factors:

>> **You're pretty darn ill during the test.** Waking up on test day with a fever of 101 degrees or getting sick during the test may warrant canceling a GMAT score.

>> **You were unable to concentrate during the test.** Unusual personal difficulties, like a death in the family or the demise of a close relationship, could distract you to the point where you freeze up in the middle of the exam.

>> **You left many questions unanswered.** If you forget the time-management techniques we discuss in Chapter 2 and you leave quite a few questions unanswered in the verbal and quantitative sections, you may consider canceling your scores.

Repeating the Process: Retaking the GMAT

Because most programs consider only your top scores, retaking the GMAT may be in your best interest if you aren't happy with your first score. The GMAT administrators let you take the test quite a few times if you want (that's pretty big of them, considering you have to pay for it every time). If you do retake the GMAT, make sure you take the process and test seriously. You should show score improvement. A college will be much more impressed with a rising score than a falling one.

WARNING

Many colleges may be turned off if they see that you've taken the GMAT more than two or three times. The key is to prepare to do your best on the first (or second) try.

REMEMBER

Official GMAT reports contain scores for every time you take the test. So if you take the GMAT twice, both scores appear on your report. It's up to the business program to decide how to use those scores. Some may take the higher score and some may take the average. Keep in mind that your new scores won't automatically be sent to the recipients of previous scores, so you'll need to reselect those programs when you retake the test.

IN THIS CHAPTER

» Checking out guessing strategies

» Managing your time like a pro

» Knowing how to recognize a wrong answer

» Avoiding worthless activities that minimize your score

» Quieting your nerves with tried-and-true relaxation techniques

Chapter 2

Maximizing Your Score on the GMAT

You enter the test center and stare down the computer. For the next three and a half hours, that machine is your adversary. The GMAT loaded on it is your nemesis. All you have to aid you in this showdown is a booklet of noteboards and your intellect. The questions come quickly, and your reward for answering a question correctly is another, usually more difficult question! Why did you give up your precious free time for this torture?

By the time you actually take the GMAT, you'll have already given up hours and hours of your free time studying for the test, researching business schools, and planning for the future. Those three and a half hours alone with a computer represent a rite of passage that you must complete to accomplish the goals you've set for yourself. And because the test is a necessary evil, you may as well get the highest score you're capable of achieving!

This chapter contains the techniques you need to apply to pull together a winning strategy for the GMAT. You already have the brains, and the test center provides the materials. In this chapter, we share with you the other tools you need to maximize your score.

Discovering Strategies for Successful Guessing

You may be surprised that we start this chapter by discussing guessing strategies. Your ideal GMAT test-day scenario probably involves knowing the answers to most of the questions right away rather than randomly guessing! The reality is that almost no one is absolutely sure of every answer to every question on the GMAT. Think back; did you have to guess at any questions on the ACT or SAT? We bet you did! We provide a few guessing strategies in the following sections to improve your chances of answering more questions correctly, even if you otherwise have no clue of the correct answer.

Forcing yourself to guess so you can move on

Remember that standardized tests aren't like tests in your undergraduate college courses. If you studied hard in college, you may not have had to do much guessing on your midterms and finals. On the GMAT, however, the computer won't allow you to skip questions. So if you stumble upon some really difficult questions that you're not sure how to answer, you have to guess and move on. Don't fall into thinking that you must know the correct answer for each question to do well on the GMAT. The GMAT is designed to test the potential of a wide range of future MBA students, so some of the questions have to be ridiculously difficult to challenge that one-in-a-million Einstein who takes the GMAT. Almost everyone incorrectly answers a few questions in each section, and almost everyone has to guess on those really difficult questions. Don't worry if you have to guess; just figure out how to guess effectively!

TIP

With the computer-adaptive test (CAT) format, developing a strategy for successful guessing in the quantitative-reasoning and verbal-reasoning sections is actually more important than ever. In these sections, as you answer questions correctly, the level of difficulty continues to increase. Although the integrated-reasoning section isn't in the CAT format, you can't skip the questions in this section, either, so be sure to apply the guessing strategies we discuss in this chapter to that section as well. Even if you do really, really well on the test, you'll probably find yourself guessing on some questions. On the GMAT, almost *everyone* guesses!

Understanding the importance of completing each section

To get the optimum score for the questions you answer correctly, you must respond to *all* the questions in each section. If you don't have time to complete the questions at the end of each section, your score is reduced in proportion to the number of questions you didn't answer. Therefore, it's important to move at a pace that allows you to get to all the questions.

WARNING

One of the ways you can get into real trouble with the CAT format is by spending too much time early on trying to correctly answer questions that are more difficult. If you're reluctant to guess and, therefore, spend more than a minute or two on several difficult questions, you may not have time to answer the relatively easy questions at the end.

TIP

Answer every question in each section! If you notice that you have only three or four minutes remaining in a section and more than five questions left, spend the remaining minutes marking an answer for every question, even if you don't have time to read them. You always have a 20 percent chance of randomly guessing the correct answer to a verbal-reasoning or quantitative-reasoning question, which is better than not answering the question at all. If you have to guess randomly at the end of the section, mark the same bubble for each answer. For example, you may choose to mark the second bubble from the bottom. Chances are that at least one in five questions will have a correct answer placed second to the end. Marking the same bubble also saves time because you don't have to choose which answer to mark for each question; you already have your guessing strategy in mind, so you don't have to think about it.

Even the GMAT folks warn of a severe penalty for not completing the test. They claim that if you fail to answer just 5 questions out of the 41 in the verbal section, your score could go from the 91st percentile to the 77th percentile. That's the kind of score reduction that could make a huge difference to your admissions chances!

Winning the Race against the Clock

Random guessing as the clock runs out serves you better than leaving the remaining questions in a section unanswered, but it's not a good way to approach the test in general. Instead, adopt a strategy of good time management that combines proper pacing, an active approach to answering questions, and appropriate guessing. We discuss all these time-management strategies in the following sections.

Giving each question equal treatment

You may have heard that you should spend a lot of time on the first ten questions because your performance on them determines your ultimate score. Although your performance on the first ten questions *does* give the computer an initial estimate of your ability, in the end, these first questions don't carry greater significance than any other questions. You'll still encounter all the questions in the section eventually, so you really have no reason to spend an unreasonable length of time on the first ten.

WARNING

If you spend too much time on the first ten questions and answer them all correctly, you'll have a limited amount of time in which to answer the 27 remaining quantitative or 31 remaining verbal questions. The computer program would give you a high estimated score after those first ten questions, but that initial estimate would then most likely fall steadily throughout the session as you would hurry through questions and guess at those you didn't have time to answer at the end. The worst outcome of all would be if you were unable to finish the section and had your score reduced in proportion to the questions you couldn't answer. You can't cheat the system by focusing on the first few questions. If you could, the very intelligent, highly paid test designers would find a way to adjust the format to thwart you.

Making time for the last ten questions

A much better approach than lavishing time on the *first* ten questions is allowing ample time to answer the *last* ten questions in both the verbal and quantitative sections. Because the best way to score well is to give adequate time to each question, guess when necessary, and complete the entire test, you shouldn't spend a disproportionate amount of time answering the early questions.

Here are the steps to follow for this approach:

1. **Work through the first 55 minutes of the quantitative and verbal sections at a good pace.**

   Plan to spend around two minutes per quantitative question and a little more than a minute and a half per verbal question.

2. **Don't spend more than three minutes on any question during the first 75 percent of the quantitative and verbal sections.**

3. **When you have ten questions remaining in the section, check the time remaining and adjust your pace accordingly.**

TIP

   Ten questions remain when you hit Question 27 of the quantitative section or Question 31 of the verbal section.

   For example, if you've answered the first 27 quantitative questions in only 50 minutes, you have a total of 25 minutes to work on the last ten questions. That means you can spend about two and a half minutes on each of the last ten questions. That extra 30 seconds per question may be what you need to answer a high percentage of those final ten questions correctly. Avoid random guesses on the last unanswered questions of either section.

WARNING

We're not suggesting that you rush through the first 55 minutes of each section so you can spend lots of time on the last ten questions. Instead, you should stick to a pace that allows you to give equal time to all the questions in a section. You can't spend five or six minutes on a single question without sacrificing your performance on the rest of the test, so stick to your pace.

If you happen to have additional time when you get to the last ten questions, by all means, use it. There's a severe penalty for not finishing a section but no prize for getting done early.

When you work steadily and carefully through the first 75 percent of each section, you're rewarded with a score that stabilizes toward the higher end of the percentile and that may rise to an even higher level at the end of the section as you spend any extra time you have getting the last questions right. Talk about ending on a high note!

Keeping track of your pace

You may think that keeping an even pace throughout the test means a lot of clock watching, but this isn't the case if you go into the test site with a plan. You can conceal the clock on the computer to keep from becoming obsessed with time, but you should periodically reveal the clock to check your progress. For example, you may plan to check your computer clock after every eight questions you answer. This means revealing the feature about five or six times during the verbal and quantitative sections. You'll spend a second or two clicking on the clock and glancing at it, but knowing that you're on pace will be worth it.

If you time yourself during practice tests you take at home, you'll probably begin to know intuitively whether you're falling behind. During the actual exam, you may not have to look at your clock as frequently. However, if you suspect that you're using too much time on a question (more than three minutes), you should check the clock. If you've spent more than three minutes, mark your best guess from the choices you haven't already eliminated and move on.

Getting Rid of Wrong Answers

We've stressed that the key to success is to move through the test steadily so you can answer every question and maximize your score. Keeping this steady pace will probably require you to make some intelligent guesses, and intelligent guesses hang on your ability to eliminate incorrect answers.

Eliminating answer choices is crucial on the verbal and quantitative sections of the GMAT. Most questions come with five answer choices, and usually one or two of the options are obviously wrong (especially in the verbal section). As soon as you know an answer choice is wrong, eliminate it. After you've eliminated that answer, don't waste time reading it again. By quickly getting rid of choices that you know are *wrong*, you'll be well on your way to finding the *right* answer! In the following sections, we show you a few elimination strategies that help you cross off wrong answers so you can narrow in on the right ones.

Keeping track of eliminated answer choices for the computer test format

You may be thinking that eliminating answer choices on a computerized test won't work. In truth, doing so is more difficult than on a paper test where you can actually cross off the entire answer in your test booklet. However, you can achieve the same results on the computerized test with a little practice. You must train your mind to look only at the remaining choices and not read every word that your eyes fall upon. You can't afford to waste time rereading a choice after you've eliminated it. That's why you need a system.

You can use the booklet of noteboards you're given at the test site to help you eliminate answers. The test administrators will replenish your noteboard supply if you fill them up, so don't be afraid to write all over your noteboards.

Here are some simple steps to help you keep track of which answers you've eliminated:

1. **At the beginning of the section (especially the verbal one, where eliminating answer choices is easier), quickly write down "A, B, C, D, and E" (or 1, 2, 3, 4, and 5 if you prefer numbers) in a vertical row on your noteboard.**

   A stands for the first answer choice, *B* for the second, *C* for the third, and so on, even though these letters don't appear on your computer screen.

2. **When you eliminate an answer choice, cross out the corresponding letter on your noteboard.**

   For example, if you're sure that the second and fifth answers are wrong, mark a line through *B* and *E* on your noteboard.

3. **If you look at your noteboard and see only one remaining answer letter, you've zeroed in on the right answer.**

   You don't need to reread the answer choices to remember which one was correct. It's listed right there on the noteboard.

4. **If you can't narrow down your choices to just one answer, eliminating three incorrect choices gives you a good chance of guessing correctly between the two options that remain.**

5. **Quickly rewrite the five letters (or numbers) for the next question and repeat the process.**

Practice this technique when you're taking your practice tests. The hard part isn't crossing out the letters on your noteboard; it's training your eyes to skip the wrong answers on the computer screen. Your brain will want to read through each choice every time you look at the answers. With the paper test booklet, you'd simply cross out the entire answer choice and then skip that choice every time you came to it. With the computerized test, you have to mentally cross out wrong answers. Developing this skill takes time. Mastering it is especially important for the verbal section, which has some long answer choices.

Recognizing wrong answers

So maybe you've mastered the art of the noteboard answer-elimination system, but you may be wondering how you know which answers to eliminate. Most of the verbal questions are best answered by process of elimination because answers aren't as clearly right or wrong as they may be for the math questions. For many math questions, the correct answer is obvious after you've performed the necessary calculations, but you may be able to answer some math questions without performing complex calculations if you look through the answers first and eliminate choices that don't make sense. So by using your common sense and analyzing all the information you have to work with (we show you how to do both in the next sections), you can reach a correct answer without knowing everything there is to know about a question.

Using common sense

Reading carefully reveals a surprising number of answer choices that are obviously wrong. In the quantitative- and integrated-reasoning sections, you may know before you even do a math calculation that one or two of the answers are simply illogical. In the verbal section, critical-reasoning questions may have answer choices that don't deal with the topic of the argument, or some sentence-correction answer choices may obviously display poor grammar or faulty sentence construction. You can immediately eliminate these eyesores from contention. If an answer is outside the realm of possibility, you don't ever have to read through it again. For example, consider the following sample critical-reasoning question.

EXAMPLE

Most New Year's resolutions are quickly forgotten. Americans commonly make resolutions to exercise, lose weight, quit smoking, or spend less money. In January, many people take some action, such as joining a gym, but by February, they are back to their old habits again.

Which of the following, if true, most strengthens the preceding argument?

(A) Some Americans do not make New Year's resolutions.

(B) Americans who do not keep their resolutions feel guilty the rest of the year.

(C) Attempts to quit smoking begun at times other than the first of the year are less successful than those begun in January.

(D) Increased sports programming in January motivates people to exercise more.

(E) People who are serious about lifestyle changes usually make those changes immediately and do not wait for New Year's Day.

Chapter 6 gives you a whole slew of tips on how to answer critical-reasoning questions, but without even looking closely at this one, you can eliminate at least two choices immediately. The argument states that people usually don't live up to New Year's resolutions and the question asks you to strengthen that argument. Two of the answer choices have nothing to do with keeping resolutions, so you can discard them right away: Choice (A) provides irrelevant information — the argument is about people who make resolutions, not those who don't — and Choice (D) brings up a completely different topic (sports programming) and doesn't mention resolutions.

Without even taxing your brain, you've gone from five choices down to three. Psychologically, dealing with three answer choices is much easier than dealing with all five. Plus, if you were short on time and had to quickly guess at this question, narrowing your choices to only three gives you a much better chance of answering it correctly.

Relying on what you know

TIP

Before you attempt to solve a quantitative problem or begin to answer a sentence-correction question, you can use what you know to eliminate answer choices.

For example, if a quantitative question asks for a solution that's an absolute value, you can immediately eliminate any negative answer choices, because absolute value is always positive. (For more about absolute value, see Chapter 12.) Even if you don't remember how to solve the problem, you can at least narrow down the choices and increase your chances of guessing correctly. If you eliminate one or two choices and if you have the time, you may be able to plug the remaining answer choices back into the problem and find the correct answer that way. So if you approach questions with a stash of knowledge, you can correctly answer more questions than you realize.

Letting the question guide you

If you've ever watched a popular TV game show, you know that the clue to the answer can sometimes be found in the question. Although the answers to most GMAT questions aren't as obvious as the answer to "in 1959, the U.S. said 'aloha' to this 50th state," you can still use clues from the GMAT questions themselves to answer them.

In the earlier critical-reasoning example on New Year's resolutions, you were left with three answer choices. Paying attention to the wording of the question can help you eliminate two more.

The question asks you to *strengthen* the argument that Americans quickly forget their New Year's resolutions. Choice (B) seriously *weakens* the argument by indicating that instead of forgetting their resolutions, Americans are haunted by failed resolutions for the rest of the year. Likewise, Choice (C) indicates that a resolution to quit smoking at the beginning of the New Year may be more successful than the same resolution at other times. Because these answers weaken the argument rather than strengthen it as the question asks, you can eliminate them, also. By process of elimination, you know that Choice (E) is the correct answer to the question, and you haven't yet seriously considered the logic of the argument!

Quickly recognizing and eliminating wrong answers after only a few seconds puts you on the path to choosing a right answer. This strategy works in the quantitative section as well. Consider this problem-solving question example.

EXAMPLE

If $\frac{1}{2}$ of the air in a balloon is removed every 10 seconds, what fraction of the air has been removed from the balloon after 30 seconds?

(A) $\frac{1}{8}$

(B) $\frac{1}{6}$

(C) $\frac{1}{4}$

(D) $\frac{5}{6}$

(E) $\frac{7}{8}$

You can immediately eliminate any choices with fractions smaller than one-half because the problem tells you that half the air departs within the first ten seconds. So you can discard Choices (A), (B), and (C). Without performing any calculations at all, you've narrowed down your choices to just two!

TIP

Another benefit of eliminating obviously wrong answer choices is that you save yourself from inadvertently making costly errors. The GMAT offers Choices (A), (B), and (C) to trap unsuspecting test-takers. If you mistakenly tried to solve the problem by multiplying $\frac{1}{2} \times \frac{1}{2} \times \frac{1}{2}$, you'd come up with $\frac{1}{8}$. But if you've already eliminated that answer, you know you've done something wrong. By immediately getting rid of the answer choices that can't be right, you may avoid choosing a clever distracter. By the way, $\frac{1}{8}$ is the amount of air remaining in the balloon after 30 seconds. After the first 10 seconds, $\frac{1}{2}$ of the air remains. After 20 seconds, $\frac{1}{2}$ of that, or $\frac{1}{4}$, remains. After 30 seconds, the balloon still has $\frac{1}{2}$ of $\frac{1}{4}$ of its air, which is $\frac{1}{8}$.

So the amount of air removed in 30 seconds is Choice (E), $\frac{7}{8}$, because $1 - \frac{1}{8} = \frac{7}{8}$.

Dealing with questions that contain Roman numerals

The GMAT presents a special type of question that pops up from time to time. This question gives you three statements marked with the Roman numerals I, II, and III and asks you to evaluate their validity. You'll find these questions in the quantitative- and verbal-reasoning sections. You're supposed to select the answer choice that presents the correct list of either valid or invalid statements, depending on what the question is looking for.

To approach questions that contain statements with Roman numerals, follow these steps:

1. **Evaluate the validity of the first statement or the statement that seems easiest to evaluate.**

2. **If the first statement meets the qualifications stated by the question, eliminate any answer choices that don't contain Roman numeral I; if it doesn't, eliminate any choices that have Roman numeral I in them.**

3. **Examine the remaining answer choices to see which of the two remaining statements is best to evaluate next.**

4. **Evaluate another statement and eliminate answer choices based on your findings.**

   You may find that you don't have to spend time evaluating the third statement.

Here's an example to show how the approach works.

If x and y are different integers, each greater than 1, which of the following must be true?

I. $x + y > 4$

II. $x - y = 0$

III. $x - y$ results in an integer

(A) II only

(B) I and II

(C) I, II, and III

(D) I and III

(E) III only

Consider the statements one by one. Start with Statement I and determine whether the expression $x + y > 4$ is true. Because x and y are greater than 1, they must be positive. The smaller of the two integers must be at least 2, and the other number can't be less than 3. So because $2 + 3 = 5$, $x + y \geq 5$, so their sum has to be greater than 4.

Don't read Statement II yet. Instead, run through the answer choices and eliminate any that don't include Statement I. Choice (A) and Choice (E) don't include Statement I, so cross out those letters on your noteboard. The remaining choices don't give you any indication which statement is best to evaluate next, so proceed with your evaluation of Statement II, which states that $x - y = 0$. This statement can't be correct because x and y have different values. The only way one number subtracted from another number can result in 0 is when the two numbers are the same. The difference of two different integers will always be at least 1.

Because Statement II isn't correct, eliminate choices that include Statement II. You can cross out Choice (B) and Choice (C), which leaves you with Choice (D). By process of elimination, Choice (D) has to be right. You don't even need to read Statement III, because you know the correct answer. Not all Roman numeral questions are so helpful, but many are, and in those cases, the strategy is a real timesaver!

Playing It Smart: A Few Things You Shouldn't Do When Taking the Test

Most of this chapter focuses on what you *should* do to maximize your score on the GMAT. However, there are also a few things you *shouldn't* do, which we discuss in the following sections. Avoid these mistakes, and you'll have an advantage over many other test-takers!

Don't lose your focus

You may be used to the fast-paced world of business or the cooperative world of group presentations that is popular in many business classes. Don't be surprised if 180 minutes of multiple-choice questions peppered with 30 minutes of essay writing gets a little boring. We know the prospect is shocking!

Don't allow yourself to lose focus. Keep your brain on a tight leash, and don't let your mind wander. This test is too important. Just remind yourself how important these three and a half hours are to your future. Teach yourself to concentrate and rely on the relaxation tips we give you later in this chapter to avoid incessant mind wandering. You'll need those powers of concentration in that MBA program you'll soon be starting!

Don't read questions at lightning speed

We hate to break it to you, but you probably aren't a superhero named "Speedy Reader." You'll be anxious when the test begins, and you may want to blow through the questions at record speed. Big mistake! You don't get bonus points for finishing early, and you have plenty of time to answer every question if you read at a reasonable pace. You may take pride in your ability to speed-read novels, and that skill may help you with the reading-comprehension passages, but don't use it to read the questions. You need to read questions carefully to capture the nuances the GMAT offers and understand exactly what it asks of you.

Many people who get bogged down on a few questions and fail to complete a section do so because of poor test-taking techniques, not because of slow reading. Do yourself a favor: Relax, read at a reasonable pace, and maximize your score!

Don't waste all your time on the hardest questions

Although you shouldn't try to work at lightning speed, remember not to get held back by a few hard questions, either. The difficulty of a question depends on the person taking the test. For everyone, even the high scorers, a few questions on a test are just harder than others. When you confront a difficult question on the GMAT, do your best, eliminate as many wrong answers as you can, and then make an intelligent guess. Even if you had all day, you might not be able to answer that particular question. If you allow yourself to guess and move on, you can work on plenty of other questions that you'll answer correctly.

Don't cheat

We aren't sure how you'd cheat on the computerized GMAT, and we won't be wasting our time thinking of ways! Spend your time practicing for the test and do your best. Cheating is futile.

Tackling a Case of Nerves with Relaxation Techniques

All this talk about time management, distracting answer choices, blind guessing, and losing focus may be making you nervous. Relax. After you've read this book, you'll have plenty of techniques for turning your quick intellect and that packet of noteboards into a high GMAT score. You may feel a little nervous on the day of the test, but don't worry about it, because a little nervous adrenaline can actually keep you alert. Just don't let anxiety ruin your performance.

You may be working along steadily when suddenly, from out of the blue, a question appears that you don't understand at all. Instead of trying to eliminate answer choices and solve the problem, you may stare at the question as if it were written in a foreign language. You may start to second-guess your performance on the test as a whole. You panic and think that maybe you're just not cut out for a graduate business degree. You're on the verge of freaking out — help!

REMEMBER

Because much of the GMAT is in CAT format, encountering a super-hard quantitative or verbal question probably means you're doing pretty well. Besides, if you do miss a question, you'll just get an easier question next — unless you're on the last question, in which case you needn't freak out at all. Heck, you're nearly done!

If you do find yourself seizing up with anxiety partway through the test, and if these facts about the CAT format don't ease your tension, try these techniques to get back on track:

» **Inhale deeply.** When you stress out, you take shallow breaths and don't get the oxygen you need to think straight. Breathing deeply can calm you and supply the air you need to get back to doing your best.

» **Stretch a little.** Anxiety causes tension, and so does working at a computer. Do a few simple stretches to relax and get the blood flowing. Try shrugging your shoulders toward your ears and rolling your head from side to side. You can put your hands together and stretch your arms above your head or stretch your legs out and move your ankles up and down (or both!). Last, shake your hands as though you've just washed them and don't have a towel.

» **Give yourself a mini massage.** If you're really tense, give yourself a little rubdown. The shoulders and neck usually hold the most tension in your body, so rub your right shoulder with your left hand and vice versa. Rub the back of your neck. It's not as great as getting a full rubdown from a professional, but you can book that appointment for after the test!

» **Think positive thoughts.** Give yourself a quick break. The GMAT is tough, but don't get discouraged. Focus on the positive; think about the questions you've done well on. If you're facing a tough question, realize that it will get better.

» **Take a little vacation.** If nothing else is working and you're still anxious, picture a place in your mind that makes you feel comfortable and confident. Visit that place for a few moments and come back ready to take charge!

Devising a Plan of Attack

The best way to avoid freaking out on exam day is to be fully prepared. So make sure you have a strategy. About two to three months before your test day, map out a regular study schedule that includes these steps:

1. **Use one of the online practice tests included with this book to take a full, timed exam.**

2. **Score your practice exam.**

3. **Based on your scores, read the chapters in this book that correspond to those areas where you need the most improvement.**

   If your verbal score is lower than your math, focus on improving your reading and grammar skills in Part 2. If your math score is closer to your total number of fingers and toes than the measure of your height in inches, open up the math review in Part 4.

4. **Once you've read through the appropriate chapters, practice what you've learned by answering practice questions.**

   Use the questions provided in the remaining five practice tests offered in this book and online. Try to spend several hours each week involved in practice. After you score your efforts, examine the questions you answer incorrectly to determine your error. Then check the answer explanations for more insight.

5. **Follow the same approach to studying your areas of strength.**

   If you've spent the previous month focusing on the math in Part 4, focus on the verbal approach offered in Part 2. If you've concentrated on the verbal questions, set your sights on the math chapters.

6. **When you've mastered the verbal and math questions, work on the AWA approach offered in Part 3 and the suggestions for integrated-reasoning practice in Part 5.**

7. **Test your skills on actual GMAT questions and get used to the online test format.**

   Supplement your practice with the most current official GMAT materials: *The Official Guide for GMAT Review, The Official Guide for GMAT Quantitative Review,* and *The Official Guide for GMAT Verbal Review.* Download the free GMATPrep software on www.mba.com. After you work through the initial practice questions in the program, reserve a three-hour block of time to take a full-length GMAT practice exam. Review concepts and strategies in this book. Then take the other full-length practice exam in the GMATPrep program.

REMEMBER

Take the GMAT as soon as you're ready. You'll lose momentum and intensity if you prepare for more than three or four months prior to your test date.

Chapter **3**

Mastering Business-School Admissions

I f you're reading a book about the GMAT, you're probably considering an MBA. Well, get ready for a great adventure. Applying to business school can be a challenge, not to be attempted by the lukewarm or ambivalent. If you're truly committed to acquiring an MBA, though, the application process may be sort of exciting. You may end up living someplace new and broadening your opportunities in ways you never considered.

In this chapter, we discuss the ins and outs of evaluating business programs and applying for admission, as well as the importance of the GMAT in this process.

Choosing a Business School

Choosing the right business school is not unlike choosing the right car or home — you're faced with numerous considerations, and what works best for, say, your sister or friend may not be the best option for you. Just as cars and houses are major investments, so is a business-school education, so just as you would likely test-drive a new car before buying it and have a home inspection performed on a house before sinking your life savings into it, you ought to conduct extensive research before deciding where to pursue that MBA.

Not all MBA programs are created equal. You may still be able to get a fine business education at most of them, but understand that different programs have different characteristics. Some are extremely competitive, while others are easier to get into. Most require attending classes on campus, but a growing number of colleges offer programs that can be completed entirely online or through a blend of online and on-campus coursework. Some have excellent practical career-oriented programs while others present a more theoretical approach to business. You need to decide what you want in a school before you let schools decide whether they have the privilege of accepting you.

As you build your application list, consider the following factors:

» **Prestige:** School prestige falls first on this list, and that isn't by accident. In a Forbes survey of about 750 GMAT test-takers, prospective students were asked which consideration was most important to them when selecting a business school. Prestige was the most common answer, and the best measure of prestige at a given school was said to be the proven success of its alumni. Why does prestige get so much credit? Primarily, because students believe that being affiliated with a particular high-ranked school will give them a foot up in many areas and help them stand out from the crowd. To be more specific, students tend to associate higher-prestige business schools with enhanced opportunities for career and business networking, and in many ways the association is justified. For example, Wall Street firms generally recruit from the top-ranked East Coast MBA programs, so if you desire to join one of these corporations, you need to apply to the programs they favor. Checking the top five rankings of MBA programs — Forbes, Businessweek, US News & World Reports, The Economist, and The Financial Times — provides you with an indication of which programs are most prestigious. An MBA school's rank may not matter to you, however, if you're already employed or are self-employed and primarily desire to acquire skills to enhance your current profession.

» **Affordability:** Obviously, it makes sense to borrow as little money as possible for business school, as you'll more than likely be committed to pay it all back, plus interest, somewhere down the line. MBA programs generally aren't cheap, however, so the trick is to not only find a school that you can afford, but uncover one that offers the biggest return on your investment (ROI). To get a sense of what that ROI may ultimately be, you'll want to take a comprehensive look at all costs associated with attending a particular institution. In addition to tuition rates, review any additional fees that contribute to the total cost of attendance, such as room and board (if applicable), textbooks and technology needs (for example, laptops and so on) and personal living expenses. Carefully assess the likelihood of receiving financial aid and merit scholarships to help offset expenses. Also, consider the wages you give up while you attend a full-time program. Ultimately, ROI comes down to whether the amount you spend for your MBA, including the lost wages, will be less than the salary increase you receive as a result of enhancing your academic credentials.

» **Selectivity:** You have to get into an MBA program before you can graduate from it. Check with admissions to determine a school's mid 50 percent and top 25 percent qualifications regarding accepted GPA and GMAT scores. Your application list should include at least one or two programs where your numbers — grades and test scores — fall within the top 25 percent. With that assurance, you can toss your hat in the ring for more selective schools.

» **Concentrations and specialties:** As with undergraduate programs, some MBA programs specialize in a particular business concentration. Do your research. If your focus is finance, apply to programs with a strong finance curriculum. If your goal is to increase your management opportunities, find programs that specialize in business management. Some universities offer dual degree programs. You can earn an MBA and a law degree in four years at some or combine an MBA with an MD. Master's degrees in a variety of areas, such as education, public policy, journalism, and so on, may be paired with an MBA. If gaining more than one degree excites you, look for schools that offer these options.

» **Special programs:** While traditional MBA programs consist of a full-time, two-year commitment, you'll find a variety of options that stray from this model. Some schools offer part-time programs that allow you to work while you earn your degree. Other programs may integrate online learning or may be offered entirely online to accommodate different schedules. You may seek a program that offers more practical application opportunities, or you may be more interested in a program with a more theoretical approach. Investigate programs to find the ones that best fit your schedule and goals.

» **Location:** Geography plays a big role in deciding where you pursue your MBA. Do you want to be near your family? Do you want to be able to drive to the beach or the mountains to get a break from your studies? Do you feel more comfortable on the East Coast or West Coast? Or are you more at home in the Midwest or South? Location may also be a factor in overall cost; living in Palo Alto, California, is more expensive than residing in Columbus, Ohio.

If you're fresh out of college and don't yet have a family, you may have more flexibility choosing a business school than you might if you own property and have children or other responsibilities that require you to stay close to your home base. Additionally, it's wise to think beyond graduation when determining where to attend business school. Often, MBA programs have tight links within their communities, meaning your best bet at landing a job through networking, interning, or networking with alumni may be in the same neighborhood as the institution. Choosing a business school may also mean choosing your future hometown.

» **Public or private:** MBA programs may be found at state university systems or in private universities. Many public schools charge less for tuition than private ones, especially for in-state residents, but more financial aid and scholarship possibilities may exist at private universities.

» **Average starting salary:** You're probably considering business school at least in part because you hope an MBA will boost your ability to secure gainful employment or command a higher salary. All MBA programs are not created equal, and (here's where "prestige" again factors in) attending a big-name school really can help you bring home the bacon, so to speak. An MBA from a highly ranked, selective business school, such as Stanford, Harvard, or Wharton, can considerably boost your ability to earn a substantial income. The average MBA starting salary is also important if you are accruing interest on student loans. Checking program rankings based on starting salary may help give you a rough idea of how long you'll be indebted.

» **Quality of life:** Some business schools are known for being competitive, even cutthroat; others embrace a more collaborative atmosphere. Examine your personality and be honest with yourself. Does competition challenge you or defeat you? Are you more comfortable working in groups or individually? Talk with current students and alumni to get an accurate assessment of a program's character to make sure it fits with yours.

» **Alumni network:** You're going to spend much more of your life as a business-school graduate than as a business-school student. The connections you make as you earn your MBA may last a lifetime, and a strong alumni network can be a valuable resource throughout your career. Consider the depth and breadth of a program's alumni when you draw up your application list.

REMEMBER

When it comes to selecting a business school, there is no "one size fits all" approach. Do your due diligence, therefore, to find the programs that best fit you. Once you have your list, your next step is to create a memorable, effective application that leaves a lasting impression.

Lining Up Your Ducks — Applying to Business Schools

Applying to MBA programs is an expensive and time-consuming process not to be entered into lightly. Each school has its own admissions requirements and components you must gather and submit according to instructions. Be sure to check each program's admission web page thoroughly, and carefully follow the instructions. Despite slight differences, most MBA admissions expect to receive by a designated deadline the application, GMAT (or GRE) scores, college transcripts, a personal essay, a list of activities and/or a resume, letters of recommendation, and the application fee.

TO GMAT OR TO GRE — THAT IS THE QUESTION

A growing trend among business schools is to accept either the GRE or the GMAT for admissions. This practice may leave you wondering which to choose. The GRE is used for most graduate programs other than the MBA, so if you aren't sure whether you want an MBA or, say, a masters in finance, or you have your heart set on a dual-degree program, it may seem that the GRE is a more efficient option. Be careful, though; business schools may view your GRE score as a lack of surety on your part regarding your dedication to an MBA. Choosing the GMAT over the GRE may help your admissions chances because it indicates a commitment to the MBA path. If an MBA is your one and only goal, the GMAT is likely a better option, and that choice may serve you well even after you graduate with potential employers who are more familiar with GMAT results in job applications.

When to apply

Most traditional MBA programs begin in the fall semester, and the application season begins the fall prior. More flexible schedules may accommodate entry at several times throughout the year, each with its own application deadline. Some schools have rolling admissions, reviewing applications as they come in and cutting off applications after a certain date. A relatively common application practice is to accept applications in two or three rounds with separate deadlines and notification dates. This practice cuts down on the time it takes for you to receive a decision.

TIP

Whether your program has one deadline or three, rolling admissions or not, it's best to get your materials in as early as possible. Early applications cut down on your competition and may make you eligible for additional scholarships and financial aid. To ready yourself for early applying, take the GMAT as soon as you decide to pursue an MBA.

What to submit

Most programs expect to see the following:

>> A completed, signed application form

>> GMAT (or GRE) score

>> Transcripts of prior academic record

>> Letters of recommendation, at least one from an immediate supervisor

>> A personal statement — an essay usually explaining why you want to earn an MBA

>> For some programs, additional essays, usually defining why you want to study at that institution

>> A hefty application fee, which can vary from around $50 to $250 or so at some selective universities

You may also have to send in documentation of state residency, financial aid forms, or other relevant information.

WARNING

If one required component of your application isn't in place by the deadline (or whenever the admissions committee stops considering applications), no one will read any of it. So if one of your recommenders forgets to send in a letter or you neglect to order an official transcript from a college you attended during the summer, your application may be jeopardized or thrown out.

REVIEW OF APPLICATIONS

Many law schools receive far more applicants than they have spaces for in an entering class. Obviously the first thing admissions committees look at is academic credentials and GMAT scores, but numbers aren't everything. Every year competitive business schools admit some students with comparatively low scores and grades and reject some with stellar numbers.

MBA programs desire to create classes that represent a diversity of backgrounds and interests and have the potential to bring them fame and fortune as successful alumni. Therefore, these factors may also contribute to a successful application:

- Geography (where students come from); schools like to get people from all over the world
- Race and ethnicity
- Unique activities or work experience

You can highlight your individual contributions in your personal statement, which is why this essay can be a very important component of your application.

Crafting Effective Business-School Essays

More people apply to MBA programs than any other post-graduate degree, which results in a large number of business-school graduates seeking positions. This fact poses a problem for business-school administrators who want to boast about their alumni's high employment rates. Therefore, MBA programs are much more likely to accept you when they see evidence of your future success. This support comes to them in your academic record, for sure, but it's also conveyed in the case you make in your personal statement.

Before you sit down to write your essay, outline your future plans. Define exactly why you want to earn an MBA and clarify specific career goals. The personal statement should not only convey what you've achieved so far, but it should also link your past accomplishments to concrete future goals, ones that require an MBA to fulfill. The essay is your chance to show admissions the unique contributions you can make to their program. To this end, here is a summary of what an appropriate personal statement is *not*:

> **The essay isn't a summary of your past education, activities, and accolades.** Your resume fulfills this task. Use the personal statement to provide deeper insight into who you are as well as what you do.

> **The essay isn't a university fan letter.** Resist the temptation to fill your personal statement with boundless praise. Your discussion of the business school should reveal your knowledge of its strengths as they relate to your particular goals. Don't tell a school about its unique concentrations and experiences; show how these opportunities align with your goals and abilities.

> **The essay isn't poetic license.** The personal statement provides an opportunity for you to convey your story in creative ways. By all means, use stories and sensory description to reveal your qualities in a very real way. But avoid overstepping the boundaries. Observe word or page limits and follow directions. An attempt to dazzle with difference may just show admissions that you have trouble following rules.

>> **The essay isn't a philosophical treatise.** Focus on what's true for you rather than what's true for the world.

>> **The essay isn't a personality assessment.** Perhaps the biggest mistake applicants make in writing their personal essays is over-generalization and under-substantiation. You don't convince others of your personal characteristics by simply telling them you're awesome or hardworking. Show who you are through carefully chosen stories that unfold through specific details. Allow the reader to draw conclusions about who you are from reading about how you interact with the world.

>> **The essay doesn't have to sugarcoat.** Don't be afraid to express some vulnerability. You aren't good at everything. If you were, you wouldn't need an advanced degree. Sometimes the best way to endear your reader is to acknowledge a shortcoming.

2

Vanquishing the Verbal Section

IN THIS PART . . .

Put your grammar skills to work to catch and correct sentence errors that GMAT writers are most fond of throwing at you.

Discover techniques to help you move through reading passages most efficiently within the time limit.

Apply our time-tested strategy for approaching critical reasoning arguments so that you get really good at evaluating the arguments and answering the questions.

Tackle a short version of a GMAT verbal section to get familiar with how all three question types come together.

Chapter **4**

Applying What You Learned (We Hope) in Grammar Class: Sentence Correction

Business success depends on a number of diverse skills, and one of the most important of these skills is the ability to communicate effectively. The GMAT can't test your speaking ability (not yet, anyway), so it focuses on your reading and writing skills. In fact, about half of the GMAT is devoted to reading and writing. And, of course, knowing the rules of standard written English is essential to good writing. The GMAT test-makers have developed diabolically effective ways to use multiple-choice questions to test your knowledge of written English. They present you with a sentence and underline a portion of it. Your job is to figure out whether the underlined part is okay the way it is. If it needs to be changed, you have to pick the answer choice that offers the proper correction.

Sentence-correction questions appear in the verbal-reasoning section along with reading-comprehension and critical-reasoning questions. You have 75 minutes to answer the 41 questions that appear in the entire section. So you have a little less than two minutes to answer each question. You'll likely need more time to ponder reading questions, so plan to spend no more than one minute answering each sentence-correction question.

Punctuation, subject-verb agreement, parallel construction, and other keys to good grammar may have you lying awake at night. Take heart. We won't let your dream of attending the business school of your choice die on the sentence-correction portion of the GMAT. Fortunately, the kinds of sentence errors that crop up on the GMAT don't change much, so you can focus your study on the common ones.

In this chapter, we review the grammar basics you should have down before test day. We also show you what sentence-correction questions look like, which common errors the GMAT likes to test, and the best way to approach the questions.

Building a Solid Foundation: Grammar Basics

Luckily, the rules of grammar are really pretty logical. After you understand the basic rules regarding the parts of speech and the elements of a sentence, you've got it made. The following sections provide what you need to know to do well on sentence-correction questions. As an added bonus, this refresher can help you write the GMAT analytical-writing essay.

Getting wordy: The parts of speech

Sentence-correction questions consist of, well, sentences. Sentences are made up of words, and each word in a sentence has a function. The parts of speech in the English language that are important to know for GMAT grammar are verbs, nouns, pronouns, adjectives, adverbs, conjunctions, and prepositions.

Acting out: Verbs

Every sentence has a verb, which means that a sentence isn't complete without one. You should be familiar with three types of verbs:

>> **Action verbs:** These verbs state what the subject of the sentence is doing. *Run, jump, compile,* and *learn* are examples of action verbs.

>> **To be:** The verb *to be* (conjugated as *am, is, are, was, were, been,* and *being*) functions sort of like an equal sign. It equates the subject with a noun or adjective. For example: *Ben is successful* means *Ben = successful. She is a CEO* means *she = CEO.*

>> **Linking verbs:** These words join (or link) the subject to an adjective that describes the condition of the subject. Like the verb *to be,* they express a state of the subject, but they provide more information about the subject than *to be* verbs do. Common linking verbs are *feel, seem, appear, remain, look, taste,* and *smell.*

Telling it like it is: Nouns

You've undoubtedly heard nouns defined as persons, places, or things. They provide the "what" of the sentence. A noun can function in a sentence in different ways:

1. The *subject* plays the principal role in the sentence. It's what the sentence is about or who is doing the action.

2. A *direct object* receives the action of an action verb.

3. An *indirect object* receives the direct object. Sentences with direct objects don't need indirect objects, but you need a direct object before you can have an indirect object.

4. The *object of a preposition* receives a preposition. (See the "Joining forces: Conjunctions and prepositions" section, later in this chapter.)

5. The *object in a verbal phrase* serves as the receiver of the *gerund* (which is a verb form that functions as a noun, like *singing*).

6. An *appositive* clarifies or renames another noun.

7. A *predicate noun* follows the verb *to be* and regards the subject.

So you can see how these different types of nouns function, we've marked their appearances in these two sentences with numbers that correspond to the preceding list:

> Being a *businesswoman (5)* with great leadership *abilities (4)*, *Anna Arnold (1)*, an *MBA (6)*, gave her *employees (3)* the *opportunity (2)* to succeed. *Anna (1)* was a supportive *supervisor (7)*.

The GMAT won't ask you to define the various noun functions, but being familiar with them helps when we talk about the different types of sentence errors you may encounter.

REMEMBER

One of the most important things to remember about nouns and verbs on the GMAT is that the subject and verb of a sentence have to agree in number. See the later section "Pointing Out Mistakes: Common Sentence-Correction Errors" for details.

Standing in: Pronouns

Pronouns figure prominently in the sentence-correction portion of the GMAT. Pronouns rename nouns and provide a means of avoiding the needless repetition of names and other nouns in a sentence or paragraph. On the GMAT, pronoun errors are common. To correct these errors, you need to be familiar with the three types of pronouns: personal, indefinite, and relative:

» **Personal pronouns:** These words rename specific nouns. They take two forms: subjective and objective.

- The subjective personal pronouns are *I, you, he, she, it, we,* and *they. Subjective personal pronouns* are used when the pronoun functions as a subject or predicate noun (see the preceding section for info on noun functions).

- The *objective* personal pronouns are *me, you, him, her, it, us,* and *them. Objective personal pronouns* are properly used when they function as an object in the sentence.

» **Indefinite pronouns:** These pronouns refer to general nouns rather than specific ones. Some common examples are *everyone, somebody, anything, each, one, none,* and *no one.* It's important to remember that most indefinite pronouns are singular, which means they require singular verbs: **One** of the employees is being laid off.

» **Relative pronouns:** These words, like *that, which,* and *who,* introduce adjective clauses that describe nouns. *Who refers to persons; which* and *that refer primarily to animals and things: He is a manager **who** is comfortable leading. The consulting work **that** she does usually saves companies money, **which** makes her a very popular consultant.*

Filling in the details: Adjectives

Adjectives describe and clarify nouns and pronouns. For example: *The secretive culture of the corporation created discontented employees. Secretive* defines the kind of culture and *discontented* describes the feeling of the employees. Without the adjectives, the sentence is virtually meaningless: *The culture of the corporation created employees.*

TIP

With sentence-correction questions, make sure adjectives are positioned correctly in the sentence so each adjective modifies the word it's supposed to. For example, *I brought the slides to the meeting that I created* makes it seem that the author of the sentence created the meeting rather than the slides. The descriptive clause *that I created* is in the wrong place. The better composition is *I brought the slides that I created to the meeting.*

Describing the action: Adverbs

Adverbs are like adjectives because they add extra information to the sentence, but adjectives usually modify nouns, and adverbs primarily define verbs. Adverbs include all words and groups of words (called *adverb phrases*) that answer the questions *where, when, how,* and *why: The stock market **gradually** recovered from the 1999 crash. Gradually defines how the stock market recovered.*

Some adverbs modify adjectives or other adverbs: *The **extremely** unfortunate plumber yodeled **very well**.*

You'll recognize many adverbs by the *-ly* ending. But not all adverbs end in *-ly*. For example, in *The company's manufacturing moved **overseas**,* the adverb *overseas* reveals where the manufacturing is located. In *The Human Resources director resigned **today**, today* explains when the director resigned.

Positioning adverbs correctly is important on the GMAT. Separating adverbs from the words they modify makes sentences imprecise.

Joining forces: Conjunctions and prepositions

Conjunctions and prepositions link the main elements of the sentence.

>> **Conjunctions:** This part of speech joins words, phrases, and clauses. The three types of conjunctions are *coordinating, correlative,* and *subordinating*. Don't worry about memorizing these terms; just remember that the three types exist.

- The seven coordinating conjunctions — *and, but, for, nor, or, so,* and *yet* — are the ones most people think of when they consider conjunctions.

- Correlative conjunctions always appear in pairs: *either/or, neither/nor, not only/but also.* These conjunctions correlate two similar clauses in one sentence. Therefore, if you use *either* as a conjunction, you have to include *or*.

- Subordinating conjunctions introduce dependent clauses and connect them to independent clauses. *Although, because, if, when,* and *while* are common examples of subordinating conjunctions. We talk more about clauses in the section "In so many words: Phrases and clauses."

>> **Prepositions:** These words join nouns to the rest of a sentence. We'd need several pages to list all the prepositions, but common examples are *about, above, at, for, in, over, to,* and *with*. A preposition can't function within a sentence unless the preposition is connected to a noun, so prepositions always appear in prepositional phrases. These phrases consist of a preposition and noun, which is called the *object of the preposition: The woman **in the suit** went **to the office** to sit down.* The preposition *in* relates its object, *suit,* to another noun, *woman,* so *in the suit* is a prepositional phrase that works as an adjective to describe *woman; to the office* is an adverbial prepositional phrase that describes where the woman went. Note that the word *to* in *to sit down* isn't a preposition; rather, it's part of the infinitive form of the verb *to sit* — the phrase doesn't have an object, so you don't have a prepositional phrase.

Prepositions often play a part in sentence-correction questions. The GMAT may provide you with a sentence that contains an improper preposition construction. Here's a simple example: *He watched the flood while sitting in the roof.* The correct preposition is *on,* not *in*. Other types of preposition questions may not be so easy, but we highlight these for you in the section "Pointing Out Mistakes: Common Sentence-Correction Errors."

Pulling together: The parts of a sentence

The parts of speech work together to form sentences. And the thrust of the sentence's information is conveyed by three main elements: the subject, the verb, and the element that the verb links to the subject. To locate the main idea of a sentence, you focus on these three elements. Other information within the sentence is secondary.

Trouble comes in threes: Subject, verb, and third element

The subject is the main character of the sentence; it's the noun that carries out the action of the sentence or whose condition the sentence describes. The verb describes the action or links the subject and predicate. Depending on the verb used, the third important part of the sentence could be a direct object, an adverb, an adjective, or a predicate noun. The third element for a sentence with a *transitive verb* (an action verb that must be followed by a direct object) is always a direct object. *Intransitive verbs* (action verbs that can't be followed by direct objects) may be completed by adverbs. You can follow the verb *to be* with either an adjective or a predicate noun. Recognizing the three main elements of the sentence helps you spot errors in the sentence-correction questions.

In so many words: Phrases and clauses

In addition to the main elements, a sentence may contain single words, phrases, or clauses that convey more information about the sentence's main message. Phrases and clauses are groups of words that work together to form a single part of speech, like an adverb or adjective. The difference between phrases and clauses is that clauses contain their own subjects and verbs, and phrases don't. A good understanding of both clauses and phrases can help you greatly on the sentence-correction portion of the GMAT.

PHRASES

Phrases are groups of words that function together as a part of speech. Many tested errors on the GMAT concern phrases, and we discuss them in more depth in the section "Pointing Out Mistakes: Common Sentence-Correction Errors."

INDEPENDENT AND DEPENDENT CLAUSES

The distinguishing characteristic of clauses is that they contain subjects and verbs. The two types of clauses are independent and dependent. Recognizing the difference between independent and dependent clauses can help you with many of the sentence-correction problems on the GMAT.

>> **Independent clauses:** These clauses express complete thoughts and could stand as sentences by themselves. Here's an example of a sentence that contains two independent clauses: *The firm will go public, and investors will rush to buy stock.* Each clause is a complete sentence: *The firm will go public. Investors will rush to buy stock.*

Punctuate two independent clauses in a sentence by joining them either with a semicolon or with a comma and a coordinating conjunction.

>> **Dependent clauses:** These clauses express incomplete thoughts and are, therefore, sentence fragments. Even though they contain a subject and verb, they can't stand alone as sentences without other information. For example, in the sentence *After the two companies merge, they'll need only one board of directors,* the dependent clause in the sentence is *after the two companies merge.* The clause has a subject, *companies,* and a verb, *merge,* but it still leaves the reader needing more information. So the clause is dependent. To form a complete sentence, a dependent clause must be paired with an independent clause.

Punctuate a beginning dependent clause by placing a comma between it and the independent clause that comes after it. If the dependent clause follows the independent clause, you don't need any punctuation: *They'll need only one board of directors after the two companies merge.*

Dependent clauses that function as adverbs begin with subordinating conjunctions and answer the questions *how, when, where,* or *why.* For example, *The woman got the job **because she was more qualified.*** The bolded portion is a dependent clause explaining *why* the woman got the job. On the other hand, an adjectival clause usually begins with a relative pronoun to provide more information about the noun it modifies, like in this sentence: *The judge is a man **who requires a silent courtroom.*** The bolded clause describes what type of man the judge is. Dependent clauses may also function as nouns: *The insurance company was focusing on **how much money the hurricane would cost.*** The dependent clause in this sentence is the object of the preposition *on.*

When you understand the difference between independent and dependent clauses, you'll be better able to recognize sentence fragments and faulty modification errors (more about those appears in the section "Pointing Out Mistakes: Common Sentence-Correction Errors").

Before we talk about the most commonly tested errors in the sentence-correction questions, we need to share one more thing about dependent clauses. Dependent clauses can be classified as either restrictive or nonrestrictive. Distinguishing between the two can be tricky.

>> **Restrictive clauses are vital to the meaning of the sentence.** Without them, the sentence's original meaning is lost. For example, in *She never wins her cases that involve the IRS,* the restrictive clause *that involve the IRS* provides essential information about the particular type of cases she never wins. The point of the sentence is that she never wins IRS cases.

>> **Nonrestrictive clauses provide clarifying information, but they aren't mandatory for the sentence to make sense.** In the sentence *She never wins her cases, which involve the IRS,* the nonrestrictive clause, *which involve the IRS,* makes a "by the way" statement. It provides additional information about what type of cases she handles. The main point of the sentence is that she never wins a case.

TIP

Note that in the preceding examples, the restrictive clause begins with *that* and the nonrestrictive clause begins with *which.* You don't use commas before clauses that begin with *that* because they're restrictive clauses and integral parts of the sentence. You should use commas to set nonrestrictive clauses apart from the rest of the sentence.

Pointing Out Mistakes: Common Sentence-Correction Errors

Sentence-correction questions test your ability to edit written material so it follows the rules of standard written English. The questions provide you with sentences that contain underlined parts. From the five provided answer choices, you have to choose the answer that expresses the underlined portion of the sentence in the way that conforms to the dictates of standard written English.

REMEMBER

The first answer choice is always the same as the underlined portion of the sentence. So if you think the sentence is fine as is, select the first answer. The other four choices present alternative ways of expressing the idea in the underlined part. Your task is to determine whether the underlined portion of the statement contains an error and, if so, which of the four alternatives best corrects the error.

You correct errors in sentence-correction sentences by applying the basic rules of English grammar. The good news is that you won't be asked to define or spell words or diagram sentences! And no question expects you to correct specific punctuation errors, though knowing the rules for placing commas helps you eliminate answer choices in some cases.

REMEMBER

The GMAT is a test for admission to business school. Therefore, sentence-correction questions center on errors that adversely affect the quality of business writing, such as improper word choices, incomplete or run-on sentences, and verb tense and agreement issues. The kind of errors you'll be asked to correct on the GMAT are the kind you should avoid if you want to write successfully in business.

Can't we all just get along? Errors in subject-verb and noun-pronoun agreement

One of the most fundamental skills in writing is the ability to make the elements of a sentence agree. If your subject is singular but your verb is plural, you've got a problem! Even in less formal kinds of communication, like quick emails, errors in subject-verb or noun-pronoun agreement can obscure the message you hope to communicate. You can be sure that the GMAT sentence-correction problems will contain some agreement errors.

Subject-verb agreement

When we say the subjects and verbs agree, we don't mean they're having a meeting of minds. We mean that plural subjects pair with plural verbs and singular subjects require singular verbs. Errors in simple constructions are pretty easy to spot. It just doesn't sound right to say *He attend classes at the University of Michigan.*

It's when the subject isn't simple or obvious that determining subject-verb agreement gets a little more difficult. For example, take a look at this sentence: *His fixation with commodities markets have grown into several prosperous ventures, including a consulting business.* The subject is *fixation*, but the prepositional phrase *with commodities markets* may confuse you into thinking that *markets* is the subject. *Markets* is a plural noun, so it would take a plural verb if it were the subject. But you know that *markets* can't be the subject of the sentence because *markets* is part of a prepositional phrase. It's the object of the preposition *with*, and a noun can't be an object and a subject at the same time. The subject has to be *fixation*, so the singular verb *has*, rather than the plural *have*, is proper.

TIP

Focus on the three main elements of any complex sentence by mentally eliminating words and phrases that aren't essential to the sentence's point. Then you can check the subjects and verbs to make sure they agree. For example, when you remove the prepositional phrase *with commodities markets* from the sample sentence we just discussed, you get *His fixation have grown*, which reveals an obvious disagreement in number between the subject and verb.

Noun-pronoun agreement

Another relationship you need to keep on track is the one between nouns and the pronouns that refer to them. A pronoun must agree in number with the noun (or other pronoun) it refers to. Plural nouns take plural pronouns, and singular nouns take singular pronouns. For example, this sentence has improper noun-pronoun agreement: *You can determine the ripeness of citrus by handling them and noting their color. Citrus* is a singular noun, so using plural pronouns to refer to it is incorrect. It would be correct to say *You can determine the ripeness of citrus by handling it and noting its color.*

Another problem with pronouns is unclear references. To know whether a pronoun agrees with its subject, you have to be clear about just what the pronoun refers to. For example, it's not clear which noun the pronoun in this sentence refers to: *Bobby and Tom went to the store, and he purchased a candy bar.* Because the subject of the first clause is plural, the pronoun *he* could refer to either Bobby or Tom or even to a third person. To improve clarity in this case, you'd use the name of the person who bought the candy bar rather than the ambiguous pronoun.

TIP

If a GMAT sentence-correction question contains a pronoun in the underlined portion, make sure the pronoun clearly refers to a particular noun in the sentence and that it matches that noun in number. Otherwise, you need to find an answer choice that clarifies the reference or corrects the number.

Here's a sample question that contains both types of agreement errors:

EXAMPLE

Much work performed by small business owners, like managing human relations, keeping track of accounts, and paying taxes, <u>which are essential to its successful operation, have gone virtually unnoticed by their employees</u>.

(A) which are essential to its successful operation, have gone virtually unnoticed by their employees

(B) which are essential to successful operations, have gone virtually unnoticed by their employees

(C) which is essential to its successful operation, have gone virtually unnoticed by its employees

(D) which are essential to successful operation, has gone virtually unnoticed by their employees

(E) which are essential to successful operation, has gone virtually unnoticed by its employees

The underlined portion contains several agreement errors, and your job is to locate and fix all of them. To accomplish this task, isolate the three main elements of this sentence:

> » The subject is *work.* None of the other nouns or pronouns or noun phrases in the sentence can be the main subject because they're all either objects *(owners, managing, keeping, paying, relations, accounts, taxes, operation, employees)* or subjects of dependent clauses *(which).*

> » The main verb is *have gone.* The other verb *(are)* belongs to the dependent clause, so it can't be the main verb.

> » The third element is *unnoticed.*

So the essential sentence states that *work have gone unnoticed.* Well, that doesn't sound right! You know you have to change the verb to the singular *has* to make it agree with the singular subject *work.* Eliminate any answer choices that don't change *have* to *has,* which leaves you with Choices (D) and (E).

TIP

You'll notice that both Choice (D) and Choice (E) contain the verb *are.* So the pronoun *which* must refer back to *managing, keeping,* and *paying* (which, together, are plural), so the verb that corresponds to *which* has to be plural, too. Also, both choices eliminate *its* before *successful operation* because it's unclear what *its* refers to.

The difference between the two choices is that Choice (E) changes *their* to *its.* Ask yourself which noun the pronoun before *employees* refers to. Who or what has the employees? The only possibility is *business owners,* which is a plural noun. So the pronoun that refers to it must also be plural. *Their* is plural; *its* is singular. Therefore, Choice (D) is the best answer: *Much work performed by small business owners, like managing human relations, keeping track of accounts, and paying taxes, which are essential to successful operation, has gone virtually unnoticed by their employees.*

Building code violations: Faulty construction

Errors in construction threaten the stability, readability, and even existence of a sentence! You have, no doubt, been told to avoid incomplete and run-on sentences. It's equally important to avoid sentences that confuse your reader. Some sentences may not contain grammatical errors, but they can be constructed so poorly that they obscure the point. Both grammatical and rhetorical constructions rely on correct punctuation, proper ordering of clauses, and parallel sentence structure.

The most commonly tested errors in grammatical construction are sentence fragments, run-on sentences, and sentences that lack parallel structure. After you get used to them, these errors are pretty easy to spot.

Sentence fragments

Sentence fragments on the GMAT usually show up as dependent clauses pretending to convey complete thoughts or as a bunch of words with something that looks like a verb but doesn't act like one (technically, a *verbal*).

>> **Dependent clauses standing alone are fragments because they don't present complete thoughts.** For example, this clause comes complete with a subject and verb: *Although many companies have failed to maintain consistent profits with downsizing.* However, it begins with a subordinating conjunction, *although,* so it leaves you hanging.

>> **Phrases with a verbal instead of a verb can appear to be complete if you don't read them carefully.** The verbal phrases in this sentence look like verbs but don't function as verbs: *The peacefulness of a morning warmed by the summer sun and the verdant pastures humming with the sound of busy bees.* *Warmed* and *humming* can function as verbs in other instances, but in this sentence, they're part of phrases that provide description but don't tell what the subjects (peacefulness and pastures) are like or what they're doing.

TIP

You get the hang of recognizing sentence fragments with practice. If you read the sentence under your breath, you should be able to tell whether it expresses a complete thought.

Correcting fragments is usually pretty simple. You just add the information that completes the thought or change the verbal phrase to an actual verb. For example, you can make *although many companies have failed to maintain consistent profits with downsizing* into a complete sentence by adding a comma and *some still try,* like so: *Although many companies have failed to maintain consistent profits with downsizing, some still try.* To complete *the peacefulness of a morning warmed by the summer sun and the verdant pastures humming with the sound of busy bees,* you can change the verbal phrases: *The peacefulness of a morning is warmed by the summer sun, and the verdant pastures hum with the sound of busy bees.*

Run-on sentences

Run-on sentences occur when a sentence with multiple independent clauses is improperly punctuated. Here's an example: *I had a job interview that morning so I wore my best suit.* Both *I had a job interview* and *I wore my best suit* are independent clauses. You can't just stick a coordinating conjunction between them to make a sentence. Here are the two rules for punctuating multiple independent clauses in a sentence:

REMEMBER

» **Independent clauses may be joined with a comma and a coordinating conjunction.** You can correct the problem by adding a comma, like this: *I had a job interview that morning, so I wore my best suit.*

» **Independent clauses may be joined by a semicolon.** The sentence can look like this: *I had a job interview that morning; I wore my best suit.*

Of course, you can change one of the independent clauses to a dependent clause, like this: *Because I had a job interview that morning, I wore my best suit.* If you do that, remember to separate the clauses with a comma when the dependent clause precedes the independent one.

TIP

The GMAT probably won't give you a run-on sentence to correct, but it may give you an answer choice that looks pretty good except that it makes the original sentence a run-on. Make sure the answer you choose doesn't create a run-on sentence.

Verb tense issues

In addition to checking for subject-verb agreement, make sure the verbs in the underlined portion of the sentence-correction question are in the proper tense. The other verbs in the sentence give you clues to what tense the underlined verbs should be in.

Lack of parallelism

You can count on several sentence-correction questions that test your ability to recognize a lack of parallel structure. The basic rule of parallel structure is that all phrases joined by conjunctions should be constructed in the same manner. For example, this sentence has a problem with parallelism: *Ann spent the morning emailing clients, responding to voice mails, and she wrote an article for the newsletter.*

The problem with the sentence is that the three phrases joined by the coordinating conjunction (*and*) in this sentence are constructed in different ways. *Emailing* and *responding* both take the gerund (or *-ing*) form, but *she wrote* initiates a clause. Changing *wrote* to its gerund form and eliminating *she* gets rid of the clause and solves the problem: *Ann spent the morning emailing clients, responding to voice mails, and writing an article for the newsletter.*

Parallel structure is also a factor when you make comparisons. The following sentence lacks parallel structure: *To be physically healthy is as important as being prosperous in your work.* The sentence compares a phrase in the infinitive form, *to be physically healthy,* with a phrase in the gerund form, *being prosperous in your work.* Changing one of the constructions to match the other does the trick: *Being physically healthy is as important as being prosperous in your work.*

TIP

When you see a sentence-correction question with an underlined list, check for lack of parallelism. Look for phrases joined by coordinating conjunctions. If the phrases or sentence parts exhibit dissimilar constructions, you have to correct the parallelism error.

Here's how the GMAT may question you about parallel structure:

EXAMPLE

The consultant recommended that the company <u>eliminate unneeded positions, existing departments should be consolidated, and use outsourcing when possible</u>.

(A) eliminate unneeded positions, existing departments should be consolidated, and use outsourcing when possible

(B) eliminate unneeded positions, consolidate existing departments, and outsource when possible

(C) eliminate unneeded positions, existing departments should be consolidated, and when possible outsourcing used

(D) eliminate unneeded positions and departments and use outsourcing when possible

(E) eliminate unneeded positions, existing departments are consolidated, and outsourcing used when possible

The underlined portion of this sentence contains a list joined by *and*, which is a pretty good clue that you should be vigilant for any lack of parallelism. Because the three phrases joined by *and* are not all constructed the same way, you know there's an error, so eliminate Choice (A).

Next, eliminate the answers that don't solve the problem. Choice (C) keeps the same faulty construction as the original statement in the first two recommendations, and it introduces even more awkwardness by changing *use* to *used* and adding it to the end of the third recommendation. You can clearly eliminate Choice (C). Get rid of Choice (E) because it's also worse than the original. Each of the three elements in Choice (E) has a completely different construction.

Both Choice (B) and Choice (D) seem to correct the error by introducing each recommendation with a similar construction, but Choice (D) creates a new error because it changes the meaning of the sentence. If you select Choice (D), you're stating that some departments are also unneeded and should be eliminated. The original, however, stated that departments should be consolidated. An answer can't be correct if it changes the meaning of the original sentence, so Choice (D) is wrong.

Choice (B) solves the problem without changing the original meaning, so it's the one to choose: *The consultant recommended that the company eliminate unneeded positions, consolidate existing departments, and outsource when possible.*

Is that a rhetorical question? Other construction errors

It may surprise you to know that a GMAT sentence can be grammatically accurate and still need correction. Sentences that exhibit awkward, wordy, imprecise, redundant, or unclear constructions require fixing. The GMAT calls these *errors in rhetorical construction*. The good news is that you can often use your ear to correct these problems. The right answer will often simply sound better to you.

» **Using passive instead of active voice makes a sentence seem weak and wordy.** Passive voice beats around the bush to make a point, so it lacks clarity. For example, this passive-voice sentence masks the doer of an action: *The speech was heard by most members of the corporation.* The sentence isn't technically incorrect, but it's better to say it this way: *Most members of the corporation heard the speech.* Notice also that the active voice sentence uses fewer words. So if all else is equal, choose active voice over passive voice.

» **Using repetitive language adds unnecessary words and seems silly.** A sentence shouldn't use more words than it needs to. For example, it's a bit ridiculous to say the following: *The speaker added an additional row of chairs to accommodate the large crowd.* The construction of *added an additional* isn't grammatically incorrect, but it's needlessly repetitive. It's more precise and less wordy to say *The speaker added a row of chairs to accommodate the large crowd.*

EXAMPLE

The bottom line is that any sentence that uses an excessive number of words to convey its message probably has construction problems. Often, wordiness accompanies another type of error in the underlined part. Look for the answer that uses the fewest words to correct the main error. Try it out with this sample question.

Recently, the price of crude oil <u>have been seeing fluctuations with</u> the demand for gasoline in China.

(A) have been seeing fluctuations with

(B) have fluctuated with

(C) fluctuate with

(D) has fluctuated with

(E) has changed itself along with

The main error in the sentence concerns subject-verb agreement. The singular subject, *price*, requires a singular verb. Additionally, the underlined portion is needlessly wordy. First, eliminate answer choices that don't correct the agreement problem. Then, focus on choices that clarify the language.

Both Choices (B) and (C) perpetuate the agreement problem by providing plural verbs for the singular subject. Eliminate those along with Choice (A), and you're left with Choices (D) and (E).

Choice (E) is constructed even more awkwardly than the original sentence, so Choice (D) is the best answer: *Recently, the price of crude oil has fluctuated with the demand for gasoline in China.*

This sample question gives you practice recognizing redundancy:

EXAMPLE

A recent survey of American colleges <u>reveal that among some of the most selective universities the acceptance rates have lowered by at least a 2 percent decrease over the last two years.</u>

(A) reveal that among some of the most selective universities the acceptance rates have lowered by at least a 2 percent decrease over the last two years

(B) reveals that among some of the most selective universities the acceptance rates have lowered by at least a 2 percent decrease over the last two years

(C) reveal that among some of the most selective universities acceptance rates have decreased by at least 2 percent over the last two years

(D) reveals that among some of the most selective universities acceptance rates have decreased by at least 2 percent over the last two years

(E) reveals that among some of the most selective universities the acceptance rates have decreased by at least a 2 percent margin over the last two years

As you examine the possible answers, first notice you have the option of either *reveal* or *reveals*. The subject is *survey*, so you can eliminate answers that provide the plural verb *reveal*. So Choices (A) and (C) are out.

In Choice (B), the verb *lowered* is sufficient to let you know that the rates have gone down; you don't also need to know that the rate was a percent decrease. The redundancy makes this answer incorrect. Choice (E) eliminates the repetition of the decrease, but it introduces another redundancy. If the rate decreased by a percentage, you don't also need to know it decreased by a margin.

The answer that corrects the verb agreement and eliminates redundant wording is Choice (D).

Follow the idiom: Correct use of standard expressions

Idiomatic expressions are constructions English speakers use because, well, those are the expressions they use. In other words, we use certain words in certain ways for no particular reason other than because that's the way we do it. However, even native English speakers often fail to use idiomatic expressions correctly. It's common to hear people use *further* instead of *farther* when they mean distance or *less* instead of *fewer* when they're talking about the number of countable items.

The GMAT tests you on your knowledge of idiomatic expressions because sentences that are idiomatically incorrect can damage your credibility and interfere with the clarity of your message. The only way to know idiomatic constructions is to memorize them. Luckily, you probably know most of them already. To help you along, Table 4-1 lists some commonly tested idioms and how to use them correctly.

TABLE 4-1 **Idiomatically Correct Constructions for the GMAT**

Expression	Rule	Correct Use
among/between	Use *among* for comparing three or more things or persons, *between* for two things or persons.	*Between* the two of us there are few problems, but *among* the four of us there is much discord.
as . . . as	When you use *as* in a comparison, use the construction of *as . . . as.*	The dog is *as* wide *as* he is tall.
being	Don't use *being* after *regard as.*	She is *regarded as* the best salesperson on the team. (Not: She is *regarded as being* the best salesperson.)
better/best and worse/worst	Use *better* and *worse* to compare two things, *best* and *worst* to compare more than two things.	Of the two products, the first is *better* known, but this product is the *best* known of all 20 on the market.
but	Don't use *but* after *doubt* or *help.*	He could not *help* liking the chartreuse curtains with the mauve carpet. (Not: He could not *help but* like the curtains.)
different from	Use *different from* rather than *different than.*	This plan is *different from* the one we implemented last year. (Not: This plan is *different than* last year's.)
effect/affect	Generally, use *effect* as a noun and *affect* as a verb.	No one could know how the *effect* of the presentation would *affect* the client's choice.
farther/further	Use *farther* to refer to distance and *further* to refer to time or quantity.	Carol walked *farther* today than she did yesterday, and she vows to *further* study the benefits of walking.
hopefully	*Hopefully* is an adverb meaning *with hope* and should never be used to mean *I hope* or *it is hoped.*	*I hope* they offer me the managerial position. (Not: *Hopefully,* they'll offer me the managerial position.)
however	*However* used at the beginning of a sentence (without a comma) means *to whatever extent.*	*However* they try to discourage his antics, he continues to engage in office pranks.
imply/infer	Use *imply* to mean to suggest or indicate, *infer* to mean deduce.	From his *implication* that the car was packed, I *inferred* that it was time to leave.
in regard to	Use *in regard to* rather than *in regards to.*	The memo was *in regard to* the meeting we had yesterday. (Not: The memo was *in regards to* the meeting.)

(continued)

TABLE 4-1 *(continued)*

Expression	Rule	Correct Use
less/fewer	Use *less* to refer to unmeasured quantity, *fewer* to refer to number.	That office building is *less* noticeable because it has *fewer* floors.
less/least	Use *less* to compare two things and *least* to compare more than two things.	He is *less* educated than his brother is, but he is not the *least* educated of his entire family.
like/as	Use *like* before simple nouns and pronouns, *as* before phrases and clauses.	*Like* Ruth, Steve wanted the office policy to be just *as* it had always been.
loan/lend	Use *loan* as a noun, *lend* as a verb.	Betty asked Julia to *lend* her a car until she received her *loan*.
many/much	Use *many* to refer to number, *much* to refer to unmeasured quantity.	For *many* days I woke up feeling *much* anxiety, but I'm better now that I'm reading *GMAT For Dummies*.
more/most	Use *more* to compare two things, *most* to compare more than two things.	Of the two girls, the older is *more* educated, and she is the *most* educated person in her family.
try/come	*Try* and *come* take the infinitive form of a subsequent verb.	*Try to* file it by tomorrow. (Not: *Try and* file it by tomorrow.)

In addition to the expressions listed in Table 4-1, you should also memorize the correlative expressions in Table 4-2, which shows you words that must appear together in the same sentence. To maintain parallel structure, the elements that follow each component of the correlative should be similar. Thus, if *not only* precedes a verb and direct object, the *but also* that follows it should also precede a verb and direct object.

TABLE 4-2 Correlative Expressions

Expression	Example
not only . . . but also	He *not only* had his cake *but also* ate it.
either . . . or	*Either* do it my way *or* take the highway.
neither . . . nor	*Neither* steaming locomotives *nor* wild horses can persuade me to change my mind.

Here are a couple of examples of how you may see idioms tested on the GMAT:

Never before had American businesses confronted <u>so many challenges as they did during the Great Depression</u>.

EXAMPLE

(A) so many challenges as they did during the Great Depression

(B) so many challenges at one time as they confronted during the Great Depression

(C) at once so many challenges as they confronted during the Great Depression

(D) as many challenges as it did during the Great Depression

(E) as many challenges as they did during the Great Depression

You've memorized that the proper comparison construction is *as . . . as*, so you know that the sentence contains an idiomatically improper construction (it also probably sounds strange to you!). Start by eliminating all answers that don't correct *so many . . . as* to *as . . . as*. Choices (A), (B), and (C) retain the improper construction, so cross them out.

Now consider Choices (D) and (E). Both maintain the original verb, which is fine. The sentence compares two different periods of time. The first portion of the sentence refers to the period before the Great Depression, which requires the past perfect verb *had . . . confronted.* The under-lined part of the sentence simply requires the past tense verb *did* to maintain the proper tense. Choice (D) creates a new error in pronoun agreement by using the singular pronoun *it* to refer to the plural noun *businesses.* Choice (E) is the correct answer: *Never before had American businesses confronted as many challenges as they did during the Great Depression.*

EXAMPLE

Experts agree that good health may result from following a regimen that <u>includes consuming less fat and calories</u>.

(A) includes consuming less fat and calories

(B) includes the consumption of less fat and calories

(C) includes consuming less fat and fewer calories

(D) including the consumption of less fat and calories

(E) including consuming fewer fats and calories

For a single quantity, use *less*; use *fewer* for plural nouns. So the proper construction is *less* fat and *fewer* calories. Choices (A), (B), and (D) are incorrect because they apply the singular *less* to the plural *calories.* Choice (C) corrects the issue by adding *fewer* before *calories*, and Choice (E) changes *fat* to *fats*, so *fewer* appropriately applies to both plural nouns. Choice (E) is wrong, however, because *including* doesn't properly follow *that.* The correct answer is Choice (C).

Implementing an Approach to Sentence-Correction Questions

The key to performing well on sentence-correction questions is to approach them systematically:

1. **Determine the nature of the original sentence's error (if one exists).**

   If a sentence has more than one error, focus on one error at a time. If you can, come up with a quick idea of how to fix the error before you look at the answers.

2. **Skim through the answer choices and eliminate any choices that don't correct the error.**

3. **Eliminate answer choices that correct the original error but add a new error or errors.**

   You should be left with only one answer that fixes the original problem without creating new errors.

4. **Reread the sentence with the new answer choice inserted just to make sure that you haven't missed something and that the answer you've chosen makes sense.**

To show you how this process works, we'll refer to this example question throughout the next few sections.

EXAMPLE

Because the company is disorganized, <u>they will never reach their goal</u>.

(A) they will never reach their goal

(B) it will never reach their goal

(C) it will never reach its goal

(D) their goal will never be reached

(E) its goal will never be reached

Spotting the error

When you read the sentence-correction question, pay particular attention to the underlined portion and look for at least one error.

> » If the underlined section contains verbs, make sure they agree with their subjects and are in the proper tense.
>
> » Check any pronouns to determine whether they agree in number with the nouns they refer to.
>
> » Look at lists to confirm that their construction is parallel.
>
> » Note any tricky idiomatic phrases to verify that they're used correctly.
>
> » Look for repetitive and otherwise wordy language.

If you don't see any obvious errors, read through the answer choices just to make sure they don't reveal something you may have missed. If you still don't see a problem, choose the first answer choice. About 20 percent of the sentence-correction sentences contain no errors.

REMEMBER

Don't look for errors in the portion of the sentence that isn't underlined. Even if you find something, you can't correct it!

The underlined portion of the sample question contains a verb (*will reach*), but it agrees with its subject and is in the proper tense. There's also a pronoun, *they*. *They* refers to company, but *company* is a singular noun and *they* is a plural pronoun. You can't have a plural pronoun refer to a singular noun. Therefore, the underlined section definitely has a pronoun agreement error.

Eliminating answers that don't correct errors

If you spot an error in the underlined portion, read through the answer choices and eliminate those that don't correct it. If you see more than one error in the underlined portion of the statement, begin with the error that has the more obvious correction. For example, if the underlined portion has both a rhetorical error and an error in subject-verb agreement, begin with the error in subject-verb agreement. Eliminating answer choices that don't address the agreement problem is quick and easy. After you've eliminated the choices that don't fix the obvious error, move on to the other error or errors. Comparing rhetorical constructions in answer choices can take a while, so eliminating choices before this step saves you time.

REMEMBER

After you've eliminated an answer choice, don't reread it! Chapter 2 gives you tips on how to "erase" wrong answer choices. Follow the guidelines in Chapter 2 to avoid wasting time on answers you've already determined are wrong.

You know the example problem has an error, so you can eliminate Choice (A). Now eliminate any choices that don't correct the incorrect pronoun reference. Choice (D) doesn't; it still uses a plural pronoun (*their*) to refer to a singular subject. Eliminate Choice (D), and don't look at it again. The other three choices, Choices (B), (C), and (E), seem to fix that particular pronoun error.

The underlined portion contains another problem with noun-pronoun agreement, though. *Their* in the original sentence is also plural but refers to the singular noun *company*. Although Choice (B) makes the first plural pronoun singular, it retains the second problem pronoun, so you can eliminate Choice (B). Only Choices (C) and (E) remain.

Eliminating choices that create new errors

The next step is to eliminate answers that create new errors.

A new error in an answer choice usually isn't the same type of error as the original one. GMAT writers know you'll look for pronoun errors if a pronoun error occurs in the original sentence, so the new error in an answer choice may be an improper expression or a verb-tense problem.

Check the remaining answer choices for new errors. Choice (E) doesn't contain an agreement error, but it changes the underlined portion of the sentence to a passive construction. On sentence corrections, active voice is always better than passive voice. Choice (C) is the answer that corrects the pronoun problem without creating new errors.

You should end up with only one answer choice that corrects the existing errors without creating new ones. If you end up with two seemingly correct answer choices, read them both within the context of the original sentence. One will have an error that you've overlooked.

Rereading the sentence

Don't skip this step! Check your answer by replacing the underlined portion with your answer choice and reading the new sentence in its entirety. Don't just check to see whether the answer sounds good in the sentence; also check for errors that you may not have noticed as you worked through the question.

Missing errors is easy when you focus only on the underlined portion of the statement. After you integrate your answer choice with the rest of the sentence, errors you've missed may suddenly become obvious. Reading the statement with your answer choice inserted is the best way to check your answer.

When you reread the sentence with Choice (C), you get this: *Because the company is disorganized, it will never reach its goal.* The corrected sentence contains the proper noun-pronoun agreement.

Reviewing the process and guessing on sentence corrections

The approach outlined in this section works well as long as you have time to determine the error in the sentence or recognize that no error exists. If you're running short on time or can't tell whether the statement is correct as written, you may need to guess. Eliminate the choices you know are wrong because they contain their own errors. Then read each of the possible choices in the context of the entire statement. You may find errors that you didn't notice before. If you still can't narrow down your choices to one answer, pick one from the remaining answers and move on.

Sentence-Correction Practice Problems with Answer Explanations

After you master the approach to sentence-correction questions, they'll seem a lot less daunting. To help you solidify your plan of attack, answer the following ten practice questions. Try to answer them in ten minutes or less. When you're finished, check your answers with the explanations that follow.

Practice problems

1. Most state governors now have the power of line item veto, <u>while the U.S. President does not</u>.

   (A) while the U.S. President does not

   (B) a power which is not yet available to the U.S. President

   (C) which the U.S. President has no such power

   (D) the U.S. President does not

   (E) they do not share that with the U.S. President

2. Although all six state governments faced budget problems after the economic downturn of 2007, the problems were <u>worse</u> in California because much of it revenue came from a large number of high-tech industries.

   (A) worse

   (B) worst

   (C) more

   (D) great

   (E) worsening

3. The PTA held monthly meetings to discuss matters concerning the schoolchildren, determine what fundraisers to implement, <u>and for coming up with ways to balance the budget</u>.

   (A) and for coming up with ways to balance the budget

   (B) and to balance the budget in creative ways

   (C) and discovering ways to balance the budget

   (D) and to determine how to come up with ways the budget should be balanced

   (E) and come up with ways to balance the budget

4. Many tourists <u>seem to be avoiding the Tijuana/Rosarito Beach area because they are experiencing an upsurge in the occurrence of border violence</u>.

   (A) seem to be avoiding the Tijuana/Rosarito Beach area because they are experiencing an upsurge in the occurrence of border violence

   (B) seem to avoid the Tijuana/Rosarito Beach area because they are experiencing an upsurge of violence on the border

   (C) avoid the Tijuana/Rosarito Beach area because they are experiencing an upsurge of border violence occurrence

   (D) seem to be avoiding the Tijuana/Rosarito Beach area because it is experiencing an upsurge in the occurrence of border violence

   (E) seem to be avoiding the Tijuana/Rosarito Beach area because it experiences an upsurge in the occurrence of border violence

5. Historians believe that roughly 600 deaths have occurred at the Grand Canyon since the 1870s; <u>many resulted from drowning, plane crashes into canyon walls</u>, and the actions of overzealous hikers.

   (A) many resulted from drowning, plane crashes into canyon walls

   (B) many of these resulting from drowning deaths, planes crashing into canyon walls

   (C) many of these deaths being the results of drowning, plane crashes into canyon walls

   (D) many of these were drowning deaths, plane crash deaths

   (E) with many as a result from drowning, planes crashing into canyon walls

6. After Great America Bank incited public outrage with its announcement of new debit-card fees, many customers withdrew their funds and joined credit unions instead, which seems <u>as if to indicate that</u> America's mistrust of big banks is still widespread.

    (A) as if to indicate that

    (B) indicative of

    (C) like an indication of

    (D) like it is indicative that

    (E) to indicate that

7. Despite arguments made by parent watch-dog groups, <u>neither violent behavior or disruptiveness have been directly linked to violent video games</u>.

    (A) neither violent behavior or disruptiveness have been directly linked to violent video games

    (B) neither violent behavior nor disruptiveness has been directly linked to violent video games

    (C) neither violent behavior or disruptiveness has been directly linked to violent video games

    (D) neither violent behavior nor disruptiveness have been directly linked to violent video games

    (E) neither violent behavior nor disruptiveness were directly linked to violent video games

8. Russell & Carmody, LLC, and Rutledge, Inc., merged in 2012 to create Russell, Carmody and Rutledge, Inc., <u>and they are now the most successful public relations firm in the metro area</u>.

    (A) and they are now the most successful public relations firm in the metro area

    (B) it is now the most successful public relations firm in the metro area

    (C) and they are now the most successful public relations firms in the metro area

    (D) which is now the most successful public relations firm in the metro area

    (E) and it is now the most successful public relations firms in the metro area

9. A transaction-broker assists the buyer or seller or both <u>throughout a real estate transaction by performing</u> terms of any written or oral agreement, fully informing the parties, presenting all offers, and assisting the parties with any contracts, including the closing of the transaction, without being an agent or advocate for any of the parties.

    (A) throughout a real estate transaction by performing

    (B) throughout a real estate transaction by the performance of

    (C) during a real estate transaction by the performance of

    (D) with a real estate transaction by accomplishing the performing

    (E) during a real estate transaction through the performance of

10. Although <u>its policy for honorary doctorates was not dissimilar to</u> Cambridge or Oxford — they gave awards to the "distinguished" in particular fields, and the person had to be "widely recognized" — it is clear that the universities were drawn to the entertainment industries to produce visible personalities for their convocation ceremonies, and the idea of "widely recognized" trumped any other distinction.

    (A) its policy for honorary doctorates was not dissimilar to

    (B) their policies for awarding honorary doctorates were not dissimilar to those of

    (C) their policies for honorary doctorates was not dissimilar from

    (D) its policy for honorary doctorates was very similar to

    (E) its policies for awarding honorary doctorates was very similar to that of

Answer explanations

1. **A.** Always begin by trying to identify the error in the underlined portion of the statement. The underlined words don't contain any pronouns and the subject and verb agree, so you don't have any agreement errors. Parallel construction doesn't seem to be an issue. The use of *while* to mean *although* may have alerted you. However, while the primary purpose of *while* is to indicate an event that happens at the same time as another, you may also use *while* to mean *although*. In fact, we just used it that way in the previous sentence!

   This question doesn't seem to have an error. But just to be sure, read each answer choice to make sure you haven't missed something. Choice (B) is wrong because it uses *which* instead of *that* to introduce a restrictive clause, and the pronoun *which* in Choice (C) has no clear reference. You can't use Choice (D) or Choice (E) because they're independent clauses. Plugging in either of these choices creates a comma splice. None of the answer choices offer a better construction for the sentence.

   TIP

   Remember that about 20 percent of the time, the underlined part contains no error. Don't assume that the sentences always contain errors.

2. **B.** This example has only one underlined word, which is nice because you know just what to focus on. If you simply go by what sounds right, you may think this example is fine the way it is. You probably hear English speakers use *worse* like this in everyday conversations. But the GMAT doesn't test common spoken English; it tests *standard written* English.

   REMEMBER

   You use *worse* to compare two entities and *worst* to compare three or more.

   The sentence talks about a situation among several state governments. *Worse* would be appropriate for a comparison between two states. But this sentence compares budget problems in *six* states, so instead use the superlative form *worst* to single out poor California. That's the answer you find in Choice (B).

   You can double-check your answer by reading through the other choices. You've found an error, so Choice (A) can't be right. Choices (C) and (D) aren't superlatives, and Choice (E) uses the progressive form *were worsening*, which changes the meaning of the sentence.

3. **E.** The underlined words are part of a series, so adjust your error antennae to feel out a parallelism problem. Check the grammatical construction of each element. The underlined portion contains the gerund form *coming*, but the other two PTA purposes are expressed in the infinitive form. All three reasons should be in the same form. Both Choices (A) and (C) use the *-ing* form, so they can't be right. Choice (D) is unnecessarily wordy, so now you know the correct answer must be either Choice (B) or Choice (E). Both choices properly use the infinitive form, but Choice (B) unnecessarily repeats *to* and it adds information to the original sentence.

4. **D.** The underlined portion is lengthy, so use your powers of concentration to home in on the potential errors. You see a couple verbs and the pronoun *they*. Check the pronoun first.

   REMEMBER

   Whenever you see an underlined pronoun, check its reference to make sure it's clear and that it agrees in number with the noun.

The pronoun *they* is plural, but the only plural noun in the sentence is *tourists*. It doesn't make sense that tourists would be experiencing an upsurge in the occurrence of border violence. It's more likely that *they* refers to the beach area, which is experiencing increased violence. Only one area is mentioned, so the pronoun should be singular, *it.* That narrows your choices considerably. The only two answers that change *they* to *it* are Choices (D) and (E). The difference between the two is that Choice (E) changes the verb tense to the simple present. The upsurge is ongoing, so the original progressive tense in Choice (D) is better.

5. **A.** The first thing you likely notice about the underlined part is that it contains a series of causes of Grand Canyon deaths. An underlined series means check for parallel structure. Each cause is presented as a noun, so there isn't a blatant problem with parallelism. Some of the answer choices change *plane crashes* to *planes crashing* to match *drowning,* but they introduce new errors. Choices (B), (C), and (E) create sentence fragments, which don't work with the semicolon. The semicolon has to be followed by an independent clause. Choice (D) unnecessarily repeats *deaths.* It doesn't make sense to say the deaths result from drowning deaths. The best answer is to leave this one exactly as it is.

6. **E.** To say that something *seems as if to* is improper, so Choice (A) is out. You can eliminate Choices (B) and (C) as well, because their use of *of* doesn't fit with the rest of the sentence. You use *like* to compare simple nouns, and Choice (D) improperly uses *like* to compare *which* to the clause *it is indicative.* The best answer has to be Choice (E). It gets rid of *as if* without creating another error.

7. **B.** The original sentence contains both a conjunction error and a subject–verb agreement error.

REMEMBER

Whenever you see *neither,* you must also see *nor.* Neither Choice (A) nor Choice (C) pairs *nor* with *neither.* Eliminate them.

You're left with Choices (B), (D), and (E). The verbs in these three choices are different. Choice (B) contains a singular verb, and the other two have plural verbs. The subject of the clause is *neither,* and *neither* is singular. Therefore, Choice (B) has to be correct because it contains the singular verb.

8. **D.** This sentence-correction question involves a commonly tested pronoun reference problem. Although the sentence initially refers to two separate companies, it then states that they merged into one firm, so the correct pronoun to use when referring to only one company is *it.* Therefore, you can eliminate Choices (A) and (C). Choice (E) contains the proper pronoun, *it,* but refers to the new company in the plural, *firms,* so you can cross that one out as well. You're left with Choices (B) and (D), but Choice (B) creates a comma splice because it's an independent clause.

9. **A.** To maintain parallel structure in the sentence's list, you need to begin the first element with an *–ing* word, so *performing* is a better choice than "the performance of." You can eliminate Choices (B), (C), and (E). Choice (D) contains *performing,* but it also adds the redundant *accomplishing.* Performing the terms of an agreement is the same as accomplishing them. So, the best answer is Choice (A). The different options for the initial preposition in the answer choices are included to distract you from the real error. Each of them works in the context of the sentence.

10. B. The answer choices provide you with either the pronoun *its* or *their*. Search the sentence to find the noun the pronoun references. The policies belong to the plural universities, so you need the plural pronoun *their*. Eliminate Choices (A), (D), and (E).

When you examine the difference between the remaining answers, you see that Choice (B) includes *awarding* and inserts "those of" in the comparison between the policies of the universities in the second part of the sentence and Cambridge or Oxford in the first part. Because you can't compare *policies* to *Cambridge* (as in Choice [C]) but must compare *policies* to *policies*, you need to add "those of" as provided by Choice (B). Choice (C) is also wrong because it's idiomatically incorrect to say that something is "dissimilar from" another thing and because the singular verb *was* is improperly paired with the plural subject *policies*.

Chapter 5

Not as Enticing as a Bestseller: Reading Comprehension

I f you find yourself reading approximately 350 words about white dwarfs in space, you're not encountering a sci-fi fable about the seven companions of an astronomical Snow White. You're more likely tackling a reading-comprehension problem on the GMAT. The GMAT test-makers present yet another way to poke and prod your intellect with several paragraphs of fascinating reading material and a few questions to test your comprehension of it. The questions may be specific and focus on highlighted portions of the passage, or they may concern general themes, like the author's main idea.

Reading-comprehension questions are designed to test how well you understand unfamiliar reading material. But you're probably less concerned with the reason these passages are included on the GMAT than you are with getting through all that reading and question-answering with enough time left over to confront those pesky sentence-correction and critical-reasoning problems. What you need is a proven strategy. And in this chapter, we deliver by introducing you to the types of passages and questions you'll encounter and telling you how to deal with them.

Judging by Appearances: What Reading-Comprehension Questions Look Like

The verbal section of the GMAT mixes reading-comprehension questions with critical-reasoning questions and sentence-correction questions. So you may correct grammatical errors in a few sentences and then come across a set of reading-comprehension questions. About one-third of the 41 questions in the verbal section are reading questions. You'll see a split screen with an article passage on the left and a question with five answer choices on the right.

Although every passage has more than one question (usually, passages have about five to eight questions), only one question pops up at a time. You read the passage (which contains about 350 words), click on the choice that best answers the question, and confirm your answer. As soon as you confirm your answer, another question pops up on the right side of the screen. The passage remains on the left. Sometimes a question refers to a particular part of the passage. For these questions, the GMAT highlights the portion of the passage you need to focus on to answer the question.

Approaching Reading Passages

Reading-comprehension questions don't ask you to do anything particularly unfamiliar. You've probably been reading passages and answering multiple-choice questions about them since you were in elementary school. If you're having difficulty answering reading-comprehension questions correctly, don't worry: Your reading skills are likely fine. You're probably just not familiar with the specific way you have to read for the GMAT.

REMEMBER

You have less than two minutes to answer each reading-comprehension question, and that includes reading the passage. Generally, you shouldn't spend more than five minutes reading a passage before you answer its questions, so you have to read as efficiently as you can. You need a plan for getting through the passage in a way that allows you to answer questions correctly and quickly. When you read a passage, focus on the following elements:

>> The passage's general theme

>> The author's tone

>> The way the author organizes the passage

TIP

Unless you have a photographic memory, you won't be able to remember all a passage's details long enough to answer the questions. Don't try to figure out the passage's minutiae while you're reading it. If you encounter a question about a little detail, you can go back and reread the relevant section. Instead of sweating the small stuff, make sure you understand the author's main point, the author's tone, and the overall way the author presents the information.

Mastering the message: The main point

Generally, people write passages to inform or persuade. Most of the passages on the GMAT are informative rather than argumentative, and even the argumentative ones are pretty tame.

REMEMBER

The main point of GMAT passages is often *to discuss a topic, to inform the reader about a phenomenon, or to compare one idea to another.* Rarely does a GMAT passage seek to condemn, criticize, or enthusiastically advocate a particular idea or position.

Because most authors present the main theme in the first paragraph or two, you'll probably figure it out in the first few seconds of your reading. If it's not clear in the first paragraphs, it probably appears in the last paragraph, where the author sums up the ideas. After you've figured out the author's overall theme, quickly jot down on your noteboard a word or two to help you remember the theme. For a passage that describes the differences between the flight patterns of houseflies and horseflies, you can write *compare flight — house/horse.* Your notation gives you something to refer to when you're asked the inevitable main theme synthesis question (which we discuss in greater detail in the later section "Getting to the point: Main-theme questions").

Absorbing the ambiance: Author's tone

In addition to understanding the author's main point, you need to know how the author feels about the issue. You get clues to the author's tone or mood by the words he uses. GMAT passages either inform the reader about something or try to persuade the reader to adopt the author's viewpoint. Informative passages are often more objective than persuasive ones, so the author's tone is usually neutral. Authors of persuasive passages may exhibit more emotion. You may sense that an author is critical, sarcastic, pessimistic, optimistic, or supportive. When you figure out how the author feels about the topic, write a short description on your noteboard, like *objective*, *hopeful*, or *mildly critical*. Knowing the tone of a passage helps you choose answers that exhibit the same tone or level of bias.

WARNING

Regardless of the author's mood, don't let your personal opinions about a passage's subject matter influence your answer. Getting emotionally involved with the content of the passage can cloud your judgment. You may subconsciously rely on your opinions as you answer questions. To avoid doing so, you may find it helpful to remind yourself that correct answers are true *according to the passage* or *according to the author*.

Finding the framework: The passage's outline

Knowing the structure of a passage is much more important than understanding its details. Instead of trying to comprehend everything the author says, focus on how the author lays out the information.

Standard essay format includes an introduction with a thesis, two or three supporting paragraphs, and a conclusion. Many GMAT passages are excerpts from larger works, so they may not exhibit exact standard essay form, but they'll contain evidence of all three elements. As you read, determine the passage's overall point and the main points of each paragraph.

TIP

You may find it helpful to construct a mini-outline of the passage as you read it. Underneath the main theme, jot down a word or two on your noteboard that describes the type of information contained in each paragraph. So under *compare flight — house/horse*, you may list a synopsis of each supporting paragraph: *difference in wingspan, size difference — horse 3x bigger, ways flight helps house*. This outline tells you that in the first supporting paragraph, you find info about how the two flies differ in wingspan. The second supporting paragraph is where you find out how the greater size of horseflies affects their flight. And from the third supporting paragraph, you find out how the housefly's flight helps it in everyday life. Although you may not understand all the fascinating details of the author's account, you know where to go in the passage if you have to answer a detail question.

Building an outline in your head or on your noteboard helps you know where in the passage you can find answers to questions about particular details. Doing so also helps you answer any questions that ask you *how* an author develops his point.

WARNING

Even though you don't need to read and understand every detail of a passage before you answer its questions, we highly recommend that you scan the entire passage before you attempt the questions. You need an idea of what a passage is about and how it's organized before you look at the questions. Any minutes you save by not reading the passage first will be wasted when you have to read and reread paragraphs because you don't know where information is located or what the passage is about.

Sticking to the Subject: Types of Passages

You may think that because the GMAT measures your aptitude for MBA programs, its reading passages deal with subjects like marketing and economics. You're wrong. Although some of the passages do concern business matters, you'll also read about topics from the natural and social sciences. The GMAT wants to see how well you analyze a variety of topics, unfamiliar and familiar, so it presents you with articles about everything from the steel-making process to the quality of artifacts from the Bronze Age.

In the following sections, we explore the types of reading passages found on the GMAT.

Experimenting with natural science passages

Physical and biological sciences mean big business. Some of the areas of commerce that depend on science include pharmaceuticals, computers, agriculture, the defense industry, household products, and materials manufacturing (such as plastics and polymers). These industries, taken together, exert a huge influence on American quality of life and the nation's bottom line. Just think of this country without computers and pharmaceuticals, not to mention modern agriculture!

Although you may concede that the natural sciences are important, you may not be eager to confront a chemistry passage halfway through the GMAT verbal section. The good news is that the reading-comprehension questions don't assume that you have any previous knowledge in the subject. If you do come across a reading passage on chemistry and it's been 20 years since you've studied the periodic table, relax. The answer to every question is located somewhere in the passage.

You really don't need to know a lot about a passage topic to answer the questions correctly. Although it's true that a chemistry major may read a passage about polymers more quickly than someone who never took a college chemistry course, that doesn't necessarily mean the chemistry expert will answer more questions correctly. The chemistry major may actually be at a disadvantage because he may try to answer questions based on outside knowledge instead of using only the information stated in the passage.

WARNING

Reading-comprehension questions test your reading skills, not the plethora of details you keep tucked away in your long-term memory. When you come across a passage on a subject that you're familiar with, don't rely on your outside knowledge to answer the question! Make sure the answers you choose can be justified by information contained in the passage.

REMEMBER

Natural science passages tend to be more objective and neutral than persuasive in tone. So usually the main theme of a natural science topic is *to explain*, *describe*, or *inform* about a scientific event.

Gathering in social circles: Social science passages

In addition to natural science passages, the GMAT presents passages about a different kind of science: social science, which includes topics like law, philosophy, history, political science, archeology, sociology, and psychology. The good news about social science passages is that their topics tend to crop up more in the news and in daily conversation than does, for example, physics! So you're more likely to be comfortable, if not necessarily familiar, with them.

Although passages about the social sciences are still mostly descriptive and informative, they're more likely to be persuasive than natural science passages, so you may see more variety in the kinds of tones these passages display.

Getting down to business passages

Business passages may be objective or persuasive and are generated from fields like economics, marketing, resource management, and accounting, among others. Finally, topics you're familiar with! You can forgo the archeology of New Zealand or an anatomy lesson on the long-horned beetle. This is business, your chosen field of study. At least it's a topic you're clearly interested in. You'll probably breeze right through most of these passages. But don't let familiarity with the topic serve as an excuse to slack off. You need your powers of concentration for every passage topic.

WARNING

If the passage is on a familiar subject, don't fall into the trap of using your own information to answer questions. Being familiar with a passage topic is an advantage, but only if you approach each question reminding yourself that the correct answer is based on information in the passage and not on what you studied last semester in your marketing courses or discussed last week in your sales meeting.

Approaching Reading-Comprehension Questions

The GMAT verbal section has 41 questions, and you're allotted 75 minutes to answer them. That comes out to less than two minutes per question. If you spend too much time answering reading-comprehension questions, you'll have less time to consider the sentence-correction and critical-reasoning questions that also comprise the verbal section. So having a system for tackling reading-comprehension questions is just as important as knowing how to read through the passages. Your approach should include

>> Recognizing the type of question

>> Quickly eliminating incorrect answer choices

>> Managing questions that ask for the answer that *isn't* supported by the passage

We show you how to do all three of these things in the following sections and provide a few examples of what to look for so you know how to answer the questions correctly.

Identifying the question type

The first step in answering a reading-comprehension question correctly is identifying the type of question. Most reading-comprehension questions fall into one of these four categories:

>> Summarizing the main theme

>> Finding specific information

>> Making inferences

>> Assessing the author's tone

Each of the four question types requires a slightly different approach. Main theme and tone questions ask you to make determinations about the passage as a whole, and specific-information and inference questions usually ask you to home in on particular parts of the passage. For example, when you know that a question is about specific details in the passage, you can focus your attention on the portion of the passage that's relevant to the information in the question.

We share all the details about each of the four categories of reading-comprehension questions in the following sections.

Getting to the point: Main-theme questions

Main-theme questions ask you to identify the primary purpose of the whole passage. Almost every passage has at least one question that asks you to identify the thesis of the passage, and often it's the first question you answer for a particular reading passage.

TIP

You can identify main-theme questions by the language they contain. Here are some examples of the ways main-theme questions may be worded:

>> The author of the passage is primarily concerned with which of the following?

>> The author's primary goal (or purpose) in the passage is to do which of the following?

>> An appropriate title that best summarizes this passage is

While you read the passage, look for its main theme because you know you'll probably be asked about it. You may even want to write a sentence that briefly states the passage's primary purpose. Then, if you're asked a question about the passage's main theme, you'll look for an answer that conveys an idea similar to your statement of the author's purpose.

TIP

The best answer to a main-theme question is general rather than specific. If an answer choice concerns information that's discussed in only one part of the passage, it probably isn't the correct answer to a main-theme question. Here are some other ways to narrow in on the correct answer for main-theme questions:

>> Eliminate answer choices that contain information that comes only from only the middle paragraphs of the passage. These paragraphs probably deal with specific points rather than the main theme.

>> Eliminate any answer choices that contain information that you can't find in the passage. These choices are irrelevant.

>> Look at the first words of the answer choices to see whether you can eliminate any answer choices based on the first words only. For example, if you're trying to find the best answer to the author's purpose in an objectively written natural science passage, you can eliminate answers that begin with less objective terms, such as *to argue that . . ., to criticize . . .,* and *to refute the opposition's position that. . . .*

Finding the details: Specific-information questions

Some GMAT reading-comprehension questions ask you about specific statements in the passage. These questions are potentially the easiest type of reading-comprehension question because the information you need to answer them is stated in the passage. You just need to find it. This information may be quantitative, such as years, figures, or numbers, or it may be qualitative, like ideas, emotions, or thoughts.

Specific-information questions are worded in many different ways, but they almost always contain some reference to the passage. For example:

>> The passage states that . . .

>> According to the passage, . . .

>> In the passage, the author indicates that . . .

TIP

To succeed on specific-information questions, read the question carefully and refer to the outline of the passage you've written on your noteboard to remind you where the passage addresses certain types of information. And keep in mind that the correct answer may paraphrase the passage rather than provide a word-for-word repeat.

Reading between the lines: Inference questions

Inference questions ask you about information that's *implied* by the passage rather than directly stated. These questions test your ability to draw conclusions, using evidence that appears in the passage. For inference questions, you're normally required to do one of these three things:

>> Identify a different interpretation of an author's statement.

>> Infer the intended meaning of a word that's used figuratively in the passage.

>> Interpret the author's statements one step beyond what is actually written.

For example, suppose you read a passage that compares the rapidity of wing beats between houseflies and horseflies. Information in the second paragraph may state that the wings of horseflies beat at 96 bps (beats per second). Information in the fourth paragraph may say that a Purple Winger is a type of horsefly. From this information, you can infer that the wings of the Purple Winger beat at a rate of 96 bps. This is an example of the third bullet: taking the author's statements one step beyond what is actually written. Note that the horsefly conclusion doesn't require that you make great leaps of logic.

TIP

When you're answering an inference question, look for the choice that slightly extends the meaning of the passage. Choices that go beyond the scope of the passage are usually incorrect. Don't choose an answer that requires you to come up with information that isn't somehow addressed by the passage.

REMEMBER

Sometimes knowing a great deal about a passage's topic can be a detriment, because you may be tempted to answer questions based on your own knowledge rather than the passage itself. Simply answer the questions as they're asked, and make inferences that can be justified by information in the passage.

The GMAT loves inference questions, so expect to see a lot of them. They're easily recognizable because they usually contain either *infer* or *imply* in the question, like these examples:

>> It can be inferred from the passage that . . .

>> The passage implies (or suggests) that . . .

>> The author brings up . . . to imply which of the following?

Sometimes, the GMAT highlights in yellow the portion of the passage that discusses the material in question. If the test highlights information for you, it's likely an inference question rather than a specific information type.

Feeling moody: Questions about the author's tone and style

As you read the passage, be sure to look for clues to the author's tone as well as her purpose. You're bound to see questions that ask you to gauge how the author feels about the topic. Tone and style questions commonly ask you to figure out the author's attitude or complete the logical flow of the author's ideas. The author may be neutral, negative, or positive and may have different attitudes about different types of information within the same passage. It's up to you to determine the nature and degree of the author's feeling from the language used in the passage. With practice, you'll figure out how to distinguish between an enthusiastic author and one who's faking enthusiasm to mock the subject of the passage.

You can recognize questions about tone and style by the way they're worded. Here are some examples of how tone and style questions may appear on the GMAT:

» The author's attitude appears to be one of . . .

» With which of the following statements would the author most likely agree?

» The tone of the passage suggests that the author is most skeptical about which of the following?

WARNING

When making determinations about the author's style and tone, consider the passage as a whole. You may find one or two examples of negative comments in an article that is otherwise overwhelmingly positive about a subject. Don't make the mistake of quickly categorizing the passage from a few words that happen to catch your attention. Instead, determine the main idea of the passage and the author's purpose (you need to do this to answer other questions, anyway) and use that information to help you discern the author's style and tone. For example, if an author's purpose is to argue against a particular point of view, critical words regarding the proponents of that viewpoint reveal an overall critical attitude. However, you wouldn't say the same about an author of a passage that supports a viewpoint overall but includes one or two criticisms about some supporters of the viewpoint.

REMEMBER

Style and tone questions may point you to a specific portion of a passage, or they may be about the entire passage. Even if a question does reference a specific part of the text, it'll do so in relation to the passage as a whole. For example, you can usually answer a question that asks you why an author chose to use certain words in a particular sentence only within the context of the entire passage. So if you know the main idea, author's purpose, and tone of the entire passage, you should be able to effectively deal with questions about the use of a particular word or phrase in one part of the passage.

Eliminating answer choices

One of the most effective ways of moving through reading-comprehension questions is to eliminate incorrect answer choices. That's because you're looking for the best answer choice, not necessarily the perfect answer choice. Sometimes, you'll have to choose the best choice out of five pretty great choices, and other times you'll choose from five really crummy ones. Because the definitive answer usually won't pop right out at you, you have to know how to eliminate obviously wrong choices. Chapter 2 gives you general tips for eliminating answer choices. In this section, we show you how to apply those techniques specifically to reading-comprehension questions.

TIP

Much of the time, you can eliminate wrong choices without having to refer back to the passage. As long as you carefully read the passage and have a good idea of the main theme, the author's purpose in writing the selection, and the author's style or tone, you should be able to recognize some wrong answers immediately.

Some common wrong answers include the following:

>> **Choices that concern information that isn't found in the passage:** Some answer choices contain information that's beyond the scope of the passage. Even if the information in these choices is true, you can't choose them. You have to choose answers based on what's stated or implied in the passage. Eliminate these choices, no matter how tempting they may be.

>> **Choices that contradict the main theme, author's tone, or specific information in the passage:** After you've read through the passage, you should be able to quickly eliminate most of the choices that contradict what you know about the passage.

>> **Choices that counter the wording of the question:** You can also eliminate some answer choices by paying careful attention to the wording of the question. For example, a question may ask about a *disadvantage* of something discussed in the passage. If one of the answer choices lists an advantage instead of a disadvantage, you can eliminate that choice without thinking too much about it. Or a question may ask you to choose which answer the author is most optimistic about. If one of the things listed is something the author is negative about, you can eliminate that choice.

WARNING

The GMAT may try to entice you with answer choices that deal with information directly stated in the passage but don't relate to the actual question at hand. Don't choose an answer just because it looks familiar. Make sure it actually answers the question.

>> **Choices that contain *debatable* words:** Question any answer choice that uses absolutes. Examples are *all, always, only, complete, first, never, every,* and *none.* An answer choice that contains a word that leaves no room for exception is probably wrong. The GMAT makers don't want you calling them up complaining that you know of a circumstance where, say, not all fire engines are red. Beware: Usually the rest of an answer choice that includes a debatable word sounds pretty good, so you may be tempted to choose it.

WARNING

Don't automatically eliminate an answer choice that contains a debatable word. If information in the passage justifies the presence of *all* or *none* in an answer choice, it may be right. For example, if a passage tells you that all horseflies beat their wings at a rate of 96 bps, the choice with *all* in it may be accurate.

Dealing with exception questions

Most questions ask you to choose the one correct answer, but some questions are cleverly disguised to ask for the *one* false answer. We call these gems *exception questions.* You'll recognize these questions by the presence of a negative word, usually *except* or *not.* When you see these words capitalized in a question, you know you're looking for the one answer choice that *doesn't* satisfy the requirements of the question.

You won't see many exception questions on the GMAT, but when you do see that negative word, take a moment to make sure you know exactly what the question is asking. Don't get confused or rush and automatically choose the first choice that looks good. *Remember:* The question is asking for the *one* answer out of five that's false or not part of the information stated or implied in the passage.

Exception questions aren't that difficult if you approach them systematically. Determining that an answer definitely isn't discussed in the passage takes time. You have to carefully look through the passage for the choice and *not* find it — then check again just to be sure. But a better way does exist: Instead of determining that an answer isn't discussed, eliminate the four true answers, which leaves you with the one false (and, therefore, correct) answer.

Identifying those choices that *do* appear in the passage is much easier than determining the one choice that isn't in the passage. After you've identified the four correct answers (remember to use your erasable noteboard to keep track), you can click on the one false answer as the choice for that question.

Take a look at two exception questions based on a fairly difficult natural science passage.

This passage is excerpted from *The Earth Through Time*, 7th Edition, by Harold L. Levin (Wiley):

Geologists have proposed the term *eon* for the largest divisions of the geologic time scale. In chronologic succession, the eons of geologic time are the Hadean, Archean, Proterozoic, and Phanerozoic. The beginning of the Archean corresponds approximately to the ages of the oldest known rocks on Earth. Although not universally used, the term *Hadean* refers to that period of time for which we have no rock record, which began with the origin of the planet 4.6 billion years ago. The Proterozoic Eon refers to the time interval from 2,500 to 544 million years ago.

The rocks of the Archean and Proterozoic are informally referred to as Precambrian. The antiquity of Precambrian rocks was recognized in the mid-1700s by Johann G. Lehman, a professor of mineralogy in Berlin, who referred to them as the "Primary Series." One frequently finds this term in the writing of French and Italian geologists who were contemporaries of Lehman. In 1833, the term appeared again when Lyell used it in his formation of a surprisingly modern geologic time scale. Lyell and his predecessors recognized these "primary" rocks by their crystalline character and took their uppermost boundary to be an unconformity that separated them from the overlying — and therefore younger — fossiliferous strata.

The remainder of geologic time is included in the Phanerozoic Eon. As a result of careful study of the superposition of rock bodies accompanied by correlations based on the abundant fossil record of the Phanerozoic, geologists have divided it into three major subdivisions, termed eras. The oldest is the Paleozoic Era, which we now know lasted about 300 million years. Following the Paleozoic is the Mesozoic Era, which continued for about 179 million years. The Cenozoic Era, in which we are now living, began about 65 million years ago.

EXAMPLE

The passage uses all the following terms to describe *eons* or *eras*, except

(A) Archean

(B) Paleozoic

(C) Holocene

(D) Phanerozoic

(E) Cenozoic

The terms in this passage may be unfamiliar to you, but if you read the passage carefully, you should be able to get a general sense of what it's talking about. For this exception question, which tests you on unfamiliar terms, the best way to approach the question is to consult the text and eliminate the four terms that it uses to describe eons or eras.

TIP

First, scan the answer choices so you have an idea of the words you're looking for. Then begin at the top of the passage and look for words that resemble the answer choices. You should be especially aware of any lists that occur in the text, because exception questions often focus on lists. It's very difficult for test-makers to come up with a good exception question without a list.

The passage contains three lists. The first one appears in the first paragraph. It names eons of geologic time. The question refers to eons, and uses four terms that certainly resemble the answer choices. Consult this first list and eliminate any choices that appear on it. The terms *Archean* and *Phanerozoic* appear, so you can eliminate Choices (A) and (D). In the second paragraph, you see the term *Precambrian* (which isn't an answer choice) and a list of geologists who have mentioned Precambrian rocks. The second paragraph doesn't help with this question, so move quickly to the third paragraph.

The third paragraph also provides a list of eras that are part of the Phanerozoic eon. In this list, you see the terms *Paleozoic, Mesozoic,* and *Cenozoic. Paleozoic* is Choice (B), and *Cenozoic* is Choice (E), so you can eliminate both of these terms. Therefore, the correct answer to this exception question is Choice (C), *Holocene,* which isn't mentioned in the passage and, in fact, is neither an eon nor an era but the epoch in which you're living!

Here's another exception question based on the same passage.

EXAMPLE

Which of the following terms is not used in the passage to describe rocks that are more than 544 million years old?

(A) Precambrian

(B) Cenozoic

(C) Primary Series

(D) Archean

(E) Proterozoic

This question is more difficult because all the terms appear in the passage, but one of them doesn't apply to rocks that are more than 544 million years old. Begin in the same way you did for the previous question, by scanning the answer choices so you know the kinds of words you're looking for.

WARNING

When you find a term, don't automatically eliminate it. In this example, you must confirm that it refers to rocks more than 544 million years old before you can cross it off.

The list in the second sentence of the first paragraph doesn't help because it has no corresponding dates for the eons. The next sentence, however, says that *Archean* rocks are the "oldest known rocks on Earth." You can probably eliminate Choice (D), but keep reading to be sure. The last sentence of the paragraph says that Proterozoic rocks are 544 million to 2,500 million (2.5 billion) years old. And because Archean rocks are older than that, you can eliminate both Choices (D) and (E).

At the beginning of the second paragraph, you discover that both Archean and Proterozoic rocks are referred to as *Precambrian.* Because both types of rock are older than 544 million years, you can also eliminate Choice (A). Finally, in the very next sentence, you find out that Precambrian rocks are also called *Primary Series* rocks, so you can eliminate Choice (C). Choice (B) is the correct answer.

You'd also know that Choice (B) is the correct answer if you happened to look at the last sentence of the passage. That sentence tells you that the Cenozoic era started just 65 million years ago. The question asks for the rocks that are *not* older than 544 million years. Clearly, Cenozoic rocks are, at most, 65 million years old. So Choice (B) must be the one.

TIP

You can definitely skip the elimination process if you happen to stumble onto the right information, but that haphazard method won't work for all exception questions. You're better off approaching the question by eliminating the four answers that you find in the passage or that satisfy the criteria and locating the exception by process of elimination.

Exception questions can take some time, but they're among the easier reading-comprehension questions because often the answers are right there in the text! So don't get in a hurry and make a mistake. Relax and use the proper approach, and you'll do exceptionally well.

Reading-Comprehension Practice Questions with Answer Explanations

To practice the approach to answering reading-comprehension questions, try your hand at these practice questions. Read the passages and answer the questions, using the techniques we've discussed in this chapter. When you're finished, read through the answer explanations that follow.

Reading-comprehension practice questions

In this practice section, we provide you with three passages, one of each of the subject types you'll see in the GMAT verbal-reasoning section. Try to answer the following ten questions within the 18-minute minimum average pace needed to finish all 41 verbal section questions before the 75 minutes are up. For each question, choose the best answer from the five options.

REMEMBER

The GMAT won't label answer choices with letters as we have here to make our explanations easier to follow. To choose an answer on the computerized test, you'll simply click on the oval next to the choice.

Answer Questions 1–3 based on the following passage.

For most Americans and Europeans, this should be the best time in all of human history to live. Survival — the very purpose of all life — is nearly guaranteed for large parts of the world, especially in the "West." This should allow people a sense of security and contentment. If life is no longer as Thomas Hobbes famously wrote, "nasty, brutish, and short," then should it not be pleasant, dignified, and long? To know that tomorrow is nearly guaranteed, along with thousands of additional tomorrows, should be enough to render hundreds of millions of people awe-struck with happiness. And modern humans, especially in the West, have every opportunity to be free, even as they enjoy ever-longer lives. Why is it, then, that so many people feel unhappy and trapped? The answer lies in the constant pressure of trying to meet needs that don't actually exist.

The term "need" has been used with less and less precision in modern life. Today, many things are described as needs, including fashion items, SUVs, vacations, and other luxuries. People say, "I need a new car," when their current vehicle continues to function. People with many pairs of shoes may still say they "need" a new pair. Clearly, this careless usage is inaccurate; neither the new car nor the additional shoes are truly "needed."

What is a need then? The Oxford English Dictionary defines the condition of "need" as "lack of means of subsistence." This definition points the way toward an understanding of what a need truly is: A need is something required for survival. Therefore, the true needs of life are air, food, water, and, in cold climates, shelter. Taken together, this is the stuff of survival. Because the purpose of life is to survive — or more broadly, to live — then these few modest requirements are all that a modern human truly needs. Other things make life exciting or enjoyable, and these are often referred to as "the purpose of life" — but this is surely an exaggeration. These additional trappings are mere wants and not true needs.

1. Which of the following most accurately states the main idea of the passage?

   (A) Modern Americans and Europeans feel unhappy and trapped because they don't distinguish true needs from mere wants.

   (B) There are no human needs, and all so-called needs are merely wants.

   (C) Human needs can never be satisfied in this life and, therefore, people will always be unhappy.

   (D) The satisfaction of human needs has resulted in nearly universal happiness for people in the United States and Europe.

   (E) There is no difference between needs and wants; the desire for wealth and power is just as real as the need for food and shelter.

2. According to the author, which of the following is an example of a fulfillment of a need?

   (A) Adding a roof to block moonlight from shining on a rudimentary sleeping structure built on a tropical island

   (B) Creating a pair of slippers from deer hide to protect one's bare feet from being cut by sharp rocks and stones

   (C) Traveling several miles through dense foliage to obtain a particular berry, known for its sweetness and antioxidant properties, to accompany one's regular bland diet of rice and beans

   (D) Climbing a steep rock face for the exhilaration and sense of accomplishment

   (E) Digging a hole to locate a new water supply after one's prior single source of refreshment has run out

3. Which of the following best defines the way the first paragraph of the passage is organized?

   (A) The author poses a question and provides context and then suggests an answer to the question.

   (B) The author presents an argument and develops that argument by referencing a famous quote that reiterates the point that precedes it.

   (C) The author presents an argument and then supports that argument by defining an essential term.

   (D) The author compares life in one area of the world to life in another area of the world and shows how one way of thinking about life is better than the other.

   (E) The author poses a rhetorical question and explains why modern humans are incapable of answering that question.

   Answer Questions 4–6 based on the following passage.

   A logarithmic unit known as the decibel (dB) is used to represent the intensity of sound. The decibel scale is similar to the Richter scale used to measure earthquakes. On the Richter scale, a 7.0 earthquake is ten times stronger than a 6.0 earthquake. On the decibel scale, an increase of 10 dB is equivalent to a 10-fold increase in intensity or power. Thus, a sound registering 80 dB is ten times louder than a 70 dB sound. In the range of sounds audible to humans, a whisper has an intensity of 20 dB; 140 dB (a jet aircraft taking off nearby) is the threshold of immediate pain.

   The perceived intensity of sound is not simply a function of volume; certain frequencies of sound appear louder to the human ear than do other frequencies, even at the same volume. Decibel measurements of noise are, therefore, often "A-weighted" to take into account the fact that some sound wavelengths are perceived as being particularly loud. A soft whisper is 20 dB, but on the A-weighted scale, the whisper is 30 dBA. This is because human ears are particularly attuned to human speech. Quiet conversation has a sound level of about 60 dBA.

Continuous exposure to sounds over 80 dBA can eventually result in mild hearing loss, while exposure to louder sounds can cause much greater damage in a very short period of time. Emergency sirens, motorcycles, chainsaws, construction activities, and other mechanical or amplified noises are often in the 80 to 120 dBA range. Sound levels above 120 dBA begin to be felt inside the human ear as discomfort and eventually as pain.

Unfortunately, the greatest damage to hearing is done voluntarily. Music, especially when played through headphones, can grow to be deceptively loud. The ear becomes numbed by the loud noise, and the listener often turns up the volume until the music approaches 120 dBA. This level of noise can cause permanent hearing loss in a short period of time, and in fact, many young Americans now have a degree of hearing loss once seen only in much older persons.

4. The primary purpose of the passage is to

   (A) argue for government mandates that decibel levels produced by headphones be reduced

   (B) compare the scale used to measure intensity of sound to the scale used to measure the strength of earthquakes

   (C) describe the way that sound intensity is measured and explain its effect on human hearing

   (D) define which volume levels and sound exposure times are safe for humans and which are harmful

   (E) warn readers about the harmful effects of continuous exposure to sounds over 80 dBA

5. The author mentions that "emergency sirens, motorcycles, chainsaws, construction activities, and other mechanical or amplified noises" fall in the 80 to 120 dBA range. It can be inferred from this statement that these noises

   (A) are unwanted, outside intrusions common in urban life

   (B) can cause hearing loss with constant exposure

   (C) are more dangerous to hearing than sounds of the same dBA level from headphones

   (D) are loud enough to cause immediate pain

   (E) have no negative impacts

6. The second paragraph of the passage states "Decibel measurements of noise are therefore often 'A-weighted' to take into account the fact that some sound wavelengths are perceived as being particularly loud. A soft whisper is 20 dB, but on the A-weighted scale the whisper is 30 dBA." Therefore, for any particular sound, the A-weighted decibel level differs from the unweighted decibel level in that

   (A) the A-weighted number is 10 points higher than the unweighted number

   (B) the A-weighted number is based on the way the noise is perceived in the human ear

   (C) the unweighted number is always higher than the A-weighted number

   (D) the A-weighted number is measured by more accurate instruments

   (E) only on the unweighted scale does a 10 dB increase in sound equal a ten-fold increase in intensity

Answer Questions 7–10 based on the following passage.

This passage is an excerpt from *Microeconomics Theory and Applications*, 9th Edition, by Edgar K. Browning and Mark A. Zupan (Wiley):

In 1980, Washington, D.C., city officials, hard-pressed for tax revenues, levied a 6 percent tax on the sale of gasoline. As a first approximation (and a reasonable one, it turns out), this tax could be expected to increase the price of gasoline by 6 percent. The elasticity of demand is a key factor in the consequences of this action, because the more sharply the sales of gasoline fall, the less tax revenue the city will raise. Presumably, city officials hoped that gasoline sales would be largely unaffected by the higher price. Within a few months, however, the amount of gasoline sold had fallen by 33 percent.[1] A 6 percent price increase producing a 33 percent quantity reduction means the price elasticity was about 5.5.

The sharp sales drop meant that tax revenue was not increased. Further indications were that when consumers had fully adjusted to the tax, tax revenues would actually decrease. (There had been a 10 cent per gallon tax before the 6 percent tax was added, so although the 6 percent levy was raising revenue, the gain was largely offset by the loss in revenue from the initial 10 cent tax following the reduction in sales.) This was not a general increase in gasoline prices but a rise only within the D.C. city limits. Gasoline sold in the District of Columbia is a narrowly defined product that has good substitutes — gasoline sold in nearby Virginia and Maryland. Higher gasoline prices in the District of Columbia, when the prices charged in Virginia and Maryland are unchanged, indicate high elasticity in the market.

No economist would be surprised at the results of this tax, but apparently city officials were. Observed one city councilman: "We think of ourselves here in the District as an island to ourselves. But we've got to realize that we're not. We've got to realize that Maryland and Virginia are right out there, and there's nothing to stop people from crossing over the line." The 6 percent gasoline tax was repealed five months after it was levied.

[1]"Barry Asks Gasoline Tax Repeal," *Washington Post*, November 2, 1980, p. A1.

7. The author is primarily concerned with doing which of the following?

   (A) Arguing for increased gas taxes

   (B) Arguing against increased gas taxes

   (C) Ridiculing all local government officials

   (D) Advancing a particular ideology

   (E) Explaining certain principles of supply and demand

8. It can be inferred from the passage that *elasticity* in the last sentence of the second paragraph refers to

   (A) fluctuations in the price of gasoline in Washington, D.C.

   (B) fluctuations in the price of gasoline in Virginia and Maryland

   (C) changes in the amount of tax collected at 6 percent

   (D) changes in the number of vehicles in the region

   (E) fluctuations in the demand for gasoline sold in Washington, D.C.

9. For which of the following reasons does the second paragraph of the passage mention the original gas tax of 10 cents per gallon?

   (A) To show that Washington, D.C., residents were already overtaxed

   (B) To distinguish between a straight 10 cent per gallon tax and a percent tax

   (C) To explain why residents should not be subjected to different kinds of taxes

   (D) To contrast the 10 cent tax that was included in the pump price and the 6 percent sales tax that was added after the sale

   (E) To show that with a sufficient decrease in gasoline sales, the city would actually lose money despite the higher tax

10. The passage suggests that a reason the tax increase failed to raise tax revenues in the District of Columbia is that

(A) District of Columbia consumers decreased the amount of fuel they purchased and limited their overall vehicle usage

(B) the amount of gas consumed by District of Columbia residents in their commute to nearby states was sufficiently negligible to justify purchasing fuel outside the city limits

(C) consumers in the District of Columbia were upset that city council members would decrease fuel taxes to increase tax revenues

(D) as a result of the tax increase, residents of Virginia and Maryland discontinued making gas purchases in the District of Columbia

(E) District of Columbia city council members failed to convince legislators in nearby states to increase their fuel taxes

Answer explanations

1. **A.** First, identify the question type. This one's pretty easy because it contains the phrase *main idea* right in the question. You're dealing with a main-theme question, so the answer concerns the general idea and purpose of the passage and is probably found in the first or last paragraphs of the passage.

Eliminate any choices that go beyond the scope of the information discussed in the passage. You recall that the passage distinguished *true needs* from *mere wants*. Choice (C) says, "Human needs can never be satisfied in this life. . . ." The reading passage never mentions anything about needs not being satisfied in this life. You may or may not agree with the statement in Choice (C), but you can eliminate it because it discusses ideas that aren't covered in the passage.

Next, look for choices that contradict what you remember from reading through the passage. Choice (B) states that "there are no human needs." The passage specifically lists human needs of food, water, shelter, and so on. So Choice (B) has to be wrong. You may also recall that this list of needs is included in a section in which the author distinguishes between needs and wants. Choice (E) says that there's "no difference between needs and wants"; you know that the passage says otherwise, so you can eliminate that option.

You're left with Choices (A) and (D). If you have trouble choosing between them, consult the passage. Concentrate on the first paragraph, which says that although Americans and Europeans should be happy, many are "unhappy and trapped." You can, therefore, eliminate Choice (D).

Choice (A) should be the correct answer. But take a moment to reread Choice (A) to make sure it makes sense as the main idea of the passage. Choice (A) says, "Modern Americans and Europeans feel unhappy and trapped because they don't distinguish true needs from mere wants." This statement agrees with the author's questioning of the reasons behind modern unhappiness found in the first paragraph and the author's distinguishing of needs from wants in the last paragraph.

2. **E.** The author describes a need as "something required for survival" and lists the true needs as "air, food, water, and, in cold climates, shelter." Eliminate answer choices that don't have something to do with air, food, water, and shelter. Climbing a rock face for the fun of it likely falls within the author's definition of a want because it makes life "exciting or enjoyable." So you can eliminate Choice (D). As nice as it would be to maintain your pedicure with a nice pair of soft deer-hide slippers, foot apparel doesn't fall within the author's criteria for survival. (Apparently, in the author's world, clothing is optional!) Cross off Choice (B).

You're left with Choice (A), which concerns shelter; Choice (C), which deals with food; and Choice (E), which regards water. Each of the remaining answer choices addresses one of the author's categories of needs, so it's up to you to determine which is required for survival. Although it would be nice to sleep peacefully without the interruption of pesky moonlight, the roof in Choice (A) is more likely a want than a need. The author clarifies that shelter is a need in cold climates, not tropical islands. Because Choice (C) tells you that the berry seekers already have a regular diet of rice and beans, you know they're not searching for the berry for survival purposes. The berry isn't necessary for survival, so it's unlikely that it fits the author's idea of a need.

By process of elimination, you settle on Choice (E) as the best answer. The purpose of the hole excavation is to find one of the author's required elements for survival: water. And you know that the exercise is urgent because the hole-digger has no other source for water.

Don't be fooled by the reference to *refreshment* in Choice (E). You may think that refreshment pertains to a want rather than a need, but the author tells you that water is necessary. Therefore, you can conclude that refreshment that refers to water is also necessary.

3. **A.** Examine the way the author introduces the point in the first paragraph of the passage. The first several sentences explain that modern humans should be happy because their daily survival is virtually guaranteed. The author inserts the Hobbes quote about how rough life used to be to show that modern life has improved considerably. The author then wonders, given how good we have it, why modern humans are unhappy. The paragraph's ending statement is the author's answer to this question. Find the answer that best describes this organization.

Choice (D) and Choice (E) are pretty easy to eliminate. The author provides an answer to the question, so modern humans aren't incapable of answering it, and Choice (E) can't be right. The author references the "West" but doesn't compare western thinking to the way people think about life in other parts of the world. Choice (D) is wrong.

You may be tempted by Choice (B). The first paragraph has a famous quote, but that quote about the nastiness of life doesn't restate the prior point that people should feel secure and content. Choice (C) may also sound good at first, but it describes the organization of the entire passage rather than just the first paragraph. The author doesn't define a need until the last paragraph.

When you're asked to evaluate the organization of reading content, make sure you know the parameters of the portion you're supposed to consider.

The best answer has to be Choice (A). The first several sentences provide background for the author's question about why modern humans aren't happy. Then the author answers the question by stating that humans aren't happy because they don't know what a need is.

4. **C.** This passage is almost exactly 350 words, so it's as long as any passage on the GMAT is going to get. Don't let the unfamiliar scientific concepts worry you. You're probably familiar with the term *decibel*, but you may have never encountered the *A-weighted decibel* or *dBA*, as it's abbreviated. Focus on the main point of the passage, which is to describe dBAs and how human ears perceive them, and what type of information appears in each paragraph so that you can approach this main-theme question systematically:

- First, check out the first word of each answer choice to find obvious incorrect answers. The tone of the passage is primarily objective and descriptive, so an answer that begins with *argue* is likely wrong. If you read Choice (A) further, you know you can eliminate it. The author doesn't mention anything about government mandates.

Natural science passages are usually objective and informative. Their primary purpose is rarely to argue in favor of or against a particular position.

- Next, eliminate answer choices that deal with information found in only one area of the passage. The scales mentioned in Choice (B) appear only in the first paragraph, so a comparison of them can't be the purpose of the passage. The author discusses the harmful effects of exposure to sound only in the last two paragraphs, so Choice (E) isn't the primary purpose. For the same reason, you can likely eliminate Choice (D). While the author does indeed define the sound exposure levels and times that are safe for humans and does warn readers about the harmful effects of sound exposure, neither Choice (E) nor Choice (D) provides the overall reason for the passage.

- Finally, choose the answer that incorporates information from the passage as a whole. Choice (C) brings together the information in the first two paragraphs (how sound intensity is measured) and the information in the last two (how sound intensity affects humans). Therefore, it's the best answer.

5. **B.** The word *infer* in the question gives you a fairly obvious clue to the type of question you're dealing with. Again, you can rely on the process of elimination to answer it.

Begin by eliminating those choices that rely on outside information. This passage focuses on noise levels and health effects. The passage doesn't mention societal concerns, such as the intrusive impacts of a plethora of noise in urban life. Therefore, you can cross out Choice (A). All the other choices have something to do with noise levels and health, so don't eliminate them yet.

Next, look for choices that contradict what you know about the passage. One of the author's purposes in writing the passage is to warn young people of the hearing loss associated with headphone use (or abuse). To say that the noises mentioned in the question are *more* dangerous than noises at the same decibel level from headphones would be contradictory. Because Choice (C) is inconsistent with what you find out from the passage, you can eliminate it.

You can use the information in the question to narrow down your choices. The question indicates that the noises mentioned are in the 80 to 120 dBA range. Even if you don't remember all the specifics of the passage, you probably remember that noises over 100 dBA are very loud. You may even remember that 120 dBA is the threshold for feeling discomfort in the ear. It's, therefore, not logical to say, as Choice (E) does, that noises in this range would have *no* health effects. Noises that loud have some impact on the ear!

You can also eliminate Choice (E) because it contains an implicit debatable word. *No impacts* in this answer choice suggests *none,* and answer choices that contain the word *none* are almost always wrong because *none* doesn't allow for any exceptions. If the answer were worded a little differently to say "may have no negative impacts," it could be correct. Short exposure to noise may, in fact, have no impact.

You're left with just two answer choices. If you happen to remember that 140 dB is the threshold for immediate pain, you can answer the question without having to refer back to the text. However, if you have any doubt, take a few seconds to be sure. Remember, with the computerized test, you can't go back to check your answers. After you confirm an answer, it can't be changed.

The last sentence of the first paragraph indicates that 140 dB is the threshold of immediate pain, and in the third paragraph, you read that 120 dBA can "eventually lead to pain." Therefore, you can eliminate Choice (D), so Choice (B) is probably the answer. Glancing at the passage confirms that it indicates that constant exposure to sounds over 80 dBA can result in hearing loss.

6. **B.** On the computerized test, the question would refer to a highlighted part of the passage on the screen instead of quoting it, but for our purposes, we use the quotation. This problem is probably a specific-information question because it refers to details of the passage without using *infer* or *imply.*

You can eliminate Choice (E) because the passage doesn't mention a difference between a 10 dB increase and a 10 dBA increase. Choice (D) also refers to information not covered in the passage. Nowhere does the reading suggest that instruments used to measure A-weighted decibels are more accurate; it just indicates that sounds are measured differently with the A-weighted scale. Cross out Choice (D). Likewise, Choice (C) is incorrect because it directly contradicts prominent information from the reading. A whisper registers a higher number on the A-weighted scale, so Choice (C) can't be correct.

The two choices that are left, Choices (A) and (B), both provide correct information, but only one answers the question. A whisper does register 30 dBA on the A-weighted scale, as opposed to 20 dB on the normal decibel scale, so Choice (A) provides good information. But if you refer back to the passage, you find that some wavelengths are heard more clearly than others. The passage specifically states that the reason for the A-weighted scale is to take into account those noises that are perceived better by the human ear, which is how the A-weighted scale differs from the unweighted scale. Because sounds other than a whisper may have more or less than 10 points difference between their A-weighted and unweighted numbers, Choice (B) is a better answer than Choice (A).

7. **E.** When you're answering a question about an author's purpose, looking at the beginning words of each answer choice can be helpful. The author doesn't appear to be particularly argumentative or condescending in this piece, so you can probably eliminate Choices (A), (B), and (C) right off the bat. Additionally, Choice (C) contains the debatable word *all*. The author doesn't talk about *all* local officials in D.C., much less *all* local officials in general.

This leaves Choices (D) and (E). You can eliminate Choice (D) because the author doesn't advance "a particular ideology." Instead, the author is stunned that the city council didn't know the basic theory of supply and demand. Choice (E) is the best answer of the five.

To double-check your answer, read through the answers you eliminated based solely on first words. Choice (A) is clearly wrong because the author shows that increased taxes actually resulted in decreased revenues. Choice (B) seems more logical because the author is showing the problems with the gas tax increase in Washington, D.C. But if you check the passage, you'll notice that the author never advocates for lower taxes in the passage. The author explains why the gas tax failed in the unique case of Washington, D.C., but that isn't enough to make Choice (B) the primary purpose for writing the passage. The author is primarily concerned with explaining the principles of supply and demand, using the Washington, D.C., gas tax as a case study.

8. **E.** That this question is an inference question is pretty obvious. Be careful not to make an inference that goes beyond the scope of what's stated in the passage.

Eliminate incorrect answer choices. Because this is an inference question, it may be hard to recognize answer choices that use outside knowledge. The point of inferring is, after all, to extend the reasoning beyond what's actually written. But one of the choices strays too far from the information in the passage. Choice (D) mentions changes in the number of vehicles in the region, but the passage says nothing about people getting rid of their cars or not driving through D.C. in reaction to the increase in the price of gas. Eliminate Choice (D).

Choice (B) is inconsistent with the passage as a whole, so you can also cross it off. The passage is about price increases in Washington, D.C., and specifically not about price increases in Maryland and Virginia. This leaves you with three possible answers, each of which could fit with the term *elasticity* in this passage. You need to go back and reread the sentence that's referenced in the question and also reread the surrounding sentences to understand the sentence's context.

The sentence clearly doesn't apply to "the amount of tax collected at 6 percent," so you can cross out Choice (C). The sentence does mention changes in price in D.C., yet if you read the entire second paragraph carefully, especially the last two sentences, you'll see that the author discusses lower demand in D.C. because of good substitutes: gas in Maryland and

Virginia. The paragraph states outright that prices have gone up in D.C. — but this is an inference question, which means you're looking for an implication. It's not the prices that are elastic, which means Choice (A) is wrong. *Elasticity* must refer to the demand for gas, because low price and demand are positively related. So Choice (E) is the best answer to this difficult question.

TIP

Don't forget to consider the context of the passage beyond the specific sentence and paragraph mentioned in the question. A valuable clue to this question can be found in the third sentence of the first paragraph, which states that "The elasticity of demand is a key factor". This indicates that *elasticity* as used in the passage will probably be associated with *demand*.

9. **E.** This question is also an inference one, even though it doesn't contain words that suggest inference. You know it's an inference question because you're asked about the reason the author mentions something, and the passage doesn't directly state the reason.

As usual, start by eliminating obviously incorrect answer choices that don't deal with the subject matter of the passage. The author doesn't mention residents being overtaxed or undertaxed; the article just mentions gas prices and shifting demand. So you can eliminate Choice (A). Choice (D) is incorrect because the passage doesn't mention collecting the taxes differently or at different times. The article makes no effort to distinguish between the straight 10 cent tax and the percentage tax, so you can also cross out Choice (B).

This leaves you with just two possible answers, Choices (C) and (E). Quickly referring to the second paragraph of the passage reveals that before the authors mention the 10-cent tax, they indicate that lower demand may actually result in lower tax revenue. To show how this could be true, the authors mention that the city was previously collecting 10 cents on each gallon. When less gasoline was sold, the city lost this revenue. Choice (E) is a better answer than Choice (C) because it pinpoints the authors' reasons for mentioning the earlier tax.

10. **B.** To answer this inference question, note that the tax increase was implemented with the intent to increase tax revenue. The passage states that tax revenues didn't increase essentially because city officials didn't account for the elasticity in the market. Consumers found equal, less-expensive substitutes in nearby gas stations outside the D.C. city limits.

TIP

Eliminate answer choices that are blatantly wrong. Choice (C) presents information that's contrary to the details of the passage. City officials didn't *decrease* fuel taxes; they increased them. You can easily narrow your choices to four.

Choice (A) provides an explanation for the decreased revenues. If consumers limited their overall gas consumption, tax revenues would fall. This isn't the reason the author suggests, however. The passage doesn't say that D.C. residents stopped buying fuel altogether. It suggests that they stopped buying fuel in D.C. and started buying it in Virginia and Maryland. Furthermore, D.C. residents may actually have been consuming more gas than usual rather than less because they were driving longer distances to fuel up. Eliminate Choice (A).

REMEMBER

Just because an answer choice makes logical sense doesn't mean it's correct. The answer has to make sense given the information in the passage.

You can also cross off Choices (D) and (E) from the list. Both answers require you to infer information that's beyond the scope of the passage. You don't know anything about the fuel-buying habits of Virginia and Maryland residents, nor can you imagine that D.C. officials tried to work with officials in neighboring states. In fact, the passage states that D.C. officials were surprised that their constituents bought gas elsewhere, so it's unlikely that they had the forethought to negotiate with other governments.

The remaining answer is Choice (B). If D.C. residents went outside of the city limits to purchase fuel, the overall cost of the trip must have been more cost effective than buying gas within the city. Otherwise, they would have continued to purchase fuel in D.C.

Chapter 6

Let's Think This Through Logically: Critical Reasoning

You're taking the GMAT to go to business school, not to get a PhD in philosophy, so you're probably wondering why you need to be tested in logic and critical reasoning. Don't worry — answering the critical-reasoning questions on the GMAT doesn't require any knowledge of formal logic. You won't be constructing syllogisms or using fancy Latin words, like *ad hominem*, for logical fallacies. The GMAT verbal section contains questions that test you on informal logic, which is a lot like the kind of reasoning you use to decide between a chocolate frosted doughnut and a bran muffin when the office pastry cart passes by. We fill you in on this logic (for the GMAT, not the pastry cart) in this chapter. The people who run the admissions offices at business schools want to make sure their future students can think through situations clearly and carefully. That's where the critical-reasoning question comes in.

About a third of the questions in the GMAT verbal section are critical-reasoning questions. This question type tests your ability to analyze an argument. The good news is that you analyze arguments all the time, even though you may not know you're doing so. When you see a commercial advertising a new product that claims it'll make your life better, you probably question that claim. If a weight-loss drug helped someone lose 50 pounds, you ask, "Is that a typical result?" If four out of five dentists recommend a chewing gum, you say, "Did they ask only five dentists?" When a mutual fund boasts of its performance, you ask, "Is that better than the market average?" You'll use this same kind of thinking to ace the critical-reasoning questions on the GMAT.

Focusing on "Critical" Concepts: An Overview

Critical-reasoning questions consist of an argument, a question, and five answer choices. You'll encounter short passages from a variety of sources, such as speeches, advertisements, newspapers, and scholarly articles. You may see an argument like this: "The local sales tax must be raised to fund city services. Admittedly, this increased sales tax will impose a greater hardship on the poorest citizens. But if the sales tax is not increased, all city services for the poor will have to be cut." The paragraph reflects the type of arguments you encounter in the news every day.

In the following sections, we clue you in on what to expect when you approach a critical-reasoning question on the GMAT — from the length and format of the argument, to the type of questions you'll be asked, to how to figure out the correct answer.

Understanding the structure of the questions

Each critical-reasoning question has essentially the same structure. The question usually begins with a two- to five-sentence paragraph that contains the argument. The question contains all the information you need to answer the question. Don't rely on any outside information! Even if you happen to be an expert in the area a question covers, don't rely on your expertise to answer the question.

The short argument paragraph is followed by a question (or possibly two questions, although the computer displays only one at a time). The questions usually fall conveniently into one of a few types. The question may ask that you weaken or strengthen an argument, draw a conclusion, analyze the structure of an argument, or identify an unstated assumption the author makes. We examine each of these question types in the section "Getting from Point A to Point B: Types of reasoning," later in this chapter.

Each question has five possible answer choices, which are often long, sometimes even longer than the argument or question. For this reason, you'll spend most of your time for each question examining the answer choices.

TIP

As with most GMAT questions, you can quickly eliminate one or two of the answers that are obviously wrong. The remaining answers will be more difficult to eliminate, so spend your time analyzing these better answer choices.

Figuring out how to answer the questions

To break down a critical-reasoning question, follow these three steps:

1. **Read the question.**

2. **Read the argument paragraph, focusing on the specific information you need to know to answer the question.**

3. **As you read the argument, look for inconsistencies and/or assumptions in the logic.**

The best way to tackle a critical-reasoning question is to read the question first to determine its type. The later section "Thinking Inside the Box: Question Types" shows you how to distinguish critical-reasoning question types. When you first read the question, don't read all the answer choices; doing so takes way too much time and clutters your thinking. You need to concentrate on only the information you need to find to answer the question.

After you figure out what kind of question you're dealing with, you can read the paragraph very carefully. Be sure to locate the conclusion of the argument. The conclusion may come at the beginning, middle, or end of the paragraph. When you've identified the conclusion, you can better understand the rest of the paragraph. As you read the paragraph, look for inconsistencies or gaps in the argument that may help you answer the question. Isolating the argument's premises, assumptions, and conclusion helps you determine the method of reasoning.

WARNING

The argument paragraph usually isn't too complicated, and therefore you may be tempted to read it too quickly. Force yourself to read slowly and carefully so you don't skim over the word or words that provide the keys to the argument. If you read thoroughly enough, you'll be able to eliminate some — or even most — of the answer choices. When you're down to two possible answers, you can then easily refer back to the text to make sure you choose the correct answer.

Making a Case: Essentials of Informal Logic

You can score well on the GMAT critical-reasoning questions without knowing the elements of informal logic, but if you understand a few terms and concepts, you can score even higher. You really just need to know the two basic components of a logical argument and a few methods of coming up with a conclusion, which we outline in the following sections.

Fighting fair: The elements of an argument

A logical argument consists of premises and a conclusion, and when you're analyzing arguments, identifying what parts are premises and what makes up the conclusion can help. The *premises* give the supporting evidence that you can draw a conclusion from. You can usually find the *conclusion* in the argument because it's the statement that you can preface with *therefore*. The conclusion is often but not always the last sentence of the argument. For example, take a look at this simple argument:

All runners are fast. John is a runner. Therefore, John is fast.

The premises in the argument are "All runners are fast" and "John is a runner." They provide the supporting evidence for the conclusion that John is fast, which is the sentence that begins with *therefore*. Not all conclusions in the GMAT critical-reasoning arguments will begin with *therefore* or other words like it (such as *thus* and *so*), but you can try adding *therefore* to any statement you believe is the conclusion to see whether the argument makes sense. We give you plenty of sample arguments in this chapter so you can use them to practice identifying premises and conclusions.

Getting from Point A to Point B: Types of reasoning

Each logical argument has premises and a conclusion, but not every argument comes to a conclusion in the same way. For the purposes of the GMAT, you should be familiar with two basic types of logical reasoning: deductive and inductive (which we explain further in the next sections). You use both types of reasoning all the time, but now you can apply definitions to your logical genius.

Elementary, my dear Watson: Deductive reasoning

In *deductive reasoning*, you come up with a specific conclusion from more general premises. The great thing about deductive reasoning is that if the premises are true, the conclusion must be true! The following is an example of a deductive reasoning argument:

All horses have hooves. (General premise)

Bella is a horse. (More specific premise)

Therefore, Bella has hooves. (Very specific conclusion)

SURE SOUNDS GREEK TO ME: ORIGINS OF LOGICAL THOUGHT

Legend has it that a Greek philosopher named Parmenides in the 5th century BC had plenty of time on his hands while living in a Greek colony off the west coast of Italy. So he whiled away the hours contemplating logical thought and became one of the first Westerners to record his findings. He penned a philosophical poem in which an unnamed goddess instructs him in the ways of determining truth about the universe. His poem explored the contrast between truth and appearance and portrayed truth to be firm and steadfast, whereas appearance (the way mortal men usually think) was unstable and wavering. Parmenides's work influenced other great Greek thinkers, like Plato, Aristotle, and Plotinus.

Unfortunately, you won't have a goddess to guide you through the critical-reasoning questions of the GMAT, but you can rely on Aristotle's method of developing syllogisms to examine GMAT arguments. He's the one who came up with this famous syllogism: "All humans are mortal; Socrates is human; therefore, Socrates is mortal."

If the premise that all horses have hooves is true, and if Bella is, in fact, a horse, then it must be true that Bella has hooves. The same holds true for all examples of deductive reasoning. Here's another example:

> All who take the GMAT must complete an analytical essay. (General premise)
>
> You're taking the GMAT. (More specific premise)
>
> Therefore, you have to complete an analytical essay. (Very specific conclusion)

This example shows the relationship between the truth of the premises and that of the conclusion. The first premise is categorically true: The GMAT requires you to write an essay. The second premise, however, may not be true. Certainly, you're thinking of taking the GMAT or you wouldn't be reading this book, but you may still decide not to take the test. This possibility doesn't affect the logic of the argument. Remember, in deductive reasoning, the conclusion must be true *if* the premises are true. If you take the test, you have to write an essay, so this argument is valid.

REMEMBER

When you analyze deductive reasoning arguments for the GMAT, the only way you can prove that a conclusion is true is by showing that all premises are true. The only way to prove that a deductive reasoning conclusion is false is to show that at least one of the premises is false.

Perhaps I'm just generalizing: Inductive reasoning

In deductive reasoning, you draw a specific conclusion from general premises. With *inductive reasoning*, you do just the opposite; you develop a general conclusion from specific premises. Inductive reasoning differs from deductive reasoning in that the conclusion in an inductive reasoning argument could be false even if all the premises are true. With inductive reasoning, the conclusion is essentially your best guess. That's because an inductive reasoning argument relies on less complete information than deductive reasoning does. Consider this example of an inductive argument:

> Bella is a horse and has hooves. (Specific premise)
>
> Smoky is a horse and has hooves. (Specific premise)
>
> Nutmeg is a horse and has hooves. (Specific premise)
>
> Shadow is a horse and has hooves. (Specific premise)
>
> Therefore, it is likely that all horses have hooves. (General conclusion)

Because inductive reasoning derives general conclusions from specific examples, you can't come up with a statement that "must be true." The best you can say, even if all the premises are true, is that the conclusion can be or is likely to be true.

Inductive reasoning arguments come in all sorts of flavors, but the folks who create the GMAT tend to favor three types: analogy, cause and effect, and statistical. To excel on the GMAT, you want to get very familiar with these three methods of inductive reasoning:

>> **Analogy arguments:** An analogy argument tries to show that two or more concepts are similar so that what holds true for one is true for the other. The strength of the argument depends on the degree of similarity between the persons, objects, or ideas being compared. For example, in drawing a conclusion about Beth's likes, you may compare her to Alex: "Alex is a student, and he likes rap music. Beth is also a student, so she probably likes rap music, too." Your argument would be stronger if you could show that Alex and Beth have other similar interests that apply to rap music, like hip-hop dancing or wearing bling. If, on the other hand, you show that Alex likes to go to dance clubs while Beth prefers practicing her violin at home, your original conclusion may be less likely.

>> **Cause-and-effect arguments:** A cause-and-effect argument concludes that one event is the result of another. These types of arguments are strongest when the premises prove that the alleged cause of an event is the most likely one and that no other probable causes exist. For example, after years of football watching, you may conclude the following: "Every time I wear my lucky shirt, my favorite team wins; therefore, wearing my lucky shirt causes the team to win." The above example is weak because it doesn't take into consideration other, more-probable reasons (like the team's talent) for the wins.

>> **Statistical arguments:** Arguments based on statistical evidence rely on numbers to reach a conclusion. These types of arguments claim that what's true for the statistical majority is also true for the individual. But because these are inductive-reasoning arguments, you can't prove that the conclusions are absolutely true. When you analyze statistical arguments on the GMAT, focus on how well the given statistics apply to the circumstances of the conclusion. For example, if you wanted people to buy clothing through your website, you might make this argument: "In a recent study of the preferences of consumers, 80 percent of shoppers surveyed spent more than six hours a day on the Internet; therefore, you'll probably prefer to buy clothes online." You'd support your conclusion if you could show that a positive correlation occurs between the amount of time people spend on the Internet and a preference for buying clothing online. If you can't demonstrate that correlation, the statistics regarding time spent on the Internet have little to do with predicting one's preference for online shopping.

To do well on the critical-reasoning questions, you need to recognize premises and conclusions in arguments, determine whether the argument applies deductive or inductive reasoning (most will be inductive), and, if the argument is inductive, figure out the method the author uses to reach the conclusion. As you can induce, knowing a little about logical reasoning is essential to scoring well on the GMAT!

Thinking Inside the Box: Question Types

When you were growing up, you probably experienced clichés. You had your jocks, your stoners, the smart kids (that was you!), and various other categories. Labels were important because they gave you clues on how to deal with someone who was a member of a particular group. You knew better than to pick a fight with a jock, and it was a good bet that you could get a match from a stoner. Well, we categorize GMAT questions for the same reason. After you figure out a critical-reasoning question's type, you know just how to deal with it. Most of the critical-reasoning questions you'll encounter on the GMAT fit into one of the following five categories:

>> **Strengthening or weakening arguments:** The argument presents premises and a conclusion and asks you to evaluate the answer choices to determine which one would best strengthen or weaken the author's conclusion.

>> **Drawing conclusions from premises:** The argument paragraph consists of a bunch of premises but doesn't provide a conclusion. Your job is to choose the best conclusion for the argument.

>> **Seeking assumptions:** This more-subtle type of question requires you to discover an essential premise of the argument that the author doesn't state directly.

>> **Making inferences:** For these less-common question types, you have to surmise information that isn't directly stated, usually about one of the premises rather than the conclusion.

>> **Finding the method of reasoning:** In these questions, you'll be asked to find an argument in the answer choices that uses the same method of reasoning as the original given argument.

Because each question type has a best way to handle it, recognizing what type of question you're dealing with before you try to answer it is important. That's why you read the question before you tackle the argument. You'll immediately know what you need to look for when you read the argument from the wording of the question.

Stalking Your Prey: How to Approach Each Question Type

Knowing the types of questions you'll face is valuable only if you know the specialized strategies for dealing with each one. The following sections give you the tips you need to make approaching each of the question types second nature. You get some practice questions, too, so you'll know just what to expect when you take the actual GMAT.

Strengthening or weakening arguments

Critical-reasoning questions that ask you how to best support or damage an argument are some of the easiest to answer, which is a good thing because they appear the most frequently. You probably analyze ideas every day and think of evidence to attack or defend those ideas. Because you already have the skill to evaluate arguments, it doesn't take much work for you to modify that skill to fit this specific GMAT question format. This question category has two subtypes: One asks you to strengthen an argument, and the other asks you to weaken it. You'll recognize these questions because they include words that mean to strengthen or weaken (like *support*, *bolster*, or *impair*), and they almost always contain an "if true" qualifier.

Here are a couple samples of the ways the questions could be worded:

>> Which of the following statements, if true, would most seriously weaken the conclusion reached by the business owners?

>> Which of the following, if true, provides the most support for the conclusion?

Nearly all these questions contain the words *if true*, but not all questions that have *if true* in them are strengthening- or weakening-the-argument types. To make sure an "if true" question is really a strengthening or weakening question, look for the identifying language that asks you to either strengthen or weaken the argument.

Here are three simple steps to follow when approaching strengthening- or weakening-the-argument questions:

1. **Read the question carefully so you know exactly what you'll be strengthening or weakening.**

   In most cases, you'll be asked to strengthen or weaken the conclusion of the main argument. But in less-frequent cases, you may be asked to support or impair a different conclusion, like the view of the author's opponent.

2. **Examine the argument to find the premises and conclusion and to determine what method of reasoning the author uses to reach the conclusion.**

   Usually the author uses inductive reasoning, so you'll need to figure out whether the argument relies on analogy, statistics, or cause and effect to arrive at the conclusion. In the following sections, we tell you what to look for in each type of reasoning.

3. **Evaluate the answer choices to determine which choice best fits with the author's conclusion and method of reasoning.**

   Assume all the answer choices are true and then determine which one best either supports or undermines the specific conclusion addressed in the question.

Always assume that all the answers to strengthening- or weakening-the-argument questions are true. Almost all these questions include the words *if true* in them to remind you that you're supposed to assume that each answer choice presents a true statement. Don't fall into the trap of trying to evaluate whether answer choices are true or false! Your only job is to determine whether the choices help or hurt the argument. This means that a statement like "humans do not breathe air" could be a correct answer choice even though you know it's not true. Perhaps you're supposed to weaken the conclusion that a company must pump air into an underwater habitat for humans. If humans don't breathe air, pumping in air may not be necessary. Make sure you don't dismiss any answer choices simply because you know they aren't usually true.

Analyzing analogy arguments

Analogy arguments rely on the similarity of the two persons, things, or ideas being compared. Therefore, if the author uses an analogy to reach a conclusion, answer choices that show similarities between the compared elements will support the conclusion, and choices that emphasize the differences between the elements will weaken the conclusion. Take a look at this example of an analogy argument.

Hundo is a Japanese car company, and Hundos run for many miles on a gallon of gas. Toyo is also a Japanese car company; therefore, Toyos should get good gas mileage, too.

The author's conclusion would be best supported by which of the following?

(A) All Japanese car manufacturers use the same types of engines in their cars.

(B) British cars run for as many miles on a tank of gas as Hundos do.

(C) The Toyo manufacturer focuses on producing large utility vehicles.

(D) Toyo has been manufacturing cars for more than 20 years.

(E) All Japanese cars have excellent service records.

Recognizing the premises and conclusion in this argument is simple. The author states directly that Hundo cars are Japanese and get good gas mileage and that Toyo cars are Japanese; therefore, Toyos also get good gas mileage. Your job is to find the answer that perpetuates the similarity between Hundos and Toyos.

TIP

You can generally eliminate answer choices that introduce irrelevant information, such as Choices (B), (D), and (E). The author compares Japanese cars, so what British cars do has nothing to do with the argument. The length of time that Toyo has been in business tells you nothing about how similar its cars are to Hundo's. And the question is talking about gas mileage, not service records, so don't spend too much time considering Choice (E).

Choice (C) tells you the focus of Toyo producers, but it doesn't give you any information about how that compares to Hundo, so the best answer is Choice (A). If all Japanese manufacturers supply their cars with the same engines and Hundo and Toyo are both Japanese manufacturers, it's more likely that Toyos will achieve a gas mileage similar to that experienced by Hundos.

Considering cause-and-effect arguments

Questions that ask you to evaluate arguments often apply cause-and-effect reasoning. If the argument uses cause and effect to make its point, focus on the causes. Almost always, the correct answer to a question that asks you to strengthen the conclusion is an answer choice that shows the cause mentioned is the most likely source of the effect. The best answer for a question for which you have to weaken the argument points to another probable cause of the effect. Here's how you'd apply this reasoning to a sample question.

EXAMPLE

Average hours of television viewing per American have rapidly increased for more than three decades. To fight the rise in obesity, Americans must limit their hours of television viewing.

Which of the following, if true, would most weaken the author's conclusion?

(A) A person burns more calories while watching television than while sleeping.

(B) Over the last 30 years, the number of fast-food restaurants in America has increased.

(C) Americans spend most of their television time watching sporting events rather than cooking shows.

(D) Television viewing in Japan has also increased over the past three decades.

(E) Studies show that the number of television commercials that promote junk food has risen over the past ten years.

To tackle this question, first identify the conclusion you're supposed to weaken and the premises the author states or implies to reach that conclusion. The conclusion is pretty easy to spot. The last thought of the argument is that Americans must limit their hours of television viewing to curb the rise in obesity. The author makes this judgment using the following evidence:

>> The author directly states that the number of television viewing hours has increased over the last 30 years.

>> According to the author, the number of obese Americans has also increased.

>> The author implies that television viewing causes obesity.

To weaken the argument that Americans have to reduce their television watching, you have to find the answer choice that shows that there's another cause for the rise in obesity.

You may have been tempted to select Choice (A) because it shows that television watching may be less fat-producing than another activity, sleeping. But it doesn't give you another reason for the rise in obesity. Choice (A) could be correct only if it showed that Americans were sleeping more than they were 30 years ago. It doesn't, so move on.

On the other hand, stating that during the same time period, the number of fast-food restaurants also increased introduces another possible cause of obesity and weakens the conclusion that Americans have to stop watching so much TV to get slimmer. Maybe it's the popularity of fast food that's the culprit! Choice (B) is a better answer than Choice (A), but read through all the possibilities before you commit. Choice (C) is wrong because there's nothing in the argument that suggests that the type of television Americans watch affects their obesity; nor does Choice (C) show that viewing patterns have changed over the last three decades. Choice (D) is also out because it doesn't correlate what's happening in Japan with what's happening in America. You don't know whether Japanese citizens weigh more now than they did 30 years ago, so the information in Choice (D) is useless.

If the question had asked you to strengthen the conclusion, Choice (E) would be a good option. It shows a reason that increased television watching could cause obesity. But the question asks you to weaken the conclusion, so Choice (B) is the best answer. It's the only one that shows that another cause could be to blame for the rise in obesity.

Taking a stab at statistical arguments

If you see statistics used to promote an argument, you're looking for an answer that shows whether the statistics actually relate to the topic of the conclusion. If they do, you'll strengthen the conclusion. On the other hand, an answer choice that shows the statistics are unrelated to the conclusion significantly weakens that conclusion. The following is an example of a statistical argument critical-reasoning question you could find on the GMAT.

EXAMPLE

In a survey of 100 pet owners, 80 percent said that they would buy a more expensive pet food if it contained vitamin supplements. Consequently, CatCo's new premium cat food should be a top-seller.

Which of the following best demonstrates a weakness in the author's conclusion?

(A) Some brands of cat food contain more vitamin supplements than CatCo's does.

(B) CatCo sells more cat food than any of its competitors.

(C) Some of the cat owners surveyed stated that they never buy expensive brands of cat food.

(D) Ninety-five of those pet owners surveyed did not own cats.

(E) Many veterinarians have stated that vitamin supplements in cat food do not greatly increase health benefits.

Because the argument hinges on statistics, eliminate answers that don't directly address the statistical evidence. Those surveyed stated that they'd pay more for pet food with vitamin supplements, but they didn't provide information on whether the amount of vitamin supplements was important. So even though Choice (A) may entice you, it isn't the best answer because it doesn't address the statistics used in the argument. Choice (B) doesn't regard the survey results, either, and it supports the conclusion rather than weakens it. The argument has nothing at all to do with veterinarians, so Choice (E) can't be right. Only Choices (C) and (D) deal with the survey the author uses to reach the conclusion that CatCo's premium cat food will be a big seller.

TIP

You can eliminate answer choices that show an exception to the statistical evidence. Exceptions don't significantly weaken a statistical argument.

Therefore, Choice (C) is wrong and Choice (D) is the best answer because it demonstrates a weakness in the statistics the author uses to support the conclusion. The preferences of dog or bird owners isn't a good indicator of the habits of cat owners.

Dabbling in deductive-reasoning arguments

Rarely will you see a strengthen- or weaken-the-argument question that uses deductive reasoning to reach a conclusion. It's just too hard to come up with challenging answer choices for weakening deductive arguments, because the only way to weaken them is to question the accuracy of the evidence, and correct answers are pretty easy to spot. The only way to strengthen a deductive argument is to reinforce the validity of the premises, which seems sort of silly. Even though GMAT creators don't want to make things too easy for you, one or two deductive arguments may crop up. To weaken an argument with a conclusion that must be true, look for an answer choice that shows that one of the premises is untrue. For example, you may see a question with the following argument:

All horses have tails. Nutmeg is a horse. Therefore, Nutmeg must have a tail.

The only way to weaken this argument is to question one of the two premises. Answer choices like "Scientists have recently developed a breed of horses that has no tail" or "Although Nutmeg looks like a horse, she's really a donkey" would weaken the conclusion.

Delving into drawing conclusions

Another common critical-reasoning question type tests your ability to draw logical conclusions (or hypotheses). The GMAT gives you a series of premises (the evidence), and you choose an answer that best concludes the information. Questions that ask you to draw conclusions from premises may be worded like this:

>> Which of the following conclusions is best supported by the preceding information?

>> Assuming the preceding statements are true, which of the following must also be true?

>> The experimental results support which of the following hypotheses?

As you read through the premises, think of a logical conclusion of your own. Then look through the answer choices to see whether one listed comes close to what you've thought up.

TIP

The key to correctly answering drawing-conclusions questions is to look for an answer choice that addresses all the information contained in the premises. Eliminate any choices that are off topic or incomplete. A conclusion that addresses only part of the information may be plausible, but it probably isn't the best answer. For example, consider the following premises:

Five hundred healthy adults were allowed to sleep no more than five hours a night for one month. Half of the group members were allowed 90-minute naps in the afternoon each day; the remaining subjects were allowed no naps. Throughout the month, the subjects of the experiment were tested to determine the impact of sleep deprivation on their performance of standard tasks. By the end of the month, the group that was not allowed to nap suffered significant declines in their performance, while the napping group suffered more moderate declines.

The best conclusion for these premises would have to address all the following:

>> The nightly sleep deprivation of healthy adults

>> The allowance for naps for half of the study group

>> The smaller decline in performance of standard tasks for the group who took naps

Any conclusion that fails to address all three points isn't the best conclusion. For example, the statement "Sleep deprivation causes accumulating declines in performance among healthy adults" wouldn't be the best conclusion because it fails to address the effect of naps. A better conclusion would be "Napping helps reduce the declines in performance caused by nightly sleep deprivation among healthy adults."

You'll often see more than one plausible conclusion among the answer choices. Your task is to identify the best choice. Don't fall for the trap of choosing an answer that just restates one of the premises. Answer choices that restate a premise may entice you because they echo part of the information in the argument, but the best choice must contain an element of each of the pieces of information presented in the question.

The process is pretty simple, really. Try this sample question to see for yourself.

Over the last eight years, the Federal Reserve Bank has raised the prime interest rate by a quarter-point more than ten times. The Bank raises rates when its Board of Governors fears inflation and lowers rates when the economy is slowing down.

Which of the following is the most logical conclusion for the preceding paragraph?

(A) The Federal Reserve should be replaced with regional banks that can respond more quickly to changing economic conditions.

(B) The Federal Reserve has raised the prime rate in recent years to try to control inflation.

(C) The economy has entered a prolonged recession caused by Federal Reserve policies.

(D) The monetary policy of the United States is no longer controlled by the Federal Reserve.

(E) The Federal Reserve has consistently raised the prime rate over the last several years.

You know from the language that this is a drawing-conclusions question, so you don't have to look for a conclusion in the argument. Just read through the premises and formulate a quick conclusion, something like "Because the Federal Reserve has raised interest rates many times over the last eight years, it must fear inflation."

Eliminate answer choices that aren't relevant or that contain information not presented by the premises. The argument says nothing about regional banks or the termination of the Federal Reserve's control over U.S. monetary policy, so you can disregard Choices (A) and (D). Then get rid of any choices that don't take all premises into consideration. Choice (E) just reiterates the first premise, so it's wrong. You're left with Choices (B) and (C), but Choice (C) contradicts the information in the premises. The problem says the Federal Reserve responds to the economy, not the other way around, so it'd be wrong to say the Federal Reserve causes a recession. Choice (B) is clearly the best answer. It takes into consideration the information that the Federal Reserve has raised rates and that raising rates is its response to inflation.

Be careful to avoid relying on outside knowledge or opinions when answering drawing-conclusions questions. You may have studied the Federal Reserve Bank and have opinions about monetary policy. Choices (A), (C), and (D) reflect some possible opinions about the Federal Reserve. Don't get trapped into choosing an answer because it supports your opinion.

Spotting those sneaky assumptions

Some GMAT critical-reasoning questions ask you to identify a premise that isn't there. For these types of questions, the author directly states a series of premises and provides a clear conclusion, but in getting to that conclusion, the author assumes information. Your job is to figure out what the author assumes to be true but doesn't state directly in drawing the conclusion to the argument. Seeking-assumptions questions may look like these:

>> The argument in the preceding passage depends on which of the following assumptions?

>> The conclusion reached by the author of the preceding passage is a questionable one. On which of the following assumptions did the author rely?

>> The preceding paragraph presupposes which of the following?

TIP

Words like *assume, rely, presuppose, depend on,* and their derivatives usually indicate seeking-assumptions questions. Remember, these questions ask you to look for the ideas the author relies on but doesn't state.

As you read seeking-assumptions questions, look for information that's necessary to the argument but isn't stated by the author. In these questions, the author always takes for granted something on which the entire argument depends. You just need to identify what that is. To do so effectively, choose an answer that links the existing premises to the conclusion. The assumption you're seeking always bears directly on the conclusion and ties in with one or more premises, often with the last premise. Therefore, the best answer often contains information from both the last premise and the conclusion.

EXAMPLE

Women receive fewer speeding tickets than men do. Women also have lower car insurance rates. It is clear that women are better drivers than men.

The preceding conclusion is based on which of the following assumptions?

I. Men and women drive cars equal distances and with equal frequency.

II. Having lower car insurance rates indicates that one is a better driver than those who have higher rates.

III. Speeding tickets are equally awarded for violations without any gender bias on the part of police officers.

(A) I only

(B) III only

(C) I and III only

(D) II and III only

(E) I, II, and III

As always, read the question first. Because it references assumptions, we bet you figured out pretty quickly that it's a seeking-assumptions question.

Next, read through the argument and try to figure out the assumption or assumptions the author makes in reaching the conclusion that women are better drivers. The author moves from the premises to the conclusion pretty quickly and assumes that fewer speeding tickets and lower car insurance rates indicate better driving skills. The author also assumes that men and women have equal driving experiences. Use this information to examine each of your options.

Look at Statement I first. It fits with your second observation that men and women experience equal driving situations, so eliminate any answer choices that *don't* include Statement I. This means that you can get rid of Choices (B) and (D), which leaves you with Choices (A), (C), and (E).

TIP

Before you continue reading through your options, examine the remaining answer choices. You'll see that it's best to examine Statement II next, because if it's true, you won't even have to read Statement III; you'll know the answer is Choice (E). You have to read Statement III only if you determine that Statement II isn't an assumption. (For more about strategies for answering Roman numeral questions, see Chapter 2.)

The information in Statement II links the author's last premise, that women have lower insurance rates, to the conclusion that women are better drivers. Thus, Statement II is also correct. You can eliminate Choices (A) and (C), and by process of elimination, the answer must be Choice (E). If you read through Statement III, you'll confirm that it, too, is an assumption the author makes about men and women having an equal playing field in the driving game.

TIP

If you find seeking-assumption questions to be tricky, try arguing the opposite position. For example, in the sample question, you could've taken the opposing view, that men are better drivers. This means you'll be looking for ways to undermine the conclusion. If you assume the premises to be true, the best way to attack the conclusion is to show that the author assumes things that aren't true. For example, you may argue that men have more accidents because they drive more, they get more tickets because police are less forgiving with male speeders, and they have higher car insurance rates because they drive more-expensive cars. Those counterarguments expose the author's assumptions!

Using your noggin to make inferences

Critical-reasoning inference questions ask you to make an inference (using inductive reasoning) based on the argument in the passage. Making-inferences questions are pretty easy to recognize because they usually include the word *infer*, such as the following examples:

>> Which of the following statements can be correctly inferred from the preceding passage?

>> Which of the following can be inferred from the preceding statements?

The key to answering these questions correctly is to know that they usually ask you to make an inference about one of the premises in the argument rather than about the entire argument or the conclusion. Because these questions usually deal with the premises and not the conclusion, you should choose an answer that makes a plausible inference about one or more of the premises. Like the correct answer choices for the drawing-conclusions questions, the best answers to this type of question don't go beyond the scope of the information provided in the paragraph. Here's what one looks like.

EXAMPLE

The highest-rated television shows do not always command the most advertising dollars. Ads that run during shows with lower overall ratings are often more expensive because the audience for those shows includes a high proportion of males between the ages of 19 and 34. Therefore, ads that run during sporting events are often more expensive than ads running during other types of programs.

Which of the following can properly be inferred from the preceding passage?

(A) Advertisers have done little research into the typical consumer and are not using their advertising dollars wisely.

(B) Sports programs have higher overall ratings than prime-time network programs.

(C) Advertisers believe males between the ages of 19 and 34 are more likely to be influenced by advertisers than are other categories of viewers.

(D) Advertising executives prefer sports programs and assume that other Americans do as well.

(E) Ads that run during the biggest sporting events are the most expensive of all ads.

You know you're dealing with an inference question before you read through the argument because you've read the question first and it contains the word *inferred*. Focus on the premises of the argument as you read it. Then look through the answer choices and eliminate any that don't address one of the premises or that present inferences that require additional information.

The argument says nothing about advertising research or whether the particular advertising practice is wise, so you can eliminate Choice (A) immediately. You're stretching beyond the scope of the information if you infer that advertisers are unwise. Likewise, Choice (D) mentions the preferences and assumptions of advertisers, but none of the premises discuss advertisers, so you can get rid of Choice (D). The inference in Choice (E) relates to the conclusion rather than any of the premises, so you can probably eliminate it right away. Furthermore, just because sporting events ads are "often more expensive" than other ads doesn't necessarily mean that they're always the most expensive. This leaves you with Choices (B) and (C).

Choice (B) contradicts information in the argument. The author implies that some sporting events have lower overall ratings even though they have higher advertising rates. You're left with Choice (C). You need an explanation for the information in the second sentence that states that advertising is often more expensive for lower-rated shows viewed by males who are between 19 and 34 years old. This practice would be logical only if males of these ages were more susceptible to advertising than other groups. It makes sense that Choice (C) is the correct answer.

WARNING

Remember to check your outside knowledge about the critical-reasoning subjects at the door! You may know that Super Bowl ads are the most-expensive ads, which may tempt you to pick Choice (E). Using your own knowledge rather than what's expressly stated in the test questions will cause you to miss questions that someone with less knowledge may answer correctly.

Making your way through method-of-reasoning questions

Method-of-reasoning questions are the rarest form of GMAT critical-reasoning question types. This type of question either directly asks you what type of reasoning the author uses to make an argument or, more often, asks you to choose an answer that uses the same method of reasoning as the argument. You may see method-of-reasoning questions phrased like these:

>> Which of the following employs the same method of reasoning as the preceding argument?

>> The author's point is made by which method of reasoning?

>> David's argument is similar to Katy's in which of the following ways?

The two types of method-of-reasoning questions may seem different, but each of them asks you to do the same thing: to recognize the type of reasoning used in the argument.

REMEMBER

For the purposes of the GMAT, the methods of reasoning are as follows:

>> Deductive, which is reaching a specific conclusion from general premises

>> Inductive, which is drawing a general conclusion from specific premises and includes the following methods:

  • Analogy, which shows that one thing is sufficiently similar to another thing such that what holds true for one is true for the other

- Cause and effect, which shows that one event resulted from another

- Statistics, which uses population samples (surveys) to reach conclusions about the population as a whole

Questions that ask you to specifically choose what kind of reasoning the author uses are straight-forward, so we focus on the other type of question, which asks you to choose an answer that mimics the reasoning method of the given argument. When you know you're dealing with this type of question, you just need to focus on the way the author makes the argument to make sure you choose an answer that follows the logic most exactly.

WARNING

Don't choose an answer just because it deals with the same subject matter as the given argument. These choices are often traps to lure you away from the answer that more exactly duplicates the author's logic but addresses another topic.

It doesn't matter whether the argument makes sense. If the given argument isn't logical, pick an answer choice that isn't logical in the same way.

TIP

You may focus on the method of reasoning better if you substitute letters for ideas in the argument. For example, say you're presented with this argument: "Balloons that contain helium float. Jerry's balloon doesn't float, so it contains oxygen rather than helium." You could state this logic with letters like this: "All A (helium balloons) are B (floaters). C (Jerry's balloon) isn't B (a floater), so C isn't A." Then you can apply that formula to your answer choices to see which one matches best.

Some of the reasoning methods may be as obscure as the one in this sample question.

EXAMPLE

A teacher told the students in her class, "The information that you read in your history book is correct because I chose the history book and I will be creating the test and assigning your grades."

The reasoning in which of the following statements most closely resembles that of the preceding argument?

(A) The decisions made by the Supreme Court are just because the Court has the authority to administer justice.

(B) The people who have fame are famous because they deserve to be famous.

(C) Those who play sports get better grades because of the link between the health of the body and the health of the mind.

(D) Because my favorite teacher chooses to drive this kind of car, I should as well.

(E) Of 100 professors surveyed, 99 agree with the conclusions reached by the scientist in his paper on global warming.

Reading the question first tells you that you'll have to analyze the way the author reaches the conclusion in the argument. As you read, you find that this illogical cause-and-effect argument states that information is correct because someone in a position of authority (the teacher) says so, so you need to find an equally illogical argument based on power and authority.

Because this is a cause-and-effect argument, you can eliminate any choices that don't use cause and effect to reach a conclusion. All choices contain an element of cause and effect except Choice (D), which presumes an analogy between a favorite teacher and the writer, and Choice (E), which uses statistical evidence. (Note that just because Choice [D] also concerns a teacher doesn't automatically make it the correct answer.) Disregard Choices (D) and (E) and examine the other three choices.

Among Choices (A), (B), and (C), the only choice that uses power to justify a cause–and–effect relationship is Choice (A). Choice (B) is faulty because it uses circular reasoning, which means it uses its conclusion as a premise, instead of using power to advance its position. Choice (C) doesn't work because its logic isn't necessarily faulty. Instead, it relies on a logical correlation between physical health and intellectual prowess. Therefore, Choice (A) is the answer that most nearly matches the kind of reasoning in the original argument.

Critical-Reasoning Practice Questions and Answer Explanations

With practice, you'll probably find that critical-reasoning questions become some of the easiest question types to master in the GMAT verbal section. To master your approach, work through these practice questions and read through the answer explanations.

Critical-reasoning practice questions

This set of 11 critical-reasoning practice questions gives you a taste of what to expect from this verbal question, which tests your ability to analyze arguments. To mimic the approximate amount of time you'll have to answer critical-reasoning questions on the actual exam, try to answer these 11 questions in about 18 minutes. Answer each question based on the passage that precedes it, and choose the best answer from the five answer choices provided.

REMEMBER

Don't expect to see letters before the answer choices on the computerized GMAT. Each answer will have an oval next to it that you select by clicking on it. We've put letters next to the answers in this practice section to make it easier to discuss the answer in the explanations that follow the questions.

1. It seems that Americans are smarter than they were 50 years ago. Many more Americans are attending college now than in the past, and the typical entry-level job in business now requires a college degree.

   Which of the following statements, if true, would most seriously weaken the argument in the preceding paragraph?

   (A) High-school courses are more rigorous now than they were in the past.

   (B) Tuition at colleges and universities has more than tripled in the past 25 years.

   (C) High-school class sizes have gotten smaller, and computers have introduced a more individualized curriculum.

   (D) Businesses are not requiring as high a level of writing or math skills as they did in past decades.

   (E) Many of the skills and concepts taught in high school 50 years ago are now taught in college.

Questions 2 and 3 are based on the following argument.

Rachel: The legal drinking age in America should remain at 21, because teens have not yet reached an age where they are able to consume alcohol responsibly. Additionally, the actions of 18-year-olds are more likely to be imitated by teens aged 15 to 17 than are the actions of those who are significantly older, so lowering the drinking age to 18 would also result in increased alcohol consumption by younger teens trying to emulate the actions of their older peers.

Mackenzie: The drinking age in America should be lowered to 18, because keeping it at 21 has not only failed to curb teen drinking but has encouraged those teens who *do* drink to do so in private, uncontrolled environments where they are more prone to life-endangering behavior. Many youths in European countries drink from an early age, and those countries have substantially fewer alcohol-related problems than we do in America.

2. Which of the following, if true, would most significantly weaken Mackenzie's argument?

(A) The idea that Europeans and other nations with low or no minimum drinking ages do not have alcohol-related problems is a myth.

(B) If Americans are allowed to give their lives for this country at age 18, then they should be considered old enough to make the proper decision as to what to put in their bodies.

(C) More American high-school students drink now than they did decades ago, when the drinking age was lower.

(D) In European culture, youths are taught at an early age that it is acceptable to either abstain from alcohol entirely or drink in moderation and that it is never acceptable for them to abuse alcohol, regardless of their age.

(E) European youths are just as likely as American youths to drink in private, uncontrolled environments.

3. Rachel's argument is based on which of the following assumptions?

(A) Those who have reached the age of 21 are able to consume alcohol more responsibly than those who are 18.

(B) When European teenagers consume alcohol, they do so in public, controlled environments.

(C) Teens who are 15 to 17 years old are more impressionable than those who are aged 18 or older.

(D) The impressionability of one's actions on others should not be a consideration when deciding the legal age to consume alcohol.

(E) Consuming alcohol in private, uncontrolled environments is not more dangerous than consuming alcohol in more public environments, such as bars or restaurants.

4. A recent census of all American females revealed that the current average age that females in America marry is 27. The average age that females have their first child is also 27. According to a census taken 20 years ago, the average ages that females married and had their first child were 23 and 25 years, respectively.

If the information recorded in the two censuses is true, which of the following must also be true about American females?

(A) Currently, more females are having their first child before they marry than they did 20 years ago.

(B) On average, females are currently waiting longer to have their first child than they did 20 years ago.

(C) Females today are more likely to complete their education before getting married and having children than they were 20 years ago.

(D) On average, females had larger families 20 years ago than they have today.

(E) Twenty years ago, most females waited at least two years after they were married to have their first child.

5. Continuous technological advances are critical to many types of business, because they allow machines to do the work previously done by humans — and they don't have to be compensated. Banking executives are always looking for ways to cut costs, so they support a heavy emphasis on automated technology in the workplace. Yet what customers look for most in their banks is to be recognized by their teller and feel a sense of familiarity and friendliness upon entering, so the reliance of banks on machines should be minimized, rather than exacerbated.

Which of the following best outlines the main idea of the argument?

(A) Banks should reduce their dependence on technology.

(B) Bank patrons desire personal attention.

(C) Machines can work faster than humans.

(D) Bank executives are a greedy bunch.

(E) Bank automation is inevitable.

6. A school board candidate has indicated that cheating through the use of cellphones in the classroom is on the rise this year and has proposed a ban on cellphones in schools altogether. School officials cite only a marginal increase in the number of students who cheat this year in comparison to the last two years, so this is just a ploy to make voters think a quality education is his top priority.

Which of the following, if true, best strengthens the conclusion of the preceding argument?

(A) The school board candidate has continuously voted down proposals to increase the budget for area schools.

(B) The school board candidate has continuously voted in favor of budget increases for area schools.

(C) This year, schools in the district have smaller class sizes and better student/teacher ratios than they have had in past years.

(D) The ratio of teachers to number of students has decreased significantly over the past several years because of a growth in number of students district-wide without a concomitant rise in the number of teachers to accommodate the increase.

(E) The school board candidate has a daughter who attends a school in the district, and he does not want her to own a cellphone.

7. Springfield is the first city to ban fast-food advertisements marketed specifically toward children. Although eating fast food has been linked to weight gain, banning these advertisements will do little to curb childhood obesity, and it should be the job of the parent, not the government, to tell children what to eat.

The argument would be most weakened if which of the following were true?

(A) Families are increasingly relying on the fast-food industry for financial reasons and will continue to frequent these establishments on their own terms, regardless of their children's preferences.

(B) Studies indicate that, generally speaking, adults tend to be more influenced by advertising than children.

(C) If children learn that adults are trying to limit their fast-food intake, they will want to consume fast food even more.

(D) Those opposed to fast-food marketing geared toward children are welcome to buy airtime for their cause, too.

(E) Watching an advertisement has been shown to increase one's desires for a product, particularly when the product is a food item.

8. Patients who feel they have a good relationship with their doctors generally show more improvement in their health than those who lack a connection with their doctors. Patients who like their doctors show improved emotional well-being, are less anxious about their symptoms, and are more likely to follow doctors' advice.

Which one of the following, if true, would provide the most support for the argument?

(A) Patients are more likely to take legal action against a doctor for malpractice if they believe that the doctor failed to establish a connection with them during their office visits.

(B) Recently, medical schools and health insurers have taken measures to improve doctor-patient communication.

(C) Doctors who work in stressful environments are much less likely to take the time to connect with patients than doctors in more relaxed settings.

(D) The average physician spends about 15 minutes with each patient during routine office visits.

(E) A large number of studies have confirmed that the more anxious a patient is, the more protracted his or her recovery from a medical condition is.

9. The legislature is considering a law banning the use of cellphones by people who are driving a moving car. Drivers texting and talking while driving are distracted by their phone conversations and can't give their full attention to driving their vehicles. Banning the use of cellphones by drivers will make the roads safer.

The argument depends on assuming which one of the following?

(A) A study by a sociologist has shown that the use of cellphones is occasionally a contributing factor in traffic accidents.

(B) The proper role of the legislature is to enact laws that protect the safety of drivers and passengers in automobiles.

(C) Drivers who hold their cellphones in their hands are more distracted than drivers who use a hands-free headset or speakerphone while driving.

(D) Because drivers talking and texting on cellphones are distracted, they are more prone to getting into accidents.

(E) Many drivers engage in behavior that distracts them from their driving, such as eating, adjusting the radio, reading maps, and talking on cellphones.

10. Many Americans do not take all the vacation time to which they are entitled. There are several reasons for this: They feel that they are indispensable at work, they fear the resentment of co-workers, or they dread discovering that their workplaces can actually function perfectly well without them. This is a mistake; vacation time gives workers a chance to rest, recover, and gain perspective that in turn can lead to more creativity and better performance at work.

The claim that many Americans don't take all the vacation time to which they are entitled plays which one of the following roles in the argument?

(A) It is a recommendation of a policy that the American workplace should implement.

(B) It is evidence of the author's claim that vacation time gives workers a chance to rest.

(C) It is the conclusion of the argument.

(D) It is a statement of a principle that the author wishes all people would observe.

(E) It is a statement of fact about which the author expresses an opinion.

11. A large Southern state university has changed its teaching practices. Formerly, instructors without PhDs taught most introductory courses; now professors with PhDs will teach all introductory classes. That means the average class size will increase from 44 students per class to 600 per class, but overall the students' learning experience should improve.

Which one of the following is an assumption required by this argument?

(A) Requiring professors with PhDs to teach all introductory classes will mean that the university must hire more faculty with doctorates.

(B) Students tend to participate in smaller classes more than they do in large lectures, even when the lectures are supplemented by weekly discussion sections.

(C) Major private universities already have implemented a format in which professors with PhDs teach all introductory classes as large lectures.

(D) A class taught by a PhD, even in a lecture format with hundreds of students, is a better learning environment than a smaller class taught by an instructor without a PhD.

(E) Services that rank colleges and universities usually consider the percentage of classes taught by PhDs when computing rank.

Answer explanations

1. E. Read the question first so you know what to focus on in the passage. Because this question asks you to weaken the argument, you know you need to figure out what the conclusion is and what kind of reasoning the author uses in moving from the premises to the conclusion.

When you examine the argument, you may notice that the conclusion actually comes first. The author concludes that Americans are smarter than they were 50 years ago and does so by contrasting current college participation and entry-level job requirements with those of the past. The method of reasoning is similar to analogy, except instead of showing similarities between Americans now and 50 years ago, the author shows the differences. To weaken the conclusion that Americans are smarter today, you need to find the answer choice that shows that things really aren't all that different today than they were 50 years ago.

First, eliminate answer choices with irrelevant information. Neither college tuition rates nor class size and curriculum have anything to do with levels of intelligence, so Choices (B) and (C) are wrong. Plus, you're looking for an answer that shows that things aren't much different between now and yesterday, and Choices (B) and (C) accentuate the difference.

Then, get rid of any answer that tends to strengthen rather than weaken the conclusion that Americans are smarter. More-difficult high-school courses seem to indicate that Americans may indeed be smarter, so disregard Choice (A). This leaves you with Choices (D) and (E), and your job is to choose the one that shows that now and then aren't all that different. Not only does Choice (D) demonstrate a difference between the eras, but it also refutes the premise that businesses are looking for the higher skill levels of a college education.

The correct answer must be Choice (E). If skills that were part of the high-school curriculum 50 years ago are now offered in college, actual education hasn't changed all that much from then to now. Americans must now attend college to acquire the high-school skills of earlier times, and businesses need to require college degrees to make sure their employees have the same skills that high-school students had in the past. If the skill levels are the same, Americans aren't really any smarter than they were 50 years ago.

You must know precisely what point a paragraph is arguing before you can strengthen or weaken that argument. Take the time to understand the premises, conclusion, and method of reasoning so you can quickly eliminate answer choices and accurately select the best answer. When you really understand the argument, attacking or defending it is fairly easy.

2. **E.** First, a quick review of Mackenzie's argument indicates that she is in *favor* of lowering the drinking age, not opposed, so you can quickly eliminate any answer choices that include support for doing so, such as Choices (B) and (C), because those choices actually strengthen Mackenzie's argument.

Now, determine which of the remaining options *best* weakens Mackenzie's argument that the legal drinking age should be lowered. The remaining answers focus on Mackenzie's premise that because European countries have lower drinking ages and fewer problems with alcohol, lowering the drinking age in America would likewise lead to fewer alcohol-related problems. She makes her argument based on an analogy between Europe and America, so weaken her contention by showing that Europe and America are substantially similar in their approach to teenage drinking. It may sound surprising to weaken an analogy with a similarity, but in this case Mackenzie's analogy seeks to liken the alleged present state of affairs in Europe to the supposed future state of affairs in America if the American drinking age is lowered. Showing a similarity between present-day Europe and present-day America can therefore weaken the argument that a change in the drinking age will reduce alcohol-related problems in America.

Mackenzie doesn't say that European countries have *no* alcohol-related problems, just that there are fewer, so Choice (A) is irrelevant to her argument. Choice (D) provides a concrete difference between European and American culture that reveals why European teens tend to be more responsible than American teens when it comes to alcohol consumption, so this is an answer choice that seems to lend support to Mackenzie's argument that a lower drinking age won't result in less-responsible drinking among American teens. On the other hand, Choice (E) reveals a similarity between European and American youth, which best serves to weaken Mackenzie's analogy between the lower drinking age in Europe and the proposed lower drinking age in America. If both European and American youths drink in private, uncontrolled environments despite the difference in the drinking ages of the two cultures, it's unlikely that changing the drinking age in America will affect the behavior that Mackenzie claims is dangerous (drinking in private).

3. **A.** Rachel argues for retaining the current legal drinking age of 21. She bases her conclusion on the premises that younger drinkers are more likely to influence the behavior of 15- to 17-year-olds and that teens haven't reached an age where they can drink alcohol responsibly.

To find the correct answer to questions that ask for an assumption, look for the answer choice that links one or more of the premises to the conclusion. Eliminate answer choices that don't relate to at least one of the premises of the argument.

Choices (B) and (E) relate to one of Mackenzie's premises, so it's unlikely that they would reveal one of Rachel's assumptions. Cross out those two answers on your noteboard.

You can also check off Choice (D) because it contradicts Rachel's premise that the effect an 18-year-old's alcohol consumption can have on younger peers is an important consideration in determining the legal drinking age. It's also unlikely that Choice (C) is correct because Rachel doesn't make comparisons regarding the impressionability of teens based on their ages. Her premise is that younger teens are more likely to be influenced by 18-year-olds than 21-year-olds. Furthermore, Choice (C) doesn't link one of Rachel's premises to her conclusion in the way that Choice (A) does.

If Rachel concludes that the legal drinking age must remain at 21 because younger drinkers don't consume alcohol responsibly, she must think that 21-year-olds have achieved some level of responsibility that's greater than those who are younger. Choice (A) links the relevance of one of Rachel's premises (a lower level of responsible drinking) to her conclusion that people who are younger than 21 shouldn't be able to legally consume alcohol. So the correct answer is Choice (A).

4. **B.** This question asks you to come up with a conclusion based on the information in the paragraph.

TIP

Notice that the question asks you for what *must* be true rather than what *could* be true. So you can cross out any answers that aren't absolutely true given the data in the paragraph.

All you know from the paragraph is the average marrying age for females today and 20 years ago and the average age that females have their first child today compared to 20 years ago. The paragraph says nothing about the number of children females have or had, so you can easily wipe Choice (D) out of contention. Furthermore, the paragraph provides no explanation for why the data has changed over the years, so you can't know the reason that the average age has increased. So Choice (C) can't be right.

WARNING

Don't choose an answer based on an assumption or your own experience. The paragraph merely reports data instead of commenting on it, and it treats the age of marrying and having one's first child as two separate statistics. You can't make assumptions about how the two sets of data are related.

That means that Choice (A) doesn't have to be true. Just because the average age for marrying and having a first child are currently the same doesn't mean that more American females are having their first child before they marry. For example, the increased marrying age could be the result of females who marry when they're older and have no children. Eliminate Choice (E) for the same reason. You can't assume from these limited statistics that the females who are 23 when they marry are the ones who are having their first child at 25. There are too many other variables in the population.

The only thing you know for sure is that, because the average age for having a first child has risen over the last 20 years, on average, females are having their first child at a later age than they did 20 years ago. Choice (B) is the only answer that must be true.

5. **A.** Asking for the main point of an argument is another sneaky way of getting you to pick out the conclusion. This paragraph makes it easy for you because the conclusion follows the *so* in the last sentence: Banks should rely less on machines. The first sentence of the argument equates machines with technological advances, which means that you can say that the main point is that banks should rely less on technology, Choice (A).

Choices (C), (D), and (E) require you to make assumptions that aren't supported by the argument. Because you read newspaper headlines, you may think that Choice (D)'s assertion about the avarice of bank executives is a foregone conclusion, but, alas, it isn't mentioned in the argument. (You should also have been alerted by the debatable word *inevitable* in Choice [E]). The paragraph does suggest that bank patrons want personal attention (Choice [B]), but this statement is a premise rather than the conclusion. So the correct answer is Choice (A).

6. **D.** The first step to answering any question that asks you to strengthen a conclusion is to figure out exactly what that conclusion is. In this case, the paragraph argues that the candidate's proposal to ban cellphones in schools is a campaign strategy to make voters think he cares about the quality of education. The argument is based on the statistic that the increase in the number of students who cheat has been insignificant. To support the author's argument, find the answer that best supports the contention that cheating really hasn't increased all that much.

Eliminate choices that don't pertain to the author's argument. You can disregard Choices (A) and (B). The argument is concerned with the implications surrounding a cellphone ban, not the candidate's position on a budget increase. You're assuming too much (or relying on your own opinion) to make a determination of whether the candidate's vote for or against a budget increase has anything to do with education quality.

Choice (E) indicates that a reason other than cheating may be the reason the candidate wishes to impose the cellphone ban, but that absurd personal reason doesn't support the author's argument that the candidate is proposing the ban for political reasons.

The answer must be either Choice (C) or Choice (D). Both deal with the number of actual students in the district, so they may reflect on the validity of the candidate's claim that cheating has increased and the author's claim that it hasn't. Having smaller class sizes tells you nothing about the overall number of students. The district could have hired more teachers to accommodate the same number of students. The only answer that relates to the cheating statistic is Choice (D). The marginal increase in cheating could be due to an increase in number of students rather than an increase in cellphone cheating, which supports the author's argument that the candidate's reason for banning cellphone use is unfounded.

7. **E.** The implication is that the advertising ban is designed to curb childhood obesity. The author states that this ban won't work, which suggests that the author thinks that the fast-food advertisements don't cause childhood obesity. To weaken this argument, show that the advertisements do indeed lead to obesity. If it's been proven that watching an ad increases one's desire for something, then banning the ads *would* reduce the desire for fast food that produces weight gain in children. Choice (E) weakens the author's argument by showing that the advertisement ban will indeed curb childhood obesity. Choice (A) seems to strengthen the author's argument, and Choices (B), (C), and (D) deal with tangents that don't relate to whether the advertisement would be effective in curbing childhood obesity. The correct answer is Choice (E).

8. **E.** The argument claims that patients do better when they feel a connection to their doctors; the premises are three factors that result from liking one's doctor. To support this argument, you need to find statements that link those factors with health improvements. Choice (A) doesn't help. It illustrates the danger of people not liking their doctors but doesn't prove the point that patients who like their doctors are healthier. Choice (B) may suggest that improving doctor-patient communication is desirable, but it doesn't specifically link improved communication to improved patient health. Choice (C) presents a reason for poor doctor-patient communication but doesn't show how that affects patient health. Choice (D) provides evidence of how the average doctor doesn't have a good relationship with patients, but it doesn't show the results of good doctor-patient rapport. Choice (E) does support the conclusion by linking one effect of liking a doctor (less anxiety) to a greater improvement in health. Choice (E) is correct.

9. **D.** You're looking for an assumption. Assumptions connect the premises to the conclusion. The conclusion that if drivers can't use cellphones, the roads will be safer is based on the evidence that drivers on phones are distracted; the author assumes that distracted drivers are unsafe drivers. (Yes, that's obvious, but the author doesn't explicitly say what the connection is, so it's an assumption.) Choice (A) is tricky and could be a possible answer if you were asked to support the legislator's argument, but information about the results of a specific cellphone use study is way too specific to be the legislator's assumption. Assumptions are rarely based on particular statistical data. See whether you can find a better answer. Choice (B) is wrong; the author probably does assume that this is the legislature's job, but this assumption isn't necessary to the specific argument connecting distraction

and road safety. Choice (C) doesn't work; the author isn't concerned with distinctions among types of cellphones users. Choice (D) is something the author assumes — it explains the connection between cellphones and distracted drivers and dangerous roads. Choice (E) contains mostly irrelevant details about other behaviors, and to the extent it addresses drivers on cellphones, it just repeats evidence the argument already explicitly states. Choice (D) is the best answer.

10. **E.** The claim in the question is a statement of fact in the first sentence that the speaker explores more thoroughly, concluding with the statement that it's a mistake. She's not suggesting that it's a good thing, so Choices (A) and (D) are wrong. It's not evidence, so Choice (B) is wrong. Her actual conclusion is that refraining from taking vacation is a mistake, so Choice (C) is wrong. The claim is a statement of fact that provides the background information for the author's opinion about what Americans should do with their vacation time, so Choice (E) is correct.

11. **D.** The author concludes that having classes taught by PhDs instead of instructors improves students' learning experience, so he must assume that PhDs, even in very large classes, are somehow better at teaching than instructors in smaller ones. Choice (A) isn't his assumption. In fact, the reference to increased class sizes suggests that the university won't be hiring more faculty. Choice (B) contradicts the author's conclusion by suggesting that student participation is a good thing. Choice (C) is interesting information but isn't essential to the conclusion about the practices of the particular Southern state university in the argument, especially because it doesn't mention students' learning experiences. Choice (D) looks like the right answer. The author does seem to think that a class taught by a PhD is somehow superior, which explains why he thinks the change would benefit students. Choice (E) explains why the university may want to increase classes taught by PhDs, but it doesn't explain how that would benefit students. Choice (D) is correct.

Chapter **7**

Bringing It Together: A Mini Practice Verbal Section

ike the real GMAT verbal section, the mini practice test in this chapter has an approximately equal distribution of each of the three types of verbal questions. It contains nine reading-comprehension questions, ten sentence-correction questions, and nine critical-reasoning questions. The total of 28 questions makes this mini verbal test a little over half the size of the 41-question GMAT verbal section. To get more practice, take the full-length practice exams included with this book.

Although we can't simulate a computer in this book, don't let that deter you. Just mark the answers right in the book, and try not to look at the answer key until *after* you've answered the questions. We designate each answer choice with a letter to make it easier to reference it in the answer explanations, but on the actual computerized exam, you'll simply click the oval that precedes each answer choice to mark your answer.

TIP

To best mimic the computer experience during this mini practice test, answer each question in sequence and don't go back and change any of your answers after you've moved on to the next question. At the actual exam, you won't have a test booklet to write in, so try not to write anything except your answers on the pages of this book. To keep your notes and record eliminated answers, use scratch paper to simulate the noteboard you'll use on test day.

TIP

Take the time to read through the answer explanations at the end of the chapter, even for the questions you get right. The explanations apply the techniques covered in the other chapters of this book and show you why a certain answer is a better choice than the others.

Working Through Verbal Reasoning Practice Questions

If you're the competitive type and want to subject yourself to a timed test, give yourself just a little less than 52 minutes to complete the 28 questions in this section.

REMEMBER

Here's a quick review of the directions for the three types of verbal questions that appear in this mini practice test (and on the real GMAT):

>> **Sentence-correction questions:** Choose the answer choice that best phrases the underlined portion of the given sentence according to the rules of standard English. The first answer choice duplicates the phrasing of the underlined portion; the other four choices provide alternative phrasings. Choose the one that rephrases the sentence in the clearest, most grammatically correct manner.

>> **Reading-comprehension questions:** Choose the best answer to every question based on what the passage states directly or indirectly.

>> **Critical-reasoning questions:** Pick the answer choice that best answers the question about the argument provided.

1. A study of energy consumption revealed that homeowners living within 100 miles of the Gulf of Mexico used less energy from November 1 to April 30 than did homeowners in any other region of the United States. The same study found that from May 1 to October 31, those same homeowners used more energy than any other homeowners.

Which of the following, if true, would most contribute to an explanation of the facts above?

(A) People who own homes near the Gulf of Mexico often own second homes in cooler locations, where they spend the summers.

(B) Air conditioning a home is a more energy-efficient process than heating a similarly sized home.

(C) Homes near the Gulf of Mexico require very little heating during the warm winters, but air conditioners must run longer in the summer to cool the warm, humid air.

(D) The average daily temperature is lower year-round near the Gulf of Mexico than in other areas of the United States.

(E) Because of the large number of refineries located in the Gulf region, the price of energy there is less than in any other area of the country.

2. A conservation group is trying to convince Americans that the return of gray wolves to the northern United States is a positive development. Introduction of the wolf faces significant opposition because of the wolf's reputation as a killer of people and livestock. So that the wolf will be more acceptable to average Americans, the conservation group wants to dispel the myth that the wolf is a vicious killer.

Which of the following, if true, would most weaken the opposition's claim?

(A) Wolves are necessary for a healthy population of white-tailed deer because wolves kill the weaker animals and limit the population to sustainable numbers.

(B) In a confrontation, black bears are much more dangerous to humans than wolves are.

(C) Wolves are superb hunters, operating in packs to track down their prey and kill it.

(D) There has never been a documented case of a wolf killing a human in the 500-year recorded history of North America.

(E) Wolves occasionally take livestock because domestic animals are not equipped to protect themselves the way wild animals are.

Questions 3–6 refer to the following passage.

This passage is excerpted from *The Big Splat, or How Our Moon Came to Be*, by Dana Mackenzie, PhD (Wiley):

It is hard for us to imagine today how utterly different the world of night used to be from the daylight world. Of course, we can still re-create something of that lost mystique. When we sit around a campfire and tell ghost stories, our goose bumps (and our children's) remind us of the terrors that night used to hold. But it is all too easy for us to pile in the car at the end of our camping trip and return to the comfort of our incandescent, fluorescent, floodlit modern word. Two thousand, or even two hundred, years ago there was no such escape from the darkness. It was a physical presence that gripped the world from sunset until the cock's crow.

"As different as night and day," we say today. But in centuries past, night and day really were different. In a time when every scrap of light after sunset was desperately appreciated, when travelers would mark the road by piling up light stones or by stripping the bark off of trees to expose the lighter wood underneath, the Moon was the traveler's greatest friend. It was known in folklore as "the parish lantern." It was steady, portable, and — unlike a torch — entailed no risk of fire. It would never blow out, although it could, of course, hide behind a cloud.

Nowadays we don't need the moon to divide the light from the darkness because electric lights do it for us. Many of us have never even seen a truly dark sky. According to a recent survey on light pollution, 97 percent of the U.S. population lives under a night sky at least as bright as it was on a half-moon night in ancient times. Many city-dwellers live their entire lives under the equivalent of a full moon.

3. The primary purpose of this passage is to

(A) compare and contrast nighttime in the modern world with the dark nights of centuries past

(B) explain why the invention of the electric light was essential to increasing worker productivity

(C) lament the loss of the dark nights and the danger and excitement that moonless nights would bring

(D) describe the diminishing brightness of the moon and the subsequent need for more electric lights

(E) argue for an end to the excessive light pollution that plagues 97 percent of the U.S. population

4. When the author says "Many city-dwellers live their entire lives under the equivalent of a full moon," he is essentially saying that

(A) city-dwellers will never be able to truly appreciate the mystique and beauty of a truly dark night

(B) there is no longer a need for moonlight because artificial light is sufficient

(C) city-dwellers are missing out on much of the beauty of the natural world

(D) the amount of artificial light that shines in cities is enough to produce the same amount of light as a full moon

(E) it is easier to view the moon from cities than from rural areas

5. The passage mentions all the following as possible ways for travelers to find the path at night *except*

   (A) piles of light-colored stones
   (B) the moon
   (C) a torch
   (D) railings made of light wood
   (E) trees with the bark stripped off

6. The author includes the statistic "97 percent of the U.S. population lives under a night sky at least as bright as it was on a half-moon night in ancient times" to primarily emphasize which of the following points?

   (A) Modern humans have the luxury of being able to see well at night despite cloud cover or a moonless night.
   (B) Most modern people cannot really understand how important the moon was to people in centuries past.
   (C) Americans are unique among the people of the world in having so much artificial light at night.
   (D) A full moon in ancient times was brighter than modern electric lights, which are only as bright as a half-moon.
   (E) Light pollution is one of the most important problems facing the United States in the 21st century.

7. The sugar maples give us syrup in March, a display of beautiful flowers in spring, and <u>their foliage is spectacular in October</u>.

   (A) their foliage is spectacular in October
   (B) spectacularly, their foliage changes color in October
   (C) has spectacular foliage in October
   (D) spectacular foliage in October
   (E) October foliage that is spectacular in orange and red

8. The Industrial Revolution required levels of financing <u>which were previously unknown</u>; for instance, Florence had 80 banking houses that took deposits, made loans, and performed many of the other functions of a modern bank.

   (A) which were previously unknown
   (B) that were previously unknown
   (C) unknown before that time
   (D) which had been unknown in earlier times
   (E) that was previously unknown

9. His efforts to learn scuba diving, a major goal Bob had set for himself for the coming year, <u>has not successfully begun, seeing as how</u> his fear of claustrophobia is triggered anytime he is underwater.

   (A) has not successfully begun, seeing as how
   (B) have not successfully begun, seeing as how
   (C) have not been successful because
   (D) has not been successful because
   (E) have not yet met with success, on account of

10. The intern's day-to-day duties varied considerably, but typically they included <u>tasks like picking up coffee, clean up the office and arranging meetings for executives</u>.

    (A) tasks like picking up coffee, clean up the office, and arranging meetings for executives

    (B) tasks like picking up coffee, cleaning up the office, and arranging meetings for executives

    (C) tasks such as picking up coffee, cleaning up the office, and arranging meetings for executives

    (D) tasks such as pick up coffee, clean up the office, and arrange meetings for executives

    (E) tasks like pick up coffee, clean up the office, and arrange meetings for executives

11. You never want to think that your spouse may be the person trying to hide assets from you, <u>but they very well might be trying too</u>.

    (A) but they very well might be trying too

    (B) but they very well might be trying to

    (C) but he or she very well might be trying to

    (D) but he or she very well might be doing so

    (E) but they very well might be doing so

12. After the move, Amanda started shopping at a grocery store that was closer to her new home, but she found it had <u>fewer produce, less varieties of fresh juice, and less options for healthy eating then her previous store of choice</u>.

    (A) fewer produce, less varieties of fresh juice, and less options for healthy eating then her previous store of choice

    (B) less produce, fewer varieties of fresh juice, and fewer options for healthy eating than her previous store of choice

    (C) less produce, fewer varieties of fresh juice, and fewer options for healthy eating then her previous store of choice

    (D) fewer produce, fewer varieties of fresh juice, and less options for healthy eating than her previous store of choice

    (E) fewer produce, fewer varieties of fresh juice, and fewer options for healthy eating than her previous store of choice

Questions 13 and 14 are based on the following information.

Tom: The unemployment rate has dropped below 5 percent, and that is good news for America. A lower unemployment rate is better for almost everyone.

Shelly: Actually, a low unemployment rate is good for most workers but not for everyone. Workers are certainly happy to have jobs, but many businesses are negatively affected by a low unemployment rate because they have fewer applicants for jobs, and to expand their workforce, they have to hire workers they would not usually hire. The wealthiest Americans also privately complain about the inability to get good gardeners, housecleaners, and nannies when most Americans are already employed. So a low unemployment rate is not, in fact, good for America.

13. Which of the following, if true, would most weaken the argument that a low unemployment rate is bad for business?

(A) Businesses must pay skilled or experienced workers higher salaries when the unemployment rate is low.

(B) The states don't have to pay unemployment compensation to as many workers when unemployment is low.

(C) Higher unemployment generally means higher enrollment levels in college and graduate school.

(D) Inflation can increase with low unemployment, making capital more expensive for any business seeking to expand.

(E) Low unemployment rates generally mean that Americans have more money to spend on the goods and services created by American businesses.

14. Shelly's conclusion that "a low unemployment rate is not, in fact, good for America" relies on the assumption that

(A) What is bad for businesses owners and the wealthy is bad for America.

(B) Fluctuations in the unemployment rate affect the number of applicants for job openings.

(C) Wealthy Americans rarely employ other Americans as housecleaners or nannies.

(D) Business owners always want what is best for their workers even when it negatively impacts the bottom line.

(E) Low unemployment hurts some workers because they would prefer to stay at home and collect unemployment checks.

15. A particular company makes a system that is installed in the engine block of a car and, if that car is stolen, relays the car's location to police via satellite. The recovery rate of stolen cars with this device is 90 percent. This system helps everyone because it is impossible for a thief to tell which cars it is installed on. For these reasons, insurance companies try to encourage customers to get this system by offering lower rates to those who have the system. Competing systems include brightly colored steel bars that attach to the steering wheel and loud alarms that go off when the car is tampered with. These systems simply encourage thieves to steal different cars, and when cars with these devices are stolen, the police rarely recover them.

Which of the following is the most logical conclusion to the author's premises?

(A) Insurance companies should give the same discount to car owners who have any protective system because their cars are less likely to be stolen.

(B) The police shouldn't allow car owners to install the loud sirens on their cars because everyone simply ignores the sirens anyway.

(C) Car owners with the system that relays location to the police should prominently advertise the fact on the side window of their cars.

(D) Thieves should simply steal the cars with loud alarms or bright steel bars because those cars probably wouldn't also have the more effective system installed.

(E) Insurance companies should give less of a discount, or no discount at all, to the siren and steering-wheel systems because they aren't as effective as the relay system.

16. The managers were asked to rate their depth of knowledge having been increased as a result of the emergency simulation, and in each area, they reported large gains.

   (A) their depth of knowledge having been increased

   (B) how much their depth of knowledge had increased

   (C) if they had more knowledge

   (D) how deep their knowledge is

   (E) their knowledge depth

17. Keeping the nose of her kayak directly into the wind, she paddled fiercely toward the safety of the harbor through the seeming endless waves, each of those larger than the last.

   (A) through the seeming endless waves, each of those larger than the last

   (B) through the seeming endless waves, each larger than the last

   (C) through the seemingly endless waves, each of those larger than the last

   (D) through the seemingly endless waves, each larger than the last

   (E) through waves that seemingly have no end, each larger than the last

18. Companies X and Y have the same number of employees working the same number of hours per week. According to the records kept by the human resources department of each company, the employees of company X took nearly twice as many sick days as the employees of company Y. Therefore, the employees of company Y are healthier than the employees of company X.

   Which of the following, if true, most seriously weakens the conclusion?

   (A) Company X allows employees to use sick days to take care of sick family members.

   (B) Company Y offers its employees dental insurance and company X doesn't.

   (C) Company X offers its employees a free membership to the local gym.

   (D) Company Y uses a newer system for keeping records of sick days.

   (E) Both companies offer two weeks of sick days per year.

   Questions 19–23 refer to the following passage.

   This passage is excerpted from *Brand Name Bullies: The Quest to Own and Control Culture*, by David Bollier (Wiley):

   For millennia, the circulation of music in human societies has been as free as the circulation of air and water; it just comes naturally. Indeed, one of the ways that a society constitutes itself as a society is by freely sharing its words, music, and art. Only in the past century or so has music been placed in a tight envelope of property rights and strictly monitored for unauthorized flows. In the past decade, the proliferation of personal computers, Internet access, and digital technologies has fueled two conflicting forces: the democratization of creativity and the demand for stronger copyright protections.

   While the public continues to have nominal fair use rights to copyrighted music, in practice the legal and technological controls over music have grown tighter. At the same time, creators at the fringes of mass culture, especially some hip-hop and remix artists, remain contemptuous of such controls and routinely appropriate whatever sounds they want to create interesting music.

Copyright protection is a critically important tool for artists in earning a livelihood from their creativity. But as many singers, composers, and musicians have discovered, the benefits of copyright law in the contemporary marketplace tend to accrue to the recording industry, not to the struggling garage band. As alternative distribution and marketing outlets have arisen, the recording industry has sought to ban, delay, or control as many of them as possible. After all, technological innovations that provide faster, cheaper distribution of music are likely to disrupt the industry's fixed investments and entrenched ways of doing business. New technologies allow newcomers to enter the market and compete, sometimes on superior terms. New technologies enable new types of audiences to emerge that may or may not be compatible with existing marketing strategies.

No wonder the recording industry has scrambled to develop new technological locks and broader copyright protections; they strengthen its control of music distribution. If metering devices could turn barroom singalongs into a market, the music industry would likely declare this form of unauthorized musical performance to be copyright infringement.

19. Which of the following most accurately states the main idea of the passage?

(A) Only with the development of technology in the past century has music begun to freely circulate in society.

(B) The recording industry is trying to develop an ever-tighter hold on the distribution of music, which used to circulate freely.

(C) Copyright protection is an important tool for composers and musicians who earn their living from their music.

(D) Technology allows new distribution methods that threaten to undermine the marketing strategies of music companies.

(E) If music is no longer allowed to flow freely through the society, then the identity of the society itself will be lost.

20. Given the author's overall opinion of increased copyright protections, what is his attitude toward "hip-hop and remix artists" mentioned in Paragraph 2?

(A) wonder that they aren't sued more for their theft of copyright-protected music

(B) disappointment that they don't understand the damage they are doing to society

(C) envy of their extravagant lifestyle and increasing popularity

(D) approval of their continued borrowing of music despite tighter copyright controls

(E) shock at their blatant sampling of the music of other artists

21. According to the passage, new technology has resulted (or will result) in each of the following *except*

(A) new locks on music distribution

(B) newcomers' competing in the music market

(C) better music

(D) democratization of creativity

(E) faster, cheaper distribution of music

22. The author of the passage would likely agree most with which of the following statements?

   (A) Small-time musicians do not benefit from strict copyright protections in the same manner as record companies do.

   (B) Copyright protections are designed to let music artists keep more of the money they earn through their talent.

   (C) Recording companies are largely undeserving of their greedy reputations.

   (D) Recording companies embrace new technologies because they help encourage the spread of music.

   (E) Copyright protections encourage creativity among musicians because the artists must find new ways to share their music with the masses.

23. The final sentence of the passage seems to imply what about the executives of the record industry?

   (A) They have found ways to make money from any performance of any music at any time.

   (B) They are boldly leading the music industry into a new technological era of vastly increased profits.

   (C) They want their music to be performed as often as possible by the maximum number of people to create greater exposure for artists.

   (D) They don't actually like music or know anything about music and are attempting to limit the society's exposure to music.

   (E) No performance of music anywhere is safe from their attempts to control the distribution of all music.

24. Five new loon pairs successfully raised chicks this year, <u>bringing</u> to 24 the number of pairs actively breeding in the lakes of Massachusetts.

   (A) bringing

   (B) and brings

   (C) and it brings

   (D) and it brought

   (E) and brought

25. New laws make it easier to patent just about anything, from parts of the human genome to a peanut butter and jelly sandwich. Commentators are concerned about the implications of allowing patents for things that can hardly be described as "inventions." However, the U.S. Patent and Trademark Office believes that allowing for strong copyright and patent protections fosters the kind of investment in research and development needed to spur innovation.

   Which of the following can be properly inferred from the preceding statements?

   (A) It was not possible in the past to patent something as common as a peanut butter and jelly sandwich.

   (B) The U.S. Patent and Trademark Office is more interested in business profits than in true innovation.

   (C) Investment in research and development is often needed to spur innovation.

   (D) The human genome is part of nature and shouldn't be patented.

   (E) Commentators who are concerned about too many patents aren't very well informed.

26. The process of "gerrymandering," or manipulating voter-district boundaries so that one party gains a considerable advantage in a district over another, is making the modern political climate more divisive than ever. It ensures that people with likeminded ideals end up densely packed in the same districts, and those people then elect officials who also share those likeminded ideals.

These elected officials are less prone to compromise, and this creates an unnecessary and harmful divide between parties.

Assuming all the following statements are true, which would most significantly weaken the argument made above?

(A) Gerrymandering sets up an unfair advantage by creating some districts that are nearly guaranteed to vote for a particular party, thereby freeing up more time and resources for that party to campaign elsewhere.

(B) People with likeminded ideals have an innate desire to live alongside others who share similar belief systems, regardless of their political affiliation.

(C) All elected officials are typically strong in their convictions.

(D) When people with likeminded ideals live in the same district, they tend to continuously elect politicians with very similar beliefs.

(E) Gerrymandering can be executed by both political parties.

27. In a recent survey, one out of six Americans were shown to have vision problems, which is a notable increase over the past two decades. The amount of time Americans spend in front of computer and television screens has risen sharply, and to reduce the number of Americans suffering from vision issues, the amount of screen exposure must also be reduced.

Which of the following, if true, would most substantially weaken the author's conclusion?

(A) Increased screen time is directly correlated with vision problems.

(B) The connection between screen time and vision problems is not entirely clear.

(C) Screen time has increased globally and not just in America.

(D) Americans can reduce their risk of vision problems caused by too much screen time by dimming the screen and using a larger font.

(E) The majority of Americans with vision problems are older people, and the percentage of people over age 60 has steadily increased over the past twenty years.

28. Despite the fact that they were colonists, <u>more Americans thought of themselves as British citizens</u>, and throughout the early years of the American Revolution, more than half of all Americans were loyal to Britain.

(A) more Americans thought of themselves as British citizens

(B) fewer Americans felt that they were British citizens

(C) most Americans thought of themselves as British citizens

(D) many of them felt like British citizens

(E) most Americans believed we were British citizens

Understanding What's Right with Answer Explanations

You can check your answers to the practice questions by reading through the following explanations. To get the most benefit, read through every explanation, even the ones for the questions you answered correctly.

1. **C.** This critical-reasoning question asks you to strengthen the argument by providing a piece to the cause-and-effect pattern. With cause-and-effect questions, you select the answer choice that could logically cause the effects noted in the premises. So for this problem, you have to decide which of the five choices helps explain why Gulf Coast homes use little energy in the winter *and* a great deal of energy in the summer. Without even looking at the answer choices, you may conclude that the Gulf Coast climate is milder than other parts of the nation in the winter and perhaps hotter in the summer. The correct answer probably addresses that issue.

   You can eliminate Choice (A) because if most Gulf Coast residents spend the summer elsewhere, their vacant homes would use less energy during summer months rather than more. This answer would produce the opposite effect of that explained in the argument. Choice (B) would also produce the opposite effect of that found in the argument. Another important reason for eliminating Choice (B) is that it doesn't provide a way of comparing energy use in the Gulf region to energy use in the rest of the country, which is the real issue in this argument.

   Choice (C) sounds like the answer we imagined before reading through the choices. It explains why the Gulf region would have lower energy use in winter and higher use in summer, which may explain why it's different from the rest of the country as a whole. Although Choice (C) is probably the correct answer, read through the remaining two choices just to be sure.

   Choice (D) doesn't work because a region that's cool year-round would have high energy consumption in the winter for heat and low consumption in the summer. And you can eliminate Choice (E) because the argument is about energy consumption, not energy price. So the correct answer is Choice (C).

2. **D.** This critical reasoning question asks you to weaken the opposition's statement that the wolf is vicious, so look for a statement that shows that the wolf isn't a danger to people or livestock. Begin by eliminating answers that don't address the appropriate conclusion. Choice (A) deals with the beneficial impact of wolves on the ecosystem but doesn't talk about their propensity toward viciousness to humans or livestock, so eliminate it. You can also eliminate Choice (C) because the hunting prowess of the wolf isn't the issue, and this choice may actually strengthen the contention that wolves are dangerous. Choice (E) also doesn't weaken the conclusion in question; it argues that wolves may threaten livestock. This leaves you with Choices (B) and (D). Choice (B) compares the danger posed by wolves with the danger posed by black bears. Even if a wolf is less dangerous than a bear, that doesn't mean a wolf isn't dangerous. The best answer is Choice (D), because it provides a statistic that weakens the opposition's argument that wolves are dangerous to humans.

3. **A.** For a primary-purpose reading-comprehension question, you're looking for the reason the author wrote the passage.

Focus on the passage as a whole and not on any particular portion. You usually can find clues to the main theme and the author's purpose in the first and last paragraphs.

The main idea of this passage is that night was very different in centuries past than it is in current times, and the author's purpose is to show how this is true. So look for an answer that reflects this purpose.

You can start by eliminating answers based on their first words. The words *compare and contrast, explain,* and *describe* reflect the author's purpose, but *lament* and *argue* imply more emotion on the part of the author than is displayed in the passage, so eliminate Choices (C) and (E). Worker productivity has nothing to do with showing how our ancestors perceived night differently, so you can eliminate Choice (B). Choice (D) is simply wrong; the author doesn't maintain that the moon is actually getting darker, just that it's become overshadowed by electric lights. So that leaves Choice (A) as the correct answer.

4. **D.** Arguably the biggest clue to Choice (D) lies in the second-to-last sentence, when the author references a "recent survey of light pollution" in cities. This implies that there is so much visible light in cities that residents need no longer "mark the road by piling up light stones or by stripping the bark off of trees to expose the lighter wood underneath" to light their way to their destination. It's always wise to consider all the other possible answer choices, though, just to make sure. Choices (A) and (C) are somewhat similar, in that they both intimate that city-dwellers are missing out on the beauty of nature and the world around them. This doesn't appear to be the focus of the passage, however; the passage is more focused on how people used to make up for the lack of light and how they no longer need to do so to function after dark. So, you can probably eliminate both options. Choice (E) doesn't make a lot of sense; it is probably easier to get a good look at the moon in a rural area, where tall buildings, pollution, and so on are less likely to block your view. You're down to either Choice (B) or (D). The two choices seem similar, but of the two, Choice (D) is the stronger option. The last sentence provides that artificial light is "equivalent" to moonlight, which is more synonymous to the "same amount" of illumination in Choice (D) than "sufficient" in Choice (B).

5. **D.** This specific-information exception question asks you to refer to the text to eliminate answers that *are* ways in the passage that travelers can find a path at night. The second paragraph specifically mentions Choice (A), light-colored stones; Choice (B), the moon; Choice (C), torches; and Choice (E), trees with the bark stripped off. Railings, Choice (D), aren't mentioned anywhere in the passage so it's the correct answer.

6. **B.** This question asks you about the use of a specific statistic. To answer this question correctly, keep in mind the author's purpose for writing the passage, which you've already considered in the third question. Find the choice that links the statistic to the author's purpose of comparing nighttime now and nighttime in centuries past. Eliminate Choice (C) because the author compares time periods, not modern countries. Because the passage doesn't indicate that the moon is brighter than electric lights, you can eliminate Choice (D). Although the 97 percent statistic may lead you to conclude that light pollution is a big problem, that's not the author's reason for using the statistic, so eliminate Choice (E). Choice (A) is a little more plausible, but Choice (B) is better because the author is more concerned with showing how night skies are different now than with showing that the modern well-lit sky is a luxury.

7. **D.** This sentence-correction question has a parallelism problem. You know this because the underlined portion is a part of a list of elements joined by a conjunction and not all the elements in the list exhibit the same construction. The third element is expressed as a clause, and the other elements are noun phrases. Because the sentence contains an error, you know Choice (A) is wrong. Choices (B) and (C) don't change the clause to a phrase. Although Choice (E) is a noun phrase, its construction is unnecessarily wordy: *foliage that is spectacular* versus *spectacular foliage*. Choice (E) also introduces new information (the colors orange and red), which alters the original sentence. Choice (D) maintains parallel construction without adding unnecessary words, so it's the correct answer.

8. **B.** This sentence-correction question has an improperly used pronoun. You use *which* to introduce nonessential clauses. Because the information after the *which* is essential to the meaning of the sentence, you have to use *that* instead. You can eliminate Choices (A) and (D) because both keep the *which* construction. Choice (C) uses too many words to mean *previously unknown*, and Choice (E) changes *which* to *that* but presents a new problem because *that* refers to *levels*, which is plural, so it requires the plural verb *have*. So Choice (B) is the only answer that corrects the problem without creating new ones.

9. **C.** The underlined portion of this sentence-correction question has problems with agreement and rhetorical construction. The plural subject *efforts* doesn't work with the singular verb *has*. Because you find an error, you automatically eliminate Choice (A). Choice (D) doesn't correct the agreement error. This leaves you with Choices (B), (C), and (E), all of which correct the agreement problem, but *because* is a better, clearer construction than *seeing as how* and *on account of*, so Choice (C) is the best answer.

10. **C.** There are two issues with the sentence about the intern's task in the original version. First, there is the issue of using *like* instead of *such as* to introduce a series of examples. Use *like* to compare two nouns: "Like Dave, Joe performs many duties."

    The second problem with the sentence is that it lacks parallelism. In the list of the intern's tasks, two of the verbs (*picking* and *arranging*) take on the gerund form (meaning they end in *-ing*) while the third verb, *clean*, doesn't. All three tasks in the series have to have the same grammatical construction, meaning *clean* must be changed to its gerund form, *cleaning*, for the sentence to be correct. The only sentence that effectively corrects both issues is Choice (C).

11. **D.** The small underlined portion of this sentence contains three errors. The first concerns the pronoun *they*, which is a plural pronoun that renames the singular noun *spouse*. Eliminate Choices (A), (B), and (E). And of course *too* in Choice (A) means *also* and thus is wrong. The other error snuck in here is the good ol' dangling preposition. Standard writing English frowns upon ending a sentence with a preposition like *to*. Of the remaining two answers, Choice (D) corrects the preposition error.

12. **B.** The sentence as written has two problems: it confuses the use of *less* and *fewer* and of *then* and *than*. The author uses *less* and *fewer* improperly. *Fewer* refers to nouns you can actually count, such as socks, lollipops, and red trucks, whereas *less* is used for items that can't be easily quantified, such as rain or sugar. Since *produce* can't be easily counted, the use of *fewer* in the original sentence is incorrect — so you can go ahead and knock out Choices (A), (D), and (E) right off the bat. "Varieties of juice" *can* be counted. Therefore, *fewer* is correct in this circumstance. You've narrowed your choices down to either Choice (B) or Choice (C). Because Choice (C) uses *then* to make a comparison, it must be wrong. *Then* references time and is never used in comparisons. Choice (B) fixes the errors.

13. **E.** This critical-reasoning question requires you to weaken Shelly's argument that a low unemployment rate is bad for business. Choices (A) and (D) give two examples of how low unemployment hurts businesses, so they actually strengthen the argument instead of weaken it. Eliminate them along with Choices (B) and (C), because these statements are basically off topic; they deal with government and universities, not businesses. Choice (E) is the correct answer, because employed American workers' buying more American products provides a significant advantage for businesses.

14. **A.** This critical-reasoning question asks you to identify an assumption that Shelly relied on in making her conclusion that a low unemployment rate isn't "good for America."

REMEMBER

When you're asked to find an assumption, look for a statement that supports the conclusion but isn't actually stated in the argument.

Eliminate choices that don't support the conclusion. Whether businesses favor workers over the bottom line may affect the unemployment rate, but it doesn't show how low unemployment isn't good for America, so Choice (D) is incorrect. Choice (E) doesn't support the conclusion, either. The conclusion is about what's good for America in general, not a select few disinclined workers.

A person's assumption wouldn't contradict a stated premise, so Choice (C) can't be right. Choice (B) may support the conclusion, but it's actually stated in the given premises and, therefore, can't be an unstated assumption. Choice (A) is the correct answer because it links Shelly's premises about businesses and wealthy Americans to her conclusion about America in general.

15. **E.** This critical-reasoning question requires you to draw a conclusion from the premises included in the argument.

REMEMBER

Look for an answer choice that addresses all the information in the premises. You can eliminate conclusions that are off topic or incomplete.

Eliminate choices that don't include all the elements of the argument. Choices (B), (C), and (D) don't mention the insurance companies that are the subject of one of the premises. This leaves you with Choice (A) and Choice (E), which offer nearly opposite conclusions. The premises indicate that one of the reasons insurance companies like the engine-block system is that thieves don't know which cars have it installed. Choice (A) concludes that cars with any protective system, including alarms and steering-wheel bars, should get a discount because those cars are less likely to be stolen. This conclusion doesn't flow logically from the premises, however, because the reasons given for the insurance discounts are a high recovery rate of stolen vehicles and the general deterrent to all car thefts. Neither of these advantages comes from the alarms or steering-wheel bars. Choice (E) addresses all the premises and logically concludes the argument, making it the correct answer.

16. **B.** The underlined portion in this sentence-correction question is passive, so you can eliminate Choice (A). Choices (C), (D), and (E) don't address both the knowledge increase *and* the knowledge depth, so you can eliminate them, too. The best answer is Choice (B). It makes the construction active and includes both the increase and depth of knowledge.

17. **D.** You probably first noticed that the underlined portion of this sentence-correction question contains a modification error. Adjectives like *seeming* modify nouns and pronouns. They can't modify other adjectives like *endless*. Adverbs must be used for that. Instead of *seeming*, you can use the adverb *seemingly*. Therefore, you know you can disregard Choice (A). You can also eliminate Choice (B) because it doesn't make the change to *seemingly*. Choices (C), (D), and (E) change *seeming* to *seemingly*.

This underlined portion also has a problem with redundancy. *Each* refers sufficiently to *waves; of those* isn't necessary. Choice (C) doesn't fix this error, so it's wrong. Choices (D) and (E) both fix each of the errors, but Choice (E) creates another. The sentence is past tense, so the verb *have* should be in past tense like this: *seemingly had no end.* Choice (D) corrects both original errors and doesn't introduce more, so it's the correct answer.

18. **A.** This critical-reasoning question asks you to weaken the conclusion that the employees of company Y are healthier than the employees of company X. The author draws the conclusion that Y's employees are healthier than X's employees based on the cause–and–effect argument that more sick days mean sicker employees.

TIP

To weaken cause-and-effect arguments, look for an answer choice that shows another cause is possible for the effect.

Choice (E) doesn't distinguish between the two companies. It can't show another cause for the different number of sick days and, therefore, can't be right. Choice (D) differentiates between the two companies' record-keeping, but it doesn't explain how company Y's new records system accounts for fewer sick days. Dental insurance shouldn't affect the number of sick days, so Choice (B) doesn't work. Choice (C) doesn't address the issue of company X's greater number of sick days, so free gym memberships don't matter. The best answer is Choice (A) because it provides a reason other than employee health for the greater number of sick days that company X's employees take.

19. **B.** This reading-comprehension question asks for the main idea of the passage.

REMEMBER

Answers to main-theme questions are usually more general than specific in their wording.

Choices (C) and (D) each focus on sub-themes in the passage but not the main idea. Copyright protection and technology are specific subjects covered in the passage, but they don't make up the main idea, which is that the music industry is trying to control distribution of music. You can eliminate Choice (A) because it's not supported by any part of the passage. The passage clearly states that music has circulated freely in society for millennia. Choice (E) is wrong because it goes beyond what's stated in the passage. The author may well imply that without the free flow of music, society will lose its identity, but this isn't the passage's main idea. So that leaves Choice (B) as the best answer.

20. **D.** This reading-comprehension question asks about the author's attitude toward *hip-hop and remix artists* as specifically mentioned in the second paragraph. The real GMAT would highlight this phrase in yellow. You've already answered a question about the main idea, so you know the author is concerned about the tightening grip the recording industry has on the distribution of music. Because the hip-hop and remix artists defy the music industry, they'll likely meet with the author's approval. Although Choice (A) may express a valid opinion, you can eliminate it because it isn't supported by the passage. The author probably approves of hip-hop and remix artists, so he or she doesn't think they're doing damage — Choice (B) is completely off base. Envy and shock are usually too strong emotions for GMAT passages, so rule out Choices (C) and (E). The correct answer is Choice (D).

21. **C.** Here's another specific-information reading-comprehension question looking for an exception. Examine the text and eliminate the answers you find there. The one that remains is your correct answer. In connection with technology, the passage mentions Choice (A), new locks on music distribution, in the second paragraph; Choice (B), newcomers' competing in the market, in the third paragraph; Choice (D), democratization of creativity, in the first paragraph; and Choice (E), faster, cheaper distribution of music, in the third paragraph. The author certainly doesn't mention better music. So Choice (C) is correct.

22. **A.** If you picked Choice (B), you may not have read closely enough, or you may have stopped reading right after the author refers to copyright protections as, ". . . a critically important tool for artists in earning a livelihood from their creativity," because the author then goes on to lament how such protections tend to benefit the recording companies more than the artists. As for Choice (C), because a key point made by the author throughout the passage is that recording companies are, in fact, greedy, and will do just about anything to make and keep as much money as possible, you can easily eliminate that answer. Choice (D), too, can be eliminated with relative ease, as the author makes several references to the fact that record companies do just the opposite of embracing new technologies. They instead seek to "ban, delay, or control" them for their own benefit. Choice (E) can also be knocked out of contention because the author doesn't go into whether artists are finding "new ways to share their music with the masses"; he instead discusses how copyright protections are intended to help recording companies maintain control of music distribution to the fullest extent possible. Choice (E) also refers to the artist's creative ways to avoid technological and legal controls rather than the creativity associated with producing the artwork itself. Choice (A) is your best option, justified by the author's statement that "the benefits of copyright law in the contemporary marketplace tend to accrue to the recording industry, not to the struggling garage band."

23. **E.** For this reading-comprehension inference question, you need to determine what the final sentence implies about recording-industry executives. The final sentence mentions that if it were possible, executives would try to stop unauthorized singalongs. This shows that the author thinks that executives will go to any length to control the distribution of music. Choices (B) and (C) paint the executives in a positive light, which is certainly not warranted by the last sentence. You can also eliminate Choice (D) because the last sentence has nothing to do with whether executives like or dislike music. Choice (A) is closer, but the sentence doesn't talk about making money from singalongs so much as stopping them altogether. That makes Choice (E) the correct answer.

24. **A.** This sentence-correction question tests your knowledge of verb forms and grammatical construction. You're not dealing with word choice, because all the answer choices include a form of the verb *to bring*. Choices (C) and (D) introduce the pronoun *it*, which has no clear reference, so they're not right. Choice (B) applies a singular verb to a plural subject. Choice (E) includes *and*, which would make the comma in the non-underlined part of the sentence improper. The sentence is best as is.

25. **A.** This critical-reasoning question asks you to draw an inference from the passage. Inference questions generally focus on a premise rather than on a conclusion. The passage implies that the patent office wants to promote invention, so Choice (B) doesn't work. Choices (D) and (E) express opinions that aren't presented in the passage. Although you may agree that the genome shouldn't be patented or that people who are concerned about patents aren't well informed, the question doesn't ask you for your opinion.

WARNING

Don't choose answer choices to critical-reasoning questions just because you agree with them. Base your answers on the opinions stated or implied by the paragraph.

Because Choice (C) is stated in the passage, it can't be an inference. The answer must be Choice (A), because it flows logically from the first premise and isn't stated in the passage.

26. **B.** Choice (A) sounds more like an additional argument *in favor* of gerrymandering creating an "unnecessary and harmful divide between parties," so that answer can't be right since it strengthens rather than weakens the original argument. The same can be said for Choice (D); if folks are electing very similar politicians in their districts and those politicians share the same ideals, this would likely contribute to the divide between parties and help eliminate the political "middle." Choice (E) is irrelevant; that both sides can take part in gerrymandering doesn't mean they do or that they do at the same time. So, that argument also falls flat. You've narrowed the options down to either Choice (B) or (C). Of the two, Choice (B) is the stronger option. It presents an alternative to gerrymandering as the reason that certain districts tend to elect people from the same party over and over again, which arguably contributes to a sharper divide between parties. Choice (B) is your best bet.

27. **E.** Choice (E) is best because it presents a logical, alternative explanation for the statistics surrounding Americans with vision problems. It isn't screen time that causes the spike in problems but, instead, a large population of aging Americans. Choice (A) would strengthen rather than weaken the initial argument, so you know that one can't be right. Choice (B) is a possibility, but you can assume the GMAT is probably looking for something a bit more precise. Choice (C) is irrelevant; the argument is specific to *American* vision problems, so it doesn't matter how much time people in other parts of the world spend looking at screens. Choice (D), too, is irrelevant. What people do to reduce vision issues doesn't call into question the role of screen time in vision problems.

28. **C.** The final sentence-correction question contains an improper comparison. The term *more* requires a comparison between two things (more Americans thought of themselves as British citizens than what?). The sentence doesn't offer a comparison. Because there's an error, eliminate Choice (A). Choice (B) uses the term *fewer*, which also requires a comparison, and this answer choice changes the meaning of the sentence. Choice (D) gets rid of *more* but introduces the pronoun *them*, which doesn't have a clear reference and, therefore, can't be right. Choice (E) also contains a pronoun error: its inclusion of the first-person pronoun *we*. We weren't around during the American Revolution, so Choice (E) is incorrect. Choice (C) changes *more* to *most*, so it eliminates the comparison problem and is the correct answer.

3

Acing the Analytical-Writing Section

IN THIS PART . . .

Gain an understanding of the AWA, including the topics you'll have to write about and what GMAT readers are looking for when they score your essay.

Craft an exemplary GMAT essay by organizing your thoughts, writing what the readers are looking for, and avoiding common grammar and mechanics errors.

Take a look at some sample AWA essays to find out what works and what doesn't.

Try your hand at some practice AWA writing prompts.

Chapter **8**

Analyze This: What to Expect from the Analytical Writing Assessment

The analytical writing assessment (or AWA, as it's affectionately known) can be intimidating. You're required to write an analytical essay on a topic that the computer reveals to you just as your time begins to tick away. To earn the top score, you're expected to provide an excellent analysis and insightful examples and demonstrate a mastery of standard written English. Did we mention that you're supposed to do this in only 30 minutes? If it seems a little overwhelming, relax. You can do it; we show you how in this chapter.

First, you need to know what you're up against, so we walk you through the AWA and let you know what to expect. Then, we give you a sneak peak at the writing task required of you. Finally, we get to the part that interests you most — how the AWA is scored.

Fitting in the AWA with the Rest of the GMAT

The AWA is a stand-alone section of the GMAT. The GMAT reports your analytical writing score separately from your integrated reasoning score and your quantitative and verbal reasoning scores. In other words, your combined total GMAT score (with a maximum of 800 points) reflects how well you do on only the multiple-choice verbal- and quantitative-reasoning sections of the test. So you can write gibberish on the essay portion of the test and still earn an 800 for your GMAT score (but we certainly don't recommend that strategy!).

Each business program determines the importance of the analytical writing section differently. Some schools may give it the same weight as your combined quantitative and verbal score. Other schools may assign it less weight. Check with the specific schools you're interested in attending to see how they use the AWA score. The bottom line is that regardless of how a business program uses your essay score, it will be reported to them. So it's to your advantage to do as well on the AWA as you can.

TIP

Another reason to be well prepared for the AWA is that it's typically the first section of the GMAT. If you feel that you did well on the essay, this confidence may sustain you through the rest of the test. However, if you're unprepared for the AWA and have a difficult time completing the essay, your bad start can have a negative impact on your entire test session.

Calling 411: Your AWA Writing Tools

The analytical writing assessment consists of one essay prompt, which the GMAT refers to as a *task*. The task requires you to write an analytical essay within 30 minutes. You type your response, using the computer software provided at the testing center. At the end of the 30 minutes, your task is complete and only what you've actually typed into the computer contributes to your score, meaning any handwritten notes or great ideas in your head don't count!

TIP

You'll be able to use typical word-processing functions like cut, paste, undo, and redo. You can access these word-processing functions with the mouse or by using special keystrokes that the GMAT specifies for you before you begin the test. You can also use your noteboard to take notes as you plan your response.

WARNING

Some of the following word-processing features you may be accustomed to won't be available:

>> **Automatic corrections:** If you regularly use a program like Word or WordPerfect, you probably don't even notice the automatic corrections anymore. You type in *comittment* and your computer displays *commitment* without you even realizing it. The GMAT won't automatically correct your mistakes.

>> **Spelling and grammar check:** You know that spelling-and-grammar-check function that has saved you from turning in some truly hideous college papers? The function tells you, for example, that you have just written a passive sentence with subject-verb agreement problems and three misspelled words. You can't count on that because spelling and grammar check won't be available, either!

>> **Synonym finder:** You won't have access to that groovy built-in thesaurus that helped you find synonyms for six of your seven uses of the word *cool* (one of which is *groovy*).

Analyzing an Argument

The analytical writing assessment task requires you to analyze an argument. The GMAT doesn't want your opinion on a topic. Instead, you're supposed to critique the way *someone else* reaches an opinion. To score well on this task, you need to analyze the reasoning behind the argument and write a critique of the argument. First, you need to briefly explain what kind of reasoning the author uses (for all about different kinds of reasoning, consult Chapter 6). Next, you point out the strengths and weaknesses of the argument. Finally, you consider the validity of the assumptions that the author makes and what effect alternative explanations would have on the author's conclusion.

Here's a paraphrase of the directions for the analysis of an argument task on the GMAT:

>> Write a critique of the argument presented but don't provide your own opinion.

>> Think for a few minutes about the argument and organize your response before you start writing. Leave time for revisions when you're finished.

You'll be scored based on your ability to accomplish these tasks:

» Organize, develop, and express your thoughts about the given argument.

» Provide pertinent supporting ideas with examples.

» Apply the rules of standard written English.

Now that you have the directions down, check out this example essay prompt:

EXAMPLE

The following is an excerpt written by the head of a governmental department:

"Stronger environmental regulations are not necessary in order to provide clean air and water. We already have lots of regulations on the books and these are not being adequately enforced. For example, the Clean Air Act amendments, adopted in 1990, have never been fully enforced and, as a result, hundreds of coal-burning power plants are systematically violating that law on a daily basis. The Clean Water Act is also not being enforced. In the state of Ohio alone there were more than 2,500 violations in just one year. Instead of passing new regulations that will also be ignored, this department should begin by vigorously enforcing the existing laws."

Examine this argument and present your judgment on how well reasoned it is. In your discussion, analyze the author's position and how well the author uses evidence to support the argument. For example, you may need to question the author's underlying assumptions or consider alternative explanations that may weaken the conclusion. You can also provide additional support for or arguments against the author's position, describe how stating the argument differently may make it more reasonable, and discuss what provisions may better equip you to evaluate its thesis.

Racking Up the Points: How the GMAT Scores Your Essay

According to the folks who make the GMAT, the AWA is designed to measure your ability to think and your ability to communicate your ideas. To assess how well you do in each of these areas, the GMAT employs the services of two separate readers (one of which may be a computer program called an automated essay-scoring engine). Based on their analysis of your written masterpiece, these readers individually assign you a score between 0 and 6, with 6 being the highest.

In the following sections, we give you the lowdown on who evaluates your AWA, what the different scores mean, and how to get a new score if the first one you receive is way off.

Getting to know your readers

Two independent readers judge your analytical writing task, and each of the readers assigns your essay a score from 0 to 6 in half-point increments. If the two readers who are scoring your essay differ by more than a single point, a third reader will adjudicate. This means that the third reader's score will be used in conjunction with the other scores.

For example, if one reader assigns your essay a 3 and the other reader gives it a 5, a third reader is brought in. If the third reader also gives your essay a 5, then the 3 would be discarded and your two scores for that essay would be 5 and 5. If, however, the third reader splits the difference and assigns you a 4, you'd have two 4s (the score from the third reader and the average of the first two scores).

REMEMBER

The benefit of having more than one reader evaluate your essay is that if one reader happens to assign you an unfairly low score, he won't be able to sabotage your score.

College and university faculty members from a variety of academic disciplines score your essays. Some are from business management programs, but you can't expect that the particular readers who score your tasks will have any special knowledge of business. So avoid using jargon or assuming that your reader has had all the same business classes that you've had.

REMEMBER

The automated scoring program that may grade your essay is designed to reflect the judgment of human readers, so it looks for the same elements that human readers do. Regardless of who (or what) reads your essay, your goal is to present quality analysis and sound reasoning with a minimum of grammatical errors. In Chapter 9, we tell you how to avoid common writing errors.

Readers look for two things when they take on your essays: clear analysis and good writing. For an essay to earn a score of 5 or 6, it must clearly analyze the argument, demonstrate good organization, and provide specific, relevant examples and insightful reasoning. The essay must demonstrate clear control of language and apply a variety of sentence structures. It can have some minor flaws in the way you use standard written English but not too many.

Keeping all these things in mind as you write your essay is a tough order for 30 short minutes. To help you through the process, consult Chapter 9, where we discuss strategies for analyzing arguments quickly and effectively and go over the most common errors test-takers make when they write under pressure.

Interpreting the scores

The GMAT reports your AWA score as a number from 0 to 6 in half-point increments. For one administration, a score of 6, the highest possible score, lands you in the 90th percentile, meaning that 90 people out of every 100 test-takers received a lower score. A score of 6 is obviously difficult to earn, and only about 10 percent of test-takers achieve that score! For the same test, a score of 5.5 puts you in the 81st percentile; a score of 5, in the 57th percentile; 4.5, the 43rd percentile; and 4, the 20th percentile.

The mean final score on the AWA is about 4.4. The typical essay, therefore, falls somewhere between 4 (adequate) and 5 (strong). A number of papers fall into the 3 (limited) category or lower, and the cream of the crop is recognized with a 6 (outstanding). To make sure your score surfaces to the creamy top, practice using the techniques we provide in Chapter 9.

Requesting your essay be rescored

After receiving your essay score, you may think it's too low. If that's the case and you truly think you wrote a better essay than your score represents, you can take advantage of the GMAT's AWA rescoring service. Within six months of your exam, you can pay $45 to have an independent reader score your essay. The new score stands, whether it increases or decreases, so requesting a new score can be risky. But if you think a real discrepancy exists, you can take your chances by sending in a rescoring request form. The new score result is sent to you and the schools that have already received your original AWA score.

REMEMBER

The rescoring service applies only to the AWA. The GMAT won't rescore the other three sections, which makes sense because you can't do much to change a multiple-choice test score!

Chapter **9**

Present Perfect Paragraphs: How to Write a GMAT Essay

Knowing what to expect from the analytical writing assessment (AWA) gives you an advantage on the GMAT, but if you want to earn a high score, you need to know what you're expected to do and how to do it. To perform well on the analytical writing task, you have to combine good analysis with a good writing style. If you lack either of these key components, your score will suffer. In this chapter, we start with common writing errors that you should avoid and then discuss the steps to writing your analysis.

Avoiding Grammar, Punctuation, and Mechanics Errors

One of the aspects of the analytical writing assessment that causes the most trouble for test-takers is the requirement that they demonstrate a good control of standard written English. Standard written English isn't so standard anymore, and it doesn't mirror the way most Americans speak (or text and email, for that matter!). Emailed messages are often sentence fragments, and you don't have to worry about things like spelling and punctuation when you text. Because you can't always rely on what sounds right to you, you have to know the writing rules.

TIP

In the following sections, we identify a few common mistakes that plague GMAT test-takers. Writers everywhere seem to repeat these same writing errors. The essay readers will notice these errors, and their presence in your essay will affect your score. If you identify the errors you make most often, you can begin to eliminate them now. Don't wait until test day to isolate your writing issues! In addition to the information we give you in this chapter, you can find more info on applying the rules of grammar and punctuation and on correcting writing problems in Chapter 4 and in *English Grammar For Dummies* by Geraldine Woods (Wiley).

Punctuation errors

The role of punctuation is to guide the reader through sentences and paragraphs. Without proper punctuation, your reader won't know where one thought ends and another begins. Punctuation errors are among the most common mistakes test-takers make on the essay portion of the GMAT, and we're not talking about simply ending a sentence with a period.

Many people confuse colons and semicolons. Semicolons join independent clauses when the thoughts they convey are related enough to keep them in the same sentence: *It's almost test day; I need to write a practice essay this weekend.* (Independent clauses can stand alone as complete sentences. For more information on the difference between independent and dependent clauses, see Chapter 4.) You can also separate two independent clauses with a colon when the second independent clause expands on or specifies the idea conveyed in the first. *Jenny learned a very important lesson: Never leave a chocolate bar on the front seat of the car on a hot day.* Independent clauses don't have to follow a colon, however. A colon can be followed by a list of examples or a pertinent phrase or clause as long as the colon is preceded by an independent clause. *Before leaving for the exam, Saul made sure he had all of his supplies: admissions voucher, photo ID, and a bottle of water to gulp during the break.* If the colon doesn't follow an independent clause, you've used it improperly, as in this incorrectly punctuated sentence. *Before leaving for the exam, Saul made sure he had: his admissions voucher, photo ID, and a bottle of water.*

The most common punctuation errors involve commas. You use commas to separate items in a series, to replace omitted words, and to set off nonessential phrases and clauses and parenthetical expressions. You also use them to separate parts of the sentence:

>> Insert a comma before the coordinating conjunction *(for, and, nor, but, or, yet,* or *so)* that joins two independent clauses: *Bailey thought she had remembered her admissions voucher, but she discovered she had left it on the printer.* (But don't place a comma before a conjunction if it joins elements that aren't independent clauses: *Bailey remembered her admissions voucher but forgot her photo ID.)*

>> Include a comma between a beginning dependent clause and an independent clause: *If Bailey had printed the voucher the day before, she could have placed it in her car.* (But you don't need a comma between the clauses if the independent clause comes first: *Bailey could have placed the admissions voucher in her car if she had printed it the day before.)*

Two comma errors GMAT essay-writers often make are comma splices and run-on sentences:

>> **Comma splices** occur when you join two independent clauses with just a comma and no coordinating conjunction, like this: *Harold made several errors in his GMAT essay, one was a comma splice.* To correct a comma splice, do one of the following:

- Make the independent clauses two separate sentences. *(Harold made several errors in his GMAT essay. One was a comma splice.)*

- Substitute a semicolon for the comma. *(Harold made several errors in his GMAT essay; one was a comma splice.)*

- Add a coordinating conjunction after the comma. *(Harold made several errors in his GMAT essay, and one was a comma splice.)*

>> **Run-on sentences** result when you join together two independent clauses with a coordinating conjunction and no comma: *Harold made several punctuation errors in his GMAT essay and one was a run-on sentence that made his writing seem needlessly wordy.*

To correct a run-on, you just add a comma before the conjunction: *Harold made several punctuation errors in his GMAT essay, and one was a run-on sentence that made his writing seem needlessly wordy.*

Sentence-structure problems

GMAT essay-readers focus on more than how you punctuate your sentences. They also notice how you form your words. To avoid a negative critique, steer clear of these two problems with sentence structure:

» **Sentence fragments:** You may be able to blame your propensity for sentence fragments on technology, but you can't translate your email and texting style to the GMAT essays. A sentence must have a subject and a verb and convey a complete thought. Watch out for dependent clauses masquerading as complete sentences. Even though they contain subjects and verbs, they can't stand alone as sentences without other information. Here are some examples:

- **A sentence and a fragment:** I will return to the workforce. After I earn my MBA.

- **A complete sentence:** I will return to the workforce after I earn my MBA.

» **Modifier errors:** Modifiers are words and phrases that describe other words. The rule of thumb is to place modifiers as close as possible to the words they modify:

- **Sloppy:** The assistant found the minutes for the meeting held on Saturday on the desk.

- **Better:** The assistant found Saturday's meeting minutes on the desk.

Faulty forming of possessives

One writing element that you may overlook when you're frantically composing a 30-minute essay is forming possessives. Although your training in putting together proper possessives likely began in elementary school, you may appreciate this refresher:

» **Standard-issue nouns:** Use the possessive form of a noun when the noun is immediately followed by another noun that it possesses. Most possessives are formed by adding an apostrophe and an *s* to the end of a singular noun: *Steve's boss*. This practice is usually true even if the singular noun ends in *s: Charles's test score*. If the possessive noun is plural and ends in *s*, you just add an apostrophe to the end of the word: *The brothers' dogs; many clients' finances*.

» **Pronouns:** The possessive forms of personal pronouns are *my, his, her, your, its, our,* and *their* for pronouns that come before the noun and *mine, his, hers, yours, its, ours,* and *theirs* for possessive pronouns that occur at the end of a clause or that function as a subject.

REMEMBER

None of the possessive personal pronouns contains an apostrophe. *It's* is a contraction of *it is*, not the possessive form of *it*. As opposed to proper pronouns, possessive indefinite pronouns do contain apostrophes: *Somebody's dog has chewed my carpet*. For information on indefinite and personal pronouns, see Chapter 4.

Spelling issues

If you're like most people in America, you've come to rely on your word-processing program to correct your errors in spelling. The spell-check feature is one of the most popular and useful tools because it allows you to take your mind off of spelling and concentrate on what you're writing. And if you use an autocorrect feature on your word-processing program, you may not even realize how often your computer corrects your misspelled words.

The bad news is that you won't have a spell-check function available when you write your essay on the GMAT. This means that when you take the GMAT, you'll be responsible for correcting your own spelling, perhaps for the first time in years! One or two spelling errors may not be enough to lower your score, but in conjunction with any of the other errors we discuss in this chapter, a few spelling mistakes can make the significant difference between one score and the next half–point higher.

TIP

A good way to avoid potential spelling errors is to steer clear of unfamiliar words. If you've never used a word before and have any doubt about its meaning or how it's spelled, avoid using it. If you use unfamiliar words, you risk not only misspelling the word but also using it inappropriately. Stick to what you know when you write your analytical essay. If you have enough time before the test, you can always broaden your vocabulary. Developing an extensive vocabulary will pay off in your career as well as on the GMAT.

More dos and don'ts

Here are a few more things to keep in mind when preparing for your essay:

> » **Use simple, active sentences.** To increase your score, keep your sentences simple and active. The more complex your sentences, the greater your chances of making mistakes in grammar. You may think that long sentences will impress your readers, but they won't. Furthermore, they may cause you to make writing errors more easily.
>
> Another important characteristic of strong, persuasive sentences is the use of active voice. Active voice is clearer and more powerful than passive voice.
>
> » **Provide clear transitions.** Use transitions to tell the reader where you're going with your argument. You need only a few seconds to provide your readers with words that signal whether the next paragraph is a continuation of the previous idea, whether it refutes the last paragraph, or whether you're moving in a new direction. Transitions are key to good organization.
>
> » **Use precise descriptions.** Use descriptive words to keep your readers interested and informed. If you use specific, well-chosen words to clearly illustrate your points and examples, your writing will have more impact and you'll earn a higher score.
>
> » **Avoid slang expressions.** Stick to formal English, and avoid contractions and slang. Your readers are professors and should be familiar with formal English, so they expect you to use it in your essays. Using sentence fragments and slang is okay when emailing a friend, but on the GMAT, employ a more professional style.

Practice makes perfect!

TIP

You can practice writing in GMAT style in creative ways. For example, if you write a lot of emails, practice writing them more formally. When your friends send you unpunctuated emails full of misspellings and grammatical errors, respond with proper punctuation, superior spelling, good grammar, and perfect paragraphs.

You can't prepare for the GMAT with emails alone, so here are some things to think about when writing practice essays:

> » Write your essay under test conditions. Give yourself a 30-minute time limit and study in a quiet environment.
>
> » Use only those items you'll have available on the test. Type on your word processor but disable your automatic spell correction, use an erasable board or a single sheet of paper for scratch, and don't use reference books.
>
> » Take your practice essays seriously (practice the way you want to perform).

Building a Better Essay: Ten Steps to a Higher Score

If you're going to write well, you need something to write about. Remember that your analytical writing score is based on the quality of your argument as well as the quality of your writing. Even though you've been writing for years in college or in the workplace, you probably haven't had to produce very many analytical essays in just 30 minutes. In this section, we take you through a ten-step process to help you create better essays in less time.

TIP

With a plan in mind, you can use your essay time more efficiently and earn a better score. Using part of your 30 minutes to develop a plan means you'll be more organized than someone who just starts writing whatever comes to mind. In fact, you'll likely type for only about 20 minutes during the 30-minute task because you'll spend 5 minutes outlining your argument and 5 minutes proofreading what you've typed.

Work out your timing during your practice tests and note the amount of time you generally need for each part of the task. Remember that you have only 30 minutes, so you'll never have all the time you want for any of the three stages, but with practice you'll find the formula that fits your strengths. For example, you may be an excellent typist who can write very fast when you get started. In that case, you can afford a little more time for pre-writing and will need additional time for proofreading all that text you typed. If, on the other hand, you write or type fairly slowly, you'll need to spend at least 20 minutes to get your great ideas on the computer screen and saved for posterity. Here are the ten steps you should follow during your 30-minute analytical writing task:

1. Read the analytical writing prompt carefully before you begin writing.

Although this step may seem obvious, you may hurry through reading the prompt in your rush to start the essay and may miss important elements of your assignment. Take enough time to truly understand the argument you're to analyze. Read the prompt more than once; read it quickly the first time to get an idea of the subject matter and then read it more slowly to catch all the details. Some of your best arguments and examples will come to you when you're reading the prompt carefully.

2. Don't waste time reading the directions.

You can make up some of the time you spend carefully reading the prompt by skimming over the directions that follow. We've paraphrased the instructions for the essay in Chapter 8 and on the practice tests, so you know what you're supposed to do. The most you need to do is skim the directions to make sure nothing has changed and move on.

3. Plan your essay format ahead of time.

Knowing how to structure your essay can help you plan it. Make sure you have an introduction that discusses and presents your position (or *thesis*), supporting paragraphs that use examples and arguments to persuade others to see your way of reasoning, and a conclusion that briefly summarizes what you've said in the previous paragraphs. The length of your essay isn't as important as the quality of your analysis. Use as many paragraphs as you need to make your point in the allotted time. Just be sure that you know what you're going to write about before you begin writing.

4. Use the erasable noteboard.

Brainstorm and write down your thoughts so you don't forget them. Don't rely on your memory; that's what the noteboard is for. Jotting down a word or two can preserve your idea until you're ready to write about it.

5. Write a brief thesis statement.

Write a brief thesis statement indicating the main points of your evaluation of the argument and why you think that way. We recommend that you actually type this statement on the computer because it's the key sentence of your introductory paragraph.

For example, say you're asked to evaluate the strength of this argument: "Corporations exist to make a profit for shareholders; therefore, the primary duty of the corporation is not to employ workers or to provide goods and services but to make as much money as possible." Your thesis may be that the argument errs in simplifying the role of corporations and failing to provide adequate support for making the simplistic assertion that corporations exist primarily for shareholder profits.

6. Create a quick outline based on your thesis.

After you've created your thesis and have typed it into the computer, return to your notepad and make a brief outline. Because your ideas are already on the noteboard, outlining is a very simple process. Select the best arguments and examples to support your thesis. Decide in what order you want to address these ideas and number them for use as the topic sentences for the supporting paragraphs of your essay. Under each topic, list several examples and anecdotes that you'll use to support your topic.

For example, your main topics in the evaluation of the purpose of corporations argument may be that (1) the conclusion is too simplistic, and (2) the argument fails to provide adequate support for its position.

7. Write your introduction.

Move from a general statement to more specific ones and end with your thesis. In fact, your introduction may consist of only two sentences: a general introduction to the topic and your thesis statement. A complete introduction for the shareholder duty argument could consist of an introductory sentence or two that restates the conclusion and premises of the original argument. Then you'd lead into the thesis statement with a statement of the problems with the argument.

8. Write your supporting paragraphs.

After you've put together an outline and written the introduction, you've completed the hardest parts of the task. Then you just need to write your supporting paragraphs clearly with as few errors as possible. Begin with the idea you designated as your first topic in Step 6 ("the conclusion is too simplistic"). Introduce the paragraph with a topic sentence, provide a few supporting examples, and conclude your point. The first supporting paragraph could point out other important considerations for corporations, such as "a duty to care for the consumer and an obligation to perform research, that supersede the dangerous desire to make as much money as possible."

Repeat the process for your remaining points.

9. Write a brief conclusion.

End your essay with a simple summary of the points you've already made. Provide a synopsis of the conclusions you reached in each of your supporting paragraphs and end with a restatement of your thesis. Move from specific statements to more general ones. Many people try to make too much out of their conclusions, but this paragraph isn't the place to introduce new ideas or argue your position. Instead, just remind the reader of your supporting points and thesis.

10. Proofread.

When you've finished writing, make sure you have time left over to read through what you've written. Look for spelling and punctuation errors and other careless mistakes that you may have made in your rush to complete the assignment on time. Concentrate on errors that you can correct in a few seconds; don't try to rewrite entire paragraphs.

If you follow these steps in your practice writings and on test day, you'll come away with an analytical writing assessment score to be proud of.

Chapter **10**

Deconstructing Sample GMAT Essays

This chapter defines analytical writing assessment (AWA) scores for you and provides you with some sample GMAT AWA essays so you can see what these babies look like and apply some elements of the examples to your own writing. By deconstructing sample essays to figure out what makes for a great essay per GMAT standards, you'll have a much better chance of constructing great essays of your own.

Defining GMAT AWA Scores

The difference between an essay that's simply adequate and one that's outstanding comes down to a few important factors. Here's how the GMAT differentiates among essays that score 4, 5, and 6, based on analysis and organization:

» An outstanding essay (score 6) thoroughly analyzes and evaluates an argument and addresses whether the case the author makes is logically sound. The analysis uses logical reasoning to identify any flaws in the argument and offers insight as to how to minimize or eliminate these flaws. The essay is thorough and organized.

» A strong essay (score 5) still offers a powerful, well-reasoned analysis, but it may not be as insightful as an outstanding (score 6) essay. The essay contains well-chosen examples for support and is also well organized, though it's likely not as tightly organized as an outstanding essay.

» An adequate essay (score 4) offers a competent analysis of an argument. This essay interprets the strength and validity of an argument made by another and supports its points with relevant examples. The analysis may not be particularly well developed, but the fact that the essay shows competence in at least attempting to validate or disprove the assertions of another distinguishes it from lower-scoring essays.

Here's how the GMAT distinguishes among the top three scores based on quality of writing:

>> An outstanding essay (score 6) demonstrates superior control of the language and employs a variety of grammatically accurate and detailed sentences. This essay uses effective transitions. Although the essay may have a few minor errors, it generally reflects a superior ability in grammar, usage, and mechanics of standard written English.

>> A strong essay (score 5) is similar to an outstanding essay, but the sentences may not have quite as much variety, and the choice of words may not convey as much detail. This essay employs transitions but not as effectively as an outstanding essay. This essay may have a few minor errors but reflects a facility for grammar, usage, and mechanics.

>> An adequate essay (score 4) lacks sentence variety and, although the diction may be accurate, the word choice isn't particularly detailed or precise. This essay may employ transitions, but they're likely to be somewhat abrupt. The adequate essay reflects a familiarity with standard written English but may contain several minor errors or a few more-serious flaws.

In addition to the top three possible scores, four lower scores reflect flaws of differing magnitudes. We give less time to describing these categories, because after you've read Chapters 8 and 9 and practiced writing essays for the exam, you aren't likely to produce one of these lower scores on the GMAT:

>> A limited essay (score 3) is like an adequate paper in most respects, but it's clearly flawed in one or more areas. This essay may make an ineffective interpretation of the argument; lack organization; fail to present relevant examples; have problems in sentence structure; or contain errors in grammar, usage, and mechanics numerous enough to interfere with conveying meaning.

>> A seriously flawed essay (score 2) demonstrates more significant errors than a limited essay. It may fail to properly follow the directions stated in the prompt, lack any semblance of organization, neglect to provide any examples, have serious problems with language or sentence structure, and contain errors in grammar, usage, or mechanics that seriously interfere with meaning.

>> A fundamentally deficient essay (score 1) provides little evidence of the ability to effectively interpret the strength of the argument in the prompt. This essay may also have grave and pervasive writing errors that seriously interfere with the meaning of the essay.

>> A no-score essay (score 0) is blank, completely off topic, or not written in English.

Taking a Look at Sample Essays

TIP

The task for the analytical writing assessment is to analyze an argument. The prompt asks you to write an essay that uses logical reasoning to critique an argument made by another. Its focus is how well you evaluate an argument instead of what your own views and opinions may be on a particular topic. In the following sections, we provide sample essay prompts as well as sample essay responses and walk you through the elements of an effective, well-written response. You'll find more opportunities to turn your logical reasoning powers into outstanding essays in the practice tests included with this book.

Sample essay #1

If you have an extra 30 minutes just lying around, you can take the time to analyze the essay prompt in this section and write a full essay before you read the sample response we provide. If not, at least take five minutes before you read the sample essay to create a quick outline, using Steps 1 through 6 from Chapter 9. Read the instructions following the argument very carefully, and remember: The idea here is to analyze the given argument, not create your own. Here's the sample prompt:

The following appeared as part of an editorial in a business newsletter:

"Gasoline prices continue to hover at record levels, and increased demand from China and India assures that the days of one dollar per gallon gasoline are over. Continued threat of unrest in the oil-producing regions of the Middle East, Africa, and South America means a perpetual threat to the U.S. oil supply. American leaders have acknowledged the need for new sources of power to fuel the hundreds of millions of cars and trucks in America. Despite this acknowledgment, the U.S. government has yet to provide substantial funding for this important research. Officials are relying on private industry and university researchers to undertake this research that is vital to the economy and national security. Given the long interval before new technologies are likely to become profitable and the tremendous cost, research into new fuels will be successful only if funded by the U.S. government using taxpayer funds."

Examine this argument and present your judgment on how well reasoned it is. In your discussion, analyze the author's position and how well the author uses evidence to support the argument. For example, you may question the author's underlying assumptions or consider alternative explanations that may weaken the conclusion. You can also provide additional support for or arguments against the author's position, describe how stating the argument differently may make it more reasonable, and discuss what provisions may better equip you to evaluate its thesis.

After you've attempted your own response to the prompt, read through this sample:

The author of this editorial presents the idea that the development of new technology for fueling the automobiles of America is an absolutely necessary project and provides substantial evidence to support this claim, for example, the rising price of gasoline, the swelling demand for oil in overseas markets, and warning signs of turbulence and instability in oil-producing countries. However, the author has not provided much evidence for or reasoning behind the statement that the U.S. government should fund this research and instead relies on certain assumptions about the reader's level of background knowledge about the issues.

The editorial states that it will take a long time and a lot of expense to develop these new technologies, but the argument fails to include evidence of this. The author is making the assumption that readers will know that private companies and universities have been working for decades on projects such as hydrogen fuel cells, bio-diesel, ethanol, and electric cars. The editorial would be much stronger if it included one or two sentences on the fact that each of these technologies is feasible and that with increased funding could be brought rapidly to market.

Furthermore, it is suggested that the development of new fuel technologies is "vital to the economy and national security" of the U.S., but this statement is neither explained nor substantiated. It seems to me that if a greater amount of government funding is dedicated to scientific research, the budgets of other programs and departments will have to be cut, which could have serious negative impacts on national security, and possibly also the economy. If the editorial were to compare the hundreds of millions needed to fund research into alternatives to oil with the hundreds of billions spent each year on national security, then the argument would be stronger.

Clearly, the author of this editorial has made several assumptions about his/her readers, the most important probably being that readers of this business newsletter are familiar with this issue and will be able to provide the details of government funding and alternative fuel research lacking in the editorial. The evidence that the author does provide is strong. The editorial's conclusions seem valid. However, the editorial lacks the necessary foundation of facts and reasoning that would demonstrate, for example, why funding alternative fuel research now will allow new fuel technologies to gradually replace dependence on oil before a crisis hits.

This editorial discusses a very important issue and raises the critical subject of government funding for research into alternative fuels. However, the author has not provided much evidence or reasoning behind the conclusion that the U.S. government should fund this research.

Discussion of sample essay #1

This response is well developed and clearly articulated. The essay begins with a very strong introductory paragraph that develops the position, credits the editorial's strong points, and then clearly states the thesis that the author has made too many assumptions and not provided the necessary evidence. From the start, this essay appears to merit at least a 4.5.

The middle three paragraphs provide specific examples of assumptions that the editorial makes and indicate how the author could strengthen the argument. The first example is the assumption that the reader will know that alternative fuel technologies take a long time to develop. This essay provides the specific examples that the editorial itself lacked. The next paragraph discusses the claim that the economy and national security depend on alternative fuels. This is probably the weakest paragraph in the essay. The essay sidesteps the editorial's point when the essay turns to the issue of reducing the budgets of other programs. Still, this is a well-written paragraph that does offer valid suggestions for strengthening the editorial. The fourth paragraph ties everything together by pointing out the specific assumptions that the editorial is making about its readers. This paragraph demonstrates the sophistication of the essay by pointing out the editorial's intended audience, the weaknesses of the assumptions it makes, its strengths, and finally, ways to make the editorial better.

This essay is strong because it's specific and well developed. The essay singles out particular points in the editorial and explains not only the weaknesses of those points but also ways to make them stronger. It provides a clear introduction and thesis statement. The conclusion is brief and fulfills its purpose of restating the thesis. The diction used in this essay is precise and descriptive. The sentences are simple but varied, and they mostly demonstrate active rather than passive voice. There are no obvious errors in grammar, usage, or mechanics. This essay overall would likely garner a 5 but definitely nothing lower than a 4.5.

Sample essay #2

Here's another prompt for you to try. Again, if possible, attempt your own essay before you read through the sample response; if you don't have time to write an entire essay, take at least five minutes to create a quick outline, using Steps 1 through 6 from Chapter 9.

The following is an excerpt from an editorial that appeared in a periodical dedicated to education topics:

"The most important factor in choosing a career should be the potential salary. It all comes down to quality of life. A high salary ensures that you'll be able to pay your bills, live in a nice house, drive a nice car, and afford a comfortable, enjoyable lifestyle that's sure to be the envy of your friends. This is most easily achieved by securing a job with the highest salary possible. Well-paid positions like those of doctors, lawyers, and architects are important to society, well respected, and profitable, so these are the types of positions you should shoot for. While many believe it is important to find a job that you enjoy first and foremost, if that job doesn't pay well, you'll be faced with numerous stresses and hardships sure to affect your overall quality of life and you will ultimately come to regret not prioritizing financial stability above all else."

Examine this argument and present your judgment on how well reasoned it is. In your discussion, analyze the author's position and how well the author uses evidence to support the argument. For example, you may question the author's underlying assumptions or consider alternative explanations that may weaken the conclusion. You can also provide additional support for or arguments against the author's position, describe how stating the argument differently may make it more reasonable, and discuss what provisions may better equip you to evaluate its thesis.

Attempt your own response to the prompt, and then read through the following sample essay:

The author of this essay clearly states his belief that, when choosing a career path, earning potential is paramount. While he offers a number of reasons as to why he feels this way, such as an improved overall quality of life, a comfortable home, and the ability to impress your friends, his arguments are based on generalizations and assumptions about what others value most in life and the overall strength of his stance suffers as a result.

For example, the author "ensures" the reader that a high salary will enable them to live a lavish lifestyle and a life of little stress and strife. Yet he doesn't take into account the fact that high-paying jobs are also often high-demand, sometimes at the expense of a happy marriage, quality time with the kids, or simply time to kick back and relax.

Furthermore, he is assuming that happiness is achieved through material comforts, such as a fancy house and car, but he fails to recognize that his idea of happiness is not necessarily shared by the rest of the population. Nor does he consider other ways of finding happiness, like, say, helping others or finding a way to make a difference in the world.

Throughout the essay, a fundamental problem with the author's reasoning is his assumption that his readers share his feelings as to what is most valuable in life. Even when he acknowledges the fact that others feel that finding a career you enjoy should be top priority, he fails to devote any time or attention to the notion that one can feel "rich" even without a thick wallet and flashy car if they're able to engage in a career that they find fulfilling and gratifying.

While the author of this essay is sure to make his personal stance known in regard to what's most important in choosing a career, he fails to offer concrete evidence or devote sufficient attention as to why what is true for him fails to be true for the masses.

Discussion of sample essay #2

How do you think this essay would likely score? The essay asserts early on that the author in the prompt fails to acknowledge the fundamental differences as to what constitutes happiness and backs this up with examples and reasoning, so it's unlikely to receive a score below 4.

The response refutes the author's assertions that happiness is achieved through finding a job with the highest possible salary and backs this up with examples, such as the fact that high-paying jobs are frequently also high-stress and that other areas of one's life are often neglected. The essay also argues against the claim that material goods are the key to quality of life by noting that one person's opinion of what constitutes a high quality of life isn't necessarily true for someone else. To improve the quality of the supporting examples, the author could have been more specific, and she could have provided more compelling evidence for her point by referring to individuals in the public spotlight. For example, the author could have talked about the recent nervous breakdown of a wealthy celebrity to show that wealth doesn't necessarily lead to a stress-free life. And the author could have supplemented her assertion that money doesn't buy happiness by expounding on the fulfilling life of Mother Theresa.

Generally, the essay makes its points, using strong, concise English with few grammatical errors, although the concluding paragraph is constructed as one long sentence that would read more clearly if it were broken down into two. And the author includes a couple of pronouns that don't agree in number with their references. For example, the author uses the plural pronoun *they* to refer to the singular noun *one* in ". . . one can feel 'rich' even without a thick wallet and flashy car if *they're* able to engage in a career that *they* find fulfilling and gratifying." The essay also paraphrases the same general idea several times when it discusses the idea that the author of the prompt's idea of happiness differs from that of others. This essay would likely score a solid 4 or, possibly, as high as a 5.

Compare what you've written in response to the prompt to the sample essay. Evaluate your masterpiece and ask yourself how it measures up to — and perhaps accomplishes more than! — the sample. Use your evaluation to perfect your writing achievement.

Sample essay #3

Read through this prompt and attempt your own essay before you read through the sample response. If you don't have time to write an entire essay, take at least five minutes to create a quick outline, using Steps 1 through 6 from Chapter 9.

The following is an excerpt from an editorial that appeared in a local city newspaper:

"Some cities have enacted bans on pit bull breeds that prohibit city residents from owning dogs that fall under the "pit bull" umbrella, and other cities across the nation should follow suit as a matter of public safety. Given that statistics show that three-quarters of all dog-inflicted deaths involve either pit bulls or Rottweilers, which many also consider a "bully" breed, it is undeniable that these animals are unnecessarily dangerous. They are also widely abused, which contributes, at least in part, to their aggressive nature. Some pit bull owners say banning an entire breed is essentially racial profiling for dogs, but what if one type of person was responsible for three-quarters of all murders in the country? Such people should not be able to roam free and endanger whomever they like, and neither should pit bulls."

Examine this argument and present your judgment on how well reasoned it is. In your discussion, analyze the author's position and how well the author uses evidence to support the argument. For example, you may question the author's underlying assumptions or consider alternative explanations that may weaken the conclusion. You can also provide additional support for or arguments against the author's position, describe how stating the argument differently may make it more reasonable, and discuss what provisions may better equip you to evaluate its thesis.

A sample response to this prompt may read like this:

Though the argument made in the prompt starts out strong by referencing key statistics about the dangers associated with pit bulls, it falters somewhat later on, when the author tries to consider the arguments of those who are against implementing pit bull bans. The fact that the author references a pit bull ban that is already in effect in a major U.S. city seems to add some validity to the overall argument against the breed, and the statistics about the percentage of canine-inflicted deaths in America offer a solid argument about why a ban might be a good idea.

The author then falters a bit when trying to drive home the point that pit bulls are also violent and dangerous because they are widely abused. While this may or may not be true, it would have strengthened the author's argument and made he or she seem more convincing if additional statistics about abuse were included here, as they were in the section regarding canine-related fatalities. Even without formal statistics, this section of the prompt would have benefitted from additional clarification about the connection between abusive owners and aggressive pit bulls.

The holes in the author's argument become increasingly apparent when he or she notes that ban opponents often compare the act of banning certain dog breeds to racial profiling. The author tries to make the point that if a certain "type" of human was responsible for the majority of all murders, that "type" of person would likely be banned, too. But the author fails to further clarify what he or she means by "type," leaving it open to interpretation and scrutiny. Is the author referencing people of a certain race, nationality or color? Or a person with a certain type of personality trait, or hair color? Without further explanation, this argument falls flat, and the author is therefore unable to effectively refute the arguments of pit bull-ban advocates. Because of this failure to effectively address the other side, the strength of the entire argument suffers.

Discussion of sample essay #3

At first glance, this response appears relatively strong. It has no glaring spelling errors and just a couple grammatical problems, and each paragraph transitions well to the next. Additionally, the author of the response takes the time to discuss both the strengths and downfalls of the editorial and back up his opinions with thoughtful reasoning. Based off this alone, the response will likely warrant a score that comes in somewhere around a 5.

The response summarizes its content in the first few lines, giving the reader an idea that the writer plans to further develop key points, such as how the initial editorial relied on statistics to strengthen its argument, later on. The writer also mentions that while the original editorial certainly had its merits, it is not without flaws, again referring to areas of the essay that would be more closely dissected further along in the content.

This response is also likely to receive a high score because the author not only points out where he believes the editorial is flawed — such as when it fails to establish a strong connection between abusive owners and aggressive pit bulls — but also because he offers ideas for how it might be strengthened (by adding strong, clarifying information about the perceived connection and adding additional statistics specific to abusive owners). The response to the original editorial is also thoughtful in that it analyzes the editorial's consideration of the other side of the argument. The editorial notes that pit bull owners often equate breed bans to racial profiling, but it makes a weak argument about why this should not be the case. The response identifies this weakness and references it when assessing the overall strength of the original argument. Because the response's author carefully considered the strengths and weaknesses of the editorial and avoided grammatical and spelling errors, this essay would likely score high.

Sample essay #4

Here is yet another prompt for you to analyze. Create a response and then read through the sample essay that follows.

The following is an excerpt from a promotional brochure for an online dating service:

"Technology and social media are intended to better-connect society and enable us as humans to maintain relationships we may otherwise not be able. However, many people try to argue that what it is really doing is inserting more wedges between us socially by limiting face-to-face interaction and keeping our faces in our phones. When it comes to forming strong relationships with other people, though, why are relationships that develop online considered any less valid than those conceived through in-person interaction? Some online relationships might actually prove stronger than those that are developed by more traditional means, because people may be more apt to reveal their true selves from behind a screen than they would otherwise. Technology also helps those who might be shy or antisocial come out of their shells by taking away the stresses associated with real human interaction, so it can actually strengthen rather than weaken social relationships."

Examine this argument and present your judgment on how well reasoned it is. In your discussion, analyze the author's position and how well the author uses evidence to support the argument. For example, you may question the author's underlying assumptions or consider alternative explanations that may weaken the conclusion. You can also provide additional support for or arguments against the author's position, describe how stating the argument differently may make it more reasonable, and discuss what provisions may better equip you to evaluate its thesis.

Read through the following sample essay in response to this prompt to see how it compares with your masterpiece.

The author of the prompt is thoughtful in his or her discussion of whether technology and social media make us less connected as a society, and he or she makes a number of strong points when supporting the argument that these resources do not, in fact, weaken social relationships. That being said, there are a number of areas in which I think the argument might have benefitted from some additional input or material.

One such area where the author might have strengthened the prompt would be at the beginning, by plainly stating his or her belief that technology does not weaken social relationships. Instead, the prompt's author "beats around the bush," so to speak. Rather than clearly state his or her opinion right off the bat and then use arguments and key points to back up the assertion, the editorial author instead starts out by refuting some of the arguments in favor of technology hindering personal relationships. He or she begins by saying, "Technology and social media are intended . . ." which actually reveals very little about his or her own personal take on the matter. While refuting the opposition's arguments is certainly important, it might have been better if this was done further on in the initial argument, after a "thesis" statement-of-sorts based on the author's own opinions had been clearly stated.

As for the argument's strengths, the author made some strong points about why technology and social media may help some people build social bridges — it's just a little regrettable that these points didn't come up until almost the end of the argument. Such points included the arguments about shy people perhaps feeling more at ease behind a computer screen, and the notion that some people were more comfortable discussing serious, emotional matters via a computer than through face-to-face interaction.

Discussion of sample essay #4

This essay presents a clear, concise assessment of the initial prompt's strengths and weaknesses, and it does so with few, if any, spelling or grammatical errors along the way. It is apparent that the essay author took the time to consider the information provided in the original prompt and suggest that the argument may have been stronger had it made its case earlier.

For example, the essay author points out that the editorial's author failed to promptly state his or her own opinion on whether technology and social media ruin relationships. Though it quickly becomes apparent that he or she does not feel online socialization is a bad thing, the essay writer was convinced the impact would have been greater if the prompt author's personal opinion had been made clear from the outset.

The essay author did, however, take the time to point out where the argument in the prompt was particularly strong, and she called out a few key examples of such arguments, indicating strong comprehension and a convincingness on the part of the prompt author, even if the essay author didn't necessarily agree with the prompt's stance.

One area where the essay author might have benefited would have been to not only point out that the prompt's ". . . argument might have benefitted from some additional input or material," but to actually provide some suggestions for such material. For example, the essay author could have suggested the use of statistics or survey results pertaining to the connection between interconnectedness and social media, or added additional arguments not made in the prompt to support the same stance. Because the essay author took a thoughtful approach when writing her essay and analyzed much of the content of the original editorial while demonstrating strong writing skills, this essay would likely score a 3.

Chapter **11**

Sampling a Series of Writing Prompts

We know you're itching to create your own essay responses to some sample AWA prompts. In this chapter, you wait no longer. Here's your chance to create your evaluations of sample arguments. For each of the following four sample prompts, follow this plan:

1. Open your word processor so that you duplicate the AWA's online format.

2. Set a timer for 30 minutes.

3. Read the sample prompt.

4. Evaluate the argument and create a quick outline.

5. Based on your outline, write a well-organized essay within the 30-minute time limit.

6. Read the sample essay and dissection that follow each prompt to help you assess your creation.

Sample Prompt #1

The following argument appeared in a plea from a politician:

"The U.S. Constitution has expressed the laws of the land for more than 225 years, and its tenets are meant to help Americans live harmoniously in the company of one another. To date, 27 amendments have been made to it to adapt it for modern life. There are two methods under which changes can be made to the Constitution, and one of them, known as an Article V convention, has never taken place. Given the current divisive political climate, however, it has never been more necessary. An Article V convention would gather states together to discuss and debate newly proposed amendments, and the states would then vote as to whether to make the proposed changes to the Constitution. The very fact that information about Article V appears in the original Constitution implies that its framers knew broad changes would, one day, be necessary. Furthermore, 38 out of 50 states would have to approve any amendments before their passage, so any changes would truly express the wishes of the American people."

Examine this argument and present your judgment on how well reasoned it is. In your discussion, analyze the author's position and how well the author uses evidence to support the argument. For example, you may question the author's underlying assumptions or consider alternative explanations that may weaken the conclusion. You can also provide additional support for or arguments against the author's position, describe how stating the argument differently may make it more reasonable, and discuss what provisions may better equip you to evaluate its thesis.

Sample response to essay #1

The author of the prompt is trying to argue that Americans should move forward with an Article V convention in order to make the contents of the U.S. Constitution more appropriate and relevant for modern society. For the most part, the prompt does a good job of making the case for the convention.

The author makes some strong points, such as when he or she notes that the Constitution has already been changed 27 times. This statement makes it seem as if changing the document is not a major deal, which might encourage more people to think in the same manner. Another strong point made in the prompt is that the very existence of Article V in the original Constitution intimates that its original creators looked ahead and foresaw necessary change on the eventual horizon.

There are, however, some areas where the prompt could have explained its arguments more clearly or eloquently. One example of this is when the prompt author refers to the "current divisive political climate," but fails to explain the statement further. What makes the current political climate divisive? Would amending the Constitution put an end to said divisiveness? The author should have provided answers to these questions.

Additionally, the prompt might have benefited from more attention to possible arguments *against* calling a convention to amend the constitution. It sounds as if this is what he or she is starting to do near the end, where it is noted that 38 out of 50 states would have to voice their approval before any changes could be made, but more depth and additional attention to counterarguments might have strengthened the argument *for* the convention in the first place.

Furthermore, the author references "two methods" through which the Constitution could be amended, but then only discusses the Article V convention. This begs the question — what is the other method, and why isn't that one being considered as a means of adapting the Constitution for modern-day relevancy? The argument would be more convincing if it provided answers to these questions and the others mentioned above.

Dissection of essay #1

In reading the essay response to the prompt, it becomes clear that the author gave the initial argument thoughtful consideration, and he was able to articulate his thoughts about the argument in thoughtful, concise prose. The author is also able to effectively refute some of the arguments that would likely be raised by the opposition, and he also makes reference to areas where the original argument may have benefited from additional material. For these reasons, this essay would likely score at least a 4.

The essay author describes in detail the merits of the original argument, such as how it referenced the fact that the Constitution has already undergone multiple revisions and that the framers seemed to have anticipated this when the document was authored. He also applauded the author of the initial argument by foreseeing the argument about conventions possibly not expressing the wishes of the American people by noting that at least 38 states would have to be on board before any changes could be made.

The essay author also points out where the initial argument falls short, such as when it fails to clarify its remarks about the divisive political climate and what the other method of amending the Constitution (as opposed to calling a convention) might be. In doing so, the essay author also outlines his thoughts about what could be added to the essay to strengthen it, demonstrating he gave considerable thought to the issue.

In addition to showing a solid understanding of the subject matter and the arguments that can be made for or against it, the author's writing is strong and consistent throughout and is largely free of any grammatical or spelling errors. The combination of thoughtful analysis, thorough assessment of the argument's strengths and weaknesses, and strong writing skills ensures that the essay should not score below a 4.

Sample Prompt #2

The following appeared in the editorial section of a city newspaper:

"As incidents of school violence continue to dominate American mainstream media, educators, legislators and parents continue to seek out methods of countering it. One proposed solution is to arm America's teachers, so that they have what they need to act fast if the need arises. The Second Amendment already grants Americans the right to bear arms, so why should teachers, who are in charge of some of society's most vulnerable, be any different? Our teachers already assume a tremendous level of responsibility simply by teaching and guiding our children during the school day, and arming them would simply make it easier for them to accept more responsibility for protecting the nation's children, if the need arises. Teachers undergo background checks before working with children, and these checks should help weed out any potential dangers or violent offenders before they get in the classroom — or get their hands on guns."

Examine this argument and present your judgment on how well reasoned it is. In your discussion, analyze the author's position and how well the author uses evidence to support the argument. For example, you may question the author's underlying assumptions or consider alternative explanations that may weaken the conclusion. You can also provide additional support for or arguments against the author's position, describe how stating the argument differently may make it more reasonable, and discuss what provisions may better equip you to evaluate its thesis.

Sample response to essay #2

The author of the prompt is trying to argue that teachers should be armed in the classroom to enhance the safety of all students and ensure a quick response in the event of an emergency or intruder. While some of the arguments made therein are strong points, the author fails to pay much attention to some of the more obvious arguments *against* arming educators — and the strength of the argument suffers as a result.

By failing to take into account oppositional arguments — such as the fact that kids have a way of getting their hands on just about anything, and there's no reason to think this wouldn't also hold true for guns — the author doesn't give himself or herself a chance to address, or better yet, refute them. Another example of this is when the author notes that teachers undergo background checks, which, he or she reasons, will keep the bad apples out of America's schools. This, however, only holds true if you believe the assumption that the only people out there with the potential to be dangerous are people who have offended before. But every offender had to have a first time, right? So this argument falls a little flat. The language the author uses "these checks *should* weed out any potential dangers" makes it sound as if even he or she isn't speaking with a whole lot of conviction.

Where the prompt does make you think is when it raises the point about how much responsibility our teachers already have every day. The very nature of the job means most parents have to have a certain amount of trust in them but the same could be said of having a babysitter — does that mean all babysitters should be armed, too? Because the author of the prompt fails to consider, address or refute the arguments on the other side, it ultimately fails to convince.

Dissection of essay #2

The essay response to the argument made in the prompt is thoughtful, analytical, and, for the most part, well-written, although there are a few small errors here and there (more on that later). The response successfully identifies the prompt's strengths and weaknesses, and the essay author also offers some strong advice about where the argument might have been strengthened, indicating strong comprehension of the subject matter.

Among the key strengths of the essay response is that the essay author references the fact that kids have the ability to get their hands on almost anything. This raises a very strong point *against* arming teachers in America's schools, and it also points out an area where the original argument was lacking. The essay makes another strong point (another argument against arming teachers) when the author mentions the fact that background checks are only going to keep out teachers who have offended before, not every possible dangerous person out there.

The areas in which the essay response falters tend to be related to grammar and style. The essay switches back and forth between the second- and third-person, which affects its overall strength (and ultimately, its score, too). While the majority of the essay is written in the third person, the author switches to second person in the second paragraph, where she says, "only holds true if *you*" and again in the third paragraph, where she says, "the prompt does make *you* think." The overall strength of the essay would have been better if the essay author had picked one point of view and stayed consistent with it throughout the copy.

There are several other grammatical errors that also distract a reader from the actual content in the essay. For example, the second-to-last sentence in the essay is missing a comma between "them" and "but." If a complete sentence appears on either side of the conjunction, a comma is needed for clarity.

Sample Prompt #3

The following argument appeared in a parenting blog:

"Americans are raising a generation of children that don't know how to lose. Nowadays, our kids receive praise in the form of trophies for just about anything, from participating to perfect attendance. Not only does this tend to make our kids more "soft" and uneasy once they make it to the "real world," where they are prone to losing at least once in a while, but it also gives our children the impression that losing is so utterly terrible that we simply cannot let it happen anymore. NOT giving awards for any and everything teaches kids that awards must be earned, and talents have to be honed. It teaches them that it can take some time to excel in a given area, and that that's just fine."

Examine this argument and present your judgment on how well reasoned it is. In your discussion, analyze the author's position and how well the author uses evidence to support the argument. For example, you may question the author's underlying assumptions or consider alternative explanations that may weaken the conclusion. You can also provide additional support for or arguments against the author's position, describe how stating the argument differently may make it more reasonable, and discuss what provisions may better equip you to evaluate its thesis.

Sample response to essay #3

The author of the prompt clearly believes that trophies and awards are too broadly distributed among today's kids and that giving awards for participation and such sends the wrong message. After an initial read, it is safe to say the author makes some compelling arguments that might even be strong enough to convince opponents that giving out awards too freely actually does children a disservice.

Among the stronger arguments made in the prompt is the fact that if children do not learn how to lose during adolescence, they may struggle with disappointment once they enter the adult world, where most everyone tends to fail or lose at one time or another. Another key point made in the prompt is when the author says that giving awards for everything gives children the impression that losing is so terrible it cannot be tolerated. In both statements, the prompt's author drives home the point that what children are taught during childhood tends to transcend into their adult lives. Just as a child who grows up in an abusive home may, too, perpetuate the cycle of abuse, a child who grow up never losing may grow up to be an adult who has tremendous struggles with failure, and his or her life may be impacted negatively as a result. The author also notes that, by NOT giving awards for participation, kids learn the value of hard work and that it takes time and practice to be the best at something.

The author's argument is sound and thoughtful, and the only area where it might have benefited from additional copy is if it had included some points that might refute arguments made on the other side. For example, youth sports are youth sports for a reason, and not every 6-year-old is dreaming of one day playing in the big leagues. Shouldn't kids who will likely never pick up a bat or ball again receive at least some level of recognition for taking part in an activity? Ultimately, however, the argument made in the prompt is quite strong, and the author evidently took the time to clearly articulate his or her thoughts.

Dissection of essay #3

Though the author of the essay response never clearly stated his own feelings about whether today's kids are awarded too many trophies just for "participating," it sounds as if he might have initially leaned toward the other side of the argument — that kids *should* be given participation trophies — but then thought twice or reconsidered after reading the argument made in the prompt.

Evidence of this can be found in the last line of the first paragraph, when the essay author notes that the prompt's compelling arguments "might even be strong enough to convince opponents." This demonstrates that the essay author had a strong, comprehensive understanding of the arguments made in the initial prompt, and that he gave them all thoughtful consideration before crafting the essay response. This attention is also evident when the essay author introduces the comparison regarding children who grow up in abusive homes. While the subject matter might be a bit of a stretch, the comparison does have merit, and some may see it as adding strength to the original argument against giving awards for just about anything.

The essay author also points out where the original prompt might have been strengthened while pointing out one of the main arguments the opposition might make, which again demonstrates that the essay author took the time to carefully consider the issue and respond appropriately. Additionally, the essay response is formulated well: It begins by briefly summarizing the issue discussed in the prompt, and then calls out the essay's key strengths as well as the areas where it faltered slightly before adding in some suggestions about how it might have been strengthened. Because the essay author formulated the response well, clearly considered the arguments made in the original prompt, and took the time to call out the strengths and weaknesses of the initial argument, it is safe to assume this essay would score around a 5. It also is largely free from spelling or grammatical errors or any glaring inconsistencies, which should also contribute to a favorable score.

Sample Prompt #4

This argument appeared in a legal motion:

"In many states, sex offenders are not allowed to use social media sites that also allow children to use them, such as Facebook, Twitter, Instagram and so on. Some believe the ban ought to be enacted at the federal level. Sex offenders, however, already face a myriad of restrictions in their day-to-day lives that impede their abilities to find employment and housing, interact socially and with loved ones, and stay current on the world around them. Once they have served their sentences and paid their debts to society, they should be allowed to reintegrate into the outside world in the same manner as other criminals. It is also often forgotten that sex offenders, too, have civil rights. Banning them from modern forms of communication is a violation of free speech and the First Amendment of the U.S. Constitution, and for that alone, it should not be tolerated."

Examine this argument and present your judgment on how well reasoned it is. In your discussion, analyze the author's position and how well the author uses evidence to support the argument. For example, you may question the author's underlying assumptions or consider alternative explanations that may weaken the conclusion. You can also provide additional support for or arguments against the author's position, describe how stating the argument differently may make it more reasonable, and discuss what provisions may better equip you to evaluate its thesis.

Sample response to essay #4

This argument sounds as if it is sympathetic to sex offenders, which is unimaginable. That being said, there are a few important points made that really make you think. Although, not enough to actually change your mind.

The most convincing argument made in the initial prompt is when the author suggests that keeping sex offenders from using social media is a violation of the First Amendment. It is very though-provoking, because when the U.S. Constitution was written, there was no internet. There was no Facebook, Twitter or Instagram, so the Constitution's framers couldn't have possibly foreseen what was coming up the pike or addressed it in any kind of appropriate manner. However, the First Amendment is undeniably about protecting certain freedoms for all Americans, and for that reason, the argument at least has merit.

However, the prompt's author seems to be making excuses for sex offenders and expressing sympathy when he or she goes on about how they already have other restrictions imposed on them that make it hard to find work and place to live, among other things. Of course they should face restrictions — they are sex offenders. They shouldn't, as the prompt states, "be allowed to reintegrate into the outside world in the same manner as other criminals," because they aren't other criminals, and many of them commit crimes against children. Therefore, the only particularly strong argument made is the one about the First Amendment.

Dissection of essay #4

Arguably, the biggest takeaway from the essay response is that the essay's author seemed to have a difficult time analyzing the strength of the argument without letting her own personal feelings about the sensitive subject matter cloud her judgment. This is apparent in statements such as, "Of course they should face restrictions — they are sex offenders" and "they aren't other criminals."

The main point of drafting the essay is to thoughtfully and analytically evaluate the strength of the argument itself — not to include your own personal opinion on the subject matter. There are also some structural and grammatical issues that will likely affect the essay writer's score. Redundancy is among the issues, as the essay references the strength of the First Amendment statement several times.

Other issues include the lack of a comma after "of course" in the final paragraph, and the sentence fragment, "Although, not enough to actually change your mind," that appears in the introductory paragraph. It's also worth pointing out that the author of the essay has a tendency to switch back and forth between second (*you, your,* and so on) and third person throughout the copy, which can be distracting. In the intro paragraph, the essayist makes statements such as "really make you think," but the entire following paragraph switches back to third person. As a general rule, it's best to pick a point of view and stick with it.

The essay isn't entirely bad — the point about how the Internet wasn't around when the Constitution was drafted, for example, is a strong one. However, the other issues will likely keep it from scoring above a 3.

4

Conquering the Quantitative Section

Dust off your basic math skills with a review of fundamental operations, fractions, and exponents.

Take a trip down memory lane with good old algebra, including quadratic equations and functions.

Get in shape for the GMAT geometry problems. Go over various formulas, including area and perimeter and the slope of a line and gain timesaving tips for finding side lengths of triangles.

Cover the ins and outs of statistics and probability, including data interpretation, combinations and permutations, and sets, from the essential concepts of mean and mode to more complex calculations of standard deviation and probability.

Understand the two varieties of GMAT math questions: the standard five-answer, multiple-choice, problem-solving kind and the less familiar data-sufficiency questions.

Take a mini GMAT math test to show off your fresh skills.

IN THIS CHAPTER

» Refreshing your memory on types of numbers and basic operations

» Getting the skinny on bases, exponents, and radicals

» Keeping order of operations in mind

» Grabbing your share of fractions, decimals, and percentages

» Making comparisons by using ratios and proportions

» Bringing numbers down to size with scientific notation

Chapter **12**

Getting Back to Basics: Numbers and Operations

Those of you who majored in math in college probably look at the math section of the GMAT like an old friend. Those of you who haven't stepped into a math class since high school are more likely dreading it. You know who you are! Don't worry, this chapter takes you back to the beginning with a review of the concepts you've learned through the years but may have temporarily forgotten. In this chapter, you see problems that test your knowledge of the math building blocks, such as number types, basic operations, exponents and radicals, fractions, and ratios. These concepts form the foundation of more complicated math problems, so this stuff is important to know. For example, you could end up with a completely wrong answer if you solve for real numbers when the question asks for integers. Some GMAT-takers may end up kicking themselves (and that looks just plain odd) for missing relatively simple problems because they were unfamiliar with some basic terminology. To avoid this unfortunate (and awkward) position, make sure you're well-heeled in math basics.

Just Your Type: Kinds of Numbers

Since the Stone Age, humans have found it necessary to rely on numbers to get through daily living. In hunter-gatherer cultures, the people made notches in bones to count, for example, the number of days in a lunar cycle or perhaps to indicate how long the nomadic tribe spent in a particular location until it found food. But through the millennia, humankind soon realized that numbers could become large and unwieldy. Hence, the advent of number classifications and operations!

Although understanding modern mathematical operations may have burst prehistoric man's cerebral cortex, it'll surely be easier for you after you complete this review. For the GMAT, you need to know the more common types of numbers, such as integers, rational numbers, real numbers, and prime numbers. And you should at least be aware of some of the less common types, such as irrational and imaginary numbers.

REMEMBER

» **Integers:** Numbers that belong to the set of all positive and negative whole numbers with 0 included. Integers can't be fractions or decimals or portions of a number. Integers include –5, –4, –3, –2, –1, 0, 1, 2, 3, 4, and 5 and continue infinitely on either side of 0. Integers greater than 0 are called *natural numbers* or *positive integers*. Integers less than 0 are called *negative integers*.

Take care when working with 0. It's neither positive nor negative.

» **Rational numbers:** Numbers that are expressed as the *ratio* of one integer to another; that is, numbers that can be expressed as fractions. Rational numbers include all positive and negative integers, zero, fractions, and decimal numbers that either end or repeat. For example, the fraction $\frac{1}{3}$ can be expressed as $0.33\overline{33}$. Rational numbers don't include numbers like π or radicals like $\sqrt{2}$ because the decimal equivalents of these numbers don't end or repeat. They're called *irrational numbers*.

» **Real numbers:** All numbers that you normally think of as numbers. Real numbers belong to the set that includes all integers, rational numbers, and irrational numbers. Think of real numbers as those numbers represented by all the points on a number line, either positive or negative or zero. Real numbers are also those numbers you use to measure length, volume, or weight. So when the GMAT asks you to give an answer expressed in terms of real numbers, just solve the problem as you normally would.

» **Imaginary numbers:** Any number that isn't a real number. So an imaginary number is a number like $\sqrt{-1}$. Think about it: You know that when you square any positive or negative real number, the result is a positive number. This means you can't find the square root of a negative number unless the root is simply not a real number. So imaginary numbers include square roots of negative numbers or any number containing *i*, which represents the square root of –1. Won't you be a fascinating conversationalist at your next soiree!

» **Prime numbers:** All the positive integers that can be divided by only themselves and 1; 1 isn't a prime number. The smallest prime number is 2, and it's also the only even prime number. This doesn't mean that all odd numbers are prime numbers, though. Also, 0 can never be a prime number because you can divide 0 by every natural number there is. To determine prime numbers, consider this series: 2, 3, 5, 7, 11, 13, 17, 19, 23, 29, and so on. What makes these numbers unique is that the only two factors for these numbers are 1 and the number itself.

You probably won't encounter this term on the GMAT, but in case it comes up at cocktail parties, you should know that 0 and positive numbers other than 1 that aren't prime numbers are called *composite numbers*. A composite number has more than two factors, so it's the product of more than simply itself and the number 1. Questions regarding prime numbers appear fairly frequently in GMAT math sections. Here's a sample of one you may see.

AN IRRATIONAL FEAT WITH AN IRRATIONAL NUMBER

Recently, a team of computer engineers in Japan calculated π out to over 1.24 *trillion* decimal digits. It still didn't end, meaning that π is truly irrational. And it may be irrational to attempt to prove otherwise! Thankfully, the GMAT won't ask you to attempt this task or anything remotely like it.

EXAMPLE

Which of the following expresses 60 as a product of prime numbers?

(A) $2 \times 2 \times 3 \times 5$

(B) $2 \times 2 \times 15$

(C) $2 \times 3 \times 3 \times 5$

(D) $2 \times 3 \times 5$

(E) $1 \times 2 \times 5 \times 6$

This question tests your knowledge of prime numbers. Because the correct answer has to be a series of prime numbers, eliminate any choice that contains a composite (or non-prime) number. So Choices (B) and (E) are out (even though the product of both is 60) because 15, 1, and 6 aren't prime numbers. Then, eliminate any answers that don't equal 60 when you multiply them. Choice (C) is 90, and Choice (D) is 30, so the answer must be Choice (A). It's the correct answer because it contains only prime numbers whose product equals 60.

It's Not Brain Surgery: Basic Operations

Now that you're a bit more comfortable with some terms, it's time to take a stab at manipulating numbers. Figuring out how to do operations, which we discuss in the following sections, is pretty simple, almost as simple as 1-2-3. It doesn't take a brain surgeon to open your mind to endless possibilities.

Adding, subtracting, multiplying, and dividing

You're probably pretty familiar with the standard operations of addition, subtraction, multiplication, and division. But even these math basics have some tricky elements that you may need to refresh your memory on.

Putting two and two together: Addition

Adding is pretty simple. Addition is just the operation of combining two or more numbers to get an end result called the *sum*. For example, here's a simple addition problem:

$3 + 4 + 5 = 12$

Addition also has two important properties that you may remember from elementary school: the associative property and the commutative property. Understanding these simple concepts for the GMAT math questions is important:

>> **Associative property:** The *associative property* states that the order in which you choose to add three or more numbers doesn't change the result. It shows how numbers can group differently with one another and still produce the same answer. So regardless of whether you add 3 and 4 together first and then add 5 or add 4 and 5 together followed by 3, you still get an answer of 12.

$(3 + 4) + 5 = 12$
$3 + (4 + 5) = 12$

>> **Commutative property:** The *commutative property* states that it doesn't matter what order you use to add the same numbers. Regardless of what number you list first in a set of numbers, they always produce the same sum. So $2 + 3 = 5$ is the same as $3 + 2 = 5$.

Depleting the supply: Subtraction

Subtraction, as you probably know, is the opposite of addition. You take away a value from another value and end up with the *difference*. So if $3 + 4 = 7$, then $7 - 3 = 4$.

In subtraction, order *does* matter, so neither the associative property nor the commutative property applies. You get completely different answers for $3 - 4 - 5$, depending on what method you use to associate the values. Here's what we mean:

$$(3 - 4) - 5 = -6$$

but

$$3 - (4 - 5) = 4$$

The order of the values counts in subtraction, too. For example, $3 - 4$ isn't the same as $4 - 3$ ($3 - 4 = -1$, but $4 - 3 = 1$).

Increasing by leaps and bounds: Multiplication

Think of multiplication as repeated addition with an end result called the *product*: 3×5 is the same as $5 + 5 + 5$. They both equal 15.

On the GMAT, you may see several signs that represent the multiplication operation. A multiplication sign can be designated by $\times$ or simply with a dot, like $\cdot$. And in many instances, especially when variables are involved (for more about variables, see Chapter 13), multiplication can be indicated by just putting the factors right next to each other. So ab means the same thing as $a \times b$, and $2a$ is the same as $2 \times a$. One of these back-to-back factors may appear in parentheses: $2(3)$ means 2×3.

Multiplication is like addition, in that the order of the values doesn't matter. So it obeys the commutative property:

$$a \times b = b \times a$$

And the associative property:

$$(a \times b) \times c = a \times (b \times c)$$

Another property associated with multiplication is the *distributive property*. So you may encounter this multiplication problem:

$$a(b + c) =$$

You solve it by distributing the a to b and c, which means that you multiply a and b to get ab and then a and c to get ac, and then you add the results together like this: $a(b + c) = ab + ac$.

Sharing the wealth: Division

Finally, there's division, which you can consider to be the opposite of multiplication. With division, you split one value into smaller values. The end result is called the *quotient*. So whereas $3 \times 5 = 15$, $15 \div 5 = 3$, and $15 \div 3 = 5$.

As in subtraction, order matters, so division doesn't follow either the commutative or associative properties. Also, just so you're familiar with any terms you may encounter on the GMAT, the number at the beginning of any equation using division (15 in the last expression) is called the *dividend* and the number that goes into the dividend is the *divisor* (3 in the last expression).

The division sign may be represented by a fraction bar. For more info on fractions, see "Splitting Up: Fractions, Decimals, and Percentages," later in this chapter.

Checking out the real estate: Properties of real numbers

In addition to basic operations, the GMAT expects you to know the fundamental properties of the numbers you're working with. These include absolute values, evens and odds, and positives and negatives.

Absolutes do exist: Absolute value

To simplify things, just think of the absolute value of any real number as that same number without a negative sign. It's the value of the distance a particular number is from 0 on a number line. The symbol for absolute value is $|\ |$, so the absolute value of 3 is written mathematically as $|3|$. And because the number 3 sits three spaces from 0 on the number line, $|3| = 3$. Likewise, because -3 sits three spaces from 0 on the number line, its absolute value is also 3: $|-3| = 3$.

WARNING

The GMAT loves to trip you up when dealing with multiple numbers and absolute values. Remember that absolute value pertains only to the value contained within the absolute value bars. So if you see a negative sign outside the bars, the resulting value is negative. For example, $-|-3| = -3$ because although the absolute value of -3 is 3, the negative sign outside the bars makes the end result a negative.

TIP

When you're working with variables in absolute-value expressions, remember that there is likely more than one solution for the variable because the value within the absolute value sign may be positive or negative, as demonstrated by this sample problem.

EXAMPLE

Which of the following is the complete set of solutions for x when $|x - 3| = 6$?

(A) $\{9\}$

(B) $\{-9, 9\}$

(C) $\{-3, 9\}$

(D) $\{3, 9\}$

(E) $\{-9, -3, 3\}$

To find one solution for x, remove the absolute-value sign and solve:

$$|x - 3| = 6$$
$$x - 3 = 6$$
$$x = 9$$

You know 9 is a solution for x, so you can eliminate Choice (E) because it doesn't contain 9. You can't end with Choice (A), though; you have to consider that the value within the absolute value signs could be negative. To accomplish this feat, multiply the terms between the bars by −1 and then solve for x:

$$|x-3| = 6$$
$$-1(x-3) = 6$$
$$-x+3 = 6$$
$$-x = 3$$
$$x = -3$$

Because the value in the absolute-value signs may be either negative or positive, x may be either −3 or 9. Choice (C) is the complete set of solutions.

A balancing act: Even and odd numbers

We're pretty sure you know that *even numbers* are integers divisible by 2: 2, 4, 6, 8, 10, and so on. And *odd numbers* are those integers that aren't divisible by 2: 1, 3, 5, 7, 9, 11, and so on.

You're probably with us so far, but what's important to remember for the GMAT is what happens to even or odd numbers when you add, subtract, or multiply them by one another.

Here are the rules regarding evens and odds for addition and subtraction:

>> When you add or subtract two even integers, your result is an even integer.

>> When you add or subtract two odd integers, your result is also even.

>> If you add or subtract an even integer and an odd integer, your result is an odd integer.

Here's what you should know about multiplying even and odd integers:

>> When you multiply an even number by an even number, you get an even number.

>> When you multiply an odd number by an even number, you also get an even number.

>> The only time you get an odd number is when you multiply an odd number by another odd number.

Division rules are a little more complex because the quotients aren't always integers; sometimes they're fractions. Here are a few rules to know:

>> When you divide an even integer by an odd integer, you get an even integer or a fraction.

>> An odd integer divided by another odd integer results in an odd integer or a fraction.

>> An even integer divided by another even integer can result in either an odd or even quotient, so that's not very helpful.

>> When you divide an odd integer by an even one, you always get a fraction; because fractions aren't integers, the quotient for this scenario is neither odd nor even.

TIP

You may be wondering why you need to know these rules. Here's why: Memorizing them can be a big timesaver when it comes to eliminating answer choices. For example, if you have a multiplication problem involving large even numbers, you know you can eliminate any odd-number answer choices without even doing the math! Here's a sample question that shows you just how valuable knowing the rules can be.

EXAMPLE

If *a* and *b* are different prime numbers, which of the following numbers must be odd?

(A) *ab*

(B) $4a + b$

(C) $a + b + 3$

(D) $ab - 3$

(E) $4a + 4b + 3$

To solve this number theory question, think of numbers for *a* and *b* that represent their possible values. Then substitute these values into the answer choices to eliminate all that can be even. When considering values for *a* and *b*, make sure to include 2 because it's the only even prime number. Neither 1 nor 0 is an option because neither is prime.

Substitute 2 for *a* or *b* in Choice (A), and you see that it can be even because the rules tell you that any time you multiply an even number by another number, you get an even number. You also know that Choice (B) can be even because 4 (an even number) times any number is an even number. If *b* = 2 and you added that to 4*a*, you'd be adding two even numbers, which always gives you an even sum. Again, if *b* = 2 in Choice (C), then *a* would have to be an odd prime number. You add *a* (odd) to *b* (even) to get an odd sum. Then you add that odd number to the odd number 3, which results in an even number. Choice (D) can be even if both *a* and *b* are odd. An odd number times an odd number is an odd number. When you subtract an odd number, like 3, from another odd number, you get an even number.

By process of elimination, the answer must be Choice (E). It doesn't matter whether *a* or *b* in Choice (E) is even or odd; 4*a* and 4*b* will always be even, because anytime you multiply an even number by another number, you get an even number. When you add two evens, you get an even number, so $4a + 4b$ is an even number. And because an even number plus an odd number is always odd, when you add that even result to 3, you get an odd number, always. The correct answer is Choice (E).

Half empty or half full: Positive and negative numbers

Positive and negative numbers have their own set of rules regarding operations, and they're even more important to remember than those for even and odd integers. Here's what you need to know for multiplying and dividing:

» When you multiply or divide two positive numbers, the result is positive.

» When you multiply or divide two negative numbers, the result is also positive.

» Multiplying or dividing a negative number by a positive number gives you a negative result (as does multiplying or dividing a positive number by a negative number).

As you may expect, you need to know some things about adding and subtracting positives and negatives:

» When you add two positive numbers, your result is a positive number.

» When you add two negative numbers, the resulting sum is negative.

» When you add a positive number to a negative number, the result is positive when the number with the largest absolute value is positive and negative when the number with the largest absolute value is negative.

» If you subtract a negative number from another number, you end up adding the positive version of the negative number to the other number. For example, $x - (-3)$ is the same thing as $x + 3$.

Using Little Numbers for Big Values: Bases and Exponents

Because multiplication can be thought of as repeated addition, you can think of exponents as repeated multiplication. This means that 4^3 is the same as $4 \times 4 \times 4$ or 64. In the example, you refer to 4 as the *base* and the superscript 3 as the *exponent*. If you add a variable into this mix, such as $4b^3$, the base becomes b and the 4 becomes what's known as the coefficient. In our example, the coefficient 4 is simply multiplied by b^3.

As a high-school algebra teacher used to scream (usually when he caught his students napping): "The power governs only the number immediately below it!" (that is, the base). So the exponent doesn't affect the coefficient. Only the base gets squared or cubed or whatever the exponent says to do.

This rule brings up some fascinating properties regarding positive and negative bases and even and odd exponents:

>> A positive number taken to an even or odd power remains positive.

>> A negative number taken to an odd power remains negative.

>> A negative number taken to an even power becomes positive.

TIP

What all of this means is that any number taken to an even power either remains or becomes positive, and any number taken to an odd power keeps the sign it began with. Another interesting tidbit to digest is that any term with an odd power that results in a negative number will have a negative root, and this is the only possible root for the expression. For example, if $a^3 = -125$, then $a = -5$. That is, the cube root of -125 is -5.

On the other hand, anytime you have an exponent of 2, you have two potential roots, one positive and one negative, for the expression. For example, if $a^2 = 64$, then $a = 8$ or -8. So 64 has two possible square roots: either 8 or -8.

In the following sections, we outline a few rules for adding, subtracting, multiplying, and dividing exponents. We also clue you in on how to figure out the powers of 0 and 1 and what to do with fractional and negative exponents.

Adding and subtracting with exponents

The only catch to adding or subtracting with exponents is that the base and exponent of each term must be the same. So you can add and subtract like terms such as $4a^2$ and a^2 like this: $4a^2 + a^2 = 5a^2$ and $4a^2 - a^2 = 3a^2$. Notice that the base and exponent remain the same and that the coefficient is the only number that changes in the equation.

Multiplying and dividing with exponents

The rules regarding multiplying and dividing exponents are pretty numerous, so to keep them straight, we've set up Table 12-1 for you. The table describes each rule and gives you an example or two.

TABLE 12-1 **Rules for Multiplying and Dividing with Exponents**

Rule	Examples
To multiply terms with exponents and the same bases, add the exponents.	$a^2 \times a^3 = a^5$
If the expression contains coefficients, multiply the coefficients as you normally would.	$4a^2 \times 2a^3 = 8a^5$
When you divide terms with exponents and the same bases, just subtract the exponents.	$a^5 \div a^2 = a^3$
Any coefficients are also divided as usual.	$9a^5 \div 3a^3 = 3a^2$
To multiply exponential terms with different bases, first make sure the exponents are the same. If they are, multiply the bases and maintain the same exponent.	$4^3 \times 5^3 = 20^3$; $a^5 \times b^5 = (ab)^5$
Follow the same procedure when you divide terms with different bases but the same exponents.	$20^3 \div 5^3 = 4^3$; $(ab)^5 \div a^5 = b^5$
When you raise a power to another power, multiply the exponents.	$(5^4)^5 = 5^{20}$; $(a^3)^5 = a^{15}$
If your expression includes a coefficient, take it to the same power.	$(2a^2)^3 = 8a^6$

Figuring out the powers of 0 and 1

Exponents of 0 and 1 have special properties that you'll have to commit to memory:

>> The value of a base with an exponent of 0 (such as 7^0) is always 1.

>> The value of a base with an exponent of 1 is the same value as the base ($3^1 = 3$).

Dealing with fractional exponents

If you see a problem with an exponent in fraction form, consider the top number of the fraction (the *numerator*) as your actual exponent and the bottom number (the *denominator*) as the root. So to solve $256^{\frac{1}{4}}$, simply take 256 to the first power (because the numerator of the fraction is 1), which is 256. Then take the fourth root of 256 (because the denominator of the fraction is 4), which is 4, and that's your answer. (Find out more about roots in the "Checking Out the Ancestry: Roots" section later in this chapter.) Here's what it looks like mathematically:

$$256^{\frac{1}{4}} = \sqrt[4]{256^1} = \sqrt[4]{256} = 4$$

The GMAT may also present you with a variable base and a fractional exponent. You handle those the same way, like this:

$$a^{\frac{2}{3}} = \sqrt[3]{a^2}$$

This is what you get when you take a to the second power and then find its cube root.

Working with negative exponents

A negative exponent works like a positive exponent with a twist. A negative exponent takes the positive exponent and then flips the base and exponent around so that together they become the reciprocal (see the section "Defining numerators, denominators, and other stuff you need to know about fractions," later in this chapter), like this:

$$3^{-3} = \frac{1}{3^3} = \frac{1}{27}$$

WARNING

When you work with negative exponents, don't fall for the trick of assuming that the negative exponent somehow turns the original number into a negative number. It ain't gonna happen! For example, $3^{-3} \neq -27$ or $\frac{1}{-27}$.

To see how the GMAT may test exponents, check out a sample problem.

EXAMPLE

If $8^{2x-3} = 1$, what is the value of x?

(A) 0

(B) 1.5

(C) 2

(D) 8

(E) 10.5

The trick to mastering this problem is to remember that a number to the power of 0 is equal to 1. So, for the expression to equal 1, 8^{2x-3} must equal 8^0. When you know that $8^{2x-3} = 8^0$, you know $2x - 3 = 0$. Solve for x.

$$2x - 3 = 0$$
$$2x = 3$$
$$x = \frac{3}{2}$$
$$x = 1.5$$

The simple answer to this perhaps initially confusing problem is Choice (B). If you picked Choice (C), you may have thought the exponent was equal to 1 instead of 0.

Checking Out the Ancestry: Roots

If you like exponents, you'll *love* roots, which are also known as *radicals*. Roots are sort of the opposite of exponents. The square root of a number is the number that you square to get that number. So because you square 3 to get 9, the square root of 9 is 3. What could be simpler?

There are as many roots as there are powers. Most of the time, the GMAT has you work with square roots, but you may also see other roots. That won't intimidate you, though. If you come upon a cube root or fourth root, you'll recognize it by the radical sign, √.

For example, the cube root of 27 is expressed as $\sqrt[3]{27}$. This expression asks what number, when raised to the third power, equals 27. Of course, the answer is 3 because $3^3 = 27$.

TIP

Radicals, even the seemingly ugly ones, can often be simplified. For example, if you come up with an answer of $\sqrt{98}$, you're not done yet. Just think of the factors of 98 that are perfect squares. You know that $2 \times 49 = 98$, and 49 is a perfect square: $7^2 = 49$. Put these factors under the radical sign: $\sqrt{49 \times 2}$. Now you can extract the 49 from the square root sign because its square root is 7. The result is $7\sqrt{2}$. Here's how you may see this situation on the GMAT.

EXAMPLE

If $\sqrt[n]{512} = 4\sqrt[n]{2}$, then $n = ?$

(A) $\frac{1}{4}$

(B) $\frac{1}{2}$

(C) 1

(D) 4

(E) 8

You can solve this equation most easily by simplifying the radical. The nth root of 512 is equal to 4 times the nth root of 2. Consider the factors of 512: $2 \times 256 = 512$, so $\sqrt[n]{256 \times 2}$, which also equals $4\sqrt[n]{2}$. $\sqrt[n]{256 \times 2} = \sqrt[n]{256} \times \sqrt[n]{2}$, so you know that $\sqrt[n]{256} = 4$, which is the same as saying $4^n = 256$. Because $4 \times 4 \times 4 \times 4 = 256$, $n = 4$, and Choice (D) is the correct answer.

Roots obey the same rules as exponents when it comes to performing operations. You can add and subtract roots as long as the roots are of the same order (that is, square root, cube root, and so on) and the same number. Here are a couple examples:

$$5\sqrt{7} + 6\sqrt{7} = 11\sqrt{7}$$
$$11\sqrt{a} - 6\sqrt{a} = 5\sqrt{a}$$

When you need to multiply or divide radicals, make sure the roots are of the same order (such as all square or all cube roots) and you're good to go! For multiplication, just multiply what's under the radical signs, like this:

$$\sqrt{9} \times \sqrt{3} = \sqrt{27}$$

Divide what's under the radical signs like this:

$$\sqrt{9} \div \sqrt{3} = \sqrt{3}$$

And here's how a question about operations with radicals may appear on the GMAT.

EXAMPLE

$\sqrt{16 + 9} = ?$

(A) 5

(B) 7

(C) $12\frac{1}{2}$

(D) 25

(E) 625

WARNING

Pay attention to the values underneath the radical. In this question, the line of the square root symbol extends over the entire expression, so you're supposed to find the square root of $16 + 9$, not $\sqrt{16} + \sqrt{9}$. It's a subtle but major difference!

First, add the values under the radical sign: $16 + 9 = 25$. The square root of 25 is 5, so Choice (A) is the correct answer. If you chose 7, you determined the square root of each of the values before you added them together. For 7 to be the correct answer, your problem should have been written with two separate square root signs, $\sqrt{16} + \sqrt{9}$.

Order of Operations: Please Excuse My Dear Aunt Sally

Basic arithmetic requires that you perform the operations in a certain order from left to right. Okay, so maybe you don't have an aunt named Sally, but this section's title is a helpful mnemonic for the order you use when you have to perform several operations in one problem. What that means is that if you have an expression that contains addition, subtraction, multiplication, division, exponents (and roots), and parentheses to boot, it helps to know which operation you perform first, second, third, and so on.

The acronym *PEMDAS* (**P**lease **E**xcuse **M**y **D**ear **A**unt **S**ally) can help you remember to perform operations in the following order:

» **P**arentheses

» **E**xponents (and roots)

» **M**ultiplication and **D**ivision

» **A**ddition and **S**ubtraction

Here's an example:

$$20\left(4-7\right)^3 + 4\left(\frac{9}{3}\right)^2 = x$$

First, evaluate what's inside the parentheses:

$$20\left(-3\right)^3 + 4\left(3\right)^2 = x$$

Then evaluate the exponents:

$$20\left(-27\right) + 4\left(9\right) = x$$

Then multiply:

$$-540 + 36 = x$$

Finally, do the addition and subtraction from left to right:

$$-504 = x$$

Splitting Up: Fractions, Decimals, and Percentages

Fractions, decimals, and percentages are interrelated concepts; they all represent parts of a whole. You'll likely need to convert from one form to the other to solve several problems on the GMAT math.

Fractions are really division problems. If you divide the value of a by the value of b, you get the fraction $\frac{a}{b}$. So $1 \div 4 = \frac{1}{4}$.

To convert the fraction to a decimal, you simply perform the division indicated by the fraction bar: $\frac{1}{4} = 0.25$.

To convert a decimal back to a fraction, you first count the digits to the right of the decimal point; then divide the original number over a 1 followed by the same number of zeroes as there were digits to the right of the decimal. Then you simplify. So $0.25 = \frac{25}{100} = \frac{1}{4}$; $0.356 = \frac{356}{1,000} = \frac{89}{250}$.

Changing a decimal to a percent is really pretty easy. Percent simply means *out of one hundred*, or times 100. To perform the conversion, you move the decimal two places to the right. Then you write the resulting number as a percent. For example, $0.25 = 25\%$, and $0.925 = 92.5\%$.

To turn a percent back into a decimal, you follow the procedure in reverse. You move the decimal point two spaces to the left and lose the percent sign, like this: $1\% = 0.01$.

TIP

The GMAT probably won't specifically ask you to express answers in all three formats (fractions, decimals, and percentages), but you need to know that answer choices can appear in any one of the three formats when you're dealing with percentage problems.

You may encounter a GMAT problem that asks you to find something like the portion of garbage that's paper when you know that out of 215 million tons of garbage, about 86 million tons of the total garbage are paper products. You should be able to express the answer as a fraction, decimal, and percent:

» As a fraction: $\frac{86}{215}$ or $\frac{2}{5}$

» As a decimal: $\frac{2}{5} = 2 \div 5 = 0.4$

» As a percent: $0.4 = 40\%$

Don't worry: We provide all the details you need to know about dealing with fractions and percentages in the following sections.

Defining numerators, denominators, and other stuff you need to know about fractions

GMAT questions may refer to the numerator or the denominator of a fraction. The *numerator* is the number on top and represents the part of the whole. The *denominator* is the number on the bottom and represents the whole.

To better understand these terms, picture a cherry pie sliced into eight equal pieces (see Figure 12-1) and a hungry family of seven, each of whom has a slice after dinner (or before dinner if they're sneaky).

The shaded pieces of pie show how much of the dessert was gobbled up by the family; the unshaded piece shows what's left of the pie when the family is finished.

To put this pie into terms of a fraction, the total number of pieces in the pie to begin with (the whole) represents the denominator, and the number of pieces that were eaten (the part of the whole) is represented by the numerator. In this case, the number of pieces that were eaten made up $\frac{7}{8}$ of the total pie, so 7 is the numerator and 8 is the denominator. To look at the scenario another way, you can say that the fraction of pie that was left is $\frac{1}{8}$ of what you started with.

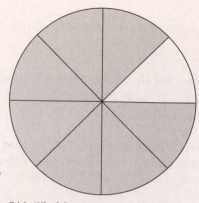

FIGURE 12-1:
Fraction of
a pie.

© John Wiley & Sons, Inc.

Here are a few other fraction definitions you should be familiar with:

>> **Proper fractions:** Fractions where the numerator is less than the denominator. Examples of proper fractions are $\frac{3}{4}$ and $\frac{13}{15}$.

>> **Improper fractions:** Fractions where the numerator is either greater than or equal to the denominator. An example is $\frac{15}{2}$.

>> **Mixed fractions:** Another way of formatting improper fractions is with a whole number and a proper fraction, such as $1\frac{2}{3}$.

>> **Reciprocal:** The flip-flop of a fraction. The numerator and denominator switch places. So the reciprocal of $\frac{3}{5}$ is $\frac{5}{3}$. To get the reciprocal of a whole number, you simply divide 1 by your number. So the reciprocal of 5 is $\frac{1}{5}$. The reciprocal of a variable a is $\frac{1}{a}$, just as long as $a \neq 0$.

TIP

When you work with fractions on the GMAT, you may have to substitute mixed fractions for improper fractions and vice versa. You'll find that changing a mixed fraction into an improper fraction before you perform operations is often easier. To change a mixed fraction to an improper fraction, you multiply the whole number by the denominator, add the numerator, and put that value over the original denominator, like this:

$$2\frac{2}{3} = \frac{8}{3}$$

You multiply the whole number (2) by the denominator (3) to get 6; add the numerator (2) to 6, which gives you 8; and place that value over the original denominator of 3.

To convert an improper fraction to a mixed number, you divide the numerator by the denominator and put the remainder over the denominator, like this:

$$\frac{31}{4} = 7\frac{3}{4}$$

First, you divide 31 by 4: 4 goes into 31 seven times with a remainder of 3 ($4 \times 7 = 28$ and $31 - 28 = 3$). Put the remainder over the original denominator, and place that fraction next to the whole number, 7.

TIP

Another thing you should know about fractions is how to simplify them. You may be thinking that fractions are simple enough, that it just can't get any easier. Simplifying a fraction means reducing it to its simplest terms. You make the larger terms smaller by dividing both the numerator and denominator by the same value. Here's an example of reducing or simplifying a fraction:

$$\frac{12}{36} \div \frac{12}{12} = \frac{1}{3}$$

The largest common factor of 12 and 36 is 12. When you divide the fraction by $\frac{12}{12}$, it's the same as dividing by 1. And any number divided by 1 equals the original number. You know that $\frac{1}{3}$ has the same value as $\frac{12}{36}$. It's just in simpler terms.

Adding and subtracting fractions

Because fractions are parts of whole numbers, they're not as easy to add together as 2 + 2. To add or subtract fractions, you must give them the same denominator. Then all you do is either add or subtract the numerators and put that value over the original denominator, like this: $\frac{2}{7} + \frac{4}{7} = \frac{6}{7}$; $\frac{6}{5} - \frac{4}{5} = \frac{2}{5}$.

WARNING

Be careful when you're asked to add and subtract fractions with different denominators. You can't just add or subtract the numerators and denominators. You have to change the fractions so they have the same denominator. So you have to find what's called the *least common denominator.* For example, if you see $\frac{2}{3} + \frac{1}{9}$, you know you have to change the denominators before you add.

To determine the least common denominator, consider values that are divisible by both 3 and 9. When you multiply 3 by 9, you get 27. So both 3 and 9 go into 27, but that's not the smallest number that both 3 and 9 go into evenly. Both 3 and 9 are factors of 9, so the least common denominator is 9 rather than 27.

Convert $\frac{2}{3}$ to $\frac{6}{9}$ by multiplying the numerator and denominator by 3. The second fraction already has a denominator of 9, so you're ready to add:

$$\frac{6}{9} + \frac{1}{9} = \frac{7}{9}$$

Multiplying and dividing fractions

Multiplying fractions is easy. Just multiply the numerators and the denominators. Reduce if you have to:

$$\frac{4}{5} \times \frac{5}{7} = \frac{20}{35} = \frac{4}{7}$$

TIP

An easier and faster (and faster is better on the GMAT) way to perform this task is to simply cancel out the fives that appear in the denominator of the first fraction and the numerator of the second one, like so:

$$\frac{4}{\cancel{5}} \times \frac{\cancel{5}}{7} = \frac{4}{7}$$

Dividing fractions is pretty much the same as multiplying them except for one very important additional step. Here's what you do to divide two fractions:

1. **Find the reciprocal of the second fraction in the equation (that is, turn the second fraction upside down).**

2. **Multiply (yes, multiply) the numerators and denominators of the resulting fractions.**

Here's an example:

$$\frac{2}{7} \div \frac{3}{5} = x$$

$$\frac{2}{7} \times \frac{5}{3} = x$$

$$\frac{10}{21} = x$$

To test your knowledge of how to perform operations with fractions, the GMAT may present you with a straightforward equation, such as the following.

$$\frac{1}{2} + \left(\frac{3}{8} \div \frac{2}{5}\right) - \left(\frac{5}{6} \times \frac{7}{8}\right) =$$

(A) $\frac{1}{8}$

(B) $\frac{15}{16}$

(C) $\frac{17}{24}$

(D) $2\frac{1}{6}$

(E) $\frac{5}{6}$

To solve this problem, you need to know how to perform all four operations with fractions. Be sure to follow the order of operations. (See the earlier section "Order of Operations: Please Excuse My Dear Aunt Sally" for details.)

First, compute the operations inside the first set of parentheses:

$$\left(\frac{3}{8} \div \frac{2}{5}\right) = \frac{3}{8} \times \frac{5}{2} = \frac{15}{16}$$

Then, figure out the value of the second set of parentheses:

$$\left(\frac{5}{6} \times \frac{7}{8}\right) = \frac{35}{48}$$

Now the equation looks like this:

$$\frac{1}{2} + \frac{15}{16} - \frac{35}{48} =$$

The least common denominator of 2, 16, and 48 is 48. To convert the denominator in the first fraction to 48, you multiply the fraction by $\frac{24}{24}$:

$$\frac{1}{2} \times \frac{24}{24} = \frac{24}{48}$$

To convert the denominator in the second fraction to 48, you need to multiply by $\frac{3}{3}$:

$$\frac{15}{16} \times \frac{3}{3} = \frac{45}{48}$$

Now you can compute the expression:

$$\frac{24}{48} + \frac{45}{48} - \frac{35}{48} = \frac{34}{48}$$

That's not one of your answer options, so you need to simplify the fraction. Divide the numerator and denominator by 2 to get $\frac{17}{24}$, which is Choice (C).

Knowing how to perform operations with fractions comes in handy for percent problems, too.

EXAMPLE

What is 75% of $7\frac{1}{4}$?

(A) $\frac{37}{130}$

(B) $5\frac{3}{4}$

(C) $5\frac{7}{16}$

(D) $7\frac{3}{4}$

(E) $21\frac{3}{16}$

This question asks you to determine a percent of a fraction. Note that the answers are in fraction form rather than decimal form, which means you need to work out the problem so it ends up as a fraction rather than a decimal.

Whenever you see the word *of* in a word problem, you know it means multiply. Therefore, you're multiplying 75 percent by $7\frac{1}{4}$. Converted to a fraction, 75 percent is $\frac{3}{4}$, so you're trying to find the answer to $7\frac{1}{4} \times \frac{3}{4}$. Converting $7\frac{1}{4}$ from a mixed fraction gives you $\frac{29}{4}$, so the answer is $\frac{29}{4} \times \frac{3}{4} = \frac{87}{16}$.

Convert to a mixed fraction: $\frac{87}{16} = 5\frac{7}{16}$. The answer is Choice (C).

TIP

You can easily eliminate Choices (D) and (E). Obviously, 75 percent of $7\frac{1}{4}$ has to be less than $7\frac{1}{4}$.

Calculating percent change

Percent change is the amount a number increases or decreases expressed as a percentage of the original number. For example, if a store normally sells tennis shoes for $72 and has them on sale for $60, what is the percent change of the markdown? To get the percent decrease, simply take the difference in price, which is $12, and divide that number by the original price:

$$12 \div 72 = 0.1667 \text{ or } 16\frac{2}{3}\%$$

WARNING

Pay careful attention when figuring percent change. For example, if the store then increases the marked down price by $16\frac{2}{3}$ percent, you may think the price returns to its original value. But that's not right. If you increase the lower price of $60 by 0.1667, you get just about a $10 increase. The price goes from $60 to just about $70: $60 \times 0.1667 = 10.002$; $60 + 10.002 = 70.002$.

How can that be? The reason the numbers don't seem to add up is because when you drop the price the first time, you take $16\frac{2}{3}$ percent of $72, which is a bigger number to take a percent from than the lower sale price.

So what percent of the marked-down price of $60 must you increase the price by in order to get the original price of $72? To find out, take the difference in price, $12, and determine what percent that is of the sale price of $60:

$$12 \div 60 = \frac{12}{60} = \frac{2}{10} = 0.20 = 20\%$$

So it's a 20 percent increase from 60 to 72.

TIP

If you know what the percent increase or decrease of an original number is and want to find out how that increase or decrease changes the original number, keep these two important details in mind:

>> To find the amount of increase, multiply the original number by 1 plus the rate as a decimal.

>> To find the amount of decrease, multiply the original number by 1 minus the rate as a decimal.

So if you increase 100 by 5 percent, you multiply 100 by (1 + 0.05):

$$100 \times (1 + 0.05) = 100 \times 1.05 = 105$$

If you decrease 100 by 5 percent, you multiply 100 by (1 − 0.05).

$$100 \times (1 - 0.05) = 100 \times 0.95 = 95$$

Try a sample percent change problem.

EXAMPLE

A file cabinet that originally cost $52 is on sale for 15% off. If the sales tax on office furniture is 5% of the purchase price, how much is the total cost of the file cabinet at its sale price?

(A) $7.80

(B) $40.00

(C) $44.20

(D) $46.41

(E) $48.23

This word problem asks you how to deal with two percentages, the subtraction of the percentage discount and the addition of the percentage sales tax. First, calculate the discount.

You can figure 15 percent in your head by knowing that 10 percent of 52 is 5.20 and half of that (5 percent) is 2.60, so the discount is $7.80. Now subtract the discount from the original price: $52.00 − $7.80 = $44.20. The discount price for the cabinet is $44.20.

You still need to calculate the sales tax, so don't choose Choice (C)! You know that 5 percent of 44.20 is half of 4.42 (10 percent), or 2.21. You add $2.21 to $44.20. The only answer that ends in 1 is Choice (D). You can do the math to verify your guess, but Choice (D) is the correct answer: $44.20 + $2.21 = $46.41. Not a bad price for some much-needed organization!

Taking it further: Repeated percent change

Now suppose you want to show a percent change repeated over a period of time, such as when you need to figure out how much interest accrues on a bank account after several years. To do so, you take the formula for percent change a step further.

Suppose you have $100 in a bank account at the end of 2012, and you want to know how much money will be in that same account at the end of 2022 at an annual interest rate of 5 percent. No fair pulling it out when the stock market is making a bull run! One way to figure this out is by using the percentage increase formula. The first step looks something like this:

$$100 \times (1 + 0.05) = 105$$

So you have $105 at the end of the first year.

WARNING

Don't make the mistake of thinking that all you have to do is multiply by 10 and you have $1,050 after 10 years. You wish! This type of question will trap anyone who isn't paying attention every time.

To get the correct answer, tweak the formula a bit by adding an exponent. The exponent will be the number of times the original number changes. The formula looks like this, where n is the number of changes:

Final Amount = Original Number $\times (1 + \text{Rate})^n$

Plug the numbers into the formula and solve:

$$100 \times (1 + 0.05)^{10} = x$$
$$100 \times 1.05^{10} = x$$
$$100 \times 1.6289 = x$$
$$162.89 = x$$

So after 10 years, you'd have $162.89 in the bank.

To show a repeated percent decrease over time, you'd use this similar formula:

$$\text{Final Amount} = \text{Original Number} \times (1 - \text{Rate})^n$$

Making Comparisons: Ratios and Proportions

A ratio is the relation between two like numbers or two like values. A ratio may be written as a fraction ($\frac{3}{4}$), as a division expression ($3 \div 4$), or with a colon ($3{:}4$), or it can be stated as "3 to 4."

Because a ratio can be regarded as a fraction, multiplying or dividing both terms of a ratio by the same number doesn't change the value of the ratio. So 1:4 = 2:8 = 4:16. To reduce a ratio to its lowest terms, simplify the ratio as you would a fraction. (See the earlier section "Defining numerators, denominators, and other stuff you need to know about fractions.")

Ratios often crop up in word problems. Suppose an auto manufacturer ships a total of 160 cars to two dealerships at a ratio of 3 to 5. This means that for every three cars that go to Dealer 1, five cars ship to Dealer 2. To determine how many cars each dealership receives, add the terms of the ratio, or 3 + 5, to get the total number of fractional parts each dealership will get: 3 + 5 = 8. The first dealership will receive $\frac{3}{8}$ of 160 cars, or $\frac{3}{8} \times 160$, which equals 60. The second dealership receives $\frac{5}{8}$ of 160 cars, or 100.

TIP

As long as the total number of *items* in a ratio problem can be evenly divided by the total number of fractional parts, you can find the total number of items that are attributable to each part.

A *proportion* is a relationship between two equal ratios. It may be written as the proportion sign :: or with an equal sign. So you can read 1:4 :: 2:8 as "1 is to 4 as 2 is to 8."

The first and last terms in a proportion are called the *extremes*, and the second and third terms are called the *means*. If you multiply the means together and multiply the extremes together and then compare the products, you find that the products are the same:

$$1 \times 8 = 2 \times 4$$

TIP

Anytime you know three terms of a proportion, you can find the missing term first by multiplying either the two means or the two extremes (depending on which are known) and then dividing the product by the remaining term. This is also known as cross-multiplying. So if you know 7:8 :: x:104, you can solve for x by using cross-multiplication:

$$\frac{7}{8} = \frac{x}{104}$$
$$8x = 7(104)$$
$$8x = 728$$
$$x = 91$$

Be sure to keep the elements of your ratios and proportions consistent. For example, if your proportion is "3 is to 4 as 5 is to x," you must set up the problem like this:

$$\frac{3}{4} = \frac{5}{x}$$

rather than this:

$$\frac{3}{4} = \frac{x}{5}$$

Here's what a GMAT ratio problem may look like.

If the ratio of $4a$ to $9b$ is 1 to 9, what is the ratio of $8a$ to $9b$?

(A) 1 to 18

(B) 1 to 39

(C) 2 to 9

(D) 2 to 36

(E) 3 to 9

At first, this problem may appear to be more difficult than it actually is. If $4a$ to $9b$ is a 1 to 9 ratio, then $8a$ to $9b$ must be a 2 to 9 ratio, because $8a$ is 2 times $4a$. If $4a$ equals 1, then $8a$ must equal 2. The answer, therefore, has to be Choice (C).

Playing the Numbers: Scientific Notation

Scientific notation is a simple way to write out humongous (technical term) or teensy weensy (another technical term) numbers so they're more manageable. You express a number in scientific notation by writing it as the product of a number and a power of 10. Simply move the decimal point so all digits except one are to the right of the decimal point; then multiply that decimal number times 10 raised to an exponent that equals the number of places you moved the decimal point. If you're working with a large number and you moved the decimal point to the left, the exponent is positive:

$$1,234,567 = 1.234567 \times 10^6$$
$$20 \text{ million } (20,000,000) = 2.0 \times 10^7$$

To display very small numbers in scientific notation, you move the decimal point to the right so one value is to the left of the decimal point. When you move the decimal point to the right, the exponent is negative. In this example, the decimal point moved six places to the right:

$$0.0000037 = 3.7 \times 10^{-6}$$

Here's how the GMAT may test you on scientific notation.

EXAMPLE

The number of organisms in a liter of water is approximately 6.0×10^{23}. Assuming this number is correct, about how many organisms exist in a covered Petri dish that contains $\frac{1}{200}$ liters of water?

(A) 6.9

(B) 3.0×10^{21}

(C) 6.0×10^{22}

(D) 3.0×10^{23}

(E) 1.2×10^{26}

This question uses many words to ask you to the find the answer to $\frac{6.0 \times 10^{23}}{200}$. If a liter of water contains a certain number of organisms, $\frac{1}{200}$ liter of water would contain the same number of organisms divided by 200. Try not to let the wording of the question confuse you.

So if 6.0 divided by 200 equals 0.03, the answer is 0.03×10^{23}, but that's not scientific notation because the decimal point is in the wrong place. Move the decimal point two places to the right and decrease the power by two (remember that when you move the decimal point to the right, the exponent is negative, so you subtract). The answer is Choice (B), 3.0×10^{21}.

IN THIS CHAPTER

» Defining variables and other fundamental algebra terms

» Solving your problems with algebraic operations

» Simplifying your life with factoring

» Getting functions to function

» Cracking the mysteries of solving algebraic equations and inequalities

Chapter **13**

Considering All the Variables: Algebra

lgebra is the study of properties of operations carried out on sets of numbers. That may sound like mumbo-jumbo, but the idea is that algebra is really just a form of arithmetic in which symbols (usually letters) stand for numbers. You use algebra to solve equations and to find the value of a variable. For example, how often have you heard the command, "Solve the equation for x"?

The algebra concepts tested on the GMAT are limited to the ones you'd use in a first-year algebra course, so you're at no disadvantage if you've never taken Algebra II. But many GMAT math problems involve basic algebra, and this chapter provides what you need to know to excel on all of them.

Defining the Elements: Algebraic Terms

Before we jump into solving algebra problems, we define some terms you need to know in the following sections. Although the GMAT doesn't specifically test you on the definitions of *variable*, *constant*, and *coefficient*, it does expect you to know these concepts when they crop up in the questions.

Braving the unknowns: Variables and constants

You'll see a lot of *variables* in algebra problems. They're the symbols that stand for numbers. Usually the symbols take the form of letters and represent specific numeric values. True to their name, variables' values can change depending on the equation they're in.

Think of variables as abbreviations for discrete things. For example, if a store charges different prices for apples and oranges and you buy two apples and four oranges, the clerk can't ring them up together by simply adding $2 + 4$ to get 6. That would be incorrectly comparing apples and oranges! So, to express the transaction in algebraic terms, you use variables to stand in for the price of apples and oranges, something like $2a$ and $4o$.

In contrast, *constants*, as their name implies, are numbers with values that don't change in a specific problem. Letters may also be used to refer to constants, but they don't change their value in an equation as variables do (for example, *a*, *b*, and *c* stand for fixed numbers in the formula $y = ax^2 + bx + c$).

Coming together: Terms and expressions

Single constants and variables or constants and variables grouped together form *terms*; terms are any set of variables or constants you can multiply or divide to form a single unit in an equation. You can combine these single parts in an equation that applies addition or subtraction. For example, the following algebraic expression has three terms: $ax^2 + bx + c$. The first term is ax^2, the second term is bx, and the third term is c.

Terms often form *expressions*. An algebraic expression is a collection of terms that are combined by addition or subtraction and are often grouped by parentheses, such as $(x + 2)$, $(x - 3c)$, and $(2x - 3y)$. Although an expression can contain just one term, it's more common to think of expressions as combinations of two or more terms. So, in the apples and oranges scenario we presented earlier, you can make an expression for combining two apples and four oranges, which may look something like this: $2a + 4o$.

A *coefficient* is a number or symbol that serves as a measure of a property or characteristic. In $2a + 4o$, the variables are *a* and *o*, and the numbers 2 and 4 are the coefficients of the variables. This means that the coefficient of the variable *a* is 2 and the coefficient of the variable *o* is 4.

In an algebraic expression, terms involving the same variable, even if they have different coefficients, are called *like terms*. For example, in the expression $3x + 4y - 2x + y$, $3x$ and $-2x$ are like terms because they both contain the single *x* variable; $4y$ and *y* are also like terms because they both contain the *y* variable and only the *y* variable.

REMEMBER

The variables must be exact matches with the same powers; for example, $3x^3y$ and x^3y are like terms, but *x* and x^2 aren't like terms, and neither are $2x$ and $2xy$.

You can combine (add/subtract) like terms together, but you can't combine unlike terms. So, in the expression $3x + 4y - 2x + y$, you can subtract the terms with the common *x* variable: $3x - 2x = x$. And you can add the like terms with the common *y* variable: $4y + y = 5y$ (if a variable has no visible numerical coefficient, it's understood that its coefficient is 1; therefore, *y* is understood to be $1y$). All this combining results in the final expression of $x + 5y$, which is a much simpler expression to work with. We work with many more algebraic expressions in the section "Maintaining an Orderly Fashion: Algebraic Operations," later in this chapter.

Knowing the nomials: Kinds of expressions

Expressions carry particular names depending on how many terms they contain. On the GMAT, you'll work with monomials and polynomials.

A *monomial* is an expression that contains only one term, such as $4x$ or ax^2. A monomial is, therefore, also referred to as a term in an algebraic expression.

Poly means many, so we bet you've already figured out that a *polynomial* is an expression that has more than one term. These multiple terms can be added together or subtracted from one another. Here are a couple of examples of polynomials:

$$a^2 - b^2$$
$$ab^2 + 2ac + b$$

Polynomials can have more specific designations, depending on how many terms they contain. For example, a *binomial* is a specific kind of polynomial, one that contains two terms, such as $a + b$ or $2a + 3$. And a *trinomial* is a polynomial with three terms, like $4x^2 + 3y - 8$.

REMEMBER

A famous trinomial that you should be very familiar with for the GMAT is the expression known as a *quadratic polynomial,* which is this trinomial expression:

$$ax^2 + bx + c$$

We discuss this very important expression in the "Solving quadratic equations" section, later in this chapter.

Maintaining an Orderly Fashion: Algebraic Operations

Symbols like $+$, $-$, $\times$, and $\div$ are common to arithmetic and algebra. They symbolize the operations you perform on numbers. Arithmetic uses numbers with known values, such as $5 + 7 = 12$, in its operations (visit Chapter 12 for more on basic arithmetic operations), but algebraic operations deal with unknowns, like $x + y = z$. This algebraic equation can't produce an exact numerical value because you don't know what x and y represent, let alone z. But that doesn't stop you from solving algebra problems as best you can with the given information. In the following sections, we show you how to add, subtract, multiply, and divide expressions with unknowns.

Adding to and taking away

From arithmetic, you know that 3 dozen plus 6 dozen is 9 dozen, or

$$(3 \times 12) + (6 \times 12) = (9 \times 12)$$

In algebra, you can write a somewhat similar equation by using a variable to stand in for the dozen: $3x + 6x = 9x$. And you can subtract to get the opposite result: $9x - 6x = 3x$.

TIP

Remember to combine positive and negative numbers according to the rules of arithmetic (see Chapter 12 if you need a refresher). If you add two or more positive numbers in an expression, they keep the positive sign. If you add a positive to a negative number, it's as though you're subtracting.

For example, to tackle the expression $7x + (-10x) + 22x$, you find the sum of the two positive numbers ($7x$ and $22x$) and then subtract the value of the negative number (because adding a negative is the same as subtracting a positive), like this:

$$7x + (-10x) + 22x =$$
$$29x - 10x =$$
$$19x$$

That's fine for adding and subtracting like terms, you may say, but what about working with unlike terms? You can't combine terms with different symbols or variables the same way you can when the symbols are the same. For instance, take a look at this example:

$$7x + 10y + 15x - 3y$$

WARNING

If you were to simply combine the whole expression by adding and subtracting without accounting for the different variables, you'd come up with a wrong answer, something like 29*xy*. (And you can bet the GMAT will offer this incorrect figure as one of the answer choices to try to trap you.) Instead, you first separate the *x*'s from the *y*'s and add and subtract to get something more manageable, like this:

$$7x + 15x = 22x$$
$$+10y - 3y = 7y$$

which gives you this final expression:

$$22x + 7y$$

TIP

If you want to get tricky and add two or more expressions, you can set them up just as you would an addition problem in arithmetic. Remember, only like terms can be combined together this way.

$$3x + 4y - 7z$$
$$2x - 2y + 8z$$
$$\underline{-x + 3y + 6z}$$
$$4x + 5y + 7z$$

Here's how an algebra problem may look on the GMAT.

EXAMPLE

For all x and y, $\left(4x^2 - 6xy - 12y^2\right) - \left(8x^2 - 12xy + 4y^2\right) = ?$

(A) $-4x^2 - 18xy - 16y^2$

(B) $-4x^2 + 6xy - 16y^2$

(C) $-4x^2 - 6xy - 8y^2$

(D) $4x^2 - 6xy + 16y^2$

(E) $12x^2 - 18xy - 8y^2$

The easiest way to approach this problem is to distribute the negative sign to the second expression (see the later section "Distributing terms") and combine the two expressions with like terms by following these steps:

1. Distribute the negative sign (multiply each term in the second expression by –1).

Remember that subtracting is the same as adding a negative number. So your problem is really $\left(4x^2 - 6xy - 12y^2\right) + -1\left(8x^2 - 12xy + 4y^2\right)$. Distributing the negative sign changes the second expression to $-8x^2 + 12xy - 4y^2$, because a negative times a positive makes a negative and two negatives make a positive.

2. Combine the expressions with like terms together:

$$4x^2 - 8x^2 - 6xy + 12xy - 12y^2 - 4y^2$$

3. Add and subtract like terms:

$$4x^2 - 8x^2 = -4x^2$$
$$-6xy + 12xy = 6xy$$
$$-12y^2 - 4y^2 = -16y^2$$

4. **Put the terms back into the polynomial:**

$$-4x^2 + 6xy - 16y^2$$

So the answer is $-4x^2 + 6xy - 16y^2$, which is Choice (B). If you chose any of the other answers, you either distributed the negative sign improperly or you added and subtracted the like terms incorrectly.

Eliminate wrong answers as you combine terms. For instance, once you determine that the first term is $-4x^2$, you can eliminate Choices (D) and (E).

After you've combined like terms, double-check that you've used the correct signs, particularly when you change all the signs like you did in the second expression. The other answer choices for the sample problem are very similar to the correct choice. They're designed to trap you in case you make an addition or subtraction error. Add and subtract carefully, and you won't fall for these tricks.

Multiplying and dividing expressions

Multiplying and dividing two or more variables works just as though you were performing these same operations on numbers with known values. So if $2^3 = 2 \times 2 \times 2$, then $x^3 = x \times x \times x$. Likewise, if $2^2 \times 2^3 = 2^5$, then $x^2 \times x^3 = x^5$. Similarly, if $2^6 \div 2^4 = 2^2$, then $y^6 \div y^4 = y^2$.

The process is pretty simple for monomials, but polynomials may be a little more complicated. In the next sections, we explore the different methods for multiplying and dividing polynomials.

Distributing terms

You can distribute terms in algebra just like you do in arithmetic. For example, when you multiply a number by a binomial, you multiply the number by each term in the binomial. In this example, you multiply $4x$ by each term inside the parentheses:

$$4x(x-3) = 4x^2 - 12x$$

With division, you do the same operation in reverse.

$$(16x^2 + 4x) \div 4x = 4x + 1$$

Here's an example of a GMAT question for which you can use distribution to answer.

For all x, $12x - (-10x) - 3x(-x + 10) = ?$

(A) $10x$

(B) $-3x^2 - 10x$

(C) $3x^2 - 52x$

(D) $3x^2 + 8x$

(E) $3x^2 - 8x$

This question tests your ability to add, subtract, and multiply terms in an algebraic expression. First, use distribution to multiply $-3x$ by $(-x + 10)$:

$$-3x(-x + 10) = 3x^2 - 30x$$

Now the equation looks like this:

$$12x - (-10x) + 3x^2 - 30x$$

Combine the terms that contain the x variable:

$$12x - (-10x) - 30x = -8x$$

So the answer to the equation is Choice (E): $3x^2 - 8x$.

Stacking terms

One easy way to multiply polynomials is to stack the two numbers to be multiplied on top of one another. Suppose you have this expression: $\left(x^2 + 2xy + y^2\right) \times \left(x - y\right)$.

You can stack this expression just like an old-fashioned multiplication problem. Just remember to multiply each of the terms in the second line by each term in the first line.

$$
\begin{array}{r}
x^2 + 2xy + y^2 \\
x - y \\
\hline
x^3 + 2x^2y + xy^2 \\
-x^2y - 2xy^2 - y^3 \\
\hline
x^3 + x^2y - xy^2 - y^3
\end{array}
$$

Line up like terms during the first round of multiplication so they match up before you add the products.

TIP

The GMAT may ask you to divide a polynomial by a monomial. Simply divide each term of the polynomial by the monomial. Here's how you'd divide the expression $\dfrac{60x^4 - 20x^3}{5x}$:

$$
\begin{aligned}
\frac{60x^4 - 20x^3}{5x} &= \frac{60x^4}{5x} - \frac{20x^3}{5x} \\
&= \left(\frac{60}{5} \times \frac{x^4}{x}\right) - \left(\frac{20}{5} \times \frac{x^3}{x}\right) \\
&= \left(12 \times x^{4-1}\right) - \left(4 \times x^{3-1}\right) \\
&= 12x^3 - 4x^2
\end{aligned}
$$

Taking a shine to the FOIL method

You can multiply binomials by using the *FOIL* method. FOIL is an acronym for *first, outer, inner, last,* which indicates the order that you multiply the terms from one binomial by the terms of the second binomial before adding their products. Take a look at this example:

$$(4x - 5)(3x + 8) =$$

Multiply the first terms in each binomial — $4x$ and $3x$.

$$4x \times 3x = 12x^2$$

Then multiply the outer terms ($4x$ and 8) to get $32x$ and the inner terms ($3x$ and -5) to get $-15x$. You can add the products at this point because they're like terms.

$$32x - 15x = 17x$$

Last, multiply the last terms.

$$-5 \times 8 = -40$$

Combine the products to form the resulting expression.

$$12x^2 + 17x - 40$$

You may recognize this expression as the quadratic polynomial we discussed in the earlier section "Knowing the nomials: Kinds of expressions."

TIP

To save time on the GMAT, you may want to commit the following factors and their resulting equations to memory:

$$(x+y)^2 = x^2 + 2xy + y^2$$
$$(x-y)^2 = x^2 - 2xy + y^2$$

So if you're asked to multiply $(x + 3)(x + 3)$, you know without using FOIL that the answer is $x^2 + 2(3x) + 9$ or $x^2 + 6x + 9$. And $(x-3)(x-3) = x^2 + -6x + 9$ or $x^2 - 6x + 9$.

If you're able to keep track of the terms, you can use FOIL to multiply terms in the proper order without taking the time to stack them. The FOIL method comes in handy for solving GMAT problems like the next one.

EXAMPLE

When the polynomials $3x + 4$ and $x - 5$ are multiplied together and written in the form $3x^2 + kx - 20$, what is the value of k?

(A) 2

(B) 3

(C) −5

(D) −11

(E) −20

This question asks you for the constant in the middle term of the quadratic expression formed by multiplying $3x + 4$ and $x - 5$. Remember with FOIL, you multiply the first, outer, inner, and last. The problem gives you the first term: $3x^2$. The last is also there: −20. Because the problem provides the product of the first terms and last terms, all you have to do to get the middle term is to multiply the outer and inner numbers of the two expressions and then add them together.

1. **Multiply the outer numbers:**

$$3x \times -5 = -15x$$

2. **Multiply the inner numbers:**

$$4 \times x = 4x$$

So the middle term of the quadratic is $-15x + 4x = -11x$. The constant k must equal −11, which is Choice (D).

Extracting Information: Factoring Polynomials

Factors are the numbers you multiply together to get a product. So, factoring a value means you write that value as a product of its factors. For the GMAT, you should know how to pull out the common factors in expressions and the two binomial factors in a quadratic polynomial. We show you how to do both in the following sections.

Something in common: Finding common factors

To simplify polynomials for complex problems, extract their common factors by dividing each term by the factors that are common to every term. You can think of the process as the opposite of distributing terms. For example, to find the common factors of the terms in the expression $-14x^3 - 35x^6$, follow these steps:

1. Consider the coefficients.

Because -7 is common to both -14 and -35, take this factor out of the expression by dividing both terms by -7. Then put the remaining expression in parentheses next to the common factor: $-7(2x^3 + 5x^6)$.

2. Now look at the variables.

Because x^3 or a multiple of it is common to both terms, divide both terms in parentheses by x^3, multiply x^3 by the other common factor (-7), and put the remaining expression in parentheses: $-7x^3(2 + 5x^3)$.

So, $-14x^3 - 35x^6 = -7x^3(2 + 5x^3)$.

Two by two: Factoring quadratic polynomials

The GMAT also expects you to know how to factor quadratic polynomials. To accomplish this task, you have to perform the FOIL operations in reverse to come up with a couple of binomial factors that look something like this: $(x \pm a)(x \pm b)$.

For example, look at the following quadratic polynomial:

$$x^2 + 5x + 6$$

To find its factors, draw two sets of parentheses: ( )( ). The first terms of the two factors have to be x and x because x^2 is the product of x and x. So you can add x as the first term for both sets of parentheses. You know that the operation in both terms must be addition because both the middle and last terms of the quadratic expression are positive:

$$(x +\ )(x +\ )$$

To find the second terms for the two factors, ask yourself which two numbers have a product of 6 (the third term of the quadratic) and add up to the number 5 (the coefficient of the quadratic's second term). The only two factors that meet these two criteria are 2 and 3. The other factors of 6 (6 and 1, -6 and -1, -2 and -3) don't add up to 5. So the binomial factors of the quadratic equation are $(x + 2)$ and $(x + 3)$.

TIP

Because you do just the opposite of what you do when you multiply binomials using the FOIL method, you can use the FOIL method to make sure the binomial factors result in the original quadratic when you multiply them together.

There's a timesaving way to factor binomials that are made up of a difference of perfect squares, such as $x^2 - 4$. Factors for these types of quadratic polynomials (known as the difference of perfect squares) result in the following form:

$$(x - a)(x + a)$$

The variable x is the square root of the first term, and a is the square root of the second term. So the factors of $x^2 - 4 = (x - 2)(x + 2)$.

This factoring technique is very easy to memorize and can help you answer some algebra questions much more quickly than if you were to take the time to carry out long calculations. For example, if you're asked to multiply factors $(x - 5)(x + 5)$, you can use the FOIL method to figure out the answer, but spotting that the correct answer will be the difference of two perfect squares is much faster. You know the correct answer is $x^2 - 25$ without performing time-consuming calculations.

Likewise, if you need to factor $x^2 - 25$, all you do is figure the square root of x^2 and the square root of 25 and enter those values into the proper factoring form for perfect square quadratics. You know right away that the factors are $(x - 5)(x + 5)$. When you break down the quadratic polynomial, you'll be able to solve quadratic equations. For more about how to do this, see the section "Solving quadratic equations," later in this chapter.

Knowing how to multiply polynomials with variables can help you more efficiently solve similar problems that don't contain variables, such as this one:

EXAMPLE

What is the solution for $\left(2 + \sqrt{3}\right)\left(2 - \sqrt{3}\right)$?

(A) −1

(B) 0

(C) 1

(D) $2\sqrt{3}$

(E) $4\sqrt{3}$

You may look at this question and think "Gee, I wish I had a calculator to help me add and subtract the stuff in the parentheses." But then you may notice that this problem looks a lot like multiplying binomial expressions. All you need is FOIL!

1. **Multiply the first terms:**

    $2 \times 2 = 4$

2. **Notice that the inner and outer terms will cancel each other because you're adding and subtracting the same terms:**

    $2\sqrt{3} - 2\sqrt{3} = 0$

3. **Multiply the last terms:**

    $\sqrt{3} \times -\sqrt{3} = -\left(\sqrt{3}\right)^2$

4. **Combine the remaining terms:**

    $4 - \left(\sqrt{3}\right)^2 = 4 - 3 = 1$

The answer is Choice (C) — no calculator needed.

Minding Your Ps and Qs: Functions

Some of the GMAT math questions involve functions. Simply put, *functions* are relationships between two sets of numbers; each number you put into the formula gives you only one possible answer. Functions may sound complicated, but they're really pretty simple. A function problem looks something like this:

$f(x) = 2x^2 + 3$. What is $f(2)$?

We explore the terminology of functions and how to find the domain and range of functions in the following sections.

Standing in: Understanding function terminology

Before we show you how to solve function problems, you need to know a few definitions. Table 13-1 gives you the terms we use when we discuss functions.

TABLE 13-1 Defining Terms for Functions

Term	Definition
Function	A rule that turns each member of one set of numbers into a member of another set.
Independent variable (input)	The number you want to find the function of; the x in $f(x)$.
Dependent variable (output)	The result of substituting the independent value into the function, $f(x)$. (This is like your y variable.)
Domain	The set of all possible values of the independent variable.
Range	The set of all possible values of the dependent variable.

Functions on the GMAT are usually displayed with the letters f or g. For example, $f(x)$ is used to indicate the function of x, and it simply means "f of x."

Don't let this language confuse you. All you really have to do is substitute the indicated value for x in the function.

WARNING

Don't think that the parentheses in the function notation mean multiplication like they do in algebraic operations. The expression $f(x)$ doesn't mean $f \times x$.

To see how functions work, consider the earlier example:

$f(x) = 2x^2 + 3$. What is $f(2)$?

The initial expression means that the function of x is to square x, multiply the result by 2, and then add 3. To calculate the function exercise with the number $f(2)$, you just substitute 2 for x in the expression and solve.

$$f(2) = 2(2)^2 + 3$$
$$f(2) = 2(4) + 3$$
$$f(2) = 8 + 3$$
$$f(2) = 11$$

So when x is 2, $f(x)$ is 11. That's all there is to it! The function notation is really just a fancy way of telling you to perform a substitution.

Here's another example.

EXAMPLE

If $g(x) = 2x^2 + 17$, what is $g(12)$?

(A) 12

(B) 17

(C) 100

(D) 288

(E) 305

If you quickly consider the situation, you can eliminate Choices (A), (B), and (C) right away. When you substitute 12 for x in the function, you square 12, which is 144. The answer then results from multiplying by and adding to that number, so you know the result will be greater than 100. Furthermore, the answer in Choice (D), 288, is just 2×144. You still have to add 17, so the answer probably isn't Choice (D) either. Without much calculation, you can eliminate enough answers to determine that Choice (E) is correct. But to do the calculations, just substitute 12 for x and solve:

$$g(12) = 2(12)^2 + 17$$
$$g(12) = 2(144) + 17$$
$$g(12) = 288 + 17$$
$$g(12) = 305$$

The answer is definitely Choice (E).

That was a pretty simple problem. But functions can get more complicated on the GMAT. Check out this example.

If $f(x) = (x-2)^2$, find the value of $f(2x - 2)$.

(A) $4x^2 - 4$

(B) $4x^2 + 4$

(C) $4x^2 - 8x + 16$

(D) $4x^2 - 16x + 16$

(E) $4x^2 - 16x - 16$

Don't try to do this one in your head. Begin by plugging in $(2x - 2)$ for x. Then solve.

$$f(2x-2) = \left[(2x-2)-2\right]^2$$
$$f(2x-2) = (2x-4)^2$$
$$f(2x-2) = (2x-4)(2x-4)$$
$$f(2x-2) = 4x^2 - (2)8x + 16$$
$$f(2x-2) = 4x^2 - 16x + 16$$

So the correct answer is Choice (D).

Taking it to the limit: Domain and range of functions

The *domain of a function* is the set of all numbers that can possibly be an input of a function, the x in $f(x)$. The *range of a function* is the set of all numbers that can possibly be an output of a function, the value for $f(x)$. In other words, if you think of the domain as the set of all possible independent variables values you can put into a function, the range is the set of all possible dependent variables values that can come out of any particular function. Domain and range questions aren't difficult, but you need to be aware of some basic rules to determine the proper limits of the domain and range. The GMAT also tests you on graphing functions on the coordinate plane, but we discuss that in Chapter 15.

Mastering the territory: Domain

Unless a problem specifies otherwise, the domain of a function includes all real numbers, which means that the only numbers that aren't included in the domain are numbers that aren't real (see

Chapter 12 for more info on imaginary and real numbers). Here are some properties of numbers that *aren't* real and, therefore, can't be part of the domain of a function:

>> A real number can't be a fraction with a denominator of 0, because then the number would be undefined.

>> A real number can't be an even-numbered root of a negative number. Even-numbered roots of negatives aren't real numbers because any number that's squared or has an even-numbered power can't result in a negative number.

For example, there's no such thing as $\sqrt{-4}$ because there's no one number that you can square that results in a negative 4. So -2×-2 will always equal positive 4.

To see how the first rule affects domain, look at this function:

$$f(x) = \frac{x+4}{x-2}$$

Normally, the domain of x in a function can contain an unlimited number of values. In the preceding example, though, you have a fraction in the function, which puts the variable x in the denominator. Because your denominator can't add up to 0, the denominator of $x - 2$ can't equal 0. This means that x can't equal 2. In terms of functions, the domain of $f(x)$ is, therefore, $\{x \neq 2\}$. That's all there is to it!

Here's a function that relates to the second rule:

$$g(n) = 3\sqrt[4]{n+2}$$

In this function, you have an even-numbered radical sign with the variable n within it. You know that the root of an even-numbered radical, in this case, the 4th root, can't be a negative number. Otherwise, you wouldn't have a real number as your final answer. Therefore, the number under the radical sign can't be less than 0. So $n \geq -2$. The result is that the domain of the function $g(n)$ is $\{n \geq -2\}$.

The GMAT may test your knowledge of domain with a problem such as the following.

EXAMPLE

Determine the domain of the function $f(x) = \dfrac{4}{x^2 - x - 2}$.

(A) $\{x \neq -1, 2\}$

(B) $\{x \neq 1, -2\}$

(C) $\{x = -1, 2\}$

(D) $\{x = -4, 2\}$

(E) $\{x \neq -4, 2\}$

This problem involves simple algebra. You know the denominator can't equal 0, so set the trinomial in the denominator equal to 0, and solve for x to find out what x can't be. We show you how to solve trinomials later in the "Solving quadratic equations" section.

$$x^2 - x - 2 = 0$$
$$(x+1)(x-2) = 0$$
$$x + 1 = 0; \ x = -1$$
$$x - 2 = 0; \ x = 2$$

WARNING

You're not finished! If you picked Choice (C) as your answer, your factoring would have been absolutely right, but your answer would be absolutely wrong. Answer Choice (C) gives you only the values for x that make the denominator equal to 0. You're trying to find the values that make the denominator *not* equal to 0.

So, the correct answer is Choice (A); x can be any real number other than −1 and 2 because if x were equal to −1 or 2, the denominator would be 0, and the value would be undefined. If you chose Choice (B), you switched the signs of the factors. If you chose Choices (D) or (E), you found the correct factors of the denominator but mistakenly divided the numerator by each root of the denominator.

Roaming the land: Range

Just as the domain of a function is limited by certain laws of mathematics, so, too, is the range. Here are the rules to remember when you're determining the range of a function:

>> An absolute value of a real number can't be a negative number.

>> An even exponent or power can't produce a negative number.

Check out some situations where these rules come into play. Look at the following functions:

$$g(x) = |x|$$
$$g(x) = x^2$$

Each of these functions can result only in an output that's a positive number or 0. So in each case, the range of the function of g is greater than or equal to 0. Here's a question that puts the range rules to work.

EXAMPLE

What is the range of the function $g(x) = 1 - \sqrt{x-2}$?

(A) $g(x) \geq -2$

(B) $g(x) \leq -2$

(C) $g(x) \geq 2$

(D) $g(x) \geq -1$

(E) $g(x) \leq 1$

TIP

First, you have to make the radical a real number. The value within the square root sign has to be equal to or greater than 0. So, x has to be equal to or greater than 2, because any value less than 2 would make the radical a negative value. To check the possible outputs, consider several values for x.

If x is the lowest value, 2, you'd figure the output of the function like this:

$$g(x) = 1 - \sqrt{2-2}$$
$$g(x) = 1 - \sqrt{0}$$
$$g(x) = 1 - 0$$
$$g(x) = 1$$

So you know that $g(x)$ can be equal to 1.

If x is a higher value than 2, say 6, then you'd calculate the output like this:

$$g(x) = 1 - \sqrt{6-2}$$
$$g(x) = 1 - \sqrt{4}$$
$$g(x) = 1 - 2$$
$$g(x) = -1$$

Now you know that any value for x that's higher than 2 results in a lower value for the output of the function. Therefore, $g(x)$ has to equal 1 or be less than 1, and the correct answer is Choice (E).

WARNING

Getting confused and looking for the domain when you should be finding the range is very easy. If you chose Choice (C), you solved for the domain of x. If you chose Choices (A) or (B), you're hung up trying to make the number under the radical a positive number. If you chose Choice (D), you simply don't know how to solve for range, so be sure to review this section.

Putting On Your Thinking Cap: Problem-Solving

You may be wondering how the GMAT tests your knowledge of algebra concepts. Well, wonder no more. The following sections present you with many of the ways you'll use algebra to solve GMAT math problems.

Isolating the variable: Linear equations

A *linear equation* is an algebra equation that contains an unknown variable and no exponent greater than 1. In other words, these equations are fairly easy.

In its simplest form, a linear equation is expressed as $ax + b = y$, where x is the variable and a and b are constants. Here are two things to keep in mind when you're solving linear equations:

» Isolate the variable in the equation you're trying to solve, which means you work to get it all by itself on one side of the equation. In other words, you're solving for x.

» Whatever operation you perform on one side of the equation, you must do to the other side.

This easy question asks you to solve a linear equation: If $4x + 10 = -38$, what is the value of x?

Solve for x by isolating the variable on one side of the equation:

1. **Eliminate 10 from the left side of the equation by subtracting it.**

(Remember that if you do something to one side of the equation, you need to do the same thing to the other side. Otherwise, your math teacher is liable to rap you on the knuckles with a slide rule.) Here's what happens when you subtract 10 from both sides:

$$4x + 10 - 10 = -38 - 10$$
$$4x = -48$$

2. **Next, divide both sides by 4, and you have your answer.**

$$\frac{4x}{4} = \frac{-48}{4}$$
$$x = -12$$

The value of x is −12.

You tackle division problems the same way. So if you're asked to solve for x in the problem $\frac{x}{4} = -5$, you know what to do. Isolate x to the left side of the equation by multiplying both sides of the equation by 4:

$$\frac{x}{4} \times 4 = -5 \times 4$$
$$x = -20$$

TIP

If the equation includes multiple fractions, you can simplify things and save precious time by eliminating the fractions. Just multiply each fraction by the *least common denominator* (which is the lowest positive whole number that each fraction's denominator divides into evenly). For example, you may have to solve for *x* in a problem like this:

$$\frac{3x}{5} + \frac{8}{15} = \frac{x}{10}$$

The lowest number that 5, 15, and 10 go into evenly is 30, so that's your least common denominator. Multiply each fraction by a fraction equivalent to 1 that will give you 30 in the denominators, like this:

$$\left(\frac{3x}{5} \times \frac{6}{6}\right) + \left(\frac{8}{15} \times \frac{2}{2}\right) = \left(\frac{x}{10} \times \frac{3}{3}\right)$$
$$\frac{18x}{30} + \frac{16}{30} = \frac{3x}{30}$$

Now you can eliminate the fractions by multiplying both sides of the equation by 30:

$$18x + 16 = 3x$$

Then just solve for *x*:

$$18x + 16 = 3x$$
$$18x - 18x + 16 = 3x - 18x$$
$$16 = -15x$$
$$\frac{16}{-15} = \frac{-15x}{-15}$$
$$-\frac{16}{15} = x$$

Bringing in the substitution: Simultaneous equations

Solving for *x* is simple when it's the only variable, but what if your equation has more than one variable? When you have another equation that contains at least one of the variables, you can solve for either variable. These two equations are called *simultaneous equations*. You just solve one of the equations for one of the variables and then plug the answer into the other equation and solve. Here's a simple example.

If $4x + 5y = 30$ and $y = 2$, what is the value of *x*?

Because the second equation tells you that *y* is 2, just substitute 2 for the value of *y* in the first equation and you're on your way:

$$4x + 5y = 30$$
$$4x + 5(2) = 30$$
$$4x + 10 = 30$$
$$4x = 20$$
$$x = 5$$

That's all there is to it!

TIP

You can also solve simultaneous linear equations by stacking them. This method works when you have as many equations as you have possible variables to solve for. So you can stack these two equations because they contain two variables:

$$6x + 4y = 66$$
$$-2x + 2y = 8$$

Your goal is to find a way to remove one of the variables. Here's how:

1. Examine the equations to determine what terms you can eliminate through addition or subtraction.

If you multiply the entire second equation by 3, you can eliminate the x terms in both equations because $2x \times 3 = -6x$, and $6x - 6x = 0$. Just be sure to multiply each term in the equation by the same value. So the second equation becomes $-6x + 6y = 24$.

2. Stack the equations, combine like terms, and solve for y.

$$6x + 4y = 66$$
$$\underline{-6x + 6y = 24}$$
$$0 + 10y = 90$$
$$y = 9$$

3. Plug the value of one variable into one of the equations and solve for the other value.

You've found that $y = 9$, so substitute 9 for the value of y in one of the equations to solve for x.

$$-2x + 2y = 8$$
$$-2x + 2(9) = 8$$
$$-2x + 18 = 8$$
$$-2x = -10$$
$$x = 5$$

Therefore, the solutions, also referred to as *roots*, to the simultaneous equations are $x = 5$ and $y = 9$.

Knowing that you can find solutions for variables when you have as many separate linear equations as the number of distinct variables they contain can help you answer some data sufficiency questions, such as this example.

EXAMPLE

What is the value of x?

1. $2x - 9y = 28$

2. $4y - 3x = 42 + y$

(A) Statement 1 is sufficient.

(B) Statement 2 is sufficient.

(C) The two statements are sufficient together.

(D) Each of the statements is sufficient alone.

(E) Neither statement nor both together is sufficient.

You can't solve for x using either of the statements by itself. The best you can do is solve for x in terms of y in either case. So the answer is either Choice (C) or (E). Without lifting a pencil, you know that the answer is Choice (C); the statements are sufficient together. Each of the two distinct equations contains the same two variables, so the conditions are met to reach a clear value for x. You don't have to take the time to actually solve for x during the exam, but we'll take you through the process in case you aren't convinced.

Combine like terms in Statement 2:

$$4y - 3x = 42 + y$$
$$-3x + 3y = 42$$

Multiply all terms in the Statement 2 equation by 3 so you can eliminate the y value when you stack the two equations:

$$3(-3x + 3y = 42)$$
$$-9x + 9y = 126$$

Stack the equations and solve:

$$2x - 9y = 28$$
$$\underline{-9x + 9y = 126}$$
$$-7x = 154$$
$$x = -22$$

Not playing fair: Inequalities

An inequality is a statement such as "x is less than y" or "x is greater than or equal to y."

In addition to the symbols for add, subtract, multiply, and divide, mathematics also applies standard symbols to show how the two sides of an equation are related. You're probably pretty familiar with these symbols, but a little review never hurts. Table 13-2 gives you a rundown of the symbols you'll deal with on the GMAT.

REMEMBER

Here are some of the more common symbols used in algebra to signify equality and inequality.

TABLE 13-2 **Mathematical Symbols for Equality and Inequality**

Symbol	Meaning
$=$	Equal to
$\neq$	Not equal to
$\approx$	Approximately equal to
$>$	Greater than
$<$	Less than
$\geq$	Greater than or equal to
$\leq$	Less than or equal to

Performing operations with inequalities

You treat inequalities a lot like equations. Isolate the variable to one side and perform the same operations on both sides of the inequality. The only difference is that if you multiply or divide by a negative number, you need to reverse the direction of the inequality sign. So, here's how you solve this inequality:

$$-2x \leq 10$$
$$x \geq -5$$

Working with ranges of numbers

You can also use inequalities to show a range of numbers. For example, the GMAT may show the range of numbers between −6 and 12 as an algebraic inequality, like this:

$$-6 < x < 12$$

To show the range between −6 and 12 including −6 and 12, you use the ≤ sign:

$$-6 \leq x \leq 12$$

You can add or subtract values within a range. For example, you add 5 to each part of $-6 < x < 12$, like this:

$$-6 + 5 < x + 5 < 12 + 5$$
$$-1 < x + 5 < 17$$

And you can perform operations between different ranges, such as $4 < x < 15$ and $-2 < y < 20$. To find the sum of these two ranges, follow these steps:

1. **Add the smallest values of each range:**

$$4 + (-2) = 2$$

2. **Add the largest values of each range:**

$$15 + 20 = 35$$

3. **Create a new range with the sums:**

$$2 < x + y < 35$$

This means that the range of values of $x + y$ is $2 < x + y < 35$.

Here's an example of how the GMAT may ask you to deal with inequalities.

EXAMPLE

If $x^2 - 1 \leq 8$, what is the smallest real value x can have?

(A) −9

(B) −6

(C) −3

(D) 0

(E) 3

This problem asks you to determine the smallest real value of x if $x^2 - 1$ is less than or equal to 8. Solve the inequality for x:

$$x^2 - 1 \leq 8$$
$$x^2 \leq 9$$
$$x \leq \sqrt{9}$$

Or $-\sqrt{9} \leq x$ because the product of two negative numbers is also positive.

So, $-3 \leq x \leq 3$. Remember that the square root of a number may be positive or negative. The square root of 9 is either 3 or −3. Because −3 is less than 3, −3 must be the smallest real value of x.

To make sure you're right, you can eliminate answer choices by using common sense. For example, −9 in Choice (A) would make $x^2 - 1$ equal 80, and −6 in Choice (B) would make $x^2 - 1$ equal 35. So neither Choices (A) nor (B) can be a solution for x. In Choice (D), 0 is a solution for x, but it isn't the smallest solution, because you know that −3 is a possibility. Choice (E) can't be right because it's larger than two other possible solutions, −3 and 0. So Choice (C) is the correct answer.

Solving quadratic equations

When you set a quadratic polynomial equal to 0, you get what's called a quadratic equation. An example of the classic quadratic form is $ax^2 + bx + c = 0$, where a, b, and c are constants and x is a variable that you have to solve for. Notice that 0 is on one side of the equation, and all non-zero terms are on the other side.

Quadratic equations may appear in slightly different forms. For example, all the following equations are quadratic equations because they contain a squared variable and equal 0:

$$x^2 = 0$$
$$x^2 - 4 = 0$$
$$3x^2 - 6x + 5 = 0$$

Factoring to find x

The GMAT may give you a quadratic equation and ask you to solve for x. The simplest way to solve a quadratic equation is to try to factor the equation into two binomials, just like you did earlier in the section "Two by two: Factoring quadratic polynomials."

$$x^2 - 6x + 5 = 0$$

To factor this trinomial, consider what numbers multiply together to become 5 that also have a sum of -6.

The two factors of 5 are 5 and 1 or -5 and -1. To get a sum of -6, you need to go with the negative values. Doing so gives these two binomial factors: $(x - 5)$ and $(x - 1)$. So the resulting equation is $(x - 5)(x - 1) = 0$.

To solve for x, you set each of the binomial factors equal to 0. You can do so because you know that one of the factors must equal 0 if their product is 0.

$$x - 5 = 0$$
$$x = 5$$

and

$$x - 1 = 0$$
$$x = 1$$

Now the solutions (or roots) to the equation are clear: $x = 1$ and $x = 5$. Both 1 and 5 are possible solutions for x in this quadratic equation.

REMEMBER Quadratic equations usually have two possible solutions.

Determining solutions for the difference of perfect squares

Finding the solution set for a quadratic equation made up of the difference of perfect squares (like $x^2 - y^2 = 0$) is simple if you remember that $x^2 - y^2 = (x + y)(x - y)$. If the GMAT presents you with the task of solving for x in an equation where the difference of perfect squares is equal to 0, you know that x equals the positive and negative values of the square root of y^2 (which is the second term).

So, if you were told to find the solution set for $x^2 - 49 = 0$, you'd determine the square root of the second term (49), which is 7. The factors, then, are $(x + 7)$ and $(x - 7)$. Therefore, the solution set for this problem is $x = -7$ and $x = 7$, which are indeed the positive and negative values of the second term's square root!

Using the quadratic formula

Solving quadratic equations is easy when the solutions come out to be nice, round numbers. But what if the ultimate solutions are harsh-looking radicals or perhaps not even real roots? For the rare GMAT occasions when you can't simply solve a quadratic equation by factoring, you may have to use the quadratic formula, which is a rearrangement of the classic equation: $ax^2 + bx + c = 0$. It looks like this:

$$x = \frac{-b \pm \sqrt{b^2 - 4ac}}{2a}$$

REMEMBER

Although this formula may look mighty unmanageable, it may be the only way to find the solution to x for quadratic equations that aren't easily factored. Here's how you'd apply the formula when asked to solve $3x^2 + 7x - 6 = 0$ for x. In this equation, $a = 3$, $b = 7$, and $c = -6$. Plug these numbers into the quadratic formula:

$$x = \frac{-7 \pm \sqrt{7^2 - 4(3)(-6)}}{2(3)}$$

$$x = \frac{-7 \pm \sqrt{49 + 72}}{6}$$

$$x = \frac{-7 \pm \sqrt{121}}{6}$$

$$x = \frac{-7 \pm 11}{6}$$

$$x = -\frac{18}{6} \text{ or } \frac{4}{6}$$

$$x = -3 \text{ or } \frac{2}{3}$$

The solutions for x are $\frac{2}{3}$ and -3. Whew! Luckily, the GMAT won't give you many quadratic equations that require you to apply this formula. But you'll know what to do if you encounter one of the few.

Reading between the lines: Word problems

The GMAT tests algebra and arithmetic concepts in word problems as well as mathematical equations. In fact, word problems are more common on the GMAT than straightforward equation-solving. So you have to know how to translate the English language into mathematical expressions. (You'll probably see a few geometry word problems, too, but algebra is more common on the GMAT.)

REMEMBER

To help you with the translation, Table 13-3 provides some of the more common words you'll encounter in word problems and tells you what they look like in math symbols.

Here's an example of how you play foreign language interpreter on GMAT word problems.

TABLE 13-3 Common Words and Their Math Equivalents

Plain English	Math Equivalent
More than, increased by, added to, combined with, total of, sum of	Plus (+)
Less than, fewer than, decreased by, diminished by, reduced by, difference between, taken away from	Minus (−)
Of, times, product of	Multiply (×)
Ratio of, per, out of, quotient	Divide (÷ or /)
x percent of y	$(x \div 100) \times y$
Is, are, was, were, becomes, results in	Equals (=)
How much, how many, a certain number	Variable (x, y)

EXAMPLE

On the first day of an alpine slalom competition, the total combined time of Grace's two runs was 1 minute and 57 seconds. If twice the number of seconds in her first run was 30 seconds more than the number of seconds in her second run, what was her time in seconds for the first run?

(A) 15

(B) 30

(C) 49

(D) 68

(E) 147

Focus on what you're supposed to figure out. The question asks for the time of Grace's first run in seconds. So you know you have to convert her total time to seconds so you're working in the correct units. A minute has 60 seconds, which means that Grace's total time was 60 + 57, or 117 seconds.

TIP

You can immediately eliminate Choice (E) because Grace's first run couldn't have been longer than the sum of her two runs. Now apply your math translation skills. You have two unknowns: the time of Grace's first run and the time of her second run. Let x stand for the first unknown and y for the second.

REMEMBER

You can solve a problem with two variables when you know two equations that involve those two variables. So search the problem for two equations.

For the first equation, the problem tells you that the total time of the two runs is 117 seconds. According to the English-to-math-translation dictionary, that means $x + y = 117$. You've got one equation!

You also know that 2 times (×) the number of seconds in her first run (x) was (=) 30 seconds more (+) than her time for the second run (y). Translation please? $2x = 30 + y$.

After you have the two equations, you can use substitution or stacking to solve for *x*. For this problem, stacking is faster. Notice that $2x = 30 + y$ is the same as $2x - y = 30$. When you stack and add the two equations, you can eliminate the *y* variable because $y - y = 0$.

$$x + y = 117$$
$$\underline{2x - y = 30}$$
$$3x = 147$$
$$x = 49$$

So, Grace ran her first race in 49 seconds, which is Choice (C). If you chose Choice (D), you solved for *y* instead of *x*. Grace's second run was 68 seconds.

Burning the midnight oil: Work problems

Work problems ask you to find out how much work gets done in a certain amount of time. You use this formula for doing algebra work problems:

$$\text{Production} = \text{Rate of Work} \times \text{Time}$$

Production means the amount of work that gets done. Because you get that quantity by multiplying two other numbers, you can say that production is the product of the rate times the time.

Here's how you'd apply the formula on a GMAT work problem.

EXAMPLE

There are two dock workers, Alf and Bob. Alf can load 16 tons of steel per day, and Bob can load 20 tons per day. If they each work eight-hour days, how many tons of steel can the two of them load in one hour, assuming they maintain a steady rate?

(A) 2.5

(B) 4.5

(C) 36

(D) 160

(E) 320

This question asks you to find the amount of production and gives you the rate and the time. But to calculate the rate properly, you must state the hours in terms of days. Because a workday is eight hours, one hour is $\frac{1}{8}$ of a day. Figure out how much Alf loads in one hour ($\frac{1}{8}$ of a day) and add it to what Bob loads in one hour.

$$\text{Total Production} = \text{Alf's Production} + \text{Bob's Production}$$
$$\text{Total Production} = \left(16 \times \frac{1}{8}\right) + \left(20 \times \frac{1}{8}\right)$$
$$\text{Total Production} = 2 + 2.5$$
$$\text{Total Production} = 4.5$$

So, Alf and Bob load 4.5 tons of steel in one hour ($\frac{1}{8}$ of a day), which is Choice (B). If you chose Choice (C), you figured out the total production for one day rather than one hour.

Going the distance: Distance problems

Distance problems are a lot like work problems. The formula for computing distance or speed problems is this:

$Distance = Rate \times Time$

Any problem involving distance, speed, or time spent traveling can be boiled down to this equation. The important thing is that you have your variables and numbers plugged in properly. Here's an example.

EXAMPLE

Abby can run a mile in seven minutes. How long does it take her to run $\frac{1}{10}$ of a mile at the same speed?

(A) 30 seconds

(B) 42 seconds

(C) 60 seconds

(D) 360 seconds

(E) 420 seconds

TIP

Before you do any calculating, you can eliminate Choice (E) because 420 seconds is 7 minutes, and you know it takes Abby less time to run $\frac{1}{10}$ of a mile than it does for her to run a mile.

The problem tells you that Abby's distance is $\frac{1}{10}$ of a mile. You can figure her rate to be $\frac{1}{7}$ because she runs 1 mile in 7 minutes. The problem is asking how long she runs, so you need to solve for time. Plug the numbers into the distance formula:

$Distance = Rate \times Time$

$\frac{1}{10} = \frac{1}{7} \times t$

You need to isolate t on one side of the equation, so multiply both sides by 7:

$\frac{1}{10} \times 7 = t$

$\frac{7}{10} = t$

So, Abby runs $\frac{1}{10}$ of a mile in $\frac{7}{10}$ of a minute. Convert minutes to seconds. There are 60 seconds in a minute, and $\frac{7}{10} \times 60 = 42$ seconds. The correct answer must be Choice (B).

Chapter **14**

Getting the Angle on Geometry: Planes and Solids

Geometry starts with the basics — plane geometry — which is the study of lines and shapes in two dimensions. From that foundation, geometry constructs increasingly complex models to more accurately portray the real world. Three-dimensional, or solid, geometry is almost as simple as plane geometry, with the added dimension of depth.

The GMAT tends to have fewer math questions about planes and solids than about algebra and statistics. Those of you who aren't particularly fond of manipulating shapes and figures can rejoice! But 20 percent of GMAT math questions cover geometry concepts, and this chapter is designed to make sure you're ready for them.

Fishing for the Answers: Lines and Angles

The building blocks for geometric forms are lines and angles, so we start by defining these fundamental elements. Understanding the meanings of these terms is an important part of solving problems on the GMAT. Here are the common terms that pop up on the test:

» **Line:** A straight path of points that extends forever in two directions. A line doesn't have any width or thickness. Arrows are sometimes used to show that the line goes on forever. See line *AB* in Figure 14-1.

» **Line segment:** The set of points on a line between any two points on the line. Basically, it's just a piece of a line from one point to another that contains those points and all the points between. See line segment *CD* in Figure 14-1.

» **Ray:** A ray is like half of a line; it starts at an endpoint and extends forever in one direction. You can think of a ray as a ray of light extending from the sun (the endpoint) and shining as far as it can go. See ray *EF* in Figure 14-1.

FIGURE 14-1:
Line, line segment, and ray.

» **Midpoint:** The point halfway (equal distance) between two endpoints on a line segment.

» **Bisect:** To cut something exactly in half, such as when a line, or *bisector,* cuts another line segment, angle, or polygon into two equal parts.

» **Intersect:** Just like it sounds — *intersect* simply means to cross; that is, when one line or line segment crosses another line or line segment.

» **Collinear:** A set of points that lie on the same line.

» **Vertical:** Lines that run straight up and down.

» **Horizontal:** Lines that run straight across from left to right.

» **Parallel:** Lines that run in the same direction, always remaining the same distance apart. Parallel lines never cross one another.

» **Perpendicular:** When two lines intersect to form a square corner. The intersection of two perpendicular lines forms a right, or 90-degree, angle.

» **Angle:** The intersection of two rays (or line segments) sharing a common endpoint. The common endpoint is called the *vertex.* The size of an angle depends on how much one side rotates away from the other side. An angle is usually measured in degrees or radians.

» **Acute angle:** Any angle measuring less than 90 degrees. Like an acute, or sharp, pain, the acute angle has a sharp point. See Figure 14-2.

FIGURE 14-2:
Acute angle.

» **Right, or perpendicular, angle:** An angle measuring exactly 90 degrees. It makes up a square corner. See Figure 14-3.

» **Obtuse angle:** An angle that measures more than 90 degrees but less than 180 degrees. The opposite of an acute angle, an obtuse angle is dull rather than sharp. See Figure 14-4.

» **Straight angle:** An angle that measures exactly 180 degrees. A straight angle appears to be a straight line or line segment.

The small square
shows that this is
a 90° angle.

FIGURE 14-3:
Right angle.

© John Wiley & Sons, Inc.

FIGURE 14-4:
Obtuse
angle.

© John Wiley & Sons, Inc.

» **Complementary angles:** Two angles that add together to total 90 degrees. Together, they form a right angle.

» **Supplementary angles:** Two angles that add together to total 180 degrees. They form a straight angle.

» **Similar:** Objects that have the same shape but may have different sizes.

» **Congruent:** Objects that are equal in size and shape. Two line segments with the same length, two angles with the same measure, and two triangles with corresponding sides of equal lengths and angles that have equal degree measures are congruent.

Two important rules for lines and angles arise from these basic definitions. You can read all about them in Table 14-1.

TABLE 14-1 **Rules for Lines and Angles**

Condition	Rule	Sample Figure
Intersecting lines	When two lines intersect, the opposite angles (across from each other) are always congruent or equal, and the adjacent angles are always supplementary. Opposite angles are also known as *vertical angles.* Adjacent angles have a common side, so they're right next to each other. In the sample figure, ∠ABC and ∠DBE are congruent; ∠ABC and ∠CBD form a straight line and are, therefore, supplementary.	
Parallel lines intersected by a transversal	When parallel lines are crossed by a third line that's not perpendicular to them (called a *transversal*), the resulting small and large angles share certain properties. Each of the small angles is equal to the other; the large angles are also equal to each other. These equal smaller and larger angles are called *corresponding* angles. The measurement of any small angle added to that of any large angle equals 180°.	

Here's how lines and angles may be tested on the GMAT math section.

EXAMPLE

In the preceding figure, line *m* is parallel to line *n* and line *t* is a transversal crossing both lines *m* and *n*. Given the information contained in this figure, what is the value of *e*?

(A) 30°

(B) 60°

(C) 100°

(D) 120°

(E) It cannot be determined from the information provided.

Because lines *m* and *n* are parallel, you know that the value of *e* is equal to the value of *c*. The angle with a value of *c* lies along a straight line with the angle with a measure of *a*, so $a + c = 180°$. Because *a* equals 60 degrees, *c* must equal 120 degrees. And because *c* equals *e*, *e* must also equal 120 degrees. The correct answer is Choice (D).

Trusting Triangles

Lines and angles form figures, and one of the most commonly tested GMAT figures is the triangle. A triangle has three sides, and the point where two of the sides intersect is called a *vertex*. You name triangles by their vertices, so a triangle with vertices *A*, *B*, and *C* is designated as $\triangle ABC$.

TIP

Many geometry questions on the GMAT involve triangles, so pay particular attention to their properties and rules.

Triple treat: Types of triangles

You can identify triangle types by the measurements of their sides and angles:

>> A *scalene triangle* has no equal sides and no equal angles.

>> An *isosceles triangle* has at least two equal sides, and the measures of the angles opposite those two sides are also equal to each other.

>> An *equilateral triangle* has three sides of equal lengths and three 60-degree angles.

>> A *right triangle* has one angle that measures 90 degrees. The side opposite the right angle is called the *hypotenuse*.

REMEMBER

These rules hold true for all types of triangles:

>> The measures of the three angles add up to 180 degrees.

>> The sum of the lengths of two sides is always greater than the length of the third side.

>> The side that's opposite of a given angle in a triangle is proportionate to that angle, as you can see in Figure 14-5. So the smallest angle faces the shortest side of the triangle. If two or more angles have the same measurement, their opposite sides are also equal.

FIGURE 14-5:
Angles of a triangle are in proportion to their opposite sides.

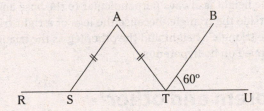

If angles $a < b < c$, then sides A < B < C

© John Wiley & Sons, Inc.

Here's an example of how this information may be tested on the GMAT.

In the preceding figure, line SA is parallel to line TB. If the measure of ∠BTU is 60 degrees, what is the measure of ∠ATB?

EXAMPLE

(A) 30°

(B) 40°

(C) 50°

(D) 60°

(E) 80°

Like a bridge over troubled water, line RU traverses the parallel lines SA and TB. Therefore, ∠BTU and ∠AST are corresponding angles and have the same measurement. Because the value of ∠BTU is 60 degrees, ∠AST must also measure 60 degrees.

You also know that line segment SA equals line segment TA, so ∆SAT is isosceles, and the angles opposite these two line segments have the same measure. One of these angles is ∠AST. ∠AST measures 60 degrees, and ∠STA has the same measurement as ∠AST. Therefore, ∠STA also measures 60 degrees.

The measures of the angles along a straight line add up to 180 degrees, so the measure of ∠ATB equals 180 less the value of ∠BTU less the value of ∠ATS. ∠BTU and ∠ATS each measure 60 degrees, so the measure of $∠ATB = 180 - 60 - 60$, which is also 60. The correct answer is Choice (D).

The area of a triangle

The GMAT will likely ask you to determine the area of a triangle, so you better be ready. Memorize this formula:

$$A = \frac{1}{2}bh$$

A stands for (what else) area, *b* is the length of the base or bottom of the triangle, and *h* stands for the height (or altitude), which is the distance that a perpendicular line runs from the base to the angle opposite the base. For a visual, check out Figure 14-6.

FIGURE 14-6:
The base and height of a triangle.

© John Wiley & Sons, Inc.

TIP

Notice that, as shown in Figure 14-6, the height is always perpendicular to the base and that the height can be placed either inside or outside the triangle. Because the legs of a right triangle are perpendicular, you can use one leg as the triangle's height and the other leg as the triangle's base (handy to remember if the triangle's flipped on its hypotenuse).

The Pythagorean theorem and other cool stuff about right triangles

You can solve GMAT problems for the lengths of the sides of right triangles by using a groovy little formula called the Pythagorean theorem and by memorizing some common right-triangle side lengths.

Digging Pythagoras and his theorem

The Pythagorean theorem simply states that the sum of the squares of the legs of a right triangle is equal to the square of the hypotenuse, or $a^2 + b^2 = c^2$, where *a* and *b* represent the two legs of the right triangle and *c* is the hypotenuse. The legs of a right triangle are simply the sides that form the right angle, and the hypotenuse is the side opposite it. (It's always the biggest side of the right triangle.) If you know the lengths of two sides of a right triangle, you can easily find the length of the other side by using this handy formula.

WARNING

Keep in mind that the Pythagorean theorem works only with right triangles. You can't use it to find the lengths of sides of triangles that don't have a right angle in them.

EXAMPLE

Which of the following is the length, in inches, of the remaining side of a right triangle if one side is 7 inches long and the hypotenuse is 12 inches long?

(A) $\sqrt{5}$

(B) 5

(C) 7

(D) 12

(E) $\sqrt{95}$

You may find it helpful to draw a right triangle on your paper to visualize the problem, but doing so isn't necessary. If the hypotenuse is 12 inches and one side is 7 inches, you figure the measurement of the remaining side by applying the formula:

$$a^2 + b^2 = c^2$$
$$7^2 + b^2 = 12^2$$
$$49 + b^2 = 144$$
$$b^2 = 95$$
$$b = \sqrt{95}$$

Pick Choice (E).

Getting hip to the common ratios of right triangles

TIP

You may find it handy to memorize some ratios based on the Pythagorean theorem. That way, you don't have to work out the whole theorem every time you deal with a right triangle.

The most common ratio of the three sides of a right triangle is 3:4:5 (3 is the measure of the short leg, 4 is the measure of the long leg, and 5 is the measure of the hypotenuse). Related multiples are 6:8:10, 9:12:15, and so on. As soon as you recognize that two sides fit the 3:4:5 ratio or a multiple of the 3:4:5 ratio, you'll automatically know the length of the third side.

REMEMBER

The hypotenuse of the triangle is always the longest side, so the largest value of the ratio (5 in this case) always corresponds to the hypotenuse when you apply this shortcut.

Other proportions of right triangles you should try to remember are 5:12:13, 8:15:17, and 7:24:25. Knowing these proportions may allow you to more quickly solve problems like the following one on the GMAT.

EXAMPLE

In the preceding figure, *AB* is 6 units long, *AC* is 8 units long, and *BD* is 24 units long. How many units long is *CD*?

(A) 26

(B) 32

(C) 80

(D) 96

(E) 100

This problem would be time consuming to solve if you didn't know the common ratios of right triangles. To determine the length of line segment *CD*, you first need to know the length of *CB*. You could use the Pythagorean theorem, but you know an easier, faster way. Because *AB* = 6 and *AC* = 8, △*ABC* is a 3:4:5 triangle times 2 — a 6:8:10 triangle. Therefore, the length of hypotenuse *BC* is 10.

Therefore, $\triangle BCD$ is a 5:12:13 triangle times 2 — a 10:24:26 triangle. So the length of $CD = 26$, and the correct answer is Choice (A).

Knowing what's neat about the 30:60:90-degree triangle

Some other handy right triangles exist. One is the 30:60:90-degree triangle. When you bisect any angle in an equilateral triangle, you get two right triangles with 30-, 60-, and 90-degree angles. In a 30:60:90-degree triangle, the hypotenuse is 2 times the length of the shorter leg, as shown in Figure 14-7. The ratio of the three sides is $s : s\sqrt{3} : 2s$, where s = the length of the shortest side.

© John Wiley & Sons, Inc.

FIGURE 14-7: The 30:60:90-degree triangle.

Feeling the equilibrium of a 45:45:90-degree triangle

If you bisect a square with a diagonal line, you get two triangles that both have two 45-degree angles. Because the triangle has two equal angles (and, therefore, two equal sides), the resulting triangle is an isosceles right triangle, or a 45:45:90-degree triangle. Its hypotenuse is equal to $\sqrt{2}$ times the length of a leg. It's important to recognize this also means that the length of a leg is equal to the length of the hypotenuse divided by $\sqrt{2}$. The ratio of sides in an isosceles right triangle is, therefore, $s : s : s\sqrt{2}$ (where s = the length of one of the legs) or $\frac{s}{\sqrt{2}} : \frac{s}{\sqrt{2}} : s$ (where s = the length of the hypotenuse). Figure 14-8 shows the formula.

© John Wiley & Sons, Inc.

FIGURE 14-8: The 45:45:90-degree triangle.

This example question shows just how helpful your knowledge of special triangles can be.

EXAMPLE

In $\triangle STR$, $\angle TSR$ measures 45 degrees and $\angle SRT$ is a right angle. If SR is 20 units long, how many units is TR?

(A) 10

(B) $10\sqrt{2}$

(C) 20

(D) $20\sqrt{2}$

(E) 40

TIP

You could draw the triangle, but with what you know about 45:45:90-degree triangles, you don't need to.

Because $\angle SRT$ is a right angle, you know that the triangle in this question is a right triangle. If $\angle TSR$ measures 45 degrees, then $\angle RTS$ must also measure 45 degrees, and this is a 45:45:90-degree triangle. So SR must equal TR. The length of line segment $SR = 20$, so $TR = 20$. The correct answer is Choice (C).

A striking resemblance: Similar triangles

Triangles are *similar* when they have exactly the same angle measures. Similar triangles have the same shape, even though their sides may have different lengths. The corresponding sides of similar triangles are in proportion to each other. The heights of the two triangles are also in proportion. Figure 14-9 provides an illustration of the relationship between two similar triangles.

FIGURE 14-9:
Similar triangles.

© John Wiley & Sons, Inc.

Knowing the properties of similar triangles helps you answer GMAT questions like the next one.

$\triangle RTS$ and $\triangle ACB$ in the preceding figure are similar right triangles with side lengths that measure as indicated. What is the area of $\triangle ACB$?

(A) 10

(B) 15

(C) 30

(D) 37.5

(E) 75

To find the area of $\triangle ACB$, you need to know the measurements of its base and height. The figure gives you the length of its height (5), so you need to find the base.

Because the two triangles are similar (and proportionate to each other), you can use what you know about $\triangle RTS$ to find the base measurement of $\triangle ACB$. TR is proportionate to CA, and RS is proportionate to AB. Set up a proportion with x representing the measure of AB, cross-multiply, and solve:

$$\frac{2}{5} = \frac{6}{x}$$
$$2x = 6 \times 5$$
$$2x = 30$$
$$x = 15$$

The base of $\triangle ACB$ is 15 inches.

Don't stop there and choose Choice (B). The question asks for the area of $\triangle ACB$, not the length of AB.

Substitute the base and height measurements for $\triangle ACB$ into the formula for the area of a triangle $A = \frac{1}{2}bh$ and solve:

$$A = \frac{1}{2}bh$$
$$A = \frac{1}{2}(5)(15)$$
$$A = \frac{1}{2}(75)$$
$$A = 37.5$$

The correct answer is Choice (D).

Playing Four Square: Quadrilaterals

A quadrilateral is a four-sided polygon, and several types of quadrilaterals exist. Your primary concern on the GMAT will be to find the measurement of a quadrilateral's area and perimeter. The following sections review what you need to know to accomplish this goal.

These two rules apply to all quadrilaterals:

>> The perimeter measure of any four-sided figure is always the sum of its side lengths.

>> The sum of the angle measures of a quadrilateral is always 360 degrees.

Drawing parallels: Parallelograms

Most of the quadrilaterals that appear on the GMAT are parallelograms.

TIP

Parallelograms have properties that are very useful for solving GMAT problems:

» The opposite sides are parallel and equal in length.

» The opposite angles are equal in measure to each other.

» The measures of the adjacent angles add up to 180 degrees, so they're supplementary to each other.

» The diagonals (designated by d_1 and d_2) of a parallelogram bisect each other. In other words, they cross at the midpoint of both diagonals.

Figure 14-10 provides a visual representation of the very important properties of parallelograms.

FIGURE 14-10:
A parallelo-
gram.

© John Wiley & Sons, Inc.

The area of any parallelogram is its base times its height ($A = bh$). You determine the height pretty much the same way you determine the height of a triangle. The difference is that you draw the perpendicular line from the base to the opposite side (instead of to the opposite angle, as in the case of a triangle). See Figure 14-11.

FIGURE 14-11:
Finding the
area of a
parallelo-
gram.

Area = base × height
or A = bh

© John Wiley & Sons, Inc.

TIP

You can use the Pythagorean theorem to help you find the height of a parallelogram. When you drop a perpendicular line from one corner to the base to create the height, the line becomes the leg of a right triangle. If the problem gives you the length of other sides of the triangle (or information you can use to determine the length), you can use the formula to find the height measurement.

Parallelograms come in various types:

» A *rectangle* is a parallelogram with four right angles. The formula for the area of a rectangle is $A = bh$, where the base and height are the measures of the rectangle's length and width.

» A *square* is a rectangle with four equal sides, which means you can easily find its area when you know the length of only one side. Keep these formulas in mind:

  • The area is $A = s^2$, where s is the length of a side.

  • The perimeter is $4s$.

>> A *rhombus* has four equal sides but not necessarily four right angles. Find the area of a rhombus by multiplying the lengths of its two diagonals (designated as d_1 and d_2) and then dividing by 2:

$$A = \frac{1}{2}d_1 d_2$$

Raising the roof: Trapezoids

A *trapezoid* is a quadrilateral with just one set of parallel sides. The parallel sides are called the bases, and the other two sides are called the legs. In an isosceles trapezoid, the legs of the quadrilateral are the same length. It looks kind of like an A-frame with the roof cut off. Check out Figure 14-12 for an example. You can find the area of a trapezoid as long as you know the length of both bases and the height. Take the average of the two bases and multiply by the height:

$$A = \frac{1}{2}(b_1 + b_2)h$$

FIGURE 14-12: The bases and height of a trapezoid.

© John Wiley & Sons, Inc.

GMAT questions about quadrilaterals, such as the following, often require you to apply the formulas for area and perimeter and what you know about triangles.

EXAMPLE

In the preceding figure, square *ABCD* has sides the length of 4 units, and *M* and *N* are the midpoints of *AB* and *CD*, respectively. What is the perimeter, in units, of *AMCN*?

(A) 6

(B) $6\sqrt{5}$

(C) $2 + 2\sqrt{3}$

(D) $4 + 4\sqrt{5}$

(E) $8\sqrt{5}$

This question asks you to determine the perimeter of parallelogram *AMCN*. To solve it, rely on what you know about triangles and simplifying radicals.

If *M* and *N* are the midpoints, then $AM = 2$ (which is $\frac{4}{2}$) and $NC = 2$. Now you know the short sides of $AMCN = 2$. You can see that each of the long sides of the parallelogram is the hypotenuse of the right triangles within the square. The lengths of the legs of the right triangles measure 2 and 4, which doesn't fit with any of the special ratios associated with right triangles. So use the Pythagorean theorem:

$$2^2 + 4^2 = c^2$$
$$4 + 16 = c^2$$
$$20 = c^2$$
$$\sqrt{20} = c$$
$$\sqrt{4 \times 5} = c$$
$$2\sqrt{5} = c$$

Each of the short sides of *AMCN* measures 2 units and each long side measures $2\sqrt{5}$. Add the sides to get its perimeter:

$$P = 2(2) + 2(2\sqrt{5})$$
$$P = 4 + 4\sqrt{5}$$

This is the answer provided by Choice (D).

Showing Their Good Sides: Other Polygons

The GMAT may throw in some other types of polygons to make things interesting. Here are some of the common ones:

» **Pentagon:** A five-sided figure

» **Hexagon:** A six-sided figure (the *x* makes it sound like *six*)

» **Heptagon:** A seven-sided figure

» **Octagon:** An eight-sided figure (like *octo*pus)

» **Nonagon:** A nine-sided figure

» **Decagon:** A ten-sided figure (like *deca*thlon)

In general, GMAT polygons will be regular polygons, which means that all the sides are the same length and all the angles are equal. Polygons with exactly the same shape and same angle measurements have proportional corresponding side lengths.

No set formula exists for determining the area of a polygon. You need to create quadrilaterals and triangles within the polygon, find their areas, and add them together to get the total area of the polygon. In addition to determining its area, you may have to come up with the sum of a polygon's interior angles.

TIP

The formula for determining the sum of the interior angles of any polygon is simple:

$$SA = (n - 2) \times 180°, \text{ where } n \text{ is equal to the number of sides.}$$

Works every time! If the polygon's regular, you can also determine the measure of each of the angles. You divide the sum of the angles by the total number of angles. So each angle in a regular pentagon measures $\frac{540}{5} = 108°$.

WARNING

The method for determining the measure of an angle in a polygon works only if the GMAT tells you that the polygon is regular.

Eating Up Pieces of Pi: Circles

A circle, by technical definition, is a set of points in a plane that are at a fixed distance from a given point. That point is called the *center*. The following sections go into detail about the kinds of questions the GMAT will ask you about circles, from knowing the measures of the circle's radius, diameter, and circumference to working with arcs, chords, inscribed figures, and tangents.

Ring measurements: Radius, diameter, and circumference

Almost any GMAT problem regarding a circle requires you to know or find its radius, diameter, circumference, and area.

» The *radius* of a circle is the distance from the center of the circle to any point on the circle. The radius is usually indicated by the letter *r*, as shown in Figure 14-13.

» The *diameter* of a circle is the length of a line that goes from one side of the circle to the other and passes through the center. The diameter is twice the length of the radius, and it's the longest possible distance across the circle. Diameter usually is indicated by the letter *d*, as shown in Figure 14-13.

» The *circumference* of a circle is the distance around the circle. The formula for finding circumference is 2 times the radius times pi: $C = 2r\pi$. Because twice the radius is the measure of the diameter, you can also figure circumference by multiplying the diameter by pi: $C = d\pi$.

» The *area* of a circle is the measure of the space inside the circle. The formula for finding area is $A = \pi r^2$.

FIGURE 14-13:
Radius and
diameter
of a circle.

© John Wiley & Sons, Inc.

Blueprints for Noah: Arcs

When it comes to angles and arcs on a circle, you should have a basic understanding of the following terms so you aren't running in circles on the GMAT math section:

» An *arc* of a circle is a portion along the circumference of the circle. See Figure 14-14.

  • A *minor arc* is less than 180 degrees.

  • A *semicircle* is equal to 180 degrees.

  • A *major arc* is greater than 180 degrees. In fact, the arc of the entire circle is 360 degrees. You're more likely to work with minor arcs than major ones on the GMAT.

>> A *central angle* of a circle is an angle that's formed by two radii; it's called a central angle because its vertex is the center of the circle. The measurement of the central angle is the same as that of the arc formed by the endpoints of its radii. So a 90-degree central angle (like the one in Figure 14-14) intercepts one-quarter of the circle, or a 90-degree arc.

FIGURE 14-14:
An arc and central angle.

Arc   Central angle

Line 'em up: Chords, inscribed and circumscribed figures, and tangents

The GMAT may toss in some extra lines and figures when it questions you about circles. The extra features may appear within or outside the circle. The next sections describe each of these extras.

Striking a chord

A *chord* is a line segment cutting across a circle that connects two points on the edge of a circle. Those two points at the end of the chord are also the endpoints of an intercepted arc. See Figure 14-15.

FIGURE 14-15:
A chord.

Moving in: Inscribed and circumscribed figures

An *inscribed figure* is any figure (angle, polygon, and so on) that's drawn inside another figure. For example, you could draw a triangle inside a circle so that all its vertices touch at points on the circle, just like Figure 14-16.

A *circumscribed figure* is one that is drawn around the outside of another shape, such as a circle drawn around a triangle so that all the vertices of the triangle touch the circle. You'd say the circle in Figure 14-16 is circumscribed around the triangle.

The only difference between an inscribed and a circumscribed figure hinges on the reference. You refer to the figure on the outside of another figure as a circumscribed figure and the figure on the inside of another figure as an inscribed figure.

FIGURE 14-16:
Inscribed and circum-scribed figures.

© John Wiley & Sons, Inc.

TIP

The GMAT may use circumscribed and inscribed figures to ask you to calculate the area of a shaded area. When you get a "shaded area" problem, calculating the area of both figures and then subtracting the area of one from the other is often the best way to solve the problem.

Going off on a tangent

A *tangent line* is one that intersects the circle at just one point. A good way to think of a tangent line in the real world is like a wheel rolling along a road. The road is tangent to the wheel. Figure 14-17 shows line *AB* tangent to the circle. The line is also perpendicular to the radius that touches the circle where the tangent intersects. To continue the wheel analogy, if that wheel had an infinite number of spokes coming from its center, only one spoke would touch (be perpendicular to) the ground at any one time.

FIGURE 14-17:
Tangent line.

© John Wiley & Sons, Inc.

The GMAT may test your knowledge of circles with a question such as this:

EXAMPLE

In the preceding figure, *A* and *B* lie on the circle with center *C*. *CA* is 9 units long, and the measure of ∠*ACB* is 40 degrees. How many units long is minor arc *AB*?

(A) π

(B) 2π

(C) 9π

(D) 18π

(E) 36π

First, determine how many degrees are in arc *AB*. Because *CA* and *CB* are radii of the circle, the degree measurement of the central angle *ACB* is the same as the measurement of the arc the ends of the radii form on the circle. So the minor arc *AB* is 40 degrees. How does that help you determine the length of the arc? Well, you know that a circle is 360 degrees, and 40 degrees is $\frac{1}{9}$ of 360 degrees. That means that arc *AB* is $\frac{1}{9}$ of the circumference of the circle. Determine the circumference:

$$C = 2r\pi$$
$$C = (2)(9)\pi$$
$$C = 18\pi$$

Then figure out $\frac{1}{9}$ of that length:

$$\frac{1}{9} \times 18\pi = x$$
$$2\pi = x$$

The correct answer must be Choice (B).

Getting a Little Depth Perception: Three-Dimensional Geometry

Three-dimensional geometry, or solid geometry, adds some depth to plane geometrical figures. You'll likely encounter no more than a handful of solid geometry questions on the GMAT, and they'll likely concern only rectangular solids and cylinders, which we discuss in the following sections.

Chipping off the old block: Rectangular solids

You make a rectangular solid by taking a simple rectangle and adding depth. Good examples of rectangular solids are bricks, cigar boxes, or boxes of your favorite cereal. A rectangular solid is also known as a *right rectangular prism* because it has 90-degree angles all around. *Prisms* have two congruent polygons on parallel planes that are connected to each other by their corresponding points. The two connected polygons make up the bases of the prism, as shown in Figure 14-18.

A rectangular solid has three dimensions: length, height, and width. You really need to worry about only two basic measurements of rectangular solids on the GMAT: total surface area and volume.

Finding volume

The volume (V) of a rectangular solid is a measure of how much space it occupies, or to put it in terms everyone can appreciate, how much cereal your cereal box holds. You measure the volume of an object in cubic units. The formula for the volume of a rectangular solid is simply its length (l) times its width (w) times its height (h): $V = lwh$.

Another way of saying this formula is that the volume is equal to the base times the height ($V = Bh$), where B is the area of the base. See what we mean in Figure 14-18.

FIGURE 14-18:
Volume of a rectangular solid.

© John Wiley & Sons, Inc.

Determining surface area

You can find the surface area (SA) of a rectangular solid by simply figuring out the areas of all six sides of the object and adding them together.

First you find the area of the length (l) times height (h), then the area of length times width (w), and finally width times height (see Figure 14-19). Now multiply each of these three area measurements times 2 (after you find the area of one side, you know that the opposite side has the same measurement). The formula for the surface area of a rectangular solid is $SA = 2lh + 2lw + 2wh$.

FIGURE 14-19:
Surface area of a rectangular solid.

© John Wiley & Sons, Inc.

You can visualize the surface area of a rectangular solid, or any solid figure for that matter, by mentally flattening out all the sides and putting them next to each other. It's sort of like taking apart a cardboard box to get it ready for recycling; only now you get to measure it. Lucky you!

TIP

Working with cubes

You can use the same formulas you used with rectangular solids to find the area and volume of a three-dimensional square, called a *cube*, shown in Figure 14-20. Because all the faces on a cube are perfect squares, you can find its measurements with some simple formulas.

>> The volume of a cube with an edge a is a^3: $V = a^3$.

>> The surface area of a cube is simply the area of one side times 6: $SA = 6a^2$.

>> The diagonal of a face on a cube (a square) measures $a\sqrt{2}$, as shown in Figure 14-20.

>> Figure 14-20 also shows that the diagonal of a cube itself measures $a\sqrt{3}$.

FIGURE 14-20:
A cube.

© John Wiley & Sons, Inc.

Sipping from soda cans and other cylinders

A cylinder is a circle that grows straight up into the third dimension to become the shape of a can of soda. The bases of a cylinder are two congruent circles on different planes. The cylinders you see on the GMAT are right circular cylinders, which means that the line segments that connect the two bases are perpendicular to the bases. Figure 14-21 shows a right circular cylinder. All the corresponding points on the circles are joined together by line segments. The line segment connecting the center of one circle to the center of the opposite circle is called the axis.

FIGURE 14-21:
A right circular cylinder.

© John Wiley & Sons, Inc.

A right circular cylinder has the same measurements as a circle. That is, a right circular cylinder has a radius, diameter, and circumference. In addition, a cylinder has a third dimension: its height, or altitude.

To get the volume of a right circular cylinder, first take the area of the base (a circle), which is πr^2, and multiply by the height (h) of the cylinder: $V = \pi r^2 h$.

If you want to find the total surface area of a right circular cylinder, you have to add the areas of all the surfaces. Imagine taking a soda can, cutting off the top and bottom sections, and then slicing it down one side. You then spread out the various parts of the can. If you measure each one of these sections, you get the total surface area.

REMEMBER

When you measure the surface area of a right circular cylinder, don't forget to include the top and bottom of the can in your calculation.

Here's the formula for the total surface area (*SA*) of a right circular cylinder — the diameter (*d*) is 2 times the radius (*r*):

$$SA = \pi dh + 2\pi r^2$$

Here's a sample question that shows how the GMAT may try to find out how much you know about three-dimensional shapes.

10 in.

A

B

D

C

EXAMPLE

The preceding figure shows a cube with an edge that measures 10 inches. If points B and D are midpoints of two of the edges, what is the measure in inches of the straight line that joins point A to point C?

(A) $5\sqrt{5}$

(B) $10\sqrt{2}$

(C) $10\sqrt{3}$

(D) $20\sqrt{5}$

(E) 125

Answering this question is easy when you know the formula for the diagonal of a cube. Each edge of the cube measures 10 inches, and the diagonal of a cube is the edge length times $\sqrt{3}$. So line AC measures $10\sqrt{3}$ inches, which is Choice (C).

WARNING

Make sure you apply the correct formula. If you pick Choice (B), you're using the formula for the diagonal of a square.

Chapter **15**

Keeping in Step: Coordinate Geometry

Coordinate geometry involves working with points on a graph that's officially known as the Cartesian coordinate plane. This perfectly flat surface has a system that allows you to identify the position of points by using pairs of numbers. In this chapter, you figure out how equations and numbers relate to geometric forms and shapes, such as a straight line or a parabola, and review the formulas you need to know to fly high on questions about the coordinate plane.

REMEMBER

You can expect to encounter coordinate geometry in roughly 10 percent of the math problems on the GMAT. So if you're not particularly savvy about coordinate geometry, it won't significantly affect your GMAT math score.

Taking Flight: The Coordinate Plane

The coordinate plane doesn't have wings, but it does have points that spread out infinitely. You may not have encountered the coordinate plane in a while (it isn't something most people deal with in everyday life), so take just a minute to refresh your memory about a few relevant terms that may pop up on the GMAT. Although you won't be asked to define the terms in the following sections, knowing what they mean is absolutely essential to answering GMAT math questions.

Line dancing: Understanding coordinate geometry

Before you get too engrossed in the study of coordinate geometry, ground yourself with an understanding of these essential terms:

» **Coordinate plane:** The coordinate plane is a perfectly flat surface where points can be identified by their positions, using ordered pairs of numbers. These pairs of numbers represent the points' distances from an origin on perpendicular axes. The coordinate of any particular point is the set of numbers that identifies the location of the point, such as (3, 4) or (x, y).

» **x-axis:** The x-axis is the horizontal axis (number line) on a coordinate plane. The values start at the origin, which has a value of 0. Numbers increase in value to the right of the origin and decrease in value to the left. The x value of a point's coordinate is listed first in its ordered pair.

» **y-axis:** The y-axis is the vertical axis (number line) on a coordinate plane. Its values start at the origin, which has a value of 0. Numbers increase in value going up from the origin and decrease in value going down. The y value of a point's coordinate is listed second in its ordered pair.

» **Origin:** The origin is the point (0, 0) on the coordinate plane. It's where the x- and y-axes intersect.

» **Ordered pair:** Also known as a *coordinate pair*, this duo is the set of two values that expresses the distance a point lies from the origin. The horizontal (x) coordinate is always listed first, and the vertical (y) coordinate is listed second.

» **x-intercept:** The value of x where a line, curve, or some other function crosses the x-axis. The value of y is 0 at the x-intercept. The x-intercept is often the *solution* or *root* of an equation.

» **y-intercept:** The value of y where a line, curve, or some other function crosses the y-axis. The value of x is 0 at the y-intercept.

» **Slope:** Slope measures how steep a line is and is commonly referred to as *the rise over the run*.

What's the point? Finding the coordinates

You can identify any point on the coordinate plane by its coordinates, which designate the point's location along the x- and y-axes. For example, the ordered pair (2, 3) has a coordinate point located two units to the right of the origin along the horizontal (x) number line and three units up on the vertical (y) number line. In Figure 15-1, point A is at (2, 3). The x-coordinate appears first, and the y-coordinate shows up second. Pretty simple so far, huh?

On all fours: Identifying quadrants

The intersection of the x- and y-axes forms four quadrants on the coordinate plane, which just so happen to be named Quadrants I, II, III, and IV (see Figure 15-1). Here's what you can assume about points based on the quadrants they're in:

» All points in Quadrant I have a positive x value and a positive y value.

» All points in Quadrant II have a negative x value and a positive y value.

» All points in Quadrant III have a negative x value and a negative y value.

» All points in Quadrant IV have a positive x value and a negative y value.

» All points along the x-axis have a y value of 0.

» All points along the y-axis have an x value of 0.

Quadrant I starts to the right of the y-axis and above the x-axis. It's the upper-right portion of the coordinate plane. As shown in Figure 15-1, the other quadrants move counterclockwise around the origin. Figure 15-1 also shows the location of coordinate points A, B, C, and D:

» Point *A* is in Quadrant I and has coordinates (2, 3).

» Point *B* is in Quadrant II and has coordinates (–1, 4).

» Point *C* is in Quadrant III and has coordinates (–5, –2).

» Point *D* is in Quadrant IV and has coordinates (7, –6).

The GMAT won't ask you to pick your favorite quadrant, but you may be asked to identify which quadrant a particular point belongs in.

© John Wiley & Sons, Inc.

FIGURE 15-1: Points on the coordinate plane.

Slip-Sliding Away: Slope and Linear Equations

One of the handiest things about the coordinate plane is that it graphs the locations of lines and linear equations. In fact, questions that expect you to know how to graph lines and equations are some of the most common GMAT coordinate geometry questions. You should know the formulas for finding the slope and the slope-intercept equation and for determining the midpoint and the distance between two points on the plane. Lucky for you, we discuss all those formulas in the following sections.

Taking a peak: Defining the slope of a line

If a line isn't parallel to one of the coordinate axes, it either rises or falls from the left-hand side of the coordinate plane to the right-hand side. The measure of the steepness of the line's rising or falling is its *slope*. In the following sections, we explain how to find the slope of a line and explore the different types of slopes on a coordinate plane.

The formula for slope

You can think of the slope as the value of the rise over the value of the run. In more mathematical terms, the slope formula looks like this:

$$slope(m) = \frac{\text{Change in Vertical Coordinates}}{\text{Change in Horizontal Coordinates}} = \frac{y_1 - y_2}{x_1 - x_2}$$

The *x* and *y* values in the equation stand for the coordinates of two points on the line. The formula is just the ratio of the vertical distance between two points and the horizontal distance between those same two points. You subtract the *y*-coordinate of one point from the *y*-coordinate of the other point to get the numerator. Then you subtract the *x*-coordinate of one point from the *x*-coordinate of the other point to get the denominator.

WARNING

When you subtract the values, remember to subtract the *x* and *y* values of the first point from the respective *x* and *y* values of the second point. Don't fall for the trap of subtracting $x_2 - x_1$ to get your change in the run but then subtracting $y_1 - y_2$ for your change in the rise. That kind of backward math will mess up your calculations, and you'll soon be sliding down a slippery slope.

The graph in Figure 15-2 shows how important it is to perform these operations in the right order.

FIGURE 15-2: Finding slope.

© John Wiley & Sons, Inc.

Figure 15-2 shows coordinate point (0, 2) as (x_1, y_1), and the coordinate point (4, 0) as (x_2, y_2). You may be tempted to subtract the 0 in each coordinate point from the corresponding greater number in the other coordinate point, but doing that switches the order of how you subtract the *x* and *y* values in the two coordinate points.

For the slope formula to work, you calculate $0 - 2$ for your $y_2 - y_1$ operation (which gives you -2), and then you take $4 - 0$ for your $x_2 - x_1$ (which gives you 4). The resulting ratio, or fraction, is $-\frac{2}{4}$, or $-\frac{1}{2}$. This gives you a slope of $-\frac{1}{2}$.

Types of slope

The line in Figure 15-2 falls from left to right. This nice ski-slope image is your visual clue that the line has a negative slope. Figure 15-3 shows how you can quickly eyeball a line to get a good idea of what kind of slope a line has.

In Figure 15-3, line *m* has a negative slope; line *n* has a positive slope; a line on the horizontal *x*-axis has a slope of 0; and a line on the vertical *y*-axis has an undefined slope.

TIP

>> A line with a negative slope falls from left to right (its left side is higher than its right), and its slope is less than 0.

>> A line with a positive slope rises from left to right (its right side is higher than its left), and its slope is greater than 0.

» A horizontal line has a slope of 0; it neither rises nor falls and is parallel to the *x*-axis.

» The slope of a vertical line is undefined because you don't know whether it's rising or falling; it has no slope and is parallel to the *y*-axis.

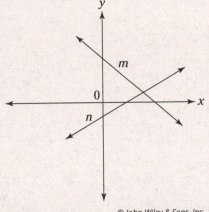

FIGURE 15-3:
Types of slope.

© John Wiley & Sons, Inc.

Using the slope-intercept form to graph lines

The characteristics of a line can be conveyed through a mathematical formula. The equation of a line (also known as the *slope-intercept form*) generally shows *y* as a function of *x*, like this:

$$y = mx + b$$

In the slope-intercept form, the coefficient *m* is a constant that indicates the slope of the line, and the constant *b* is the *y*-intercept (that is, the point where the line crosses the *y*-axis). The equation of the line in Figure 15-2 is $y = -\frac{1}{2}x + 2$, because the slope is $-\frac{1}{2}$ and the *y*-intercept is 2. The equation $y = 2$ indicates a horizontal line that intersects the *y*-axis at point (0, 2). The equation $x = 3$ indicates a vertical line that intersects the *x*-axis at point (3, 0). A line with the formula $y = 4x + 1$ has a slope of 4 (which is a rise of 4 and run of 1) and a *y*-intercept of 1. The line is graphed in Figure 15-4.

The GMAT may give you an equation of a line and ask you to choose the graph that correctly grids it. You can figure out how the line should look when it's graphed by starting with the value of the *y*-intercept, marking points that fit the value of the slope, and then connecting these points with a line.

TIP

Whenever you get an equation for a line that doesn't neatly fit into the slope-intercept format, go ahead and play with the equation a little bit (sounds fun, doesn't it?) so it meets the $y = mx + b$ format that you know and love. For instance, to put the equation $\frac{1}{3}y - 3 = x$ in slope-intercept form, you simply manipulate both sides of the equation and solve for *y*, like this:

$$\frac{1}{3}y - 3 = x$$
$$\frac{1}{3}y = x + 3$$
$$y = 3(x + 3)$$
$$y = 3x + 9$$

FIGURE 15-4:
The graph of
$y = 4x + 1$.

© John Wiley & Sons, Inc.

The new equation gives you the slope of the line, 3, as well as the y-intercept, 9. Pretty handy! Here's a sample question to give you a taste of how the slope-intercept form may be tested on the GMAT.

EXAMPLE

What is the equation of a line with a slope $-\frac{3}{4}$ and a y-intercept of 8?

(A) $4x + 3y = 32$

(B) $-3x + 4y = 16$

(C) $3x - 4y = 32$

(D) $3x + 4y = 16$

(E) $3x + 4y = 32$

REMEMBER

In the slope-intercept form, $y = mx + b$, m is the slope, and b is the y-intercept. Plug the values the problem gives you into the equation:

$$y = -\frac{3}{4}x + 8$$

This isn't an answer choice, but all options have the same format of $ax + by = c$. So you need to convert your equation to that format. Move the terms around by multiplying all terms on both sides by 4 and adding 3x to both sides, like this:

$$y = -\frac{3}{4}x + 8$$
$$4y = -3x + 32$$
$$4y + 3x = 32$$

Choice (E) is the correct answer.

Graphing a linear inequality is almost exactly the same as graphing the equation of a line, except a linear inequality covers a lot more ground on the coordinate plane. While the graph of an equation for a line simply shows the actual line on the coordinate plane, the graph of a linear inequality shows everything either above or below the line on the plane. The graph appears as a shaded area to one side of the line. Figure 15-5 shows the graphs of several inequalities.

$y = 2x - 4$

$y > 2x - 4$

$y \geq 2x - 4$

$y \leq 2x - 4$

© John Wiley & Sons, Inc.

FIGURE 15-5:
Graphing lines and inequalities.

Meeting in the middle

If the GMAT asks you for the midpoint coordinates of a line segment on the coordinate plane, you simply apply the *midpoint formula:*

$$M = \left(\frac{x_1 + x_2}{2}, \frac{y_1 + y_2}{2} \right)$$

M stands for midpoint and the *x* and *y* variables are the *x* and *y* coordinates of the line's two endpoints. So, to figure out the midpoint of a line segment that ends at points *A* (2, 3) and *B* (−1, 4), use the formula:

$$M = \left(\frac{2 + (-1)}{2}, \frac{3 + 4}{2} \right)$$

$$M = \left(\frac{1}{2}, \frac{7}{2} \right)$$

$$M = \left(\frac{1}{2}, 3\frac{1}{2} \right)$$

TIP

To help you remember the midpoint formula, think of it as the average of the two *x* coordinates and the average of the two *y* coordinates of the line segment's endpoints.

Going the distance

Some of the questions on the GMAT may ask you to calculate the distance between two points on a line. You can solve these problems with coordinate geometry.

To answer these questions, use the *distance formula*. Assume you have two points, $A(x_1, y_1)$ and $B(x_2, y_2)$, on a line. The formula to find the distance between A and B is this:

$$AB = \sqrt{(x_2 - x_1)^2 + (y_2 - y_1)^2}$$

Look at the graph in Figure 15-6 to see how the distance formula actually works.

FIGURE 15-6: Finding the distance between two points.

© John Wiley & Sons, Inc.

Notice that Point A has coordinates $(2, 1)$ and Point B has coordinates $(6, 4)$. To find the distance between these two points, you plug these numbers into the distance formula:

$$AB = \sqrt{(x_2 - x_1)^2 + (y_2 - y_1)^2}$$
$$AB = \sqrt{(6-2)^2 + (4-1)^2}$$
$$AB = \sqrt{(4)^2 + (3)^2}$$
$$AB = \sqrt{16 + 9}$$
$$AB = \sqrt{25}$$
$$AB = 5$$

If you're thinking this formula looks familiar, you're absolutely right. It's another use for the good old Pythagorean theorem: $c = \sqrt{a^2 + b^2}$. (If this theorem is only vaguely familiar to you, check out Chapter 14.) Connecting points A and B to a third point, C, as shown in Figure 15-5, gives you a right triangle, which in this case happens to be your tried-and-true 3:4:5 right triangle.

Here's a sample problem that asks you to find the distance between two points.

What is the distance in units of a line segment that connects the origin to the coordinate point $(-2, -3)$?

EXAMPLE

(A) $\sqrt{5}$

(B) $\sqrt{13}$

(C) 5

(D) 8.94

(E) 13.42

Use the distance formula to figure out the distance between the coordinates of the origin (0, 0) and the endpoint (−2, −3):

$$\overline{AB} = \sqrt{\left(x_2 - x_1\right)^2 + \left(y_2 - y_1\right)^2}$$

$$\overline{AB} = \sqrt{\left(-2 - 0\right)^2 + \left(-3 - 0\right)^2}$$

$$\overline{AB} = \sqrt{\left(-2\right)^2 + \left(-3\right)^2}$$

$$\overline{AB} = \sqrt{4 + 9}$$

$$\overline{AB} = \sqrt{13}$$

Choice (B) is the answer. If you chose Choice (C), you simply took the coordinates for the endpoint, (−2, −3), and added them together to get distance, which, of course, isn't the proper method. Choice (A) results from failing to square the differences of the coordinates. You can guess that Choices (D) and (E) are probably incorrect because uncovering their values requires using a calculator, which you won't have available on the GMAT quantitative section.

TIP

Notice that order doesn't matter when you subtract the x- and y-coordinate points from each other — you end up squaring their difference, so your answer will always be a positive number.

WARNING

Keep in mind that, in the end, the distance between two points is always a positive number. If you ever see zero or a negative number as an answer choice for a distance question, just let your mouse scoot on by.

Considering other shapes on the coordinate plane

Occasionally, the GMAT may ask you coordinate geometry questions that deal with shapes other than straight lines.

» **Circles:** The equation of a circle is $\left(x - h\right)^2 + \left(y - k\right)^2 = r^2$, where the center of the circle is point (h, k) and r is the circle's radius. If the origin is the center of the circle, the equation would be $x^2 + y^2 = r^2$.

» **Parabolas:** When you graph a quadratic equation, it appears as a *parabola,* a curve shape that opens either upward or downward. Two important properties of parabolas are

  • The *axis of symmetry*: This is the vertical line that bisects the parabola so that each side is a mirror image of the other.

  • The *vertex*: This is the rounded end of the parabola, which is the lowest point on a curve that opens upward and the highest point on a curve that opens downward. It's where the parabola crosses the axis of symmetry.

The equation for a parabola is $y = a\left(x - h\right)^2 + k$, where the coordinate point (h, k) is the vertex. The vertical line $x = h$ is the axis of symmetry. If a is a positive number, the parabola opens upward. If a is negative, it opens downward. Figure 15-7 shows the graph of $y = x^2$. The values for h and k are 0, so the vertex is at the origin. The parabola opens upward because a is 1, a positive number.

FIGURE 15-7:
A parabola with its vertex on the origin.

(h,k)

© John Wiley & Sons, Inc.

Here's a sample question that requires to you apply the parabola formula.

EXAMPLE

What is the vertex of the graph of the equation $y = -2(x-3)^2 - 4$?

(A) $(-3, -4)$

(B) $(3, 4)$

(C) $(3, -4)$

(D) $(-3, 4)$

(E) $(-6, -4)$

Remember the equation of a parabola: $y = a(x-h)^2 + k$. The vertex of the parabola is (h, k). The h value in the equation is 3, and the k value is -4. So the vertex of the graph of the equation in the question is $(3, -4)$. The correct answer is Choice (C).

WARNING

Choice (D) is a trap answer. Note that the value of h is 3 and not -3. The only way that the value of h could be -3 is if the original equation were $y = -2[x - (-3)]^2 + 4$. Then you'd have to switch the sign to put the equation into the correct form for the equation of a parabola.

Fully Functioning: Graphing Functions

Coordinate geometry and functions are connected. You can actually evaluate functions on the coordinate plane. By looking at a graph of a function, you can tell something about the function and its domain and range. The GMAT may give you a graph of a function and ask you to determine whether a statement about the function is true or false. In the following sections, we give you the info you need to know to get these questions right.

When you graph a function $f(x)$ on the coordinate plane, the x value of the function (the input, or the domain, of the function) goes along the horizontal (x) axis, and the $f(x)$ value of the function goes along the vertical (y) axis. Anytime you see a coordinate pair that represents a function, for example (x, y), the x value is the domain, or input, of the function and the y value is the output, or range, of the function. (For more info on functions, see Chapter 13.)

Passing the vertical line test

A function is a distinct relationship between the x (input) value and the y or $f(x)$ (output) value. For every x value, there's a distinct y value, and only one y value, that corresponds to the x value.

The vertical line test is one way to look at a graph and tell whether it's a graph of a function. This test states that no vertical line intersects the graph of a function at more than one point.

For example, the graphs in Figure 15-8 show two straight lines that pass the vertical line test and, therefore, represent functions.

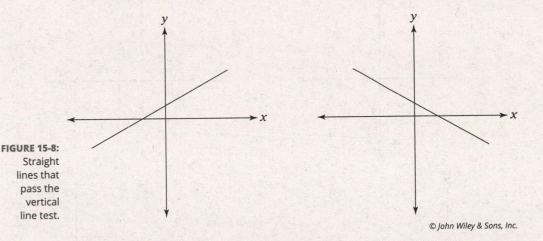

FIGURE 15-8:
Straight lines that pass the vertical line test.

© John Wiley & Sons, Inc.

The two lines in Figure 15-8 go on infinitely in both directions. Any vertical line you draw on the graph intersects the graphed line at only one point. For every x value along the line in each of these graphs, a separate and distinct y value corresponds to it. These lines pass the vertical line test, which means they represent functions.

TIP

You probably already know that most lines are functions — after all, the equation of a line is $y = mx + b$. Now you can see it for yourself graphically. The only straight line that isn't a graph of a function is a vertical line. A bazillion y values exist along a vertical line, but the line has only one x value.

Not all lines are straight. Sometimes you see graphs of curved lines. Take a look at the two graphs in Figure 15-9 and determine which of them graphs a function.

FIGURE 15-9:
Graphs of curved lines (parabolas).

© John Wiley & Sons, Inc.

The curves in Figure 15-9 are parabolas, a shape we discuss in more detail in the upcoming section about graphing domain and range. The curve in the left graph opens downward, so it goes on infinitely downward and outward. For every x value on that curve, there's a separate and distinct y value. This curve passes the vertical line test and, therefore, graphs a function. The curve in the right graph is almost like the first one, except that it opens sideways. One vertical line *can* cross the path of this curve in more than one place. Therefore, this curve isn't the graph of a function.

Questions that ask you to recognize the graph of a function appear rarely on the GMAT, but if you see one, you'll know what to do.

Which of the following graphs is *not* a graph of a function?

This question is easy when you're familiar with the vertical line test. Choice (E) has to be the correct answer because it's a curve that sort of doubles back from right to left. A vertical line can intersect that curve at more than one point. The other graphs in this question show curves, lines, or some other shape that a vertical line wouldn't pass through at more than one point. All the graphs except Choice (E) pass the test and are graphs of functions.

Feeling at home with domain and range

The GMAT expects you to be able to look at a graph of a function and have a pretty good idea of what the domain and the range of that particular function are. Figures 15-10, 15-11, and 15-12 are examples of what some of these graphs may look like.

FIGURE 15-10:
Domain and range demonstrated by a parabola.

© John Wiley & Sons, Inc.

Figure 15-10 shows you a parabola. Its vertex is the coordinate point (0, 2). The graph extends outward infinitely from side to side, so this function contains all possible values of x, which means its domain is all real numbers. The graph also extends downward infinitely, but because the y value in this function is limited on the upward side and doesn't extend above the point (0, 2), its range is $\{y : y \leq 2\}$.

In Figure 15-11, you see a straight line that goes on forever from left to right. This line also extends infinitely upward on the left side and infinitely downward on the right side. The domain and range of this linear function are also all real numbers. There's no artificial limit to the x and y values in this graph.

FIGURE 15-11: Domain and range demonstrated by a sloping straight line.

In Figure 15-12, the horizontal line extends infinitely from right to left, but it has only one value on the y-axis. Its y value is limited to -3, so the equation for this line is $y = -3$, and the range is limited to simply $\{y : y = -3\}$. Because the line goes on forever from left to right, it includes every possible x value, which means the domain of this linear function is all real numbers.

FIGURE 15-12: Domain and range demonstrated by a horizontal line.

That's really all there is to it. See how easy determining domain can be with the following question.

EXAMPLE

Which of the following answers could be the domain of the function of the figure?

(A) $\{x : x \neq 0\}$

(B) $\{x : x \neq -3\}$

(C) $\{x : x = 0\}$

(D) $\{x : x \leq 3\}$

(E) $\{x : x < 0 < x\}$

WARNING

This question asks for the *domain*, not the *range*, so don't let the fact that the upper limit of the *y* value is just shy of 3 distract you from looking for all the possible *x* values that make up the domain. You should toss out any answer choice that refers to the value 3, so get rid of Choices (B) and (D) right away.

The empty circle point (0, 3) means that you don't count that point in your answer. So Choice (C) is exactly the opposite of what you're looking for. Also, Choice (C) limits your domain to only one value: 0. Because the value of 0 is actually *excluded* from the function, Choice (C) simply can't be right. The way Choice (E) is formatted doesn't make sense at all. Set your sights on Choice (A) as the answer of the hour. The domain, or *x* value, isn't equal to 0.

IN THIS CHAPTER

» **Getting a grip on group problems**

» **Excelling with sets and Venn diagrams**

» **Arranging groups with permutations and combinations**

» **Managing means, modes, and medians**

» **Solving standard deviations**

» **Prospering on probability problems**

Chapter **16**

Manipulating Numbers: Statistics and Sets

From the time you mastered the ability to tie your shoes, you had to figure out how to work and play in groups. The GMAT tests what you know about groups of numbers, or sets. These question types are usually pretty easy, so you could probably work out the answers to most of the GMAT set questions given enough time. But, of course, you don't have all the time in the world on the GMAT, so in this chapter, we provide some shortcuts to help you answer set questions quickly.

You may find the statistics and probability questions on the GMAT a little more challenging. But don't worry: In this chapter, we go over the concepts you need to know, which include determining probability, statistical averages, and variations from the average. The statistics questions you'll encounter on the GMAT aren't particularly complex, but giving this subject your full attention will pay off.

Joining a Clique: Groups

Group problems regard populations of persons or objects and the way these populations are grouped together into categories. The questions generally ask you to either find the total of a series of groups or determine how many people or objects make up one of the subgroups.

You can find the answer to most group problems by using your counting skills, but counting is time-consuming, and you want to work smarter, not harder, to solve these questions. Solving group problems comes down to applying simple arithmetic in a handy formula and nothing else.

TIP

Here's the formula for solving group problems:

$$Group\,1 + Group\,2 - Both\,Groups + Neither\,Group = Grand\,Total$$

So if you're told that out of 110 students, 47 are enrolled in a cooking class, 56 take a welding course, and 33 take both cooking and welding, you can use the formula to find out how many students take neither cooking nor welding. Let Group 1 be the cooks and Group 2 the welders. The variable is the group that doesn't take either the cooking or welding class. Plug the known values into the formula and set up an equation to solve:

$$Group\,1 + Group\,2 - Both\,Groups + Neither\,Group = Grand\,Total$$
$$47 + 56 - 33 + x = 110$$
$$70 + x = 110$$
$$x = 40$$

Of the 110 students, 40 take neither the cooking class nor the welding class. Here's an example of how group problems may appear on the GMAT.

EXAMPLE

One-third of all U. S. taxpayers may deduct charitable contributions on their federal income tax returns. Forty percent of all taxpayers may deduct state income tax payments from their federal returns. If 55 percent of all taxpayers may not deduct either charitable contributions or state income tax, what portion of all taxpayers may claim both types of deductions?

(A) $\dfrac{3}{20}$

(B) $\dfrac{9}{50}$

(C) $\dfrac{1}{5}$

(D) $\dfrac{7}{25}$

(E) $\dfrac{17}{60}$

Use the formula to determine the correct percentage of taxpayers who may claim both deductions. Group 1 can be the $\frac{1}{3}$ who claim charitable deductions, and Group 2 can be those who deduct state income tax payments. The unknown is those who make up both groups.

TIP

Before you begin calculating, check the answer choices. Every answer appears as a fraction. Because your final answer will be in the form of a fraction, change references to percentages into fractions. Converting percentages to fractions is easy; put the value of the percentage over a denominator of 100.

So 40 percent is the same as $\frac{40}{100}$, which reduces to $\frac{2}{5}$. Fifty-five percent is the same as $\frac{55}{100}$, which equals $\frac{11}{20}$. Plug in the values and solve the formula:

$$Group\,1 + Group\,2 - Both\,Groups + Neither\,Group = Grand\,Total$$
$$\frac{1}{3} + \frac{2}{5} - x + \frac{11}{20} = 1$$

To add and subtract fractions, you have to find a common denominator for all fractions and then convert the fractions so all have the same denominator (see Chapter 12 for more about performing operations with fractions). The common denominator for this problem is 60.

$$\frac{20}{60} + \frac{24}{60} - x + \frac{33}{60} = \frac{60}{60}$$

$$\frac{77}{60} - x = \frac{60}{60}$$

$$x = \frac{17}{60}$$

The correct answer is Choice (E).

WARNING

Compute accurately. Another reason for working with fractions instead of percentages in this problem is that it helps you perform accurate calculations. You may be fooled into thinking that the one-third of the taxpayers who can claim charitable contributions equals 33 percent of tax-payers. Although $\frac{1}{3}$ is very close to 33 percent, it isn't exactly that amount. If you used 33 percent instead of one-third, you may have calculated the group as $0.33 + 0.4 + 0.55 - x = 1$ and incorrectly chosen Choice (D). If you convert $\frac{1}{3}$ to 33 percent, you're sacrificing accuracy to save time.

Setting Up Sets

Groups are related to sets. A *set* is a collection of objects, numbers, or values. The objects in a set are the *elements*, or *members*, of the set. An *empty set*, or *null set*, means that nothing is in that set. GMAT questions about sets are usually pretty simple to answer as long as you know a little terminology and how to read a Venn diagram. The following sections explore all you need to know about sets.

Set terminology

The terms *union*, *intersection*, *disjoint sets*, and *subset* describe how two or more sets relate to one another through the elements they contain.

>> **A *union* of two sets contains the set of all elements of both sets.** For example, the union of sets $A = \{0, 1, 2, 3, 4, 5, 6, 7, 8, 9\}$ and $B = \{2, 4, 6, 8, 10\}$ is $S = \{0, 1, 2, 3, 4, 5, 6, 7, 8, 9, 10\}$.

>> **An *intersection* of two sets is the set of the elements that are common to both sets.** For example, the intersection of sets $A = \{0, 1, 2, 3, 5, 6, 7, 8, 9\}$ and $B = \{2, 4, 6, 8, 10\}$ is $S = \{2, 6, 8\}$.

>> ***Disjoint sets* are two or more sets with no elements in common.** For example, set A and set B are disjoint sets if set $A = \{0, 2, 6, 8\}$ and set $B = \{1, 3, 5, 7\}$.

>> **A *subset* is a set whose elements appear in another, larger set.** If all the elements of set $B = \{2, 3, 5, 7\}$ also appear in set $A = \{0, 1, 2, 3, 5, 6, 7, 8, 9\}$, you'd say that set B is a *subset* of set A.

Getting a visual: Venn diagrams

The GMAT often illustrates the concept of sets with Venn diagrams, such as those presented in Figure 16-1. Venn diagrams provide visual representations of union, intersection, disjoint sets, and subsets. You can draw Venn diagrams to help you answer GMAT questions about sets.

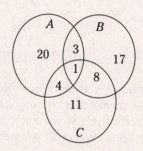

FIGURE 16-1:
Venn diagrams showing the union and intersection of sets.

© John Wiley & Sons, Inc.

GMAT quantitative reasoning questions regarding sets are usually pretty straightforward. Here's an example.

EXAMPLE

Given the Venn diagram, what are the number of elements in the intersection of sets A and B?

(A) 0

(B) 3

(C) 4

(D) 16

(E) 53

The number of elements in the intersection of sets *A* and *B* is the number of elements that are common to both sets. The portion of the diagram that represents the intersection is where the *A* circle and the *B* circle overlap. When you add the values in this intersection, you find that the number of elements that are common to both set *A* and set *B* is 4. The correct answer is Choice (C).

WARNING

If you chose Choice (B), you ignored the one element that's common to all three sets. You must include that one element, however, because it's a common element of sets *A* and *B*. Choice (E) conveys the number of elements in the union of sets *A* and *B* rather than their intersection.

Making Arrangements: Permutations and Combinations

The GMAT may test you on the arrangement of groups and sets, so you're likely to see some permutation and combination problems. When you calculate *permutations*, you figure out the number of ways the elements of a set can be arranged in specific orders. Determining *combinations* is similar to finding permutations, except that the order of the arrangements doesn't matter. In the following sections, we provide explanations and examples of each type of problem.

Positioning with permutations

Permutations problems ask you to determine how many arrangements of numbers are possible given a specific set of numbers and a particular order for the arrangements. For example, figuring out the number of possible seven-digit telephone numbers you can create is a permutation problem. And the answer is huge (10^7) because you have 10 possible values (the integers between 0 and 9) to fill each of the seven places.

REMEMBER

Order matters when you set up permutations. Even though two different phone numbers may have the same combination of numbers, such as 345-7872 and 543-7728, the numbers ring two different phones because you input them in a different order.

Consider the elements of $S = \{a, b, c\}$. You can arrange these three elements in six different ways:

a b c

a c b

b a c

b c a

c a b

c b a

Even though each group contains the same elements, these groupings are completely different permutations because they convey different orderings of the three elements. Writing out the number of possible orderings of a set of three letters isn't too difficult, but what if you had to figure out the number of orderings for a set of 11 numbers? That problem would take more time than anyone would care to spend and certainly more time than you have to finish the GMAT. Luckily, you can rely on factorials to figure out permutations.

TIP

A *factorial* is the product of all natural numbers in the set of numbers from 1 through a particular number (n), which is the number of the factorial. The number of permutations of n objects is expressed as $n!$. The ! symbol indicates a *factorial*, and you read the expression as "n factorial." So 5! is a way of expressing $5 \times 4 \times 3 \times 2 \times 1$.

Instead of writing the possible permutations for the set of three letters $\{a, b, c\}$, use a factorial. Three different elements (the letters in the set) arranged in as many different orders as possible look like this: 3!, which is equal to $3 \times 2 \times 1$, which is equal to 6. So 3! = 6. The three elements have six permutations.

Suppose you have more than three elements. Maybe a photographer wants to know how many different ways she can arrange five people in a single row for a wedding photo. The number of possible arrangements of the five-person wedding party is 5! or $5! = 5 \times 4 \times 3 \times 2 \times 1 = 120$.

The factorial of 0 is written as 0!, which always equals 1.

As you can see, more possible arrangements exist as the number of objects in the arrangement increases. That's the information you need to know to answer basic permutation questions, such as the following one. Give it a shot!

Alice received a bracelet with four distinct removable charms. How many different ways can she arrange the four charms on her new bracelet?

(A) 4

(B) 8

(C) 24

(D) 100

(E) 40,320

Because the bracelet has four charms, the number of arrangements or permutations is 4!: $4 \times 3 \times 2 \times 1$.

Then just multiply the numbers to get the number of possible arrangements (the order you multiply them in doesn't matter): $4 \times 3 = 12$ and $12 \times 2 = 24$. Because $24 \times 1 = 24$, the correct answer is Choice (C).

You can eliminate Choices (A) and (B) because they're too small. You know that more than four arrangements must exist, because you have four charms. Choice (B) is 4×2, which isn't much better. In permutations, you know the number gets pretty large in a hurry, but not as large as Choice (E), which is 8!.

Permutations get a little more challenging when you have a fixed number of objects, n, to fill a limited number of places, r, and you care about the order the objects are arranged in.

For example, consider the predicament of the big-league baseball coach of a 20-member baseball team who needs to determine the number of different batting orders that these 20 ball players can fill in a 9-slot batting lineup. The coach could work this permutation out by writing all the factors from 20 back 9 places (because 20 players can fill only 9 slots in the batting order), like this:

$$20 \times 19 \times 18 \times 17 \times 16 \times 15 \times 14 \times 13 \times 12 = x$$

But this time-consuming process isn't practical in the middle of a game. Luckily, the coach can rely on a permutation formula.

The number of permutations of n things taken r at a time is stated as $_nP_r$. (To help you remember the formula, think of a certain public radio station that has these call letters.) The permutation formula for n objects taken r at a time looks like this:

$$_nP_r = \frac{n!}{(n-r)!}$$

Apply the formula to figure out the possible number of batting orders:

$$_nP_r = \frac{n!}{(n-r)!}$$

$$_nP_r = \frac{20!}{(20-9)!}$$

$$_nP_r = \frac{20!}{11!}$$

The GMAT doesn't allow you to use calculators, so it won't expect you to calculate the permutation beyond this point. Here's an example of how complex permutations may appear on the GMAT.

EXAMPLE

A lawn care company has five employees that it schedules on a given day to work the lawns of any ten possible homes. How many different ways can the company assign the five employees to the ten homes if each employee provides lawn care service for just one home?

(A) 50

(B) $\frac{2!}{1!}$

(C) 120

(D) $\frac{10!}{5!}$

(E) $10!$

This question may seem counterintuitive to the formula, which calculates *n* number of things taken *r* at a time to get the number of permutations. This problem appears to be taking a smaller number of things, *r* (the number of employees), and finding out how many times they can be spread around a greater number of places. That's what makes this question a little tricky.

TIP

This problem may look backward, but it really follows the same formula. Rather than thinking of how to spread five workers over ten houses, think of how many ways you can arrange the ten houses over the more limited number of workers and apply the formula:

$$_nP_r = \frac{n!}{(n-r)!}$$

$$_nP_r = \frac{10!}{(10-5)!}$$

$$_nP_r = \frac{10!}{5!}$$

The correct answer is Choice (D). With a calculator, you can figure out that 30,240 ways exist to assign employees. If you chose Choice (A), you simply multiplied the number of workers times the number of houses. But that's not the correct calculation. Choice (C) is what you get if you calculated 5!, which isn't the complete answer. Likewise, Choice (E) is incomplete.

WARNING

Don't let Choice (B) trip you up. You can't simplify factorials like you can common fractions: $\frac{10!}{5!} \neq \frac{2!}{1!}$

If this problem was difficult for you, take heart: You won't see too many of these kinds of questions on the GMAT.

Coming together: Combinations

Combinations are a lot like permutations, only easier. You form a *combination* by extracting a certain number of persons or things from a larger total sample of persons and things. Unlike permutations, the order doesn't matter with combinations, so combinations result in fewer possibilities than permutations.

A combination problem may ask you to find how many different teams, committees, or other types of groups can be formed from a set number of persons. For example, if you're asked to select as many teams as you can from a set number of people and the order of the team members doesn't matter, you're finding the total number of combinations of different teams.

Consider how many three-member committees you can form with Tom, Dick, and Harry. Tom, Dick, and Harry don't line up in any particular order while they're convening, so the way you list them doesn't matter. A committee composed of Tom, Dick, and Harry is the same as a committee composed of Tom, Harry, and Dick or one composed of Dick, Tom, and Harry. So only one possible combination exists of this three-member committee. If Tom, Dick, and Harry were asked to participate in a lineup, you'd have a permutation and six different possible arrangements, but because order doesn't matter when you're forming the committee, you have only one possible combination.

You can apply a formula to figure out the number of combinations. The formula is the number of ways to choose r objects from a group of n objects when the order of the objects doesn't matter, and it looks like this:

$$_nC_r = \frac{n!}{r!(n-r)!}$$

TIP

You can see right away that this formula is different from the one for permutations. Because you have a larger number in the denominator than you'd have with a permutation, the final number will be smaller.

Suppose a pollster randomly approaches three different people from a group of five mall walkers. To figure out how many possible combinations of three different people the pollster can annoy, use the combination formula:

$$_nC_r = \frac{n!}{r!(n-r)!}$$
$$_nC_r = \frac{5!}{3!(5-3)!}$$

The factorial of 5! is 120 ($5 \times 4 \times 3 \times 2 \times 1$), and the factorial of 3! is 6 ($3 \times 2 \times 1$). So here's the resulting equation:

$$_nC_r = \frac{120}{6(5-3)!}$$

Subtract the values in the parentheses to get 2!. The value of 2! is 2 (because $2 \times 1 = 2$):

$$_nC_r = \frac{120}{6(5-3)!}$$
$$_nC_r = \frac{120}{6(2 \times 1)}$$
$$_nC_r = \frac{120}{12}$$
$$_nC_r = 10$$

Therefore, from the five mall walkers, the pollster can create ten different combinations of three people to poll.

Because you can't use a calculator, GMAT combination problems won't get too complex. The test-makers won't make you perform overly complex calculations on your low-tech noteboard.

Here's an example of what you can expect from GMAT combination problems.

Some fourth-graders are choosing foursquare teams at recess. What is the total possible number of combinations of four-person teams that can be chosen from a group of six children?

EXAMPLE

(A) 6

(B) 15

(C) 120

(D) 360

(E) 98,280

Apply the formula for combinations and see what happens:

$$_nC_r = \frac{n!}{r!(n-r)!}$$

$$_nC_r = \frac{6!}{4!(6-4)!}$$

$$_nC_r = \frac{6!}{(4!)(2)!}$$

$$_nC_r = \frac{6 \times 5 \times 4 \times 3 \times 2 \times 1}{(4 \times 3 \times 2 \times 1)(2 \times 1)}$$

$$_nC_r = \frac{6 \times 5}{2 \times 1}$$

$$_nC_r = \frac{30}{2}$$

$$_nC_r = 15$$

After you perform the calculations, you find that the correct answer is Choice (B).

If you went for Choice (D), you calculated a permutation instead of a combination.

WARNING

Meeting in the Middle: Mean, Median, and Mode

At least a few GMAT math problems will require you to evaluate sets of numbers. To evaluate data correctly, you need to know the *central tendency* of numbers and the dispersion of their values. A measurement of central tendency is a value that's typical, or representative, of a group of numbers or other information. Common tools for describing a central tendency include average (arithmetic mean), median, mode, and weighted mean.

TIP

» *Average* **(also referred to as *arithmetic mean*) is the most commonly tested tendency value.** To find the average (arithmetic mean) of a set of numbers, add the numbers and divide by the quantity of numbers in the group:

$$Average = \frac{Sum\ of\ All\ Numbers\ in\ the\ Set}{Number\ of\ Members\ in\ the\ Set}$$

You can plug known values into this formula to solve for the other values. For example, if the GMAT gives you the average and the sum of a group of numbers, you can use the formula to figure out how many numbers are in the set.

» **The *median* is the middle value among a list of several values or numbers.** To find the median, put the values or numbers in order, usually from low to high, and choose the value that falls exactly in the middle of the other values. If you have an odd number of values, just select the middle value. If you have an even number of values, find the two middle values and average them. The outcome is the median.

>> **The *mode* is the value that occurs most frequently in a set of values.** Questions about mode may contain words like *frequency* or ask you how often a value occurs. For example, you may be asked what income occurs most frequently in a given population or sample. If more people in the population or sample have an income of $30,000 than any other income amount, the mode is $30,000.

>> **You determine a *weighted mean* when some values in a set contribute more to the final average than others.** Multiply each individual value by the number of times it occurs in a set of numbers. Then, you add these products together and divide the sum by the total number of times all the values occur.

For example, suppose you're asked to calculate Becky's overall grade point average from Table 16-1, which charts the grades in all her classes and the number of credits for each.

TABLE 16-1 **The Weighted Mean of Grade Point Averages**

Class	Number of Credits	Grade	Total Grade Points
Statistics	5	3.8	19
English	5	1.9	9.5
Speech	4	2.3	9.2
Bowling	1	4.0	4
Total	15	2.78 GPA	41.7

First, you multiply the individual values (the grades) by the number of times they each occur (the credits) to get total grade points for each class. Then, you add the total grade points for all classes (41.7) and divide by the total number of times they all occur (which is the number of total credits, 15): $\frac{41.7}{15} = 2.78$ GPA.

You'll likely see a bunch of questions on the GMAT that ask you to figure out the central tendency of a set of values. Here's an example of one that asks for mean.

EXAMPLE

George tried to compute the average (arithmetic mean) of his 8 statistics test scores. He mistakenly divided the correct sum of all his test scores by 7 and calculated his average to be 96. What was George's actual average test score?

(A) 80

(B) 84

(C) 96

(D) 100

(E) 108

The question asks you for George's average score on eight tests and gives the average of those eight scores when they're divided by 7. You know that his average must be less than 96 because you're dividing by a larger number, so you can automatically eliminate Choices (C), (D), and (E). Just use the formula for averages to determine George's average score for eight tests.

1. **Figure out the sum of all George's test scores, using what you know from his incorrect calculation.**

$$96 = \frac{x}{7}$$
$$672 = x$$

2. **Find George's actual average based on the sum of all his scores.**

$$A = \frac{672}{8}$$
$$A = 84$$

The correct answer is Choice (B).

Straying from Home: Range and Standard Deviation

Besides knowing the main concepts of central tendency, you also need to know about *variation* or *dispersion* of values in statistics. The two types of dispersion you'll deal with on the GMAT are *range* and *standard deviation*, which we explore in the following sections. Dispersion tells you how spread out the values are from the center. If dispersion is small, the values are clustered around the mean. But a wide dispersion of values tells you that the mean average isn't a reliable representative of all the values.

Scouting out the range

The easiest measure of dispersion to calculate is the *range.* You can say that the range is the difference between the highest and lowest values in the set of data. The range of values in statistics can come from either a population or a sample. The *population* is the set of all objects or things, that is, the total amount of all data considered. A *sample* is just a part of the population.

Here's an example of how to find the range of a set of values: If the highest test score in a math class was 94 percent and the lowest was 59 percent, you'd subtract the low from the high to get the score range (94 − 59 = 35). The range of test scores is 35. Simple as that!

Watching out for wanderers: Standard deviation

Another form of dispersion you need to know for the GMAT is *standard deviation*. The standard deviation expresses variation by measuring how spread out the distribution is from the mean. Although the range (see preceding section) can give you an idea of the total spread, standard deviation is a more reliable indicator of dispersion because it considers all the data, not just the two on each end. Standard deviation is the most widely used figure for expressing how much the data is dispersed from the mean.

For example, suppose you get a grade of 75 on a test where the mean grade is 70 and the vast majority of all the other grades fall between 60 and 80. Your score is comparatively better in this situation than if you get a 75 on the same test, where the mean grade is still 70, but most of the grades fall between 45 and 95. In the first situation, the grades are more tightly clustered around the central tendency. A standard deviation in this case is a small number. Your grade is higher compared to all the other test-takers' grades in the first group than your grade would be in the second scenario. In the second scenario, the standard deviation is a bigger number, and a grade of 75 isn't as good relative to the others.

You've probably had a statistics class by this time in your career, and you probably had to calculate standard deviation in that class. The GMAT won't ask you to actually calculate standard deviation, but it will expect you to know how to use standard deviation.

TIP

It's a good idea to be able to recognize that a *normal distribution* creates a symmetrical bell curve such as the one in Figure 16-2. The standard deviation in a normal distribution is a constant. The average (arithmetic mean) appears as an *x* with a line over it and appears in the exact middle of all the values. If you stray 1 standard deviation in either direction from the mean, you'll have netted 68 percent of all the values. Going another standard deviation away from the center, you pick up another 27 percent of all values, giving you about 95 percent of all values. Finally, when you go ±3 standard deviations from the mean, you now have about 99.7 percent of all the values in your population or sample.

FIGURE 16-2: Distribution of the standard deviation from the mean.

© John Wiley & Sons, Inc.

If the curve in Figure 16-2 showed a group of test scores, it would mean that more than a majority of test-takers scored within 1 standard deviation of the mean (68 percent is more than 51 percent). The vast majority scored within 2 standard deviations, and virtually everyone scored within 3 standard deviations. Say that the mean test score is 80, and one standard deviation may be 10 points on either side. This means that 68 percent of the students scored between 70 and 90. If the second standard deviation was another 5 test points in either direction, you could say that 95 percent of the students scored between 65 and 95 on the test. Finally, you could say that the third standard deviation is another 4 points away from the mean, which means that 99.7 percent of the students scored between 61 and 99.

TIP

A small value for the standard deviation means that the values of the group are more tightly clustered around the mean. A greater standard deviation means that the numbers are more scattered away from the mean. The greater the standard deviation for a group of values, the easier deviating from the center is. The smaller the standard deviation, the harder it is to deviate from the center.

Here's what a standard deviation question on the GMAT may look like.

(I) {55, 56, 57, 58, 59}

(II) {41, 57, 57, 57, 73}

(III) {57, 57, 57, 57, 57}

Which of the following lists Sets I, II, and III in order from least standard deviation to greatest standard deviation?

(A) I, II, III

(B) I, III, II

(C) II, III, I

(D) III, I, II

(E) III, II, I

The set with the least standard deviation is the one that has the least amount of difference from the highest to the lowest values. The values in Set III are all the same, so Set III has the least standard deviation and should be listed first. Eliminate Choices (A), (B), and (C) because they don't list Set III first.

Set II (41 and 73) has a greater difference between the high and low values than Set I (55 and 59). So the set with the greatest standard deviation is Set II, which means it should be listed last. Choice (D) lists the sets in their proper order from least standard deviation to greatest standard deviation, so it's the correct answer.

Predicting the Future: Probability

Probability is the measure of how likely a particular event will occur, but figuring probability is a bit more scientific than telling fortunes and reading tarot cards. You express probability as a percentage, fraction, or decimal. You'd say that the probability of an event's occurring falls between 0 percent and 100 percent or between 0 and 1. If the probability of an event's occurrence is 0, or 0 percent, it's impossible for the event to occur. If the probability is 1, or 100 percent, the event is certain to occur. Few things in life are certain, other than death and taxes. For an event to be impossible is also rare. Therefore, the probability of the occurrence of an event usually falls somewhere between 0 and 1, or 0 and 100 percent.

Probability questions may ask you to determine the probability of one event or multiple events. We show you how to determine the probability for each type of question in the following sections.

Finding the probability of one event

Probability deals with *outcomes* and *events*. For situations where all possible outcomes are equally likely, the probability (P) that an event (E) occurs, represented by $P(E)$, is defined as

$$P(E) = \frac{\text{Number of Outcomes Involving Occurrences of } E}{\text{Total Possible Number of Outcomes}}$$

Because you express probability as a fraction, it can never be less than 0 or greater than 1. Getting both heads and tails with one flip of a coin is impossible, so the probability of that particular event occurring is 0. If you used a coin with heads on both sides, the probability of getting heads on one flip would be 1, because the number of possible outcomes is exactly the same as the number of outcomes that will occur.

Finding the probability of many events

You can find the probability of multiple events by following several rules. Table 16-2 lists and describes each rule, shows the corresponding formula, and provides an example of when you'd use it.

TABLE 16-2 **Finding the Probability of the Occurrence of Multiple Events**

Rule	Circumstance	Formula	Example
Special Rule of Addition	The probability of the occurrence of either of two possible events that are mutually exclusive	$P(A \text{ or } B) = P(A) + P(B)$	The probability of rolling a 5 or 6 on one roll of one die
General Rule of Addition	The probability of the occurrence of either of two possible events that can happen together	$P(A \text{ or } B) = P(A) + P(B) - P(A \text{ and } B)$	The probability of drawing a playing card that displays a club or a queen
Special Rule of Multiplication	The probability of the occurrence of two events at the same time when the two events are independent of each other	$P(A \text{ and } B) = P(A) \times P(B)$	The probability of rolling a 5 and a 6 on one roll of two dice.
General Rule of Multiplication	The probability of the occurrence of two events when the occurrence of the first event affects the outcome of the second event	$P(A \text{ and } B) = P(A) \times P(B/A)$	The probability of first drawing the queen of clubs from a pack of 52 cards, keeping the queen of clubs out of the pack, and then drawing the jack of diamonds on the next try

Applying the special rule of addition

You use the special rule of addition to figure out the probability of rolling a die and coming up with either a 1 or a 2. You can't get both on one roll, so the events are mutually exclusive. Therefore, the probability of rolling a 1 or a 2 in one roll is $P(A) + P(B)$:

$$P(A \text{ or } B) = \frac{1}{6} + \frac{1}{6}$$

$$P(A \text{ or } B) = \frac{2}{6}$$

$$P(A \text{ or } B) = \frac{1}{3}$$

Applying the general rule of addition

You use the general rule of addition to figure probability in the case of choosing sodas from a cooler. Imagine that three types of sodas are in a cooler. Colas are numbered consecutively 1 through 5, orange sodas are numbered 1 through 7, and grape sodas are numbered 1 through 8. Let event *A* stand for when a cola is taken out of the cooler and event *B* represent when a can with a number 2 is taken out. You want to know the probability of picking out *either* a cola *or* a can with the number 2 on it but *not* specifically a cola with the number 2 on it. Five of the 20 cans are colas, three display the number 2, and only one can is a cola with the number 2. So $P(A)$ is $\frac{5}{20}$, $P(B)$ is $\frac{3}{20}$, and $P(A \text{ and } B)$ is $\frac{1}{20}$. Plug the values in to the formula and solve:

$$P(A \text{ or } B) = P(A) + P(B) - P(A \text{ and } B)$$

$$P(A \text{ or } B) = \frac{5}{20} + \frac{3}{20} - \frac{1}{20}$$

$$P(A \text{ or } B) = \frac{7}{20}$$

You can also express this probability as 0.35 or as 35 percent.

Applying the special rule of multiplication

The probability of multiple events occurring together is the product of the probabilities of the events occurring individually. For example, if you're rolling two dice at the same time, here's how you find the probability of rolling a 1 on one die and a 2 on the other:

$$P(A \text{ and } B) = \frac{1}{6} \times \frac{1}{6}$$

$$P(A \text{ and } B) = \frac{1}{36}$$

Applying the general rule of multiplication

Suppose the outcome of the second situation depends on the outcome of the first event. You then invoke the general rule of multiplication. The term $P(B|A)$ is a conditional probability, where the likelihood of the second event depends on the fact that A has already occurred. For example, to find the odds of drawing the ace of spades from a deck of 52 cards on one try and then drawing the king of spades on the second try — with the ace out of the deck — apply the formula, like this: $P(A \text{ and } B) = P(A) \times P(B / A)$.

WARNING

The line between the B and A stands for "B given A"; it doesn't mean divide!

$$P(A \text{ and } B) = P(A) \times P(B / A)$$

$$P(A \text{ and } B) = \frac{1}{52} \times \frac{1}{51}$$

$$P(A \text{ and } B) = \frac{1}{2,652}$$

We wouldn't bet against the house on that outcome! The probability of drawing the king of spades on the second draw is slightly better than the probability of drawing the ace on the first draw, because you've already removed one card from the deck on the first draw. Here's a sample of how the GMAT may test your knowledge of probability rules.

EXAMPLE

A candy machine contains gumballs: three blue, two red, seven yellow, and one purple. The machine distributes one gumball for each dime. A child has exactly two dimes with which she will purchase two gumballs. What is the chance that the child will get two red gumballs?

(A) $\frac{2}{169}$

(B) $\frac{1}{13}$

(C) $\frac{2}{13}$

(D) $\frac{1}{156}$

(E) $\frac{1}{78}$

TIP

You need to treat getting the two red gumballs as two events. The occurrence of the first event affects the probability of the second because after the child extracts the first red gumball, the machine has one fewer gumball. So you apply the general rule of multiplication.

The chance of getting a red gumball with the first dime is 2 (the number of red gumballs) divided by 13 (the total number of gumballs in the machine), or $\frac{2}{13}$. If the child tries to get the second gumball, the first red gumball is already gone, which leaves only 1 red gumball and 12 total gumballs in the machine, so the chance of getting the second red gumball is $\frac{1}{12}$. The probability of both events happening is the product of the probability of the occurrence of each event:

$$P(A \, and \, B) = P(A) \times P(B \, / \, A)$$
$$P(A \, and \, B) = \frac{2}{13} \times \frac{1}{12}$$
$$P(A \, and \, B) = \frac{2}{156}$$
$$P(A \, and \, B) = \frac{1}{78}$$

Choice (E) is the correct answer. Choice (A) is $\frac{2}{13} \times \frac{1}{13}$, which would look right if you didn't subtract the withdrawn red gumball from the total number on the second draw. Choice (B) is the chance of drawing one red gumball from a machine with 13 gumballs and only 1 red gumball. In this problem, $\frac{1}{13}$ is also the chance of drawing the purple gumball. If you picked Choice (C), you found the chance of drawing the first red gumball.

Chapter 17

It's All in the Presentation: GMAT Quantitative Question Types

Y ou need more than just math skills to excel on the quantitative section; you also need to know how to approach the questions. This chapter tells you what to expect from the math sections and how to work through the unique ways the GMAT presents the questions.

REMEMBER

The kinds of math questions that appear on the GMAT test your ability to reason and think on your feet as you make use of the information you're given.

Two basic types of questions are intermingled throughout the quantitative section of the GMAT: data-sufficiency questions and problem-solving questions. Both types of questions require similar skills, but they demand different approaches. In this chapter, we show you how to ace both kinds of questions.

Enough's Enough: Data-Sufficiency Questions

The quantitative section has 37 questions, and about half of them are presented in a unique form called data sufficiency. These questions aren't particularly hard if you understand how to approach them before you walk into the testing center. However, if you don't know much about these questions, getting confused and making careless mistakes are easy. Fortunately, you've decided to read this book to get a sneak peek. Your knowledge should be more than sufficient for data sufficiency!

You don't need the solution to find the answer

Unlike the traditional math problems you've seen throughout your life, data-sufficiency questions don't actually require you to solve the problem. Instead, you have to evaluate two statements and determine which of those statements provides *sufficient* information for you to answer the question.

For each data-sufficiency problem, you have a question and two statements, labeled (1) and (2). Your job is to decide whether each of the statements gives you enough information to answer the question with general math skills and everyday facts (such as the number of days in a month and the meaning of *clockwise*). If you need a refresher in the math concepts tested on the GMAT, read Chapters 12, 13, 14, 15, and 16.

WARNING

Don't make foolish assumptions when you answer data-sufficiency questions. Keep in mind that your job is to determine whether the information given is sufficient, not to try to make up for the lack of data! You're used to having to come up with an answer to every math problem, so if the statements lack just a little information, you may be tempted to stretch the data to reach a solution. Don't give in to temptation. For example, if a data-sufficiency question provides a four-sided figure, don't assume that it's a square unless the data tells you it's a square — even if knowing that the figure is a square would allow you to solve the problem. Deal only with the information expressly as it's stated without making unwarranted assumptions.

The answer choices for data-sufficiency questions are the same for each question:

(A) Statement (1) *alone* is sufficient, but Statement (2) *alone* is *not* sufficient to answer the question asked.

(B) Statement (2) *alone* is sufficient, but Statement (1) *alone* is *not* sufficient to answer the question asked.

(C) *Both* Statements (1) and (2) *together* are sufficient to answer the question asked, but *neither* statement *alone* is sufficient.

(D) *Each* statement *alone* is sufficient to answer the question asked.

(E) Statements (1) and (2) *together* are *not* sufficient to answer the question asked, and additional data are needed.

The computer doesn't actually designate the answer choices with the letters A through E, but the choices appear in this order (you choose the correct one with your mouse or keyboard), and we refer to them as A, B, C, D, and E to make the discussion simpler.

It's possible that just one of the statements gives enough data to answer the question, that the two statements taken together solve the problem, that both statements alone provide sufficient data, or that neither statement solves the problem, even with the information provided by the other one. That's a lot of information to examine and apply in two minutes! Don't worry. You can eliminate brain freeze by following a step-by-step approach to these questions.

Steps to approaching data-sufficiency problems

Take a methodical approach to answering data-sufficiency questions, and follow this series of steps:

1. Evaluate the question to make sure you know exactly what you're supposed to solve, and, if you can, decide what kind of information you need to solve the problem.

2. **Examine one of the statements and determine whether the data in that one statement is enough to answer the question.**

Start with the first statement or whichever one seems easier to evaluate. Record your conclusion on the noteboard.

3. **Examine the other statement and determine whether it has enough information to answer the question.**

Record your conclusion on the noteboard.

4. **Evaluate what you've written on your noteboard.**

- If you recorded *yes* for both statements, pick the fourth answer, which we designate as Choice (D).

- If you recorded *yes* for (1) and *no* for (2), select the first answer, Choice (A) in this book.

- If you recorded *no* for (1) and *yes* for (2), choose the second answer, Choice (B) for our purposes.

- If you've written *no* for both statements, go on to the next step.

5. **Examine the statements together to determine whether the data given in both is enough information to answer the question.**

- If the answer is *yes,* select the third answer, our Choice (C).

- If the answer is *no,* choose the last answer, the one we've designated as Choice (E).

You can boil this method down to a nice, neat chart, like the one shown in Figure 17-1.

Data Sufficiency Answer Elimination Chart

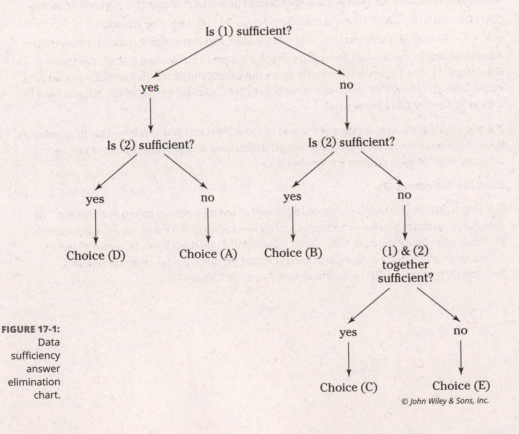

FIGURE 17-1:
Data sufficiency answer elimination chart.

© *John Wiley & Sons, Inc.*

Don't think *too* hard about whether an answer provides sufficient information to solve a problem. Data-sufficiency questions aren't necessarily designed to trick you. For example, you deal only with real numbers in these questions, and if a line looks straight, it is.

TIP

A statement is sufficient to answer the question if it provides only one possible answer for the question. If the information in a statement allows for two or more answers, the statement isn't sufficient.

EXAMPLE

David and Karena were among a group of runners who were raising money for a local charity. If David and Karena together raised $1,000 in the charity race, how much of the money did Karena raise?

1. David raised $\frac{4}{5}$ as much money as Karena did.

2. David raised 5 percent of the total money raised at the event.

Use the steps and/or the chart in Figure 17-1 to solve the problem:

1. Know what you have to solve for.

The question asks you to figure out how much money Karena raised for charity. The question gives you the total money raised by David and Karena together ($D + K = \$1,000$) but doesn't specify how much David raised. Check out the statements to see whether either or both of them let you know how much David came up with. If you have David's figure, you only need to subtract it from $1,000 to get Karena's figure.

2. Consider Statement (1) to determine whether it lets you solve for Karena's total.

You determined that you needed data that would allow you to separate the money raised by Karena from that raised by David. Knowing that David raised $\frac{4}{5}$ as much money as Karena allows you to set up a formula to solve for Karena's portion. Let K stand for Karena's contribution and substitute $\frac{4}{5}K$ for D in the equation $D + K = \$1,000$. Your new equation is $\frac{4}{5}K + K = \$1,000$. This equation has only one variable, and that variable stands for how much Karena raised. Therefore, you know you can solve the problem by using just the data from Statement (1). You don't need to actually figure out what K stands for. Just write $1 = $ *yes* on your noteboard. You know that the correct answer is either Choice (A) or Choice (D), but you have to look at Statement (2) to know which.

TIP

If a question like this one appears at the end of the section and you're pressed for time, you can guess between Choices (A) and (D), knowing that you have a 50 percent chance of answering correctly without even reading Statement (2).

3. Examine Statement (2).

Statement (2) tells you that David raised 5 percent of the total money raised at the event. The question doesn't tell you how much total money was raised at the event, so you can't use this information to figure out how much David raised. And if you don't know how much David raised, you can't figure out how much Karena raised. Jot down $2 = $ *no* on the noteboard. Because (1) is a *yes* and (2) is a *no,* the answer has to be Choice (A).

TIP

If you've read both statements and determined that either Statement (1) or Statement (2) is sufficient alone, two things are true:

» You're done with the question and can move on the next one.

» The answer can't be Choice (C) or Choice (E).

Both Choices (C) and (E) apply to the statements when they're considered together. You don't need to consider the statements together if either statement is sufficient alone. Your only possible choices if *either* statement is sufficient are Choice (A) if only Statement (1) is sufficient, Choice (B) if only Statement (2) is sufficient, and Choice (D) if each statement alone is sufficient.

WARNING

Don't evaluate whether both statements together answer the problem unless you've determined that neither is sufficient alone. The only time you consider (1) and (2) together is when you've answered *no* to both statements. For instance, say the example question replaced Statement (1) with this data: "The event raised a total of $10,000." Statement (1) wouldn't be enough to answer the question. But because Statement (2) tells you that David raised 5 percent of the total event money, you can answer the question using the data from both statements. Statement (1) provides the total amount, and Statement (2) allows you to figure out how much David raised based on that amount. If you subtract that amount from $1,000, you'll have Karena's total.

Choice (E) would be correct if Statement (1) said, "The event raised more money this year than last year." In this case, neither statement, nor the two together, could answer the question.

Don't waste time trying to come up with the actual numeric answer if you don't have to. When you look at a question like the example, you may be tempted to solve the equation and figure out how much Karena raised. Don't give in! Finding the number just wastes precious time, and no one gives you extra credit for solving the problem! Instead, use your valuable time to solve other questions in the quantitative section.

Taking a Look at Data-Sufficiency Practice Problems

The best way to master the steps for solving data-sufficiency questions is to practice on sample problems. Use the set of questions in this section to hone your skills. Make sure you have a piece of scratch paper nearby to simulate the noteboard. You can check your answers by reading through the explanations that follow the questions.

Practice questions

The GMAT gives you about two minutes to answer each quantitative question. So set your timer for ten minutes to get a feel for the time limit you'll be facing on the actual test. Follow the chart in Figure 17-1 to work your way through the answer choices. If you need to refresh your memory of the answer choices before you begin, see the earlier section "You don't need the solution to find the answer."

1. What's the value of the two-digit integer x?

   1. The sum of the two digits is 5.

   2. x is divisible by 5.

  (A) Statement (1) *alone* is sufficient, but Statement (2) *alone* is *not* sufficient to answer the question asked.

  (B) Statement (2) *alone* is sufficient, but Statement (1) *alone* is *not* sufficient to answer the question asked.

  (C) *Both* Statements (1) and (2) *together* are sufficient to answer the question asked, but *neither* statement *alone* is sufficient.

  (D) *Each* statement *alone* is sufficient to answer the question asked.

  (E) Statements (1) and (2) *together* are *not* sufficient to answer the question asked, and additional data are needed.

2. Office Solutions employs both male and female workers who work either full time or part time. What percentage of its employees work part time?

   1. Twenty percent of the female employees at Office Solutions work part time.

   2. Thirty percent of the workforce at Office Solutions is male.

  (A) Statement (1) *alone* is sufficient, but Statement (2) *alone* is *not* sufficient to answer the question asked.

  (B) Statement (2) *alone* is sufficient, but Statement (1) *alone* is *not* sufficient to answer the question asked.

  (C) *Both* Statements (1) and (2) *together* are sufficient to answer the question asked, but *neither* statement *alone* is sufficient.

  (D) *Each* statement *alone* is sufficient to answer the question asked.

  (E) Statements (1) and (2) *together* are *not* sufficient to answer the question asked, and additional data are needed.

3. What is the value of $2(x + y)$ in the preceding figure?

   1. $y = 120$

   2. $BC \parallel AD$

  (A) Statement (1) *alone* is sufficient, but Statement (2) *alone* is *not* sufficient to answer the question asked.

  (B) Statement (2) *alone* is sufficient, but Statement (1) *alone* is *not* sufficient to answer the question asked.

  (C) *Both* Statements (1) and (2) *together* are sufficient to answer the question asked, but *neither* statement *alone* is sufficient.

  (D) *Each* statement *alone* is sufficient to answer the question asked.

  (E) Statements (1) and (2) *together* are *not* sufficient to answer the question asked, and additional data are needed.

4. Joe uses three different modes of transportation to travel a total of 225 kilometers to visit his aunt. How many kilometers does Joe travel by bus?

   1. Joe rides his bike 5 kilometers to the bus station where he boards the bus to take him to the train station. He then takes the train 10 times the distance he has traveled by bus.

   2. The distance Joe travels by bike is $\frac{1}{4}$ the distance he travels by bus, and his train ride is 40 times longer than his bike ride.

   (A) Statement (1) *alone* is sufficient, but Statement (2) *alone* is *not* sufficient to answer the question asked.

   (B) Statement (2) *alone* is sufficient, but Statement (1) *alone* is *not* sufficient to answer the question asked.

   (C) *Both* Statements (1) and (2) *together* are sufficient to answer the question asked, but *neither* statement *alone* is sufficient.

   (D) *Each* statement *alone* is sufficient to answer the question asked.

   (E) Statements (1) and (2) *together* are *not* sufficient to answer the question asked, and additional data are needed.

5. If x and y are real numbers and $(a)^{2x}(a)^{2y} = 81$, what is the value of $x + y$?

   1. $a = 3$
   2. $x = y$

   (A) Statement (1) *alone* is sufficient, but Statement (2) *alone* is *not* sufficient to answer the question asked.

   (B) Statement (2) *alone* is sufficient, but Statement (1) *alone* is *not* sufficient to answer the question asked.

   (C) *Both* Statements (1) and (2) *together* are sufficient to answer the question asked, but *neither* statement *alone* is sufficient.

   (D) *Each* statement *alone* is sufficient to answer the question asked.

   (E) Statements (1) and (2) *together* are *not* sufficient to answer the question asked, and additional data are needed.

Answer explanations

The following answer explanations provide not only the correct answer for the data-sufficiency practice questions in the preceding section but also additional insight into how to approach this unique question type. So be sure to read all the info provided here.

1. **C.** Apply the steps:

   1. **Find out what to solve for.**

      This short question gives you little information about x; all you know is that it's a two-digit integer.

   2. **Examine Statement (1).**

      Statement (1) tells you that the sum of the digits is 5. Several two-digit numbers are composed of digits that when added together equal 5: 14, 23, 32, 41, and 50. Statement (1) narrows the field of two-digit numbers down to just these five possibilities, but that's not good enough. Because you don't have a single answer, Statement (1) isn't sufficient. Write down 1 = *no*. You've just eliminated Choices (A) and (D).

3. **Evaluate Statement (2).**

Statement (2) says that x is divisible by 5. You probably realize immediately that every two-digit number ending in 0 or 5 is divisible by 5, so the possibilities are 10, 15, 20, 25, and so on. Clearly, Statement (2) isn't sufficient, because $\frac{1}{5}$ of all two-digit numbers are divisible by 5. Write down 2 = *no*. You've just eliminated Choice (B).

4. **Check out what you've written.**

You have double *nos,* so you have to consider both statements together.

5. **Evaluate the two statements together.**

Statement (1) narrows the two-digit numbers down to five possibilities: 14, 23, 32, 41, and 50. Statement (2) narrows the list to those numbers that are divisible by 5. The only possibility from Statement (1) that ends in 0 or 5 is 50. Because 50 is divisible by 5 and the digits add up to 5, it answers the question. The two statements together provide enough information to answer the question. *Correct answer:* Choice (C).

TIP

You'll notice that, for this question, you had to find the actual answer to the question to determine whether the information was sufficient. Sometimes doing so is the quickest way to determine whether statements provide enough data. An equation may exist that you could've set up (and not solved) that would have told you that you had sufficient information. However, on questions like this one, just applying the information to the question is often simpler and quicker. Solving the actual problem is okay *if it's the quickest way to determine that you have enough information.* Just remember to stop solving the problem as soon as you determine whether the information is sufficient!

2. **E.** Here's an example of how word problems may appear as data–sufficiency questions. Apply the steps in the same way you do for solving linear equations:

1. **Find out what to solve for.**

The question asks you to find the percentage of part-time employees at Office Solutions. You know two facts at this point: (1) Office Solutions employs a certain number of males (m) and a certain number of females (f), and (2) a certain number of employees work either full time (F) or part time (P). That creates four unknown variables. The question doesn't tell you anything about how many total people (T) Office Solutions employs, so you have another unknown. Here's what you know in mathematical terms: $F + P = T$ and $f + m = T$.

2. **Examine Statement (1).**

The first statement gives you the percentage of female part-time employees but tells you nothing about the percentage of male part-time employees. It takes care of only two of the unknown variables; you're missing half of what you need to solve the problem. Statement (1) isn't sufficient. Write down 1 = *no*, and eliminate Choices (A) and (D).

3. **Evaluate Statement (2).**

This statement concerns male employees at Office Solutions, but not females, so it's insufficient by itself. Record your finding as 2 = *no*. The answer can't be Choice (B).

4. **Check out what you've written.**

You have double *nos,* so consider Statement (2)'s sufficiency when paired with Statement (1).

5. **Evaluate the two statements together.**

One statement provides a percentage for females and the other offers a percentage for males. You may be on your way to finding the percentage for both.

WARNING

Read the statements carefully. You may be tempted to think that Statement (2) offers the other half of the solution, but this statement tells you the percentage of *all* males who work at the company, not just the ones who work part time.

You can't determine the total percentage of part-time workers if you don't know the ratio of male full-time to male part-time workers. Neither statement is sufficient and the two together don't cut it. *Correct answer:* Choice (E).

3. B. For this problem, you evaluate a four-sided geometric figure:

1. Find out what to solve for.

You know that the sum of the interior angles of four-sided figures is 360 degrees and that x and y are the measures of two of these interior angles, but that's not enough to determine the value of $2(x+y)$. But you knew that. Data sufficiency questions never give you enough information to solve them without considering the statements. So check out what they have to offer.

2. Examine Statement (1).

Statement (1) gives you the value of y. You may have examined the figure, assumed that it was a parallelogram, and deduced that x and y are, therefore, angles formed by parallel lines cut by a transversal. That makes them supplementary angles that add to 180 degrees. So if $y = 120$, $x = 60$, and $2(x+y) = 360$. Problem solved!

WARNING

Not so fast. You can't assume information about a GMAT figure by looking at it. If the figure is supposed to be a parallelogram, the GMAT will give you the information you need to know that. Nothing to this point has indicated that BC and AD are parallel lines, so you have to write *no* next to Statement (1).

3. Evaluate Statement (2).

Well, here you go. Now you know expressly that AB is a transversal that passes through two parallel lines. The two angles x and y are supplementary.

Were you tempted at this point to pick Choice (C)? It's true that both statements together give you the value of x, but you aren't looking for the value of x. You're asked to find the value of $2(x+y)$. All you need is Statement (2). If the value of $x+y$ is 180, the value of $2(x+y)$ is 360. Write *yes* next to Statement (2) on your noteboard and pick Choice (B). You're done!

REMEMBER

You only pick Choice (C) if *neither* of the two statements by itself solves the problem. After you've determined that one of the statements works and the other doesn't, you know the answer can't be Choice (C). Follow the line of questions in the chart in Figure 17-1 and you'll be fine.

4. D. This data-sufficiency question is essentially a simple addition problem.

1. Find out what to solve for.

You know the total distance Joe travels to his aunt's is 225 kilometers and that he takes different types of transportation, one of which is a bus. Lucky guy! The question asks for the length of Joe's bus ride. That's your unknown, so designate the bus ride as x.

2. Examine Statement (1).

From the first statement, you learn that the other modes of transportation are bike (b) and train (t). Great news! It also tells you the exact length of Joe's bike ride (5 kilometers) and that his train ride is 10 times his bus ride. So $t = 10x$. You can set up an equation with this information: $5 + x + 10x = 225$. The equation has only one variable, the unknown length of the bus ride. You know you can solve a linear equation with only one variable, so Statement (1) is sufficient. Write *yes* next to (1) on your noteboard and eliminate Choices (B), (C), and (E).

3. Evaluate Statement (2).

Create an equation from the information in the second statement. If Joe's bike ride (b) is $\frac{1}{4}$ as long as his bus ride (x), then $b = \frac{1}{4}x$. If the train trip (t) is 40 times the length of the bike ride (b), then $t = 40b$. This gives simultaneous equations. Substitute $\frac{1}{4}x$ for t in the train ride equation: $t = 40\left(\frac{1}{4}x\right)$. So the equation for the bike ride plus the bus ride plus the train trip is this:

$$\frac{1}{4}x + x + 40\left(\frac{1}{4}x\right) = 225$$

This equation has only one variable, so you know you can solve for x. You don't have to actually solve for x; you just need to know that you can to know that Statement (2) is also sufficient. Write *yes* next to (2). *Correct answer:* Choice (D).

5. A. The last question in the practice set contains a bunch of unknown variables, so you may think you can't solve for much. You may be surprised!

1. Find out what to solve for.

Take a few seconds to evaluate the equation. You're given two factors with exponents, and their product is equal to a perfect square. Both factors have the same base (a), and both contain an exponent with a factor of 2. The problem asks you to find the sum of the other two factors in the exponents of the terms.

2. Examine Statement (1).

From the information in the first statement, you can substitute 3 for a in the equation:

$$(3)^{2x}(3)^{2y} = 81$$

The terms have the same base, so you add the exponents when you multiply the terms:

$$3^{2x+2y} = 81$$

Now extract the common factor in the exponent:

$$3^{2(x+y)} = 81$$

Square 3 to get 9:

$$9^{(x+y)} = 81$$

Because $9^2 = 81$, you know that the exponent ($x+y$) must equal 2.

You could also find the value of $x + y$ by rewriting 81 as a base and exponent:

$$3^{2x+2y} = 3^4$$

When the bases are equal, the exponents are equal:

$$2x + 2y = 4$$
$$x + y = 2$$

Either way, the information in Statement (1) is sufficient to tell you the value of $x + y$. Write *yes* next to (1) on your noteboard and eliminate Choices (B), (C), and (E).

3. Evaluate Statement (2).

This statement tells you that x and y are equal, so you may be tempted to draw from the information in the last statement and assume that x and y each equal 1. Well, that could be true if $a = 3$. But you no longer know that $a = 3$.

WARNING

You can't carry over the information from one statement to evaluate the sufficiency of the other. It's true that x and y could each equal 1, but they could also each equal 0.5. Start fresh with each statement.

If x and y are equal, then you can substitute x for y in the equation, simplify, and solve for a:

$$(a)^{2x}(a)^{2x} = 81$$
$$a^{4x} = 81$$
$$a^{4x} = 3^4$$
$$a^x = 3$$
$$a = \sqrt[x]{3}$$

Since a is equal to the xth root of 3, the possible values of x, y, a, and, of course, $x + y$, are infinite. For example, if $x = 2$, then so does y, and $a = \sqrt{3}$. If x and y each equal 3, then $a = \sqrt[3]{3}$, and so on. Because Statement (2) results in more than one value for $x + y$, it can't be sufficient to answer the question. Write *no* next to (2) on your notebook. *Correct answer:* Choice (A).

Houston, We Have a Problem: Problem-Solving Questions

About half of the 37 math problems on the GMAT quantitative section are data sufficiency. The other half are problem-solving questions, which (not surprisingly!) require you to apply your mathematical skills to solve a problem. These questions are more like the ones you've seen on other standardized tests, like the SAT and ACT. They present you with a question and provide five possible answer choices from which you select the correct answer.

The approach to regular old problem-solving questions is less clear-cut than the one for data-sufficiency problems, but you should still follow an approach. Arriving at the test center with a practice problem-solving plan not only provides you with a groovy little alliteration but also gives you a real edge for answering standard math questions. These techniques apply more directly to some questions than others, but learn all of them so you're prepared for all types of problem-solving questions:

>> **Examine all the data the question provides to make sure you know exactly what you're asked to do.** Some problems present you with figures, graphs, and scenarios, and some with just an equation with an equal sign. Don't jump into the answer choices until you've given the question a little thought. Isolate exactly what the problem asks you to solve for and what information the problem provides you. Especially for more complex questions and word problems, use your noteboard to keep track of what you know and what you have to find out.

>> **Eliminate obviously incorrect answer choices if possible.** Before you begin solving a more complex math problem, look at the answer choices to root out any clearly illogical options. You can then focus your problem-solving, and you won't pick these answers later through mistaken calculations. You can find more tips for eliminating answer choices in Chapter 2.

>> **Use the information in the problem.** The GMAT rarely presents you with the answer choice that states, "It cannot be determined from the information." Almost every problem-solving question contains enough information for you to figure out the correct answer. But you need to use what you're given. Pull out the numbers and other terms in a problem and write them on your noteboard in a way that makes the numbers meaningful. Depending on the problem, you may show relationships between quantities, draw simple diagrams, or organize information in a quick table.

>> **Find the equation.** Some GMAT problems provide the equation for you. Others, such as word problems, require you to come up with an equation using the language in the problem. Whenever possible, formulate an equation to solve from the information provided in the problem and write it down on your noteboard.

>> **Know when to move on.** Sometimes you may confront a question that you just can't solve. Relax for a moment and reread the question to make sure you haven't missed something. If you still don't know what to do or if you can't remember the tested concept, eliminate all the answers you can and record your best guess.

Apply the process to a sample problem.

EXAMPLE

A survey reveals that the average income of a company's customers is $45,000 per year. If 50 customers respond to the survey and the average income of the wealthiest 10 of those customers is $75,000, what is the average income of the other 40 customers?

(A) $27,500

(B) $35,000

(C) $37,500

(D) $42,500

(E) $50,000

Scan the question to get an idea of what it's asking of you. The word problem talks about surveys and averages, so it's a statistics question. It asks for the average income of 40 out of 50 customers when the average of the other 10 is $75,000 and that the average of all 50 is $45,000.

You can eliminate Choice (E) off the bat because there's no way that the 40 customers with lower incomes have an average income that's more than the average income of all 50 customers. Choice (D) is probably wrong, too, because the top ten incomes carry such a high average compared to the total average. You know the answer is either Choice (A), (B), or (C), and you haven't even gotten down to solving yet!

TIP

Quickly eliminating answers before you begin can save you from choosing an answer that comes from making a math error. Sometimes, the test-makers are tricky; they anticipate the kinds of little mistakes you'll make and offer the resulting wrong answers as distracters in the answer choices. So be sure to eliminate illogical answers before you begin a problem.

You can find the total income of all 50 customers and the total income of the wealthiest 10 customers by using the formula for averages. The average equals the sum of the values in a group divided by the number of values in the group. Apply the formula to find the total income for the group of 50. Then find the total income for the group of 10. Subtract the total income of the 10 from the total income of the 50 to find the total income of the 40. Then you can divide by 40 to get the average income for the group of 40. Here's how you do it:

TIP

Your calculations may be easier if you drop the three zeroes from the salaries. For this problem, shorten $45,000 to $45 and $75,000 to 75. Just remember to add the zeroes back on to your solution when you find it!

1. **Find the total income for the group of 50.**

   The average income is $45 and the number of group members is 50, so use the formula to find the sum of all incomes (x):

   $$\text{Average} = \frac{\text{Sum of Values}}{\text{Number of Values}}$$

   $$45 = \frac{x}{50}$$

   $$2{,}250 = x$$

2. **Find the total income for the group of 10.**

   The average income is $75 and the number of group members is 10, so use the formula to find the sum (y):

   $$75 = \frac{y}{10}$$

   $$750 = y$$

3. **Find the total income for the group of 40.**

   Subtract the total income of the group of 10 (y) from the total income for the group of 50 (x):

   $$2{,}250 - 750 - 1{,}500$$

4. **Find the average income of the group of 40.**

   The sum of the incomes in the group is $1,500, and the number of group members is 40, so apply the average formula:

   $$\text{Average} = \frac{1.500}{40}$$

   $$\text{Average} = 37.5$$

Add three decimal places for the three zeroes you excluded in your calculations, and you have your answer. The average income of the 40 customers is $37,500, which is Choice (C).

Trying Out Some Problem-Solving Practice Problems

Here are a few practice questions to help you master the approach to problem-solving questions in the quantitative section. When you're finished answering them, read through the answer explanations to see how you've fared.

Practice questions

Try to answer these practice problems in the same amount of time you'll experience on the actual GMAT (give yourself about ten minutes to answer all five questions). Remember to keep track of the information you know and the information you have to figure out as you work through the problems. Use a piece of scratch paper to simulate the noteboard as you work out the answers.

1. An electronics firm produces 300 units of a particular MP3 player every hour of every day. Each unit costs the manufacturer $60 to produce, and retailers immediately purchase all the produced units. What is the minimum wholesale price (amount the manufacturer receives) per unit that the manufacturer should charge to make an hourly profit of $19,500?

   (A) $60

   (B) $65

   (C) $95

   (D) $125

   (E) $145

2. If $x \neq 0$, what is the value for x in the equation $\dfrac{2x}{4+2x} = \dfrac{6x}{8x+6}$?

   (A) −3

   (B) 1

   (C) 2

   (D) 3

   (E) 6

3. $g(r) = \begin{cases} 4|r| & \text{if } r \geq 2 \\ -|r| & \text{if } r < 2 \end{cases}$

   Given the above, evaluate $g(-r)$ if $r = -7$.

   (A) −28

   (B) −14

   (C) −7

   (D) 7

   (E) 28

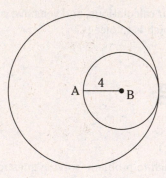

4. In the preceding figure, the circle centered at B is internally tangent to the circle centered at A. The smaller circle passes through the center of the larger circle, and the length of AB is 4 units. If the smaller circle is removed from the larger circle, how many square units of the area of the larger circle will remain?

   (A) 16π

   (B) 36π

   (C) 48π

   (D) 64π

   (E) 800π

5. A line with the equation $y - 2x + 3 = 0$ for all real numbers would pass through which quadrants on the coordinate plane?

(A) I, II, and III only

(B) III and IV only

(C) I, II, III, and IV

(D) I, III, and IV only

(E) II and IV only

Answer explanations

1. D. Note what the question gives and what it's asking for. It provides units per hour and cost per unit. It also tells you the total desired hourly profit. You're supposed to find the price per unit.

The first thing to do is eliminate obviously incorrect answer choices. You know that you're looking for the wholesale price that will yield a profit (which results from price minus cost to produce) of $19,500 per hour. Because the answers given are wholesale prices, you can eliminate Choices (A) and (B). The cost to produce each unit is $60. If the company charged the same amount for the MP3 players as it spent to produce them, it would make no profit, so Choice (A) is obviously incorrect. Choice (B) isn't much better. At a profit of just $5 per unit and 300 units per hour, the firm would make only $1,500 per hour.

You've eliminated two answer choices. Evaluate the data to find the correct answer from the remaining three. You know that 300 units are produced every hour and that those 300 units have to net a profit of $19,500. If you knew the amount of profit per unit, you could add that to the amount each unit costs to produce and get the minimum wholesale price. Set up an equation with x as the profit per unit. Remember that *per* means to *divide:*

$$x = \frac{\$19,500}{300}$$
$$x = 65$$

The firm needs to make a profit of $65 per unit.

You can't stop here and pick Choice (B). You're not done yet, but you know that because you've already eliminated Choice (B).

You have to add profit to the per-unit production cost to get the final wholesale price:

$$\$60 + \$65 = \$125$$

Correct answer: Choice (D).

TIP

You could use estimation to solve this problem by rounding $19,500 up to the nearest convenient multiple of 300, which is $21,000, and then dividing 21 by 3 in your head and getting 7. This would tell you that you need a little less than $70 profit from each unit, or a little under $130 as the wholesale price (because $60 + $70 = $130).

2. D. Here's a relatively simple question that asks you to solve for x. The only element that makes it a little complex is that you're dealing with variables in fractions. Take a moment to consider the equation. The numerator in the fraction on the right is 3 times the numerator in the fraction on the left. Multiplying the numerator of the left-side fraction would make it equal to the numerator on the right side.

REMEMBER

When the numerators of two fractions are equal, their denominators are also equal, so creating equal numerators allows you to set the denominators equal to each other. Then just solve for x.

1. **Multiply the left-side fraction by $\frac{3}{3}$.**

This doesn't change the value of the fraction, because multiplying by $\frac{3}{3}$ is the same as multiplying by 1.

$$\frac{2x}{4+2x} \times \frac{3}{3} = \frac{6x}{12+6x}$$

2. **Set the denominators equal to each other and solve for x:**

$$12+6x = 8x+6$$
$$6x = 8x-6$$
$$-2x = -6$$
$$x = 3$$

Correct answer: Choice (D).

You can also solve this question by cross-multiplying opposite numerators and denominators:

$$2x(8x+6) = 6x(4+2x)$$
$$16x^2 + 12x = 24x + 12x^2$$
$$4x^2 = 12x$$
$$x^2 = 3x$$
$$x = 3$$

TIP

You can solve many GMAT problems by using more than one method. Go with the one that's easiest for you.

3. **E.** This function problem provides you with two outputs depending on the value of the input. If the input is greater than or equal to 2, the output is 4 times the absolute value of the input. If the input is less than 2, the output is the negative of the absolute value of the input.

WARNING

Don't let the negative signs mess you up. If $r = -7$, then $g(-r)$ is the same as saying $g(7)$, because $-(-7)$ is 7. So the value of the input in this problem is 7.

Because 7 is greater than 2, you'll look to the first rule of the function $g(r)$. The solution to $g(r) = 4|7|$ is simply $4 \times 7 = 28$. *Correct answer:* Choice (E).

If you confuse the signs, you'll come up with the negative version of the correct answer, which is Choice (A). You get the other answer choices when you use the incorrect rule.

4. **C.** This geometry question asks you to find the area of the large circle less the area of the small circle. Apply the formula for finding the area of a circle: $A = \pi r^2$.

Because the smaller circle passes through the center of the larger one, the radius of the larger circle is two times the radius of the smaller one: The radius of the larger circle equals 8. Apply the area formula to the larger circle:

$$A = \pi(8)^2$$
$$A = 64\pi$$

Determine the area of the smaller circle in the same way:

$$A = \pi r^2$$
$$A = \pi(4)^2$$
$$A = 16\pi$$

Now subtract the two areas:

$$64\pi - 16\pi = 48\pi$$

Correct answer: Choice (C).

5. **D.** This coordinate geometry problem requires you to know the slope-intercept form: $y = mx + b$. But before you do any calculations, go ahead and eliminate Choice (C). No way can a straight line pass through all four quadrants of the coordinate plane. When you rearrange the equation into the slope-intercept form by isolating the y variable on the left side, you get $y = 2x - 3$. The slope-intercept form gives you the y-intercept and slope of the line. The value of b is the y-intercept, and the value of m is the slope.

TIP

For this kind of question, you may want to draw on your noteboard a coordinate plane graph and label the quadrants I, II, III, and IV. Nothing fancy, mind you, just enough to get your bearings. Now, draw a point below the origin on the y-axis representing −3, the y-intercept. Then draw a line that travels upward from left to right rising two units toward the top of the paper for every one unit to the right. Your figure doesn't have to be perfect. From a rudimentary drawing, you can immediately see that the line passes through Quadrants I, III, and IV.

So Choice (D) is your best choice. Choice (A) would be correct if you had a parallel line with a positive y-intercept. Choice (B) is possible for a line parallel to the x-axis with a negative y-intercept. Choice (E) would require a line with a negative slope passing through the origin.

TIP

Any line must travel through at least two quadrants, unless the line runs directly on top of either the x- or y-axis. A line that lies directly on top of an axis doesn't go *through* any quadrant. The lines that travel through only two quadrants are those that pass through the origin or are parallel to either the x- or the y-axis. All other lines must eventually travel through three quadrants.

Correct answer: Choice (D).

Chapter **18**

All Together Now: A Mini Practice Quantitative Section

Here's a chance to test your GMAT math skills before you embark on the real adventure of taking the test. This chapter contains only the types of math questions you'll see on the GMAT, so it's kind of like a mini practice test. To get a better idea of the time restrictions you'll face on test day, try to complete the questions in the following section in about 48 minutes. If you want to avoid the time pressure for now, feel free to just focus on answering the questions. You'll have the opportunity to time yourself again when you take the full-length practice tests included with this book.

TIP

Read through all the answer explanations (even the ones for the questions you answered correctly), because you want to make sure you know why you got the answer you did and because you may see something in the explanations that can help you with other questions.

Tackling GMAT Math Practice Questions

Here are 24 practice questions for the GMAT math section. Grab your pencil, set your timer for 48 minutes, and get started. (Try not to peek at the answers until you've come up with your own.)

1. If $\left(\dfrac{3}{y}+2\right)(y-5)=0$ and $y \neq 5$, then $y =$

   (A) $-\dfrac{3}{2}$

   (B) $-\dfrac{2}{3}$

   (C) $\dfrac{2}{3}$

   (D) $\dfrac{3}{2}$

   (E) 6

2. If Esperanza will be 35 years old in 6 years, how old was she x years ago?

   (A) $41 - x$

   (B) $x - 41$

   (C) $35 - x$

   (D) $x - 29$

   (E) $29 - x$

3. What is the value of $\dfrac{x}{3}+\dfrac{y}{3}$?

   (1) $\dfrac{x+y}{3}=6$

   (2) $x+y=18$

   (A) Statement (1) ALONE is sufficient, but Statement (2) ALONE is NOT sufficient to answer the question asked.

   (B) Statement (2) ALONE is sufficient, but Statement (1) ALONE is NOT sufficient to answer the question asked.

   (C) Both statements TOGETHER are sufficient, but NEITHER statement ALONE is sufficient to answer the question asked.

   (D) Each statement ALONE is sufficient to answer the question asked.

   (E) Statements (1) and (2) TOGETHER are NOT sufficient to answer the question asked.

4. Sofa King is having "a sale on top of a sale!" The price of a certain couch, which already had been discounted by 20%, is further reduced by an additional 20%. These successive discounts are equivalent to a single discount of which of the following?

   (A) 40%

   (B) 38%

   (C) 36%

   (D) 30%

   (E) 20%

5. If x is a member of the set {44, 45, 47, 52, 55, 58}, what is the value of x?

   (1) x is even.

   (2) x is a multiple of 4.

   (A) Statement (1) ALONE is sufficient, but Statement (2) ALONE is NOT sufficient to answer the question asked.

   (B) Statement (2) ALONE is sufficient, but Statement (1) ALONE is NOT sufficient to answer the question asked.

   (C) Both statements TOGETHER are sufficient, but NEITHER statement ALONE is sufficient to answer the question asked.

   (D) Each statement ALONE is sufficient to answer the question asked.

   (E) Statements (1) and (2) TOGETHER are NOT sufficient to answer the question asked.

6. In a given year, the United States census estimated that there were approximately 6.5 billion people in the world and 300 million in the United States. Approximately what percentage of the world's population lived in the United States that year?

   (A) 0.0046%

   (B) 0.046%

   (C) 0.46%

   (D) 4.6%

   (E) 46%

7. The symbol β represents one of the following operations: addition, subtraction, multiplication, or division. What is the value of $4\beta5$?

   (1) $0\beta1 = 0$

   (2) $0\beta1 = 1$

   (A) Statement (1) ALONE is sufficient, but Statement (2) ALONE is NOT sufficient to answer the question asked.

   (B) Statement (2) ALONE is sufficient, but Statement (1) ALONE is NOT sufficient to answer the question asked.

   (C) Both statements TOGETHER are sufficient, but NEITHER statement ALONE is sufficient to answer the question asked.

   (D) Each statement ALONE is sufficient to answer the question asked.

   (E) Statements (1) and (2) TOGETHER are NOT sufficient to answer the question asked.

8. How many burritos did Dave's Wraps sell today?

   (1) A total of 350 burritos was sold at Dave's Wraps yesterday, which is 100 fewer than twice the number sold today.

   (2) The number of burritos sold at Dave's Wraps yesterday was 20 more than the number sold today.

   (A) Statement (1) ALONE is sufficient, but Statement (2) ALONE is NOT sufficient to answer the question asked.

   (B) Statement (2) ALONE is sufficient, but Statement (1) ALONE is NOT sufficient to answer the question asked.

   (C) Both statements TOGETHER are sufficient, but NEITHER statement ALONE is sufficient to answer the question asked.

   (D) Each statement ALONE is sufficient to answer the question asked.

   (E) Statements (1) and (2) TOGETHER are NOT sufficient to answer the question asked.

9. To boost sales around the holidays, the government of the fictional country of Capitalitamia dictates that a citizen may purchase goods up to a total value of $1,000 tax-free but must pay a 7% tax on the portion of the total value in excess of $1,000. How much tax must be paid by a citizen who purchases goods with a total value of $1,220?

   (A) $14.00

   (B) $15.40

   (C) $54.60

   (D) $70.00

   (E) $87.40

10. In the preceding figure, $\frac{a+b}{b} = \frac{5}{2}$, what does b equal?

    (A) 108

    (B) 99

    (C) 81

    (D) 72

    (E) 63

11. Is the value of x closer to 75 than it is to 100?

    (1) $100 - x > x - 75$

    (2) $x > 85$

    (A) Statement (1) ALONE is sufficient, but Statement (2) ALONE is NOT sufficient to answer the question asked.

    (B) Statement (2) ALONE is sufficient, but Statement (1) ALONE is NOT sufficient to answer the question asked.

    (C) Both statements TOGETHER are sufficient, but NEITHER statement ALONE is sufficient to answer the question asked.

    (D) Each statement ALONE is sufficient to answer the question asked.

    (E) Statements (1) and (2) TOGETHER are NOT sufficient to answer the question asked.

12. How long did it take Ms. Nkalubo to drive her family nonstop from her home to Charlestown, West Virginia?

    (1) Ms. Nkalubo's average speed for the trip was 45 miles per hour.

    (2) If Ms. Nkalubo's average speed for the trip had been $1\frac{1}{4}$ times faster, the trip would have taken three hours.

    (A) Statement (1) ALONE is sufficient, but Statement (2) ALONE is NOT sufficient to answer the question asked.

    (B) Statement (2) ALONE is sufficient, but Statement (1) ALONE is NOT sufficient to answer the question asked.

    (C) Both statements TOGETHER are sufficient, but NEITHER statement ALONE is sufficient to answer the question asked.

    (D) Each statement ALONE is sufficient to answer the question asked.

    (E) Statements (1) and (2) TOGETHER are NOT sufficient to answer the question asked.

13. The arithmetic mean and standard deviation for a certain normal distribution are 9.5 and 1.5, respectively. Which of these values is more than 2.5 standard deviations from the mean?

(A) 5.75

(B) 6

(C) 6.5

(D) 13.25

(E) 13.5

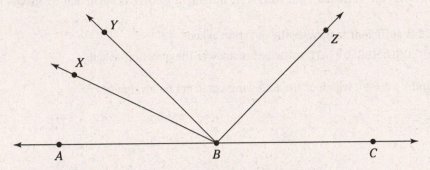

14. What is the measure of ∠ABX in the preceding figure?

(1) BX bisects ∠ABY and BZ bisects ∠YBC.

(2) The measure of ∠YBZ is 60 degrees.

(A) Statement (1) ALONE is sufficient, but Statement (2) ALONE is NOT sufficient to answer the question asked.

(B) Statement (2) ALONE is sufficient, but Statement (1) ALONE is NOT sufficient to answer the question asked.

(C) Both statements TOGETHER are sufficient, but NEITHER statement ALONE is sufficient to answer the question asked.

(D) Each statement ALONE is sufficient to answer the question asked.

(E) Statements (1) and (2) TOGETHER are NOT sufficient to answer the question asked.

15. On her annual road trip to visit her family in Seal Beach, California, Traci stopped to rest after she traveled $\frac{1}{3}$ of the total distance and again after she traveled $\frac{1}{4}$ of the distance remaining between her first stop and her destination. She then drove the remaining 200 miles and arrived safely at her destination. What was the total distance in miles from Traci's starting point to Seal Beach?

(A) 250

(B) 300

(C) 350

(D) 400

(E) 550

16. In the fraction $\frac{a}{b}$, where a and b are positive integers, what is the value of b?

(1) The lowest common denominator of $\frac{a}{b}$ and $\frac{1}{5}$ is 10.

(2) $a = 3$

(A) Statement (1) ALONE is sufficient, but Statement (2) ALONE is NOT sufficient to answer the question asked.

(B) Statement (2) ALONE is sufficient, but Statement (1) ALONE is NOT sufficient to answer the question asked.

(C) Both statements TOGETHER are sufficient, but NEITHER statement ALONE is sufficient to answer the question asked.

(D) Each statement ALONE is sufficient to answer the question asked.

(E) Statements (1) and (2) TOGETHER are NOT sufficient to answer the question asked.

17. If n is a positive integer and $x + 3 = 4^n$, which of the following could *not* be a value of x?

(A) 1

(B) 13

(C) 45

(D) 61

(E) 253

18. What is the value of b?

(1) $3^{(b^2 - 4)} = 1$

(2) $3^{(b-4-2c)} = 9^{(b-c)}$

(A) Statement (1) ALONE is sufficient, but Statement (2) ALONE is NOT sufficient to answer the question asked.

(B) Statement (2) ALONE is sufficient, but Statement (1) ALONE is NOT sufficient to answer the question asked.

(C) Both statements TOGETHER are sufficient, but NEITHER statement ALONE is sufficient to answer the question asked.

(D) Each statement ALONE is sufficient to answer the question asked.

(E) Statements (1) and (2) TOGETHER are NOT sufficient to answer the question asked.

19. This stem-and-leaf plot shows the number of automobiles sold by 22 sales associates of a Ace Auto Sales during the month of January. Next month, management wants to increase its average number of automobiles sold per salesperson to 35. If the number of sales associates remains at 22, on average how many additional automobiles will each salesperson need to sell next month for management to reach this goal?

Number of Automobiles Sold per Sales Associate in January	
1	2 5 7 8 8
2	2 3 3 4 5 5 5
3	2 4 4 4 8 9 9
5	0 2
6	1

(A) 3

(B) 5

(C) 32

(D) 35

(E) 110

20. For all $a \neq 0$ and $b \neq 0$, $\dfrac{(4a^4b^3)^2}{2a^2b^{-2}} = ?$

(A) $8a^6b^8$

(B) $8a^6b^4$

(C) $8a^4b^7$

(D) $2a^6b^8$

(E) $2a^4b^7$

21. What is the ratio of a to b?

(1) The ratio of $0.25a$ to $2b$ is 2 to 3.

(2) a is two more than four times b.

(A) Statement (1) ALONE is sufficient, but Statement (2) ALONE is NOT sufficient to answer the question asked.

(B) Statement (2) ALONE is sufficient, but Statement (1) ALONE is NOT sufficient to answer the question asked.

(C) Both statements TOGETHER are sufficient, but NEITHER statement ALONE is sufficient to answer the question asked.

(D) Each statement ALONE is sufficient to answer the question asked.

(E) Statements (1) and (2) TOGETHER are NOT sufficient to answer the question asked.

22. Akhil invests $1,200 in a certificate of deposit (CD) that earns 1.05% in interest compounded biannually, which means that he earns 1.05% of his existing money twice per year. The money he makes in interest is added to his account balance and rounded to the nearest cent. After two years, the CD matures. Akhil decides to use $400 of the funds to purchase a tablet and invest the remaining balance in another CD. How much money did Akhil invest in this second CD?

(A) $800.00

(B) $850.40

(C) $851.20

(D) $1,250.40

(E) $1,251.20

23. What is the slope of a line on the (xy) coordinate plane with endpoints of $(2, 5)$ and $(10, 4)$?

(A) -8

(B) $-\dfrac{1}{8}$

(C) $\dfrac{1}{8}$

(D) $\dfrac{4}{3}$

(E) 8

24. A downtown theater sells each of its floor seats for a certain price and each of its balcony seats for a certain price. If Matthew, Linda, and Jake each buy tickets for a particular performance at this theater, how much did Jake pay for one floor seat and one balcony seat?

(1) Matthew bought four floor seats and three balcony seats for $82.50.

(2) Linda bought eight floor seats and six balcony seats for $165.

(A) Statement (1) ALONE is sufficient, but Statement (2) ALONE is NOT sufficient to answer the question asked.

(B) Statement (2) ALONE is sufficient, but Statement (1) ALONE is NOT sufficient to answer the question asked.

(C) Both statements TOGETHER are sufficient, but NEITHER statement ALONE is sufficient to answer the question asked.

(D) Each statement ALONE is sufficient to answer the question asked.

(E) Statements (1) and (2) TOGETHER are NOT sufficient to answer the question asked.

Checking Out the Answer Explanations

1. A. The GMAT usually starts with a question of medium difficulty, and this one is in that range. If the product of two factors equals 0, then at least one of the factors must be 0 (because anything times 0 equals 0). Therefore, one of the factors in this equation must equal 0. You know it isn't the second one, because y doesn't equal 5, and y would have to equal 5 for the second term to result in 0.

Therefore, you need to create an equation that sets the first factor equal to 0 and then solve for y. Here's what you get for the first factor:

$$\frac{3}{y} + 2 = 0$$

$$\frac{3}{y} = -2$$

Cross-multiply (because $-2 = -\frac{2}{1}$) and solve:

$$3 = -2y$$

$$-\frac{3}{2} = y$$

2. E. If Esperanza will be 35 years old in 6 years, she is 29 right now ($35 - 6 = 29$). Therefore, to determine how old she was x years ago, simply subtract x from her current age of 29: $29 - x$.

3. D. This problem is simple when you recognize that because the two fractions have a common denominator, $\frac{x}{3} + \frac{y}{3}$ is the same thing as $\frac{x+y}{3}$.

Statement (1) says that $\frac{x+y}{3} = 6$, and because $\frac{x}{3} + \frac{y}{3} = \frac{x+y}{3}$, $\frac{x}{3} + \frac{y}{3}$ must also equal 6. So you know that Statement (1) is sufficient to answer the question and that the answer must be either Choice (A) or Choice (D). To figure out which it is, consider Statement (2). If it's sufficient, the answer is Choice (D). If not, the answer is Choice (A).

Because $\frac{x}{3} + \frac{y}{3} = \frac{x+y}{3}$, and Statement (2) tells you the value of $x + y$, you can substitute 18 for $x + y$ in the expression and solve for a known value ($18 \div 3 = 6$). So Statement (2) also provides sufficient information to answer the question.

4. C. This is a percent decrease question. You can apply a formula to solve it, but a faster and easier method is to apply actual numbers to the circumstances. To simplify your life, use a nice, round figure like $100.

If the couch originally cost $100 but was discounted by 20 percent, you'd multiply $100 by 20 percent (0.20) and subtract that from $100 to find the price after the first discount ($100 \times 0.20 = 20$, and $100 - 20 = 80$). After the first round of discounts, the couch cost $80.

However, the couch was discounted an additional 20 percent. Now, you have to repeat the process, this time using $80 as the original price ($80 \times 0.20 = 16$, and $80 - 16 = 64$). After both discounts, the couch cost $64.

But you're not finished yet. You need to calculate the total discount. The couch originally cost $100 and later cost $64. The discount, in dollars, is $100 - 64$, which is $36. To find the percentage of the full discount, simply divide $36 by the original price of $100 ($\frac{36}{100} = 0.36$ or 36 percent).

5. E. Evaluate Statement (1). Knowing that x is even doesn't help you much. Three numbers in the set are even: 44, 52, and 58. So Statement (1) doesn't allow you to narrow down the value of x to one number. The answer can't be Choice (A) or Choice (D).

Consider Statement (2). Two numbers in the set are multiples of 4: 44 and 52. So even when you know that x is a multiple of 4, you can't come up with a fixed value for x. Statement (2) by itself isn't sufficient, so the answer can be only Choice (C) or (E). You still have one more evaluation: whether the two statements together provide sufficient information.

Multiples of 4 are always even, so the two statements together don't point you to the value of x. So the correct answer is Choice (E).

6. D. This question requires you to work with very large numbers, so you need to know what large numbers look like.

REMEMBER

One billion = 1,000,000,000, and 1 million = 1,000,000. In other words, 1 billion is 1,000 million.

Now, look at the question at hand: 6.5 billion is written as 6,500,000,000. Writing out 6 billion is obvious, and 0.5 billion is one-half of 1,000 million, which is 500 million, or 500,000,000. You write 300 million like 300,000,000. To solve for the percentage, simply divide 300,000,000 by 6,500,000,000, using the fraction form:

$$\frac{300,000,000}{6,500,000,000}$$

Simplify things by canceling out eight zeros on the top and bottom. (This step is legal because you're just reducing your fraction.) Then divide 3 by 65.

TIP

You don't actually have to complete the mathematical calculation, because all the answer choices are derivatives of 46. You do need to know, though, that when you divide 3 by 65, your answer will have three places after the decimal. If you can't figure this in your head, quickly set up the division problem on your noteboard and mark where the decimal will be in your answer.

So $\frac{3}{65} = 0.046$, but the question asks for a percentage. To convert the decimal to a percentage, move the decimal point two places to the right and add a percentage sign. The answer is 4.6 percent.

TIP

You can also use estimation to narrow down the answers. $\frac{3}{65}$ is about $\frac{3}{60}$, which reduces to $\frac{1}{20}$, or 0.05. The answer has to be slightly smaller than 0.05 because $\frac{3}{65}$ is less than $\frac{3}{60}$, The answer that is slightly less than 0.05 is 0.046 or 4.6%

7. **B.** To determine the value of $4\beta5$, you have to figure out which of the four operations the symbol represents. The way to do so is to plug each of the operations into the equations offered by each of the two statements and see whether either of them allows you to narrow the symbol down to just one operation.

Statement (1) gives you $0\beta1 = 0$. Plug in each operation to see whether any make the equation true. You know addition and subtraction don't work because you can't add or subtract 1 to or from a number and end up with the same number. Both multiplication and division work: $0 \times 1 = 0$, and $0 \div 1 = 0$. So Statement (1) isn't sufficient because it doesn't allow you to narrow the symbol down to just one operation. The answer, then, can't be Choice (A) or Choice (D).

Statement (2) offers $0\beta1 = 1$. The only difference between this equation and the one in Statement (1) is the answer. You know that multiplication and division don't work, because they already produced an answer of 0. Subtraction results in −1, so the only operation that works is addition ($0 + 1 = 1$). This means that Statement (2) alone gives you enough information to determine which operation the symbol stands for, which allows you to figure out the value of $4\beta5$.

WARNING

Data sufficiency questions don't ask for the actual numeric answer, so don't take the time to determine the actual value of the operation (not that it would take you long to do so for this question).

8. **A.** Evaluate each statement to determine whether it allows you to figure out the exact number of burrito sales for the day.

You can construct a mathematical equation from the language in Statement (1). The unknown is the total number of today's burrito sales. Let b = today's burritos. *Fewer* means subtraction, so yesterday's sales equal $2b - 100$. The equation then looks like this:

$$350 = 2b - 100$$

This equation has only one variable, so you know you can easily solve this equation to find out how many burritos left the shop today. (Don't take the time to actually figure it out, though!) Statement (1) is sufficient, and the answer is either Choice (A) or Choice (D). To determine which it is, evaluate Statement (2).

Statement (2) tells you that the number of burritos sold at Dave's Wraps yesterday was 20 more than the number sold today, but this statement gives you two variables. You don't know how many burritos were sold today, *and* you don't know how many went out the door yesterday. If y stands for yesterday's burrito sales, the equation would look something like this: $y = 20 + b$. You can't definitively solve an equation with two variables without more information, so Statement (2) isn't sufficient. The correct answer is Choice (A).

(Oh, and if you won't be able to sleep unless we confirm for you the number of burritos sold today, it's 225: $450 = 2b$, so $225 = b$. Now be sure to get your sleep; you need it for the GMAT!)

9. **B.** The first thing that should jump out at you is that the first $1,000 of purchases is tax-free, so you don't need to consider the first $1,000. Subtract $1,000 from $1,220 to get the value of purchases that will actually be taxed: $220.

TIP

To find the amount of tax due, you multiply 220 by 7 percent (or 0.07), but you don't have to take the time to fully work out the calculation. To make things simple, you can estimate: 200 is close to 220, and $200 \times 0.07 = 14.00$, so the amount has to be just a little more than $14.

The only answer that's just a little more than $14 is Choice (B). If you take the time to multiply 220 and 0.07, you'll find that it's exactly $15.40. But because this is a test where saving time is crucial, avoid making full calculations whenever possible.

10. D. The key to solving this problem is to recognize that a and b are supplementary angles, which means they add up to 180 degrees: $a + b = 180$. (Chapter 14 has more information on shapes and angles.)

Now all you have to do is substitute 180 for $a + b$ in the original equation and solve:

$$\frac{a+b}{b} = \frac{5}{2}$$
$$\frac{180}{b} = \frac{5}{2}$$
$$5b = 360$$
$$b = 72$$

So the correct answer is Choice (D).

11. A. To solve this problem, recognize that the halfway point between 100 and 75 is 87.5, so if x is greater than 87.5, it's closer to 100. If it's less than 87.5, it's closer to 75. (If it equals 87.5, it's the same distance from both.)

If the difference between 100 and x ($100 - x$) is greater than the difference between x and 75 ($x - 75$), then x must be less than 87.5, because values greater than 87.5 would make $100 - x$ less than $x - 75$. Therefore, you absolutely know from Statement (1) that x is closer to 75. It's sufficient to answer the question, and the answer is either Choice (A) or Choice (D).

Now, look at Statement (2). Knowing that $x > 85$ doesn't help, because values above 87.5 would make x closer to 100 and values between 85 and 87.5 would make it closer to 75. Statement (2) isn't sufficient. For more about inequalities, consult Chapter 13.

12. B. This is a distance problem, so to determine the time of Ms. Nkalubo's trip, you have to use the distance equation.

The formula for distance is $r \times t = d$, which stands for Rate × Time = Distance (see Chapter 13 for details about this formula).

Statement (1) is pretty easy to evaluate. Knowing that her average speed was 45 miles per hour gives you the rate value for the equation but nothing more, so you're left with an unknown distance and an unknown amount of time. You can't solve an equation with two variables without more information. Therefore, you can't calculate her time. Statement (1) isn't sufficient, so the answer can't be Choice (A) or Choice (D).

Statement (2) takes a little more thought. At first it may not appear to give you enough information to figure out time. But if you look further, you'll see that it enables you to set up two simultaneous equations, and when you have two simultaneous equations with two variables, you can find the value of either variable. Here's how: The first equation is for Ms. Nkalubo's actual trip, which you can denote as Trip 1 (we've used a subscript 1 to show the values for Trip 1). Use the standard formula for distance:

$$r_1 \times t_1 = d_1$$

That's as much as you know about Trip 1 for now.

The second equation is for the theoretical trip proposed in the problem, which you can call Trip 2 (which we've denoted with a subscript 2). Start with the standard distance formula:

$$r_2 \times t_2 = d_2$$

Take the equation further with the information provided by Statement (2). Begin with the easy value. Trip 2 would take 3 hours, so $r_2 \times 3 = d_2$. You also know that Ms. Nkalubo's rate for Trip 2 was $\frac{5}{4}$ the rate of Trip 1. So $r_2 = \frac{5}{4}r_1$. Substitute this value for rate into the equation for Trip 2:

$$\frac{5}{4}r_1 \times 3 = d_2$$

TIP

You should also recognize that d_1 and d_2 have the same value because the distances of the two trips are the same (it's the same trip!). Therefore, you can set the left side of the first equation equal to the left side of the second and divide the rate variable from both sides.

At this point, you have an equation with only one variable, so you know you can solve for the exact length of Ms. Nkalubo's trip. Statement (2)'s information is sufficient to answer the question, so the correct answer is Choice (B).

For those of you who hate to be left hanging and need to see how the equation turns out, we'll finish the calculations. Just remember, you shouldn't do this part for the test; it's a waste of time. Here's what the solution looks like:

$$r_1 \times t_1 = \frac{5}{4} r_1 \times 3$$

$$t_1 = \frac{5}{4} \times 3$$

$$t_1 = \frac{15}{4}$$

$$t_1 = 3\frac{3}{4}$$

The time is $3\frac{3}{4}$ hours, which is equal to 3 hours and 45 minutes. The family was probably ready for some action after almost four hours in the car!

13. **E.** Don't let the language of this problem scare you. You're really just applying basic operations.

The arithmetic mean is 9.5 and the standard deviation is 1.5, so you'll use a deviation of 1.5 to find values that stray from the mean. This means that the values that are 1 standard deviation from the mean are 11 and 8, which is the mean (9.5) plus or minus the standard deviation (1.5). The values that are 2 standard deviations from the mean are 12.5 and 6.5, which you get from adding and subtracting 3 (2×1.5) from the mean of 9.5. The values that are 3 standard deviations from the mean are 14 and 5, which you derive by adding and subtracting 4.5 (3×1.5) from the mean.

So to solve this problem, you find that the values that are 2.5 standard deviations from the mean are 13.25 and 5.75, because $2.5 \times 1.5 = 3.75$. Look for an answer choice that's more than 13.25 or less than 5.75. The answer is 13.5, Choice (E).

14. **C.** The four angles lie along a straight line, so they add up to 180 degrees. (If you need a refresher on the properties of angles, read Chapter 14.)

Although it's lovely to know that *BX* bisects (which means cuts exactly in half) the two angles on the left side and that *BZ* bisects the two angles on the right side, without the measure of at least one of the angles, you have no way of knowing the measurements of any of the angles. So Statement (1) isn't sufficient, and the answer has to be Choice (B), Choice (C), or Choice (E).

Statement (2) gives you only one of the angle measures, which by itself doesn't clarify the measure of ∠*ABX* any better than Statement (1) does. Statement (2) isn't sufficient.

But remember that we said that for Statement (1) to work, you just need a value for at least one of the angles. Well, Statement (2) provides that value. Taken together, the two statements allow you to solve for the measure of ∠*ABX*. You can stop right there. The correct answer is Choice (C).

You don't have to actually figure out the measurement of the angle, but because we're so thorough, we're going to go through the calculations for you anyway. This step is unnecessary on test day. Knowing that *BZ* bisects ∠*YBC* and that ∠*YBZ* measures 60 degrees allows you to deduce that $\angle ZBC$ is also 60 degrees. Additionally, you've now accounted for 120 of the total 180 degrees allotted for the four angles, which leaves you 60 degrees to play with. Finally, because BX bisects $\angle ABY$, two equal angles remain. Two equal angles that together equal 60 degrees must equal 30 degrees each, because $\frac{60}{2} = 30$.

15. **D.** To find the total distance of Traci's trip, set up an equation that expresses the sum of the three separate trip portions. Let x equal the total distance in miles. Traci stopped to rest after she traveled $\frac{1}{3}$ of the total distance, so the first part of the trip is $\frac{1}{3}x$. She stopped again after she traveled $\frac{1}{4}$ of the distance remaining between her first stop and her destination, which is the total distance she traveled minus the first part of her trip. You can represent the second part of the trip mathematically, like this:

$$\frac{1}{4}\left(x - \frac{1}{3}x\right)$$

The third part of the trip is the remaining 200 miles. Add up the three parts of the trip to set up the equation and solve for total distance:

$$x = \frac{1}{3}x + \frac{1}{4}\left(x - \frac{1}{3}x\right) + 200$$

$$x = \frac{1}{3}x + \frac{1}{4}\left(\frac{3}{3}x - \frac{1}{3}x\right) + 200$$

$$x = \frac{1}{3}x + \frac{1}{4}\left(\frac{2}{3}x\right) + 200$$

$$x = \frac{1}{3}x + \frac{1}{6}x + 200$$

TIP

At this point, you can make it easier on yourself by multiplying each expression on both sides by 6 to get rid of the fractions:

$$2x + x + 1{,}200 = 6x$$

$$3x + 1{,}200 = 6x$$

$$1{,}200 = 3x$$

$$400 = x$$

Traci traveled a total distance of 400 miles, so the correct answer is Choice (D).

16. **E.** This problem seems simple, but if you try to solve it too quickly, you may miss something. So consider all possibilities.

WARNING

Evaluating Statement (1) can be tricky. Don't jump to the conclusion that if the lowest common denominator (LCD) of the two fractions is 10, then $\frac{a}{b}$ must have a denominator of 10 and, therefore, $b = 10$.

The value of b could also equal 2, and the two fractions would still have an LCD of 10. Because b has two possible values, Statement (1) is insufficient. Therefore, the answer is Choice (B), Choice (C), or Choice (E).

Statement (2) is easier to evaluate. The value of the numerator has no bearing on the value of the denominator, so the fact that $a = 3$ is irrelevant to the value of b. Statement (2) is also insufficient, which means the answer is either Choice (C) or Choice (E).

Knowing that $a = 3$ tells you nothing about whether b is 10 or 2, which means that the two statements together are still insufficient to answer the question.

17. **C.** You could try to solve for n, but a faster and easier way to approach this problem is to plug each of the answer choices into the given equation and pick the one that doesn't make the expression true:

- Choice (A) gives you 1. Plug in 1 for x in the equation: $1 + 3 = 4^n$. Doing so makes $n = 1$, which is a positive integer. Because 1 is a possible value for x, Choice (A) is wrong.

- If you substitute 13 from Choice (B), you get $13 + 3 = 4^n$. And $13 + 3$ is 16 and $4^2 = 16$. If $n = 2$, it's a positive integer, so eliminate Choice (B).

- For Choice (C), you substitute 45 into the equation: $45 + 3 = 4^n$. The equation comes out to $48 = 4^n$, and although it may seem like 4 could be a root of 48, it's not. There's no way n could be a positive integer when $x = 45$. Choice (C) is the correct answer. You can choose Choice (C) and go on, or you can check the last two answers just to be sure. Your decision depends on how much time you have remaining.

- If you plug in 61 from Choice (D) into the equation, you get $61 + 3 = 4^n$. And $61 + 3 = 64$, which is 4^3. But 3 is a positive integer, so Choice (D) can't be right.

- Choice (E) is 253, and $253 + 3 = 256$. And $256 = 4^4$, which would make $n = 4$, a positive integer. Choice (E) makes the equation true, so it's the wrong answer.

Be careful when you answer questions that ask you to find the answer that *can't* be true. In these cases, if an answer choice works, you have to eliminate it rather than choose it. Keep reminding yourself of your goal.

18. **B.** The first statement provides an equation that contains b, but notice that b is squared, so it's likely the solution for b in this equation could be either positive or negative. You can perform a quick check to be sure. The left side of the equation equals 1, so the exponent must equal 0. Any value to the power of 0 is equal to 1. When you set the exponent equal to 0 and solve, you get two possible values for b:

$$b^2 - 4 = 0$$
$$b^2 = 4$$
$$b = \pm\sqrt{4}$$
$$b = \pm 2$$

Statement (1) isn't sufficient, so eliminate Choices (A) and (D).

At first glance, Statement (2) appears insufficient as well because it contains more than one variable, but check it to be sure. First, make the bases equal:

$$3^{(b-4-2c)} = 9^{(b-c)}$$
$$3^{(b-4-2c)} = 3^{2(b-c)}$$

Then set the exponents equal to each other to discover whether you can solve for b:

$$b - 4 - 2c = 2(b - c)$$
$$b - 4 - 2c = 2b - 2c$$
$$b - 4 = 2b$$
$$-4 = b$$

The minute you realize that the c values cancel, you know that you can solve for b. The answer must be Choice (B).

19. **B.** Apply the average formula to find the current month's average number of automobiles sold. To find the sum, you need to add all the values represented on the plot. This stem-and-leaf plot presents a set of values in terms of their tens and ones digits. The left column is the tens digit, and the right column is the ones digit for each of the numbers of automobiles sold. Use data to find the sum:

$$12 + 15 + 17 + (2 \times 18) + 22 + (2 \times 23) + 24 + (3 \times 25) + 32 + (3 \times 34)$$
$$+ 38 + (2 \times 39) + 50 + 52 + 61 = 660$$

Enter this data into the average formula:

$$A = \frac{\text{sum of autos}}{\text{\# of autos}}$$
$$A = \frac{660}{22}$$
$$A = 30$$

At this point, you may notice that to obtain an average of 35 autos, each sales associate needs to sell 5 additional autos.

If this isn't obvious at first, you can apply the formula again to determine the total number of additional autos the sales associates need to sell next month to achieve an average of 35 autos sold per salesperson:

$$35 = \frac{660 + x}{22}$$
$$770 = 660 + x$$
$$110 = x$$

This number is the total number of additional autos the sales associates need to sell next month to reach management's goal, but the question asks for the average number each sales associate needs to sell to achieve an average of 35 autos per salesperson. So divide 110 by 22:

$$\frac{110}{22} = 5$$

On average, each sales associate needs to sell 5 additional automobiles to reach an average of 35 autos per salesperson.

20. **A.** This question requires basic simplification. Begin by canceling terms. Because the whole numerator is squared, you first need to factor every term in the parentheses. Take them one-by-one and apply process of elimination to the answer choices as you go.

$$4^2 = 16$$

Divide the coefficients of 16 and 2 to get 8 and eliminate Choices (D) and (E) because they don't have a coefficient of 8. Continue by squaring the variables in the numerator. When you take an exponent to another power, you multiply the exponents:

$$(a^4)^2 = a^8$$
$$(b^3)^2 = b^6$$

The new expression is $8\left(\dfrac{a^8 b^6}{a^2 b^{-2}}\right)$.

Divide the variables by subtracting the exponents:

$$\frac{a^8}{a^2} = a^6$$

$$\frac{b^6}{b^{-2}} = b^8$$

Combine the components to get a final answer of $8a^6 b^8$.

If you picked Choice (B), you subtracted the 2 from 6 when you worked with the *b* exponents. When you subtract a negative value, you actually add the value. If you picked Choice (C), you added the exponents when you squared them instead of multiplying them.

21. **A.** Notice the first statement gives you a ratio that contains both *a* and *b*. This looks promising. Set up the ratio by translating English to math: $\frac{0.25a}{2b} = \frac{2}{3}$. It should be clear that you can solve this equation for $\frac{a}{b}$, but if you want to sure, here's this solution:

$$\frac{0.25a}{2b} = \frac{2}{3}$$
$$0.75a = 4b$$
$$0.75\frac{a}{b} = 4$$
$$\frac{a}{b} = \frac{4}{0.75}$$

Statement (1) is sufficient, so you eliminate Choices (B), (C), and (E) and move on to Statement (2). When you translate Statement (2) into a math equation, you get $a = 4b + 2$, which you can solve for *a* or *b*, but not for $\frac{a}{b}$:

$$a = 4b + 2$$
$$a - 2 = 4b$$
$$\frac{a-2}{b} = 4$$

Statement (2) isn't sufficient, so Choice (D) is out, and Choice (A) is the answer.

22. **C.** Akhil begins with an initial CD investment of $1,200. Every six months he makes 1.05% on his existing money. So after the first six months, Akhil has 1.0105 times the $1,200 initial investment, or $1,212.60. But the balance doesn't increase by $12.60 every six months because Akhil makes 1.05% on the new existing balance, So after one year, he has 1.0105 times $1,212.60 instead of $1,200, which is a balance of $1,225.33. At a year and a half, Akhil has 1.0105 times $1,225.33, or $1,238.20. Six months later the CD matures after another 1.05% is added to Akhil's balance. $1,238.20 × 1.0105 = $1,251.20.

The amount Akhil invests into a second CD is $1,251.20 less the $400 he uses to purchase the tablet: $1,251.20 − $400 = $851.20. Pick Choice (C).

TIP

You can save some time by making a comparison between what Ahkil earns from compounded interest to what he would earn from simple interest. The amount of compounded interest earned in a certain time period should be greater than that earned from simple interest. By multiplying $1,200 by 0.0105, you know he earns $12.60 each 6 months. Multiplying $12.60 times 4 give you $50.40 earned from simple interest in 2 years, which would make Ahkil's balance $1,250.40. When you subtract $400 for the tablet, you learn that Ahkil would have $850.40 to invest in the second CD if he had earned simple interest. You can eliminate Choice (B) because he would have earned slightly more with compound interest but not so much more that you can justify Choices (D) or (E). Choice (C) is the only value that fits that description!

23. **B.** The equation to find slope is $m = \frac{y_1 - y_2}{x_1 - x_2}$. Simply plug in values in this question. When you plug the values into the slope equation and solve, you get this:

$$m = \frac{5-4}{2-10}$$
$$m = -\frac{1}{8}$$

Pick Choice (B) and move on to the next question!

24. E. This is the last question, and it happens to be one of the most difficult ones of the bunch. At first, you may think that you can solve this question with two simultaneous equations. However, when you take a closer look, you see this isn't the case. To get started, let f = the cost of a floor seat and b = the cost of a balcony seat. Then evaluate the statements.

If you write out Matthew's information in Statement (1) in mathematical terms, you get an equation with two variables:

$$4f + 3b = 82.50$$

As we've said before, you can't solve an equation with two variables without additional information. This statement alone isn't sufficient, so the answer is either Choice (B), (C), or (E).

Likewise, Statement (2)'s information leads to an equation with two variables:

$$8f + 6b = 165$$

This equation alone isn't enough to solve the problem, so the answer has to be Choice (C) or Choice (E).

Here's where you may have gotten prematurely excited. You may have thought that Statements (1) and (2) provided simultaneous equations that could be manipulated to give you the value of one of the variables. But if you look more closely, you'll see that the equations are exactly the same. When you reduce the second equation or expand the first, you have identical equations. Look at the second equation:

$$8f + 6b = 165$$

Divide both sides by 2:

$$4f + 3b = 82.50$$

You don't have simultaneous equations at all, and the two statements together won't enable you to solve the problem. Mark Choice (E).

WARNING

Be aware of data-sufficiency questions that ask you to find the sum (or difference, product, or quotient) of two variables rather than the individual value of one or both because the rule of thumb that two equations are needed to solve for two unknowns may not apply in such a case. If Matthew had purchased an equal number of floor seats and balcony seats, let's say 4 of each, the equation for his information would have looked like this: $4f + 4b = 82.50$. Since the questions asks for the value of $f + b$, the equation for Matthew's information would be sufficient by itself because you could solve for $f + b$ by factoring 4 from both sides of the equation.

5
Excelling on the Integrated-Reasoning Section

Chapter **19**

Best of Both Worlds: The Integrated-Reasoning Section

I ntegrated-reasoning (IR) questions appear right after the analytical-writing section. The IR section throws you something completely different from the five-answer multiple-choice questions you're probably used to. The 12 questions in the integrated-reasoning section are formatted in a variety of ways and include tables and graphs to test how well you apply reasoning skills to different scenarios. A lot goes on at once in this section, and this chapter gives you the information you need to manage it all successfully within the 30-minute time limit.

Understanding What the IR Section Is All About

True to its name, the integrated-reasoning section combines the critical-reasoning skills tested in the verbal-reasoning section with some of the math skills you use to solve quantitative-reasoning questions. Therefore, if you're well prepared for the GMAT's math and verbal sections, you should do well in the IR section, too. We explain the details of the IR section and the purpose behind it in the next two sections.

Skills tested

The most common math computations in the IR section involve these areas:

>> Basic statistics, such as average, median, mode, and range

>> Percentages

>> Rate and distance

>> Functions

>> Geometry formulas

You'll need to apply these essentials of critical reasoning:

>> Basic elements of logical arguments: premises, conclusions, and assumptions

>> How to strengthen and weaken an argument

>> Argument types: cause and effect, analogy, and statistical

You can review the necessary math concepts in Chapters 12, 13, and 14. Read more about evaluating logical arguments in Chapter 6.

Question format

The IR section presents you with 12 questions, one question at a time, and you have 30 minutes to answer them. Almost every question has multiple parts. To get credit for answering a question correctly, you have to answer *all* its parts correctly. You don't receive partial credit for getting one part of the question correct. Unlike the verbal- and quantitative-reasoning sections, the IR section isn't computer adaptive. So the order in which you receive questions is preordained and not based on your performance.

Your IR score is based on your answers to four types of questions. On average, you can expect to come across about three of each question type on the GMAT, but the actual number of questions of each type and the order in which they appear may vary. So count on seeing at least a couple of each of these four question types crop up on your test:

>> **Table analysis:** This three-part IR question offers you a spreadsheet of values that you can order in different ways by clicking the heading of each column. You use the data to make judgments about three pieces of information; each of your judgments has to be correct to get credit for the question.

>> **Two-part analysis:** Based on a short written explanation of a phenomenon, situation, or mathematical problem, you come up with the proper assertions or mathematical expressions that meet the two interrelated criteria presented in the question.

>> **Graphics interpretation:** A graph or chart gives you all the data you need to complete the two missing pieces of information in one or two statements. You choose from a pull-down menu of several answer options to record your answers.

>> **Multi-source reasoning:** These properly named questions present you with several sources of information, such as short passages, graphs and charts, and business documents, from which you draw logical conclusions to answer questions in either of two formats: standard five-answer multiple-choice questions and three-part questions that ask you to evaluate statements.

USING THE GMAT CALCULATOR

The calculator in the GMAT IR section looks a lot like the calculator you can purchase at your local dollar store or the one that appears when you access the Microsoft calculator accessory. It has minimal features but everything you need to work out the calculations in the IR section. When you click on *Calculator* at the top of your screen, the tool pops up. You can move it anywhere on the screen by dragging it with your mouse. It stays open until you close it by clicking the *X* in the upper-right corner of the tool.

The number and operation keys work just like a regular calculator. You can clear a single entry with the CE key or just the right digit with the ← key. Start over again from scratch by clicking the C key, which wipes out the entry and all its associated computations.

Unlike a scientific calculator, the GMAT calculator doesn't follow the order of operations. So if you enter $4 + 5 * 10$, you get 90 instead of 54. To get the right value, you have to enter the values in the proper order, $5 * 10 + 4$.

The MS key stores a value to the memory. You can add values to the memory with the M+ key and subtract them with the M- key. To access the value in the memory, click MR. To clear it, click MC.

The $\pm$ changes a positive value to negative and a negative value to positive. The / key means divide, and the * key multiples. To find the square root of 34, you enter 34 and click on $\sqrt{}$. To find 35 percent of 70, you enter $7 * 35$ and hit the % key. Though we doubt you'll use it much, the $1/x$ key finds the reciprocal of any integer. To find the value of the reciprocal of 4, for example, you enter 4 and click the $1/x$ key — voila! — 0.25 appears.

We cover the steps to answering each question type in the section "Approaching Each Question Type," later in this chapter.

To assist you with the mathematical computations you may need to make for some of the IR questions, the GMAT software provides you with a simple calculator. Whenever you need it, you click the box labeled *Calculator* and something that looks like Figure 19-1 appears. You select its functions by using your mouse. Don't get too attached to it, though; the calculator is available only for IR questions, so you won't be able to use it in the quantitative–reasoning section. If you want more information on the calculator's features, see the nearby sidebar "Using the GMAT calculator."

FIGURE 19-1: The GMAT calculator.

© John Wiley & Sons, Inc.

Because using a computer calculator can be awkward, you'll likely answer most IR questions more quickly by using estimation or working out calculations by hand on your noteboard. Save the calculator for only the most complex or precise computations.

Figuring Out How the IR Section Is Scored

Like the score you receive for the analytical-writing section, your integrated-reasoning score has no influence on your overall GMAT score, which consists of the combination of only your quantitative-reasoning and verbal-reasoning scores. Based on your performance in the IR section, your raw score is converted to a scaled score that ranges in whole numbers from 1 to 8 and is recorded separately from all the other scores.

MBA programs decide how they use your IR score and may choose to disregard it altogether. So your IR score is unlikely to make much of an impression unless it's unusually low, in the 1 to 3 score range, or really high, such as the rare 7 or 8. A midrange score of 4, 5, or 6 likely won't significantly hurt or help your chances of admission.

Making the Most of Your Time

If you've already calculated that answering 12 questions in 30 minutes gives you 2.5 minutes to answer each question, you may be celebrating the fact that that gives you even more time per question than you have for the quantitative- and verbal-reasoning sections. Don't get too excited just yet. Almost every IR question has multiple parts, and you have to answer all parts of the question correctly to be credited with a correct answer. When you consider the average number of sub-questions contained within each of those 12 questions, the actual number of IR answers you have to come up with in 30 minutes may be as high as 30. Therefore, you have to use your time wisely as you move through the section.

You'll likely feel the time crunch more fiercely in this section than the others. We provide some coping skills to help you through it:

>> **Conceal the timer.** To maintain your sanity, refrain from constant clock-watching. Hide the timer on the computer by clicking on it. After you answer about three questions, reveal the timer by clicking on it again. It counts down from 30 minutes, so if you're at 22 minutes, you're cruising comfortably. If you're at 21 or fewer, you may need to make some more calculated guesses to move through the section at a successful pace.

>> **Know when to move on.** Discipline yourself to submit your best stab at an answer if you find yourself spending more than several minutes on any one question. You don't want to sacrifice getting to an easy, less-time-consuming question because you've worked too long on a harder question. You can't go back and revisit questions after you submitted your answers, so this practice may be difficult for you, especially if you tenaciously seek perfection. Take a deep breath, mark your best guess, and move on to what lies ahead.

>> **Write stuff down.** Don't be afraid to spend a little time upfront analyzing the loads of data in some IR questions. Unless you're someone who can juggle a lot of details in your head, you should write on your noteboard as you think. A little note-taking may save you from reading information over again, which is a real time-waster.

> » **Whisper to yourself.** Studies show that processing information is easier if you speak out loud. Don't be afraid to whisper your way through some of the more complex problems the IR section throws at you. You'll likely take the test in a cubicle-like setting, so if you speak quietly, you won't disturb anyone.

Approaching Each Question Type

Each of the four IR question types tests your analytical ability in a slightly different way, so your approach depends on the question format. This section outlines the important considerations for handling each type.

Table analysis

Table-analysis questions present you with a table that contains several columns of data, similar to the one in Figure 19-2. As you can see, a little bit of explanatory material precedes the table, but don't waste too much time reading those words. Usually, everything you need to answer the question appears in the data table.

The *Sort By* feature at the top of the table allows you to organize the information by column heading, an element that comes in handy when you analyze the three statements that follow the table. When you click on *Sort By*, a drop-down menu of all column headings appears. Clicking on the column heading in the menu causes the table to rearrange its data by that category. So if you were to click on *Cuisine Type* in the drop-down menu in Figure 19-2, the table would rearrange the order of the rows alphabetically so that all the American restaurants would be listed first, followed by the Asian, Italian, Latin, Mexican, Steakhouse, and Seafood restaurants, respectively.

Using the information in the table, you decide whether the proper response to each statement is *True* or *False*, *Inferable* or *Not Inferable*, *Yes* or *No*, or some other similar either/or answer choice dictated by the specifications of the question. Then you indicate your choice by clicking on the circle next to the appropriate answer.

These questions require you to manipulate data and make observations and calculations. Some of the most common calculations are statistical ones, such as percentages, averages, medians, and ratios, so table-analysis questions can be some of the easiest questions to answer in the IR section. Here's how to make sure you get them right:

> » **Jump to the question immediately.** Most of the information you need appears in the table, so you rarely need to read the introductory paragraph that comes before the table. Glance at the column headings to get an idea of the type of information the table provides, and then move promptly to the question.
>
> » **Read the question carefully.** You're most likely to get tripped up on these questions simply because you haven't read them carefully enough to figure out exactly what data they ask you to evaluate.
>
> » **Isolate the relevant column heading.** Often, the key to answering a table-analysis question is ordering the data properly. Quickly figure out which column provides you with the best way to arrange the data and sort by that column. For example, if you were asked for the neighborhood on the list with the most participating restaurants, you'd sort by *Neighborhood*.

During Lexington Restaurant Week, participating eateries design a three-course meal that they will offer throughout the week at a set price of either $20, $30, or $40 a person, excluding drinks (unless otherwise noted), tax, and tip, as reported on the following table.

Sort By:	Restaurant
	Cuisine Type
	Price Per Meal
	Neighborhood
	Wine Included? (Y/N)
	Average Daily Number of Meals Sold

Restaurant	Cuisine Type	Price Per Meal	Neighborhood	Wine Included? (Y/N)	Average Daily Number of Meals Sold
Bendimere's	Steakhouse	$40	Downtown	N	150
Big Ben's Bistro	American	$30	Central	Y	175
Chang's	Asian	$20	Chinatown	N	142
Frank's House	American	$20	Downtown	N	175
Hadley's on the Beach	Seafood	$40	Uptown	Y	160
Meritage	American	$40	Uptown	N	152
Ocean View	Seafood	$40	Uptown	N	151
Pesce Blue	Seafood	$40	Downtown	Y	164
The Purple Parrot	Latin	$30	Northwest	Y	134
Sorbello's	Italian	$40	Old Town	Y	175
Sushi Fusco	Asian	$30	Old Town	N	100
Thai Time	Asian	$20	Northwest	N	87
Valenzuela's	Mexican	$20	Downtown	N	113

FIGURE 19-2: Sample table-analysis format.

© John Wiley & Sons, Inc.

» **Make accurate computations.** Determine exactly what calculations the question requires and perform them accurately, either in your head or on the calculator. Based on Figure 19-2, for example, you could easily figure the restaurant with the greatest average daily number of meals sold by sorting by that column and glancing at the highest number. However, calculating which participating restaurant in the Downtown neighborhood brought in the greatest average daily gross revenue may require the calculator to multiply each restaurant's price per meal by its average daily number of meals sold.

» **Make use of your noteboard.** Keep track of more complex calculations on your noteboard. As you calculate each Downtown restaurant's average daily gross revenue, for example, record the results on your noteboard. Then you can easily compare the four values without having to memorize them.

You can apply these strategies to a sample question.

EXAMPLE

For each of the following statements, select *Yes* if the statement is true based on the information provided in Figure 19-2. Otherwise, choose *No*.

Yes	No	
○	○	A. The average price per meal for all participating restaurants in the Downtown neighborhood was approximately $30.
○	○	B. The average price per meal for participating restaurants in the Old Town neighborhood was less than the average price per meal in the Downtown neighborhood.
○	○	C. Participating restaurants that included wine with the meal in the Uptown neighborhood sold more meals on average per day than participating restaurants that did not include wine with the meal.

Statement (A) references two columns, *Price Per Meal* and *Neighborhood*. Sorting by *Neighborhood* makes more sense because it lists all Downtown restaurants together so that you may better view and compare each Downtown restaurant's price per meal. After you've sorted by *Neighborhood*, the table looks like this:

Restaurant	Cuisine Type	Price Per Meal	Neighborhood	Wine Included? (Y/N)	Average Daily Number of Meals Sold
Big Ben's Bistro	American	$30	Central	Y	175
Chang's	Asian	$20	Chinatown	N	142
Bendimere's	Steakhouse	$40	Downtown	N	150
Frank's House	American	$20	Downtown	N	175
Pesce Blue	Seafood	$40	Downtown	Y	164
Valenzuela's	Mexican	$20	Downtown	N	113
The Purple Parrot	Latin	$30	Northwest	Y	134
Thai Time	Asian	$20	Northwest	N	87
Sorbello's	Italian	$40	Old Town	Y	175
Sushi Fusco	Asian	$30	Old Town	N	100
Hadley's on the Beach	Seafood	$40	Uptown	Y	160
Meritage	American	$40	Uptown	N	152
Ocean View	Seafood	$40	Uptown	N	151

This arrangement allows you to see that two participating restaurants in the Downtown neighborhood charged $20 per meal and two charged $40 per meal. The number of $20 meals sold by both restaurants is 288, and the number of $40 meals sold at the two other restaurants is 314. To find the weighted average, multiply $20 by 288 and $40 by 314. Add the two products and divide by the total number of meals sold (602):

$$A = \frac{(20 \times 288) + (40 \times 314)}{602}$$

$$A = \frac{5,760 + 12,560}{602}$$

$$A = 30.43$$

Because $30.43 is approximately $30, you can say that the average price of a Downtown meal was $30. The answer is *Yes*.

You've already figured out the second calculation for Statement (B). The average price per meal at a Downtown restaurant is about $30. You can write $D = 30$ on your noteboard to remind you. All the Uptown restaurants charged $40 per meal, so the average price per meal in Uptown is greater than the average price in Downtown. Select *No*.

Statement (C) again focuses on one neighborhood, so you don't have to resort to the table. The one restaurant that included wine in the meal price sold 160 meals on average per day, which is more than the 152 and 151 sold by the other two restaurants in the neighborhood. The answer is *Yes*.

REMEMBER

Table-analysis questions may not require that you use all the data provided. For example, you didn't need to evaluate *Cuisine Type* for any of the question parts in the example question. Don't worry if you don't use the data in some columns at all. Part of the task in answering table-analysis questions is knowing what data is important and what's irrelevant.

Two-part analysis

When you see a paragraph or two of information that sets you up to choose two pieces of information from a table with three columns, you know you're dealing with a two-part analysis question. You select the answer for the first part of the question in the first column and the answer to the second part in the second column. The third column provides the set of possible answer choices for each part.

REMEMBER

Reading the explanatory paragraph for these questions is absolutely essential. It provides the conditions you need to consider and clarifies what each part of the question asks for. Read each possibility in the third column carefully. Often, the differences among the options are subtle.

The GMAT usually uses the two-part analysis question to test mathematical skills (such as figuring functions and the properties of geometric shapes) and verbal logical reasoning abilities (such as strengthening and weakening arguments). Often the best way to figure out the answer for the math variety is to try each of the possible values to see which ones fulfill the requirements. Usually, the best way to answer the verbal type is by process of elimination.

The following two sample questions give you an example of a math two-part analysis and a verbal two-part analysis.

EXAMPLE

A set of expressions consists of a total of four expressions: these three expressions $\{2n+8, n+4, 6n-2\}$ and one additional expression. From the following expressions, select the one that could be the fourth expression in the set and the one that could be the resulting arithmetic mean of the four expressions in the set. Make only one selection per column.

Fourth Expression of the Set	Arithmetic Mean of the Set	
○	○	A. $2n$
○	○	B. $3n + 2$
○	○	C. $3n - 2$
○	○	D. $12n + 8$
○	○	E. $48n + 32$
○	○	F. $4n + 8$

Approach this question by trying out the possible answer choices as potential fourth expressions to see which, when it's included with other expressions in the set, results in an arithmetic mean that's another of the possible answer choices.

First, evaluate the three provided expressions. All contain one-digit values that are multiplied by n and then have a one-digit value added or subtracted from that term. So evaluate similar expressions, such as Choices (B), (C), and (F) before you consider less similar expressions, such as Choices (A), (D), and (E).

If Choice (B), $3n+2$, were the fourth expression, the average mean of the set would be the result of applying the average formula:

$$\frac{(2n+8)+(n+4)+(6n-2)+(3n+2)}{4}=A$$

$$\frac{12n+12}{4}=A$$

$$3n+3=A$$

Because $3n+3$ isn't one of the answer choices, you know that $3n+2$ can't be the fourth expression.

Try Choice (C), $3n-2$. If you wrote your calculations for $3n+2$ on your noteboard, you know that the first term of the average mean is the same because the $3n$ doesn't change.

$$\frac{(2n+8)+(n+4)+(6n-2)+(3n-2)}{4}=A$$

$$\frac{12n+8}{4}=A$$

$$3n+2=A$$

This value is a possible option. When the fourth expression in the set is $3n-2$, the average mean of the set is $3n+2$. Select Choice (C) for the first column and Choice (B) for the second. Only one possible set of answers exists, so if you're confident about your calculations, you don't have to consider the other expressions. Submit your answer and move on.

EXAMPLE

Joseph: Health insurance premiums are growing at an alarming rate. This is, in part, because many hospitals and clinics bill for unnecessary diagnostics and tests that inflate the subsequent amount that insurers pay out to them. These expenses are then passed on to consumers in the form of increased insurance premiums. Therefore, reducing the number of unnecessary tests performed by hospitals and clinics will effectively curb the rise in health insurance premiums.

Ronald: Often, the unnecessary diagnostics that you speak of are the result of decisions made by doctors on behalf of their patients. Doctors usually choose the diagnostics that allow them to bill insurers for more money but may not necessarily benefit the patient in a meaningful way or influence the course of treatment chosen. As a result, in order to succeed in reducing the number of unnecessary tests, patients should be allowed to decide which course of diagnostics they would like to undergo.

In the following table, identify the unique assumption upon which each argument depends. Make only one selection in each column: one in the first column for the best representation of Joseph's assumption in his argument and one in the second column for the best representation of Ronald's.

Joseph	Ronald	
○	○	A. Doctors are generally able to determine with great reliability which diagnostic procedures and tests will yield the most effective results.
○	○	B. Tests and diagnostic procedures make up a significant portion of the bills that are sent to insurers.
○	○	C. Insurance companies in other industries, such as auto and home, have been able to reduce costs by reducing the number of unnecessary repairs and replacements on claims for automobiles and homes.
○	○	D. Patients are not as likely as doctors to choose the most expensive diagnostics and tests.
○	○	E. Health insurance premiums have increased twice as fast in the past 5 years as they have over an average of the past 25 years.

Whereas the sample math two-part analysis question required you to figure out the answers to both parts at the same time, this verbal-reasoning sample question is more easily handled one column at a time. First, consider the assumption that's most likely part of Joseph's argument. Then consider the one that pertains to Ronald's.

REMEMBER

The assumption is usually the statement that best links the premises of the argument to its conclusion. For details on evaluating arguments, see Chapter 6.

Following are the premises of Joseph's argument:

» Hospitals and clinics are billing health insurance companies for unnecessary and expensive tests.

» This practice has caused health insurance companies to pay inflated rates to hospitals and clinics.

» The result is that health insurance companies are compensating by raising consumers' health insurance premiums.

Based on these premises, Joseph concludes that reducing unnecessary tests will significantly control the rise in health insurance premiums.

To find the assumption that provides a link between the cessation of the unnecessary tests and a significant effect on increasing healthcare premiums, begin by narrowing your options. Joseph doesn't mention doctors in his argument, so you can eliminate Choices (A) and (D). Choice (E) addresses healthcare premiums but not unnecessary tests, so it's out. Choice (C) concerns other insurance industries, so it has nothing to do with Joseph's argument about healthcare premiums. The best option for Joseph is the assumption that unnecessary tests make up a significant portion of insurance billing. If they make up just a small portion, eliminating tests wouldn't have a significant impact on the rising cost of healthcare premiums. Mark Choice (B) in the column for Joseph.

Now evaluate Ronald's argument. Here are his premises:

» Doctors order unnecessary tests to increase their earnings.

» Patients should be able to choose their tests.

» Putting the decision regarding diagnostics and tests in the patients' control would reduce the number of unnecessary tests.

So you're looking for the assumption that links patients' decisions to fewer unnecessary tests.

Notice that Ronald doesn't address healthcare premiums at all, so you can confidently eliminate Choice (E). Choice (B) is out because you've already attributed it to Joseph. Choice (C) doesn't work for the same reason that it doesn't work for Joseph. Ronald's argument concerns only healthcare. Of the two remaining options (Choices [A] and [D]), only Choice (D) relates to patients' decisions. Only if patients make decisions differently than doctors do would putting patients in control lessen the number of unnecessary tests. So you mark Choice (D) in the column for Ronald.

Graphics interpretation

Not surprisingly, graphics interpretation questions require you to interpret graphs. You may see line graphs, bar graphs, pie charts, Venn diagrams, and so on. Based on the information displayed in the graph, you fill in two separate blanks by selecting the best option from a drop-down menu for each blank. (In the example question later in this section, we include the answer options in parentheses.) You have to complete both blanks correctly to get credit for one graphics interpretation question.

The information you need to fill in the blanks comes primarily from the graph, so make sure you know how to read charts and graphs. Chapter 20 provides a review of the most common GMAT charts and graphs to refresh your memory.

TIP

Here are some other tips to help you efficiently move through graphics interpretation questions:

» **Analyze the graph or chart to determine exactly what information it provides and how.** Observe the labels and examine the numerical increments carefully.

» **Click on Select One to view all the answer options.** To see the possible answers in the drop-down menu for each blank, you have to click on the box that says Select One. Filling in the blank is much easier when you're limited to just the several available choices. Don't attempt to answer the question without seeing the answer choices first.

» **Eliminate illogical answer choices.** Approach the two parts of a graphics interpretation question much like you would a standard multiple-choice question. Eliminate obviously incorrect options and use your reasoning skills to select the best answer from the remaining choices.

» **Make estimations.** The data in charts and graphs are rarely precise, so most of your calculations are estimates or approximations that you can work out on your noteboard or in your head rather than on the calculator.

EXAMPLE

Here's a sample graphics interpretation question to consider.

Scientists, health professionals, and life insurance agents are interested in examining the percentage of people in a population who will live to a certain age. One way to measure this information is to look at the percentage of the population who has died after a certain number of years. The following graph displays the results of such a study.

Approximately _____ (10, 40, 60, 80) percent of the population lives to at least 80 years of age. A person who was a member of the study population would still have an 80 percent chance of being alive at around a maximum age of _____ (15, 35, 55, 80) years.

Filling the first blank in the question tests your graph-reading skills. Find 80 years of age on the horizontal axis. Move your finger from the 80-year mark upward on the graph until you reach the plotted curve. Move your finger to the left to see that at 80 years, about 60 percent of people have died. Don't stop there and choose 60 percent, however. The question asks for how many are alive at the 80-year mark. Subtract 60 from 100 to get that approximately 40 percent of the population lives to at least 80 years. The correct answer is 40 percent.

To complete the second blank, make sure you look at the answer choices first. Because the statement concerns the *maximum* value, consider higher ages first. The oldest option is 80, but it's very unlikely that 80 percent of people are alive at age 80, so try the next highest age, 55. Move along the graph until you reach 55 years. At 55 years of age, 20 percent have died, leaving a maximum of 80 percent alive. Ages above 55 can't be right, so 55 is the correct answer.

If you start with the first option of 15 years, you may be misled. Note that the graph shows you that at about 15 years of age, less than 5 percent of people have died, which means that more than 95 percent of the population are still alive. That's more than 80 percent, but the statement regards the *maximum* age where 80 percent of the population is still kicking, so 15 can't be correct.

Multi-source reasoning

The only IR question type with more than one question that pertains to a set of data is the multi-source reasoning question. For this question type, the GMAT presents different kinds of information in a series of two or three tabs. Each tab conveys a relevant aspect of a set of circumstances. The topics of the scenarios vary greatly. You may have information concerning a certain scientific phenomenon, such as black holes or plant photosynthesis, or you may be asked to apply data that relates to business situations, such as hiring decisions or event planning.

At least one of the tabs in the set contains several paragraphs of written information on a subject. Others may contain additional paragraphs or data contained in tables, charts, or graphs. You use the resources in all tabs to answer several questions, most of which have several parts. For example, Figure 19-3 shows you the first tab for a sample multi-source reasoning scenario regarding guest reservations for a hotel's wedding block. The e-mail in this tab sets up the situation and provides you with the guidelines for the reservation.

| Background Information | Contract Paragraph 3 | Guest List |

The Pearson family is hosting the destination wedding of their daughter Emily and her fiancé, Matthew Voorhies. The event will take place on Saturday, September 8th, at the popular Grand Maryvale Resort, which is located on a tropical island accessible only by airplane. The resort has provided a block of rooms at a discounted rate to accommodate the wedding guests. The terms of the room discount are outlined in Paragraph 3 of the contract between the resort and Emily's father.

The Pearson and Voorhies families want to make sure that all who attend their wedding have accomodations at the resort because the island has few other hotels, and those are shabby and located far away from the resort. The resort is known to be fully booked on weekends in September. Therefore, Emily and Matthew have contacted each guest regarding their room reservation status and have recorded their statuses as of August 1st on a spreadsheet entitled Guest List.

FIGURE 19-3: Sample multi-source reasoning format, background tab.

© John Wiley & Sons, Inc.

Figure 19-4 shows what you find when you click on the second tab: language from the contract between the Pearson family and the resort.

| Background Information | Contract Paragraph 3 | Guest List |

III. For the Pearson/Voorhies Wedding, a hotel room block has been reserved at the Grand Maryvale Resort for the nights of September 7, 8, and 9. Instead of the regular room rate of $175 per night, guests who book as a part of the block for all three nights can pay a special rate of only $135 per night. Those who book for less than three nights will be charged $150 per night. Those who book rooms for the nights before or after the three nights specified by the hotel block must pay the regular nightly room rate for nights stayed beyond the three-night block discount. We can hold five rooms at a time for the attendees of the Pearson/Voorhies wedding – once the first five are filled, we will be able to release five more. We do not guarantee accommodations to wedding guests beyond these specifications.

FIGURE 19-4: Sample multi-source reasoning format, contract tab.

© John Wiley & Sons, Inc.

When you click on the final tab, you may see a table with relevant data, such as the one in Figure 19-5, which shows the wedding guest list and their reservation status.

Name	Number Attending	Number of Rooms Needed	Nights Staying at Resort	Reservations Made?
The Rose Family	4	1	3	N
The Crawford Family	6	2	2	Y
The Fishers	2	1	1	Y
The Ball Family	5	2	3	Y
The Ranks Family	6	2	3	N
The Keppners	2	1	1	Y
The Albertsons	4	1	1	N
....	....	....	....	....

Tabs above table: Background Information / Contract Paragraph 3 / Guest List

FIGURE 19-5: Sample multi-source reasoning format, guest list tab.

© John Wiley & Sons, Inc.

The multi-source reasoning questions appear in one of two formats: three-part table (similar to table-analysis questions) or standard five-answer multiple-choice. Keep in mind that you have to answer all three parts of the first format to get credit for the one question. The multiple-choice format may be one of the easiest questions to answer in the IR section. You can use the process of elimination to narrow the answers, and you have to choose only one correct answer to get full credit for the question.

The trickiest aspect of answering multi-source reasoning questions is sifting through the plethora of information to discover what's relevant. Depending on the scenario, you may have to juggle information in tables, diagrams, articles, and so on to come up with correct answers.

TIP

Here are some pointers to help you with the task:

>> **Summarize each tab.** As you read through the information in each tab for the first time, record pertinent points to help you remember which tab holds what type of data. That way you don't have to continually flip back and forth between screens as you answer questions. For example, summarize the contract details in Figure 19-4 on your noteboard with quick notations such as *9/7, 8, & 9 = $135/night; < 3 nights = $150/night; before/after 9/7 or 9/9 = $175/night.*

>> **Make connections.** After you've seen the information in each tab, synthesize facts and figures from one tab with correlative data from another. Keep track of your findings on your noteboard. For example, you should notice as you read the information in Figures 19-4 and 19-5 that you can correlate the data in the table in the final tab with the room-charge specifications in the second tab to figure out how much each guest will pay for resort rooms.

>> **Rely on what the test gives you.** Some of the topics in multi-source reasoning scenarios may be familiar to you. Although familiarity may make the information more accessible to you, it may also influence you to answer questions based on what you know instead of what the exam tells you. For example, you shouldn't answer any questions about the Pearson wedding sample scenario based on what you know about hotel booking from your own experience as a front-desk manager.

Here's another sample multi-source scenario with a couple of questions to help you get more acquainted with the question type. This scenario has only two tabs, each conveying an opposing opinion from two scientists on a specific scientific phenomenon.

Scientist 1

Ancient ice cores from Antarctica indicate that the concentration of carbon dioxide in the atmosphere and global mean temperatures have followed the same pattern of fluctuations in levels over the past 160,000 years. Therefore, the increase in atmospheric carbon dioxide concentration from 280 parts per million to 360 parts per million that has occurred over the past 150 years points to significant and detrimental climatic changes in the near future. The climate has already changed: The average surface temperature of the earth has increased 0.6°C in the past hundred years, with the ten hottest years of that time period all occurring since 1980. Although 0.6°C may not seem large, changes in the mean surface temperature as low as 0.5°C have dramatically affected crop growth in years past. Moreover, computer models project that surface temperatures will increase about 2.0°C by the year 2100 and will continue to increase in the years after even if concentration of greenhouse gases is stabilized by that time. If the present trend in carbon dioxide increase continues, though, carbon dioxide concentration will exceed 1,100 parts per million soon after 2100 and will be associated with a temperature increase of approximately 10.0°C over the present mean annual global surface temperature.

Scientist 2

The observed increases in minor greenhouse gases such as carbon dioxide and methane will not lead to sizeable global warming. Water vapor and clouds are responsible for more than 98% of the earth's greenhouse effect. Current models that project large temperature increases with a doubling of the present carbon dioxide concentration incorporate changes in water vapor, clouds and other factors that would accompany a rise in carbon dioxide levels. The way these models handle such feedback factors is not supported by current scientific knowledge. In fact, there is convincing evidence that shows that increases in carbon dioxide concentration would lead to changes in feedback factors that would diminish any temperature increase associated with more carbon dioxide in the atmosphere. The climatic data for the last hundred years show an irregular pattern in which many of the greatest jumps in global mean temperature were too large to be associated with the observed increase in carbon dioxide. The overall increase of 0.45°C in the past century is well under what the models would have predicted given the changes in carbon dioxide concentration. As with the temperature models, recent increases in atmospheric carbon dioxide have not risen to the extent predicted by models dealing solely with carbon dioxide levels. The rate of carbon dioxide concentration increase has slowed since 1973. Improved energy technologies will further dampen the increase so that the carbon dioxide concentration will be under 700 parts per million in the year 2100.

Consider each of the following statements about atmospheric carbon-dioxide levels and determine whether Scientists 1 and 2 are both likely to agree by marking either *Yes* or *No*:

EXAMPLE

Yes	No	
○	○	A. Increasing carbon dioxide levels affect other factors.
○	○	B. Humans will never be able to stabilize atmospheric carbon dioxide levels.
○	○	C. The rate of increase in carbon dioxide levels will rise throughout the next 100 years.

Statement (A) is a nice, noncontroversial statement with which both scientists would agree. Scientist 1 stresses that rising carbon dioxide is linked to higher temperature (another factor), while Scientist 2 discusses *feedback factors,* which are factors that respond to carbon-dioxide changes and will, in turn, affect the carbon dioxide. Select *Yes* for Statement (A).

To answer Statement (B), notice that Scientist 2, who refers to improved energy technology, clearly disagrees with the statement, but so does Scientist 1, who mentions the possibility that carbon-dioxide levels will stabilize. Neither scientist would agree with Statement (B), so the answer is *No.*

Scientist 2 disagrees with Statement (C) and actually discusses a slowing down in the rate of carbon-dioxide-level increase. Because at least one of the scientists would disagree with the statement, the answer to Statement (C) is *No.*

The next question is in multiple-choice format.

EXAMPLE

Which of the following statements does only Scientist 1 support?

(A) A change in atmospheric water vapor could significantly affect global temperatures.

(B) The increase in atmospheric carbon-dioxide concentration from 280 parts per million to 360 parts per million that has occurred over the last 150 years is not expected to affect climactic change negatively in the future.

(C) Recent increases in atmospheric carbon dioxide have surpassed those predicted by temperature models dealing solely with carbon-dioxide models.

(D) Temperature fluctuations will match carbon-dioxide changes when carbon-dioxide changes are abrupt.

(E) Increases in carbon-dioxide concentration would lead to changes in feedback factors that would compound any temperature increase associated with more carbon dioxide in the atmosphere.

Focus on the information in the first tab. Scientist 1 mentions a match between carbon dioxide and temperature variations and then uses the recent large change in carbon-dioxide levels as evidence that significant changes in temperature will occur. Scientist 1 goes on to discuss how continued sharp increases in atmospheric carbon dioxide will lead to similar dramatic temperature increases. Scientist 1 implies that the recent carbon-dioxide changes have been unprecedented. The data during the past 160,000 years show a correspondence between temperature and carbon-dioxide fluctuations, but this correspondence has occurred in the absence of the dramatic changes the earth is now and soon will be experiencing. For Scientist 1 to use the fluctuation correspondence as evidence for what will soon happen, she must assume that the correspondence will continue in light of current and near-future sharp changes. So Choice (D) is correct.

Choice (A) is supported by Scientist 2, and neither scientist would support Choices (B), (C), or (E). In fact, Scientist 1 actually says that an increase in atmospheric carbon-dioxide concentration from 280 parts per million to 360 parts per million can cause "significant and detrimental climactic changes in the near future."

Chapter **20**

Deciphering Data in Charts and Graphs

N ot every integrated-reasoning question relies on a chart or graph, but most do. This chapter reviews the characteristics of the ways the GMAT represents data in the integrated-reasoning section and explains how to read each type in the most efficient way.

The charts and graphs you'll encounter on the GMAT integrated-reasoning section display data in a variety of formats. You interpret the data provided in tables, bar graphs, line graphs, scatter plots, pie charts, or Venn diagrams, and then you apply your analysis to draw conclusions about a bunch of scenarios. You get to compare statistics, identify trends or lapses in trends, make predictions for the future, and so on.

Approaching Integrated-Reasoning Data in Five Easy Steps

Most integrated-reasoning questions contain a chart or graph. You won't have much time to waste, so it's a good idea to know how to extract data from the various types of charts and graphs before you sit down in front of the computer on exam day. Regardless of the graph or chart you're working with, you'll follow a similar, five-step approach:

1. **Identify the type of chart or graph.**

Graphs display data in different ways, so start by recognizing which graph or chart type you're dealing with. To make this step easy, we provide detailed information on each of the most common charts and graphs on the GMAT in this chapter.

2. **Read the accompanying question and determine what it asks.**

Before you attempt to read the chart or graph, examine the question to figure out exactly what kind of information you need to answer it.

3. **Isolate what you need to get out of the chart or graph to successfully answer the question.**

Refer to the chart or graph to discover where it conveys the specific data you need to answer the question.

4. **Read the chart or graph properly.**

Examine the chart or graph carefully to spot trends and note where the quantities associated with each variable appear and how the value of each increment is displayed.

5. **Solve the problem.**

Use the data you've carefully extracted from the chart or graph to come up with the correct answer to the question.

The remaining sections in this chapter show you how to apply this approach to reading a variety of charts and graphs.

Translating Information in Tables

Tables report, organize, and summarize data and allow you to view and analyze precise values. For example, a table can be an effective way of presenting average daily high and low temperatures in a given area, the number of male and female births that occur each year within a population, or the ranking of a band's top-ten hits.

The sample table in Figure 20-1 records the four individual event and all-around scores for five gymnasts in a local meet. Its data is precise rather than approximated, which allows you to come up with accurate analyses of the values. For example, you can see from the table that Kate just barely edged out Jess on the balance beam by a 0.005 difference in scores.

FIGURE 20-1:
You're likely to see a table like this one as part of a GMAT integrated-reasoning question.

Bayside Gymnastics Club Score Report					
Name	Vault Score	Uneven Bars Score	Balance Beam Score	Floor Exercise Score	All-Around Score
Kelsea Moore	16.25	15.5	15.1	14.985	61.835
Adrianne Rizzo	15.9	14.975	15.225	15.325	61.425
Kate McCaffery	16.0	14.6	15.0	13.995	58.595
Jess Hartley	15.875	13.966	14.995	15.0	59.836
Maggie Birney	16.1	13.92	15.1	13.87	58.990

© John Wiley & Sons, Inc.

REMEMBER

When you evaluate a table, pay particular attention to the column labels to determine exactly what kind of information and values it displays. Read carefully to differentiate values and determine, say, whether the numbers represent percentages or actual figures. For example, a few seconds of careful consideration of the values in the sample table in Figure 20-1 tells you that the gymnasts' all-around score is the sum of the other scores rather than their average. So if a question asked you about a particular gymnast's average score for all events, you'd know you'd have to compute this calculation rather than report the provided all-around score.

Not surprisingly, tables are the primary source of information in the integrated-reasoning table-analysis question type. These questions use tables to display data, usually a lot of it. You may also find tables in multi-source reasoning and two-part analysis questions. (Chapter 19 provides more detail on how to answer all four integrated-reasoning question types.)

Making Comparisons with Bar Graphs

Bar graphs (also sometimes called bar charts) have a variety of uses. They're especially good for comparing data and approximating values. As the name suggests, they use rectangular bars to represent different categories of data (either horizontally or vertically); the height or length of each bar indicates the corresponding quantity for that category of data.

You see bar graphs most frequently on the GMAT in graphics interpretation questions, but they may also appear in multi-source reasoning and two-part analysis questions. Simple bar graphs present the relationship between two variables. More complex bar graphs show additional data by displaying additional bars or by segmenting each individual bar. We show you how to read simple and complex bar graphs in the following sections.

Simple bar graphs

Bar graphs provide an excellent way to visualize the similarities and differences among several categories of data. Even a simple bar graph, such as the one in Figure 20-2, can convey a whole bunch of information.

The chart heading in Figure 20-2 defines the overall category of information: 2009 activity ticket sales for Pleasantdale High School by group. You don't need a title for the horizontal axis. It's obvious from the chart heading that each bar provides the data for each school group. From the vertical axis title, you discover that the data represents number of tickets sold rather than the total revenue from those tickets. *In Thousands* means that each major horizontal gridline represents 1,000 tickets. Each of the four minor gridlines between each major gridline represents 200 tickets (the four lines divide the segments between the whole number into five parts, and $\frac{1,000}{5} = 200$). So the graph indicates that the number of drama club tickets sold was approximately 3,700 because the *Drama Club* bar ends between the third and fourth minor gridlines above the 3,000 mark. To find the total number of drama club tickets sold, add 200 for each of the three minor gridlines and half of that (100) as represented by the half space between the third and fourth minor gridlines: $3,000 + 3(200) + 100 = 3,700$.

Some GMAT bar graphs may display information for a range of values. An example appears in Figure 20-3. Based on this graph, you can figure that the minimum total number of tickets sold by all groups in 2009 was the sum of the lowest number for each group $(4,000 + 5,000 + 6,000)$, or 15,000 tickets. The maximum possible total of tickets sold by the three groups combined was the sum of the highest value for each category: $5,000 + 6,000 + 7,000$, or 18,000.

Graphs with many bars

Altering the design of a bar graph allows you to convey even more information. Graphs with multiple bars reveal data for additional categories. For example, Figure 20-4 compares the ticket sales totals for the three groups by year for three years.

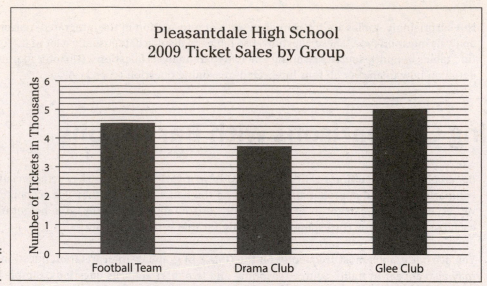

FIGURE 20-2:
Simple bar graph.

© John Wiley & Sons, Inc.

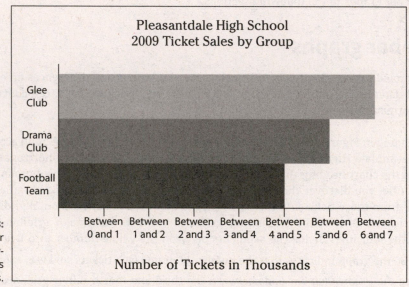

FIGURE 20-3:
Simple bar graph showing ranges of values.

© John Wiley & Sons, Inc.

The legend designates which group the bars stand for. This graph allows you to easily make comparisons over the years and among the three groups. For example, it's easy to see that in 2009, glee club ticket sales were not only greater than they had been in previous years but also exceeded sales for either of the other two groups. Perhaps sales were influenced by the launch of a popular TV show featuring a high–school glee club!

Segmented bar graphs

Graphs with segmented bars display the characteristics of subcategories. Each bar is divided into segments that represent different subgroups. The height of each segment within a bar represents the value associated with that particular subgroup. For example, Pleasantdale High can provide more specific comparisons of the ticket sales during different times of the year by using a segmented bar graph, such as the one in Figure 20-5.

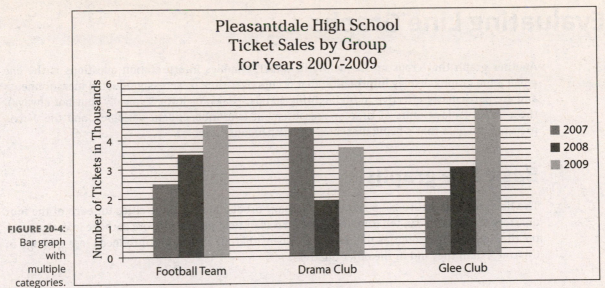

FIGURE 20-4: Bar graph with multiple categories.

Pleasantdale High School Ticket Sales by Group for Years 2007-2009

© John Wiley & Sons, Inc.

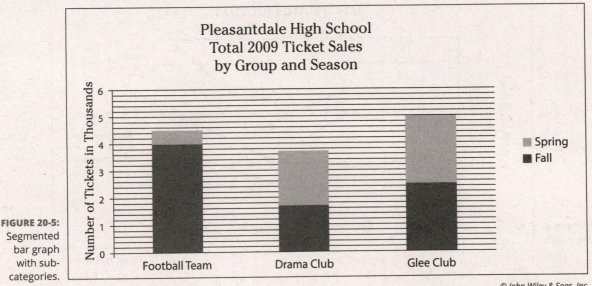

FIGURE 20-5: Segmented bar graph with sub-categories.

Pleasantdale High School Total 2009 Ticket Sales by Group and Season

© John Wiley & Sons, Inc.

You apply subtraction to read a segmented graph. The top of each bar is the total from which you subtract the designations for each subcategory. So for the *Football Team* bar in Figure 20-5, the total number of tickets sold in 2009 was 4,500. The number of tickets sold in the fall is represented by the lower segment, which climbs up to about the 4,000 mark. The number of tickets sold in the spring is the difference between the approximate total number of tickets (4,500) and the approximate number of fall tickets (4,000), which is about 500. The graph also reveals that activity sales for the glee club and drama club occur more consistently across both seasons than for the football team, which sells many more tickets in the fall than it does in the spring.

REMEMBER

Whenever you reference data from a bar graph, you speak in estimates. Bar graphs don't provide exact values; that's not their job. They allow you to make comparisons based on approximations.

Evaluating Line Graphs

Another graph that crops up frequently in GMAT graphics interpretation questions is the *line graph*. Line graphs display information that occurs over time or across graduated measurements and are particularly effective in highlighting trends, peaks, or lows. Typically (but not always), the x-axis displays units of time or measurement (the independent variable), and the y-axis presents the data that's being measured (the dependent variable).

Basic line graphs

The line graph in Figure 20-6 shows the garbage production for three cities for each of the four quarters of 2011. You can tell from the graph that Plainfield produced more garbage in every quarter than the other two cities did, and it's evident that all three cities produced less garbage in Quarter 3 than they did in the other quarters.

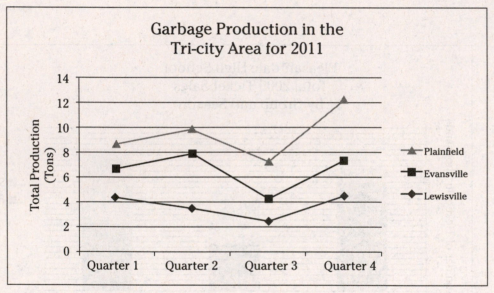

FIGURE 20-6: Line graph.

© John Wiley & Sons, Inc.

Scatter plots

Line graphs are extensions of *scatter graphs*, or *scatter plots*, which display the relationship between two numerical variables. These graphs display a bunch of points that show the relationship between two variables, one represented on the x-axis and the other on the y-axis. For example, the scatter plot in Figure 20-7 plots each city's population on the x-axis and its garbage production on the y-axis. Scatter plots show you trends and patterns. From Figure 20-7, you can figure out that, generally, a direct or positive relationship exists between a city's population and the amount of garbage it produces. The graph indicates that this is the case because the data points tend to be higher on the y-axis as they move to the right (or increase) on the x-axis. You can also surmise that of the 20 cities listed, more have fewer than 200,000 people than have greater than 200,000 people. That's because the graph shows a greater number of points that fall to the left of the 200,000 population line than to the right.

Scatter plots also convey trend and pattern deviations. The GMAT may provide a scatter plot with or without a *trend line*. The trend line shows the overall pattern of the data plots and reveals deviations. The scatter plot in Figure 20-7 doesn't display a trend line, so you have to imagine one. You can lay your noteboard along the graph to help you envision the trend line if one isn't provided. Figure 20-8 shows you the trend line for the garbage production graph. With the trend line in place, you can more easily recognize that the largest city in the county deviates from the trend somewhat considerably. Its garbage production is less in proportion to its population than that of most other cities in the county. You know that because its data point is considerably below the trend line.

FIGURE 20-7:
Scatter plot or scatter graph.

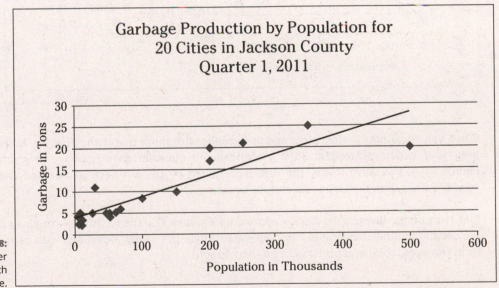

FIGURE 20-8:
Scatter plot with trend line.

Complex scatter plots

Sometimes the GMAT crams even more information on a scatter plot by introducing another variable associated with the data. The values for this variable appear on the *y*-axis on the right side of the graph. This type of graph is just a way of combining information in one graph that could appear on two separate graphs.

Figure 20-9 shows you an example of a complex scatter plot. It adds another variable (average yearly income by population) to the mix. The average annual income for each city lies on the y-axis. The points for one set of data have different symbols than those for the other so that you can distinguish between the two sets. The legend at the right of the graph in Figure 20-9 tells you that garbage production is represented by diamonds, and the symbol for income is a square. The trend line for the relationship between city population and average yearly income has a negative slope, which shows you that the smaller the population, the greater the average yearly income. This trend indicates an inverse relationship between city population and average yearly income.

REMEMBER

The GMAT may ask you to identify the relationship between two variables as positive, negative, or neutral. If the trend line has a positive slope, the relationship is positive; if it has a negative slope, the relationship is negative. If the trend line is horizontal or the points are scattered without any recognizable pattern, the relationship is neutral, meaning that no correlation exists between the variables.

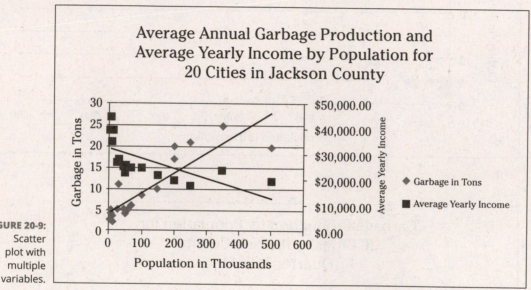

FIGURE 20-9:
Scatter plot with multiple variables.

WARNING

When you encounter scatter plots and line graphs with more than two variables, make sure you keep your variables straight. So if you're asked a question about garbage production, using Figure 20-9, you have to use the data represented by the left vertical axis and the diamond symbol rather than the right axis and the squares.

Like bar graphs, line graphs display approximate values. Use the technique explained in the earlier section "Simple bar graphs" to help you estimate the values associated with each data point from the axes labels and grid marks on these graphs.

Clarifying Circle Graphs (Also Known as Pie Charts)

Circle graphs, also known as *pie charts*, show values that are part of a larger whole, such as percentages. The graphs contain divisions called *sectors*, which divide the circle into portions that are proportional to the quantity each represents as part of the whole 360-degree circle. Each sector becomes a piece of the *pie*; you get information and compare values by examining the pieces in relation to each other and to the whole pie.

When a graphics-interpretation question provides you with a circle graph and designates the percentage values of each of its sectors, you can use it to figure out actual quantities. The circle graph in Figure 20-10 tells you that Plainfield has more Republican affiliates than Democrat and that Democrats constitute just over twice as many Plainfield residents as Independents do.

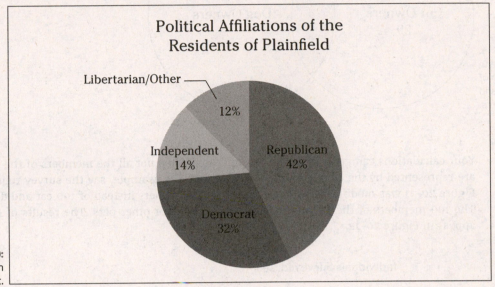

FIGURE 20-10:
Circle graph
or pie chart.

© John Wiley & Sons, Inc.

When you know one of the quantities in a circle graph, you can find the value of other quantities. For example, if a multi-source reasoning question in the integrated reasoning section provides you with both the scatter plot in Figure 20-7 and the circle graph in Figure 20-10 and tells you that the city of Plainfield was the city in Figure 20-7 with the highest population, you can use information from both graphs to discover the approximate number of Plainfield residents who are registered Democrats. The city with the largest population in Figure 20-7 has around 500,000 residents. Figure 20-10 tells you that 32 percent of Plainfield residents are Democrats. So just about 160,000 ($500,000 \times 0.32$) Democrats reside in Plainfield.

Extracting Data from Venn Diagrams

Venn diagrams, such as the one in Figure 20-11, are made of interconnected circles — usually two or three — and are a great way to show relationships that exist between sets of data. Each data set is represented by a circle; the interaction of the circles shows how the data relates.

You see Venn diagrams most often in graphics-interpretation questions. For example, the GMAT could tell you that the Venn diagram in Figure 20-11 represents the results of a survey of 100 cat and dog owners. You know from the diagram that 29 of those surveyed own cats, but no value appears for the number of dog owners. The shaded portion represents the intersection: the four members of the survey who own both cats and dogs. If you need to find the number of those surveyed who own dogs, you can't simply subtract 29 from 100 because that doesn't take into consideration the four people who own both types of pets. The total number of people in the survey who own dogs is actually (100 − 29) + 4, or 75.

Individuals Surveyed: 100

FIGURE 20-11:
Venn
diagram of
100 cat and
dog owners.

© John Wiley & Sons, Inc.

Your calculations can get a little more complicated when not all the members of the general set are represented by the circles in the Venn diagram. For example, say the survey represented in Figure 20-11 was modified a bit to represent 100 pet owners instead of 100 cat and dog owners. The 100 members of the survey could own cats, dogs, or other pets. The results of this survey appear in Figure 20-12.

Individuals Surveyed: 100

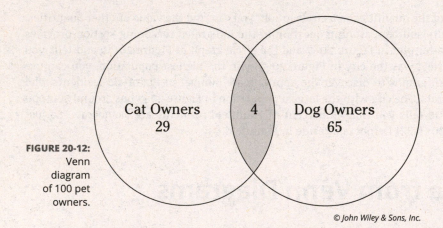

FIGURE 20-12:
Venn
diagram
of 100 pet
owners.

© John Wiley & Sons, Inc.

Based on this diagram, the GMAT could pose questions that ask for the number of people who own only cats but not dogs, the number of people who own at least one cat or one dog, or the number of those surveyed who own neither a cat nor a dog. Here's how you'd solve for these three cases:

>> The number of people who own cats but not dogs is simply the difference between the quantity in the cat-owner circle and the quantity of members who own both cats and dogs: 29 – 4 = 25. Of the 100 people surveyed, 25 own cats but don't own dogs.

» To find how many of the surveyed pet owners own at least a cat or a dog, you just need to add the values in each circle and subtract the quantity in the shaded intersection: $(29 + 65) - 4 = 90$. Of the 100 people surveyed, 90 owned at least one cat or one dog.

» Figuring the number of pet owners who own neither a cat nor a dog means that you're looking for the quantity that exists outside of the two circles. The number of people represented inside the circles plus the number of people outside of the circles is equal to 100, the total number of people surveyed. You know the number of people represented by the space inside the circle; it's the same number as those who own at least a cat or a dog (90). If x represents the number of pet owners who don't have a cat or a dog, the equation would be $90 + x = 100$. When you solve for x, you figure out that 10 people in the survey owned some pet other than a dog or cat.

So to evaluate Venn diagrams correctly, keep track of the total members in the set and what they represent. Information in the question will allow you to assess whether the circles represent the total number of members or whether a subset of members resides outside of the circle, so reading carefully will allow you to accurately interpret the Venn diagram. When you've successfully figured out the general set and the subsets, extracting information from Venn diagrams is easy.

6
Practice Makes Perfect

Bring all your new skills to the table and take a complete GMAT practice test.

Go over the answers and explanations to find out how you did and where you need to improve. Understand why the right answers were right and the wrong answers were wrong so that you can answer more GMAT questions with confidence.

Remember: When you're ready for more, be sure to take the other online practice tests available with this book. You can find instructions for accessing these tests in the Introduction.

Chapter **21**

GMAT Practice Test

The more practice you get answering GMAT questions before you take the test, the better you'll do on exam day. Increase your chances for a top score with the following practice exam, consisting of three sections of multiple-choice questions and an analytical-writing prompt. You have to write an essay in 30 minutes, finish 12 integrated-reasoning questions (located only on the online version of this test) in 30 minutes, complete 37 math questions in 75 minutes, and answer 41 verbal questions in 75 minutes.

To make the most of this practice exam, take the test under conditions similar to those you'll face on test day:

>> Find a place where you won't be distracted (preferably as far from your refrigerator as possible).

>> If possible, take the practice test at approximately the same time of day as when you'll be taking the actual GMAT.

>> Use a timer to keep track of the time limits for each section.

>> Take no more than two eight-minute breaks.

>> Mark your answers by circling the appropriate letters in the text. (On the actual GMAT, you'll mark your answer by clicking the oval next to the correct answer.)

>> Use a blank piece of paper to simulate the noteboard for keeping notes and making calculations.

>> If possible, complete your essay on a computer with the grammar and spelling correction functions turned off.

>> When your time is up for each section, put down your pencil and stop working.

After you finish, turn to Chapter 22 to check your answers with the answer key and read through the answer explanations — even the ones for the questions you got right. The explanations may present a way of approaching a problem that you haven't considered.

TIP

If you want to practice taking the test electronically, go to www.dummies.com and use your pin code to activate the online access that accompanies the purchase of this book. (Instructions are in the Introduction.) You'll find this test, along with five others for even more practice. You can answer the questions digitally, and the software tabulates correct and incorrect responses. This summary provides you with a snapshot of which areas you excel in and which areas you may need to review again.

Answer Sheet

The test is divided into four sections, though only three of the sections appear here in the book. (You can find the Integrated Reasoning section in the online version of this practice test.). Section 1 requires you to write an essay within 30 minutes. Sections 3 and 4 ask you to select the best answer among answer choices.

Section 1: Analytical Writing Assessment

Section 3: Quantitative

1. Ⓐ Ⓑ Ⓒ Ⓓ Ⓔ   9. Ⓐ Ⓑ Ⓒ Ⓓ Ⓔ   17. Ⓐ Ⓑ Ⓒ Ⓓ Ⓔ   25. Ⓐ Ⓑ Ⓒ Ⓓ Ⓔ   33. Ⓐ Ⓑ Ⓒ Ⓓ Ⓔ
2. Ⓐ Ⓑ Ⓒ Ⓓ Ⓔ   10. Ⓐ Ⓑ Ⓒ Ⓓ Ⓔ   18. Ⓐ Ⓑ Ⓒ Ⓓ Ⓔ   26. Ⓐ Ⓑ Ⓒ Ⓓ Ⓔ   34. Ⓐ Ⓑ Ⓒ Ⓓ Ⓔ
3. Ⓐ Ⓑ Ⓒ Ⓓ Ⓔ   11. Ⓐ Ⓑ Ⓒ Ⓓ Ⓔ   19. Ⓐ Ⓑ Ⓒ Ⓓ Ⓔ   27. Ⓐ Ⓑ Ⓒ Ⓓ Ⓔ   35. Ⓐ Ⓑ Ⓒ Ⓓ Ⓔ
4. Ⓐ Ⓑ Ⓒ Ⓓ Ⓔ   12. Ⓐ Ⓑ Ⓒ Ⓓ Ⓔ   20. Ⓐ Ⓑ Ⓒ Ⓓ Ⓔ   28. Ⓐ Ⓑ Ⓒ Ⓓ Ⓔ   36. Ⓐ Ⓑ Ⓒ Ⓓ Ⓔ
5. Ⓐ Ⓑ Ⓒ Ⓓ Ⓔ   13. Ⓐ Ⓑ Ⓒ Ⓓ Ⓔ   21. Ⓐ Ⓑ Ⓒ Ⓓ Ⓔ   29. Ⓐ Ⓑ Ⓒ Ⓓ Ⓔ   37. Ⓐ Ⓑ Ⓒ Ⓓ Ⓔ
6. Ⓐ Ⓑ Ⓒ Ⓓ Ⓔ   14. Ⓐ Ⓑ Ⓒ Ⓓ Ⓔ   22. Ⓐ Ⓑ Ⓒ Ⓓ Ⓔ   30. Ⓐ Ⓑ Ⓒ Ⓓ Ⓔ
7. Ⓐ Ⓑ Ⓒ Ⓓ Ⓔ   15. Ⓐ Ⓑ Ⓒ Ⓓ Ⓔ   23. Ⓐ Ⓑ Ⓒ Ⓓ Ⓔ   31. Ⓐ Ⓑ Ⓒ Ⓓ Ⓔ
8. Ⓐ Ⓑ Ⓒ Ⓓ Ⓔ   16. Ⓐ Ⓑ Ⓒ Ⓓ Ⓔ   24. Ⓐ Ⓑ Ⓒ Ⓓ Ⓔ   32. Ⓐ Ⓑ Ⓒ Ⓓ Ⓔ

Section 4: Verbal

1. Ⓐ Ⓑ Ⓒ Ⓓ Ⓔ   10. Ⓐ Ⓑ Ⓒ Ⓓ Ⓔ   19. Ⓐ Ⓑ Ⓒ Ⓓ Ⓔ   28. Ⓐ Ⓑ Ⓒ Ⓓ Ⓔ   37. Ⓐ Ⓑ Ⓒ Ⓓ Ⓔ
2. Ⓐ Ⓑ Ⓒ Ⓓ Ⓔ   11. Ⓐ Ⓑ Ⓒ Ⓓ Ⓔ   20. Ⓐ Ⓑ Ⓒ Ⓓ Ⓔ   29. Ⓐ Ⓑ Ⓒ Ⓓ Ⓔ   38. Ⓐ Ⓑ Ⓒ Ⓓ Ⓔ
3. Ⓐ Ⓑ Ⓒ Ⓓ Ⓔ   12. Ⓐ Ⓑ Ⓒ Ⓓ Ⓔ   21. Ⓐ Ⓑ Ⓒ Ⓓ Ⓔ   30. Ⓐ Ⓑ Ⓒ Ⓓ Ⓔ   39. Ⓐ Ⓑ Ⓒ Ⓓ Ⓔ
4. Ⓐ Ⓑ Ⓒ Ⓓ Ⓔ   13. Ⓐ Ⓑ Ⓒ Ⓓ Ⓔ   22. Ⓐ Ⓑ Ⓒ Ⓓ Ⓔ   31. Ⓐ Ⓑ Ⓒ Ⓓ Ⓔ   40. Ⓐ Ⓑ Ⓒ Ⓓ Ⓔ
5. Ⓐ Ⓑ Ⓒ Ⓓ Ⓔ   14. Ⓐ Ⓑ Ⓒ Ⓓ Ⓔ   23. Ⓐ Ⓑ Ⓒ Ⓓ Ⓔ   32. Ⓐ Ⓑ Ⓒ Ⓓ Ⓔ   41. Ⓐ Ⓑ Ⓒ Ⓓ Ⓔ
6. Ⓐ Ⓑ Ⓒ Ⓓ Ⓔ   15. Ⓐ Ⓑ Ⓒ Ⓓ Ⓔ   24. Ⓐ Ⓑ Ⓒ Ⓓ Ⓔ   33. Ⓐ Ⓑ Ⓒ Ⓓ Ⓔ
7. Ⓐ Ⓑ Ⓒ Ⓓ Ⓔ   16. Ⓐ Ⓑ Ⓒ Ⓓ Ⓔ   25. Ⓐ Ⓑ Ⓒ Ⓓ Ⓔ   34. Ⓐ Ⓑ Ⓒ Ⓓ Ⓔ
8. Ⓐ Ⓑ Ⓒ Ⓓ Ⓔ   17. Ⓐ Ⓑ Ⓒ Ⓓ Ⓔ   26. Ⓐ Ⓑ Ⓒ Ⓓ Ⓔ   35. Ⓐ Ⓑ Ⓒ Ⓓ Ⓔ
9. Ⓐ Ⓑ Ⓒ Ⓓ Ⓔ   18. Ⓐ Ⓑ Ⓒ Ⓓ Ⓔ   27. Ⓐ Ⓑ Ⓒ Ⓓ Ⓔ   36. Ⓐ Ⓑ Ⓒ Ⓓ Ⓔ

Section 1: Analytical Writing Assessment

1. Essay Topic: "Charter schools, which are learning institutions that are publicly funded but privately operated, were devised to offer new opportunities for teachers and to give students and families alternatives to traditional, public school settings. They are supposed to be locally managed to ensure the same level of accountability to which public schools are held. Increasingly, however, America's charter schools are being run by private companies without local interests, and accountability at the local level is suffering as a result. Statistics also indicate that nearly half of all new charter school teachers leave within one year of hiring, so charter schools have simply not lived up to all they promised."

Examine this argument and present your judgment on how well reasoned it is. In your discussion, analyze the author's position and how well the author uses evidence to support the argument. For example, you may question the author's underlying assumptions or consider alternative explanations that may weaken the conclusion. You can also provide additional support for or arguments against the author's position, describe how stating the argument differently may make it more reasonable, and discuss what provisions may better equip you to evaluate its thesis.

Section 2: Integrated Reasoning

TIME: 30 minutes for 12 questions

DIRECTIONS: Follow these directions for each of the four question types:

1. For graphics interpretation questions, examine the graph or chart and select the answer from the list that most accurately completes the statement.

2. The two-part analysis questions have two solutions. Select one choice from the list in the first column and one choice from the list in the second column to provide a complete answer for the question.

3. Analyze the data in the table analysis problems to determine which of the two opposing answer choices most clearly defines the accuracy of the statements.

4. The multi-source reasoning questions present you with several sets of different data. Read through the data and select the information you need to answer the questions.

NOTE: To simulate the look and feel of the integrated reasoning section on the actual GMAT, we include these questions in the online practice exams only.

Section 3: Quantitative

TIME: 75 minutes for 37 questions

DIRECTIONS: Choose the best answer from the five choices provided.

1. If a doughnut-making machine is operated for three hours, how many cases of doughnuts will the machine be able to produce?

   1. The machine produces doughnuts at a rate of five doughnuts per minute.

   2. The doughnut company sells cases of doughnuts in two sizes: cases of 80 doughnuts, and cases of 240 doughnuts.

   (A) Statement (1) *alone* is sufficient, but Statement (2) *alone* is *not* sufficient to answer the question asked.

   (B) Statement (2) *alone* is sufficient, but Statement (1) *alone* is *not* sufficient to answer the question asked.

   (C) *Both* statements *together* are sufficient, but *neither* statement *alone* is sufficient to answer the question asked.

   (D) *Each* statement *alone* is sufficient to answer the question asked.

   (E) Statements (1) and (2) *together* are *not* sufficient to answer the question asked.

2. The figure depicts a rectangle and a circle. Point A is the corner of the rectangle and the center of the circle. Point B, where the shapes intersect, bisects the length of the rectangle. What is the area of the circle?

   1. $y = 6$

   2. The area of the rectangle is 18.

   (A) Statement (1) *alone* is sufficient, but Statement (2) *alone* is *not* sufficient to answer the question asked.

   (B) Statement (2) *alone* is sufficient, but Statement (1) *alone* is *not* sufficient to answer the question asked.

   (C) *Both* statements *together* are sufficient, but *neither* statement *alone* is sufficient to answer the question asked.

   (D) *Each* statement *alone* is sufficient to answer the question asked.

   (E) Statements (1) and (2) *together* are *not* sufficient to answer the question asked.

3. $\dfrac{10xy + 15x}{2y + 3} + 3y = 1$

   If $x = 4$ and $y \neq -1.5$, what is the value of y?

   (A) $-\dfrac{19}{3}$

   (B) $-\dfrac{3}{19}$

   (C) $\dfrac{3}{19}$

   (D) $\dfrac{1}{3}$

   (E) $\dfrac{19}{3}$

4. A stand at a farmer's market is selling peaches individually and in cartons. An individual peach costs $1. When bought in a carton of 30, the price of each peach is discounted by 10 percent. Since it is the end of the growing season, there is a sale going on where the price is further discounted by 60 percent. What is the price of two cartons of peaches?

   (A) $9.00

   (B) $10.80

   (C) $18.00

   (D) $21.60

   (E) $32.40

5. If $y = 4$, what is the value of $2x + 7y$?

   1. $x + 3y = 2$
   2. $2x + 5y = 0$

   (A) Statement (1) *alone* is sufficient, but Statement (2) *alone* is *not* sufficient to answer the question asked.

   (B) Statement (2) *alone* is sufficient, but Statement (1) *alone* is *not* sufficient to answer the question asked.

   (C) *Both* statements *together* are sufficient, but *neither* statement *alone* is sufficient to answer the question asked.

   (D) *Each* statement *alone* is sufficient to answer the question asked.

   (E) Statements (1) and (2) *together* are *not* sufficient to answer the question asked.

6. The table shows the peak price each year for stocks from five different companies. Which stock had the greatest increase in peak price from Year 1 to Year 3?

	Year 1	Year 2	Year 3	Year 4	Year 5
OMK	$5.12	$6.86	$9.12	$6.20	$7.31
RRW	$30.51	$32.84	$45.18	$40.08	$47.12
LKP	$15.12	$25.32	$32.10	$31.12	$34.19
AWL	$130.54	$162.18	$154.96	$151.83	$183.39
TCK	$62.48	$71.31	$73.99	$79.42	$83.14

   (A) OMK

   (B) RRW

   (C) LKP

   (D) AWL

   (E) TCK

GO ON TO NEXT PAGE

7. How many kilometers does a bullet train travel to get from Tokyo to Kyoto?

 1. It takes the bullet train two hours to get from Tokyo to Kyoto.

 2. The bullet train travels at an average speed of 250 kilometers per hour from Tokyo to Kyoto.

 (A) Statement (1) *alone* is sufficient, but Statement (2) *alone* is *not* sufficient to answer the question asked.

 (B) Statement (2) *alone* is sufficient, but Statement (1) *alone* is *not* sufficient to answer the question asked.

 (C) *Both* statements *together* are sufficient, but *neither* statement *alone* is sufficient to answer the question asked.

 (D) *Each* statement *alone* is sufficient to answer the question asked.

 (E) Statements (1) and (2) *together* are *not* sufficient to answer the question asked.

8. If $y = 1$, what is the value of the following expression: $4^{y+z} \times 16 \times 4^{-z}$?

 (A) 4

 (B) 16

 (C) 64

 (D) 128

 (E) 256

9. When $x \neq 0$, $\left(\frac{2}{x} + \frac{1}{3} \right)\left(\frac{x}{2} \right)$ can be simplified to which of the following?

 (A) $1 + \frac{x}{6}$

 (B) $\frac{3x - 2}{3}$

 (C) $\frac{1}{6} + x$

 (D) $\frac{1}{3}$

 (E) $\frac{3x}{2x + 6}$

10. Sophia is buying a smartphone and a phone charger at an electronics store for a total price of $630. This price reflects a discount from the original prices of both devices due to a sale the store is offering. Assuming no taxes or other fees are involved, what was the original price of the phone charger alone?

 1. The sale that the store is offering is 15 percent off a total purchase of $500 or more or 20 percent off a total purchase of $800 or more.

 2. The original price of the smartphone alone was $720.

 (A) Statement (1) *alone* is sufficient, but Statement (2) *alone* is *not* sufficient to answer the question asked.

 (B) Statement (2) *alone* is sufficient, but Statement (1) *alone* is *not* sufficient to answer the question asked.

 (C) *Both* statements *together* are sufficient, but *neither* statement *alone* is sufficient to answer the question asked.

 (D) *Each* statement *alone* is sufficient to answer the question asked.

 (E) Statements (1) and (2) *together* are *not* sufficient to answer the question asked.

11. A line passes through the points $(-2, 2)$ and $(-1, -3)$. At what point does this line intersect the line with the equation $y = x - 8$?

 (A) $(-5, 3)$

 (B) $(0, -8)$

 (C) $(-3, 5)$

 (D) $\left(\frac{3}{5}, \frac{14}{3} \right)$

 (E) $\left(\frac{8}{3}, \frac{16}{3} \right)$

12. If $y = \frac{x}{2}$ and $x \neq 0$, which of the following is equal to $\frac{y}{2x} + \frac{x}{4}$?

 (A) $\frac{4x^2 + x}{4}$

 (B) $\frac{x + 1}{4}$

 (C) $\frac{x + 4}{2x}$

 (D) $x^2 + 1$

 (E) $\frac{1}{4}$

13. In a survey of 20 families living on Oak Street, 17 said they had previously shopped at Fresh Food Mart, and 12 said they had previously shopped at Sally's Market. How many families said they had shopped at both stores?

  1. Fifteen percent of the families surveyed said they had not shopped at either store.

  2. All of the families that said they had shopped at Sally's Market also said they had shopped at Fresh Food Mart.

  (A) Statement (1) *alone* is sufficient, but Statement (2) *alone* is *not* sufficient to answer the question asked.

  (B) Statement (2) *alone* is sufficient, but Statement (1) *alone* is *not* sufficient to answer the question asked.

  (C) *Both* statements *together* are sufficient, but *neither* statement *alone* is sufficient to answer the question asked.

  (D) *Each* statement *alone* is sufficient to answer the question asked.

  (E) Statements (1) and (2) *together* are *not* sufficient to answer the question asked.

14. Anthony runs a business manufacturing machine parts. If Anthony's business manufactured 80,000 machine parts last year and 88,000 machine parts this year, how many parts will the business need to produce next year to maintain the same percent growth from year to year?

  (A) 88,000
  (B) 88,800
  (C) 96,000
  (D) 96,800
  (E) 100,000

15. What is the surface area of a right circular cylinder with a height of 3 and a diameter of 1?

  (A) 3.5π
  (B) 3.75π
  (C) 7π
  (D) 8π
  (E) 12.25π

16. If x and y are positive integers, is $\frac{x}{y} > 1$?

  1. $x + 3 = y$
  2. $\frac{x+5}{y} > 1$

  (A) Statement (1) *alone* is sufficient, but Statement (2) *alone* is *not* sufficient to answer the question asked.

  (B) Statement (2) *alone* is sufficient, but Statement (1) *alone* is *not* sufficient to answer the question asked.

  (C) *Both* statements *together* are sufficient, but *neither* statement *alone* is sufficient to answer the question asked.

  (D) *Each* statement *alone* is sufficient to answer the question asked.

  (E) Statements (1) and (2) *together* are *not* sufficient to answer the question asked.

17. Patrick and Mel are each selling shirts at a rock concert to promote their favorite bands. It costs each of them the same amount to produce each shirt. Mel is selling her shirts for $60. If Patrick is making 20 percent more profit than Mel, and his profit is $24 per shirt, how much is Patrick charging for his shirts?

  (A) $48.00
  (B) $62.00
  (C) $64.00
  (D) $68.80
  (E) $72.00

18. If $7\left(\frac{x}{2} + \frac{x}{5}\right) = 3$, what is the value of x?

  (A) $\frac{3}{49}$
  (B) $\frac{30}{49}$
  (C) 1.5
  (D) $\frac{15}{7}$
  (E) $\frac{49}{3}$

GO ON TO NEXT PAGE

19. $f(x,y) = x^3 + x + 3y$. If $y = 1$, what is the value of $f(x,y)$?

1. $\dfrac{(y+1)^2}{2} = 2$

2. $x + 4y = 5$

(A) Statement (1) *alone* is sufficient, but Statement (2) *alone* is *not* sufficient to answer the question asked.

(B) Statement (2) *alone* is sufficient, but Statement (1) *alone* is *not* sufficient to answer the question asked.

(C) *Both* statements *together* are sufficient, but *neither* statement *alone* is sufficient to answer the question asked.

(D) *Each* statement *alone* is sufficient to answer the question asked.

(E) Statements (1) and (2) *together* are *not* sufficient to answer the question asked.

20. In the triangle in the figure, what is the length of side m?

1. $p = 4$

2. $\angle A = 90°$

(A) Statement (1) *alone* is sufficient, but Statement (2) *alone* is *not* sufficient to answer the question asked.

(B) Statement (2) *alone* is sufficient, but Statement (1) *alone* is *not* sufficient to answer the question asked.

(C) *Both* statements *together* are sufficient, but *neither* statement *alone* is sufficient to answer the question asked.

(D) *Each* statement *alone* is sufficient to answer the question asked.

(E) Statements (1) and (2) *together* are *not* sufficient to answer the question asked.

21. Given $\dfrac{3-5x}{2} + 4 < \dfrac{x+2}{3}$, which of the following describes the possible values for x?

(A) $x < \dfrac{29}{17}$

(B) $x < \dfrac{3}{14}$

(C) $x < \dfrac{29}{17}$

(D) $x > \dfrac{29}{17}$

(E) $x > \dfrac{1}{6}$

22. Roland and Felicia are testing circuit boards for wiring errors. Working together, they can test a circuit board in eight minutes. How many circuit boards can Felicia test in an hour on her own?

1. Felicia can test circuit boards twice as fast as Roland.

2. If Roland and Felicia get their friend Cory to help them, they can all work together to test a circuit board in seven minutes.

(A) Statement (1) *alone* is sufficient, but Statement (2) *alone* is *not* sufficient to answer the question asked.

(B) Statement (2) *alone* is sufficient, but Statement (1) *alone* is *not* sufficient to answer the question asked.

(C) *Both* statements *together* are sufficient, but *neither* statement *alone* is sufficient to answer the question asked.

(D) *Each* statement *alone* is sufficient to answer the question asked.

(E) Statements (1) and (2) *together* are *not* sufficient to answer the question asked.

23. A parking lot contains ten cars. The average age of the cars is seven years. If the average age of nine of the cars is six years, what is the age of the remaining car in years?

(A) 3

(B) 7

(C) 10

(D) 16

(E) 20

24. If Cindy ran at 7.5 miles per hour for 16 minutes, and then ran at 6 miles per hour for 10 minutes, how far in miles did she run total?

(A) 2.5

(B) 2.8

(C) 3

(D) 3.5

(E) 5

25. If $a = 0.01b + 3.5 \times 10^{-2}$, what is the value of a?

1. $300a - 3b = 10.5$

2. $100a + 10b = 58.5$

(A) Statement (1) *alone* is sufficient, but Statement (2) *alone* is *not* sufficient to answer the question asked.

(B) Statement (2) *alone* is sufficient, but Statement (1) *alone* is *not* sufficient to answer the question asked.

(C) *Both* statements *together* are sufficient, but *neither* statement *alone* is sufficient to answer the question asked.

(D) *Each* statement *alone* is sufficient to answer the question asked.

(E) Statements (1) and (2) *together* are *not* sufficient to answer the question asked.

26. What is the perimeter of the shape in the figure?

1. All angles in the figure are right angles.

2. $t = 2$

(A) Statement (1) *alone* is sufficient, but Statement (2) *alone* is *not* sufficient to answer the question asked.

(B) Statement (2) *alone* is sufficient, but Statement (1) *alone* is *not* sufficient to answer the question asked.

(C) *Both* statements *together* are sufficient, but *neither* statement *alone* is sufficient to answer the question asked.

(D) *Each* statement *alone* is sufficient to answer the question asked.

(E) Statements (1) and (2) *together* are *not* sufficient to answer the question asked.

27. Jerry is moving from his current apartment into a house. He is spending a total of $2,000 on moving expenses. These expenses are distributed between buying moving supplies, hiring labor for moving his items, and renting a truck. Ten percent of his moving expenses were spent on supplies, and the truck rental cost five times as much as hiring labor. How much did Jerry spend on his truck rental?

(A) $300

(B) $500

(C) $1,200

(D) $1,500

(E) $1,800

28. The figure shows a right triangle with base x and height y. If y is doubled, by what percent does x need to be increased to triple the area of the triangle?

(A) 20 percent

(B) 50 percent

(C) 100 percent

(D) 150 percent

(E) 200 percent

GO ON TO NEXT PAGE

29. At Bailey's bike shop, 75 percent of the bikes sold are mountain bikes, and the rest are road bikes. What percentage of the bikes sold are mountain bikes for kids?

1. Twenty percent of the bikes sold are for kids and 80 percent are for adults.

2. Twenty percent of the bikes sold are road bikes for adults.

(A) Statement (1) *alone* is sufficient, but Statement (2) *alone* is *not* sufficient to answer the question asked.

(B) Statement (2) *alone* is sufficient, but Statement (1) *alone* is *not* sufficient to answer the question asked.

(C) *Both* statements *together* are sufficient, but *neither* statement *alone* is sufficient to answer the question asked.

(D) *Each* statement *alone* is sufficient to answer the question asked.

(E) Statements (1) and (2) *together* are *not* sufficient to answer the question asked.

30. Using the expression $4x + 3y + z = 8$, what is the value of x?

1. $x = y = z$

2. $z = 4 - 3y$

(A) Statement (1) *alone* is sufficient, but Statement (2) *alone* is *not* sufficient to answer the question asked.

(B) Statement (2) *alone* is sufficient, but Statement (1) *alone* is *not* sufficient to answer the question asked.

(C) *Both* statements *together* are sufficient, but *neither* statement *alone* is sufficient to answer the question asked.

(D) *Each* statement *alone* is sufficient to answer the question asked.

(E) Statements (1) and (2) *together* are *not* sufficient to answer the question asked.

31. George's Gas Station gets fuel from two different fuel suppliers: Dyon and Brian's Biofuels. Each supplier provides fuel with a different percentage of ethanol, and George mixes them together in his supply tank. If George currently has 1,000 gallons of fuel at 11 percent ethanol in his supply tank, how much fuel from Brian's Biofuels would he need to add to achieve a final mixture that is 12 percent ethanol?

1. Brian's Biofuels provides fuel with 80 percent ethanol.

2. The mixture currently in George's supply tank has 10 gallons of fuel from Brian's Biofuels and 990 gallons of fuel from Dyon.

(A) Statement (1) *alone* is sufficient, but Statement (2) *alone* is *not* sufficient to answer the question asked.

(B) Statement (2) *alone* is sufficient, but Statement (1) *alone* is *not* sufficient to answer the question asked.

(C) *Both* statements *together* are sufficient, but *neither* statement *alone* is sufficient to answer the question asked.

(D) *Each* statement *alone* is sufficient to answer the question asked.

(E) Statements (1) and (2) *together* are *not* sufficient to answer the question asked.

32. If the hypotenuse of the triangle in the figure has a length of 9, what is x?

(A) 4.5

(B) 6

(C) $\sqrt{40.5}$

(D) $\sqrt{45}$

(E) $\sqrt{162}$

33. Taco Fusion restaurant served a total of 60 guests for lunch today. Twenty of the guests ordered sushi, and 45 of the guests ordered tacos. If five of the guests didn't order tacos or sushi, how many of the guests ordered both?

(A) 0

(B) 5

(C) 10

(D) 15

(E) 20

34. The population of Greenvale increases by 10 percent each year. Assuming constant growth, how many people will be living in Greenvale at the end of this year?

1. Over a two-year period, the population growth in Greenvale is 21 percent.

2. At the beginning of last year, there were 10,000 people living in Greenvale.

(A) Statement (1) *alone* is sufficient, but Statement (2) *alone* is *not* sufficient to answer the question asked.

(B) Statement (2) *alone* is sufficient, but Statement (1) *alone* is *not* sufficient to answer the question asked.

(C) *Both* statements *together* are sufficient, but *neither* statement *alone* is sufficient to answer the question asked.

(D) *Each* statement *alone* is sufficient to answer the question asked.

(E) Statements (1) and (2) *together* are *not* sufficient to answer the question asked.

35. The figure depicts a triangle with a base of *x* and a height of *y*. What is the value of the area of the triangle?

1. $xy = 100$

2. $y = 10$

(A) Statement (1) *alone* is sufficient, but Statement (2) *alone* is *not* sufficient to answer the question asked.

(B) Statement (2) *alone* is sufficient, but Statement (1) *alone* is *not* sufficient to answer the question asked.

(C) *Both* statements *together* are sufficient, but *neither* statement *alone* is sufficient to answer the question asked.

(D) *Each* statement *alone* is sufficient to answer the question asked.

(E) Statements (1) and (2) *together* are *not* sufficient to answer the question asked.

GO ON TO NEXT PAGE

36. A company is selling liquid nitrogen at a price of $2.00 per gallon. If they want to make a profit of 25 percent of their cost of production, how much can they spend on production of each gallon of liquid nitrogen?

(A) $1.25

(B) $1.50

(C) $1.60

(D) $1.75

(E) $1.80

37. Jack's morning routine includes three activities: taking a shower, drinking coffee, and walking to work. He does each activity in sequential order without overlapping. Assuming no gaps between each activity, it takes him 45 minutes to complete his routine. How long does it take him to drink coffee?

1. It takes him four times as long to walk to work as it takes him to drink coffee.

2. Showering and drinking coffee take him a total of 25 minutes.

(A) Statement (1) *alone* is sufficient, but Statement (2) *alone* is *not* sufficient to answer the question asked.

(B) Statement (2) *alone* is sufficient, but Statement (1) *alone* is *not* sufficient to answer the question asked.

(C) *Both* statements *together* are sufficient, but *neither* statement *alone* is sufficient to answer the question asked.

(D) *Each* statement *alone* is sufficient to answer the question asked.

(E) Statements (1) and (2) *together* are *not* sufficient to answer the question asked.

Section 4: Verbal

TIME: 75 minutes for 41 questions

DIRECTIONS: Follow these directions for each of the three question types:

- **Sentence-correction questions:** Choose the answer choice that best phrases the underlined words according to the rules of standard English. The first answer choice duplicates the phrasing of the underlined portion; the other four choices provide alternative phrasings. Choose the one that rephrases the sentence in the clearest, most grammatically correct manner.

- **Reading-comprehension questions:** Choose the best answer to every question based on what the passage states directly or indirectly.

- **Critical-reasoning questions:** Pick the answer choice that best answers the question about the argument provided.

Questions 1–6 refer to the following passage, which is excerpted from *Playing against Nature: Integrating Science and Economics to Mitigate Natural Hazards in an Uncertain World,* by Seth Stein and Jerome Stein (Wiley 2014).

Natural hazards are the price we pay for living on an active planet. The tectonic plate subduction producing Japan's rugged Tohoku coast gives rise to earthquakes and tsunamis. Florida's warm sunny weather results from the processes in the ocean and atmosphere that cause hurricanes. The volcanoes that produced Hawaii's spectacular islands sometimes threaten people. Rivers that provide the water for the farms that feed us sometimes flood.

Humans have to live with natural hazards. We describe this challenge in terms of hazards, the natural occurrence of earthquakes or other phenomena, and the risks, or dangers they pose to lives and property. In this formulation, the risk is the product of hazard and vulnerability. We want to assess the hazards — estimate how significant they are — and develop methods to mitigate or reduce the resulting losses.

Hazards are geological facts that are not under human control. All we can do is try to assess them as best we can. In contrast, risks are affected by human actions that increase or decrease vulnerability, such as where people live and how they build. We increase vulnerability by building in hazardous areas, and decrease it by making buildings more hazard resistant. Areas with high hazard can have low risk because few people live there. Areas of modest hazard can have high risk due to large population and poor construction. A disaster occurs when — owing to high vulnerability — a natural event has major consequences for society.

The harm from natural disasters is enormous. On average, about 100,000 people per year are killed by natural disasters, with some disasters — such as the 2004 Indian Ocean tsunami — causing many more deaths. Although the actual numbers of deaths in many events, such as the 2010 Haiti earthquake, are poorly known, they are very large.

Economic impacts are even harder to quantify, and various measures are used to try to do so. Disasters cause losses, which are the total negative economic impact. These include direct losses due to destruction of physical assets such as buildings, farmland, forests, etc., and indirect losses that result from the direct losses. Because losses are hard to determine, what is reported is often the cost, which refers to payouts by insurers (called insured losses) or governments to reimburse some of the losses. Thus, the reported cost does not reflect the losses to people who do not receive such payments.

GO ON TO NEXT PAGE

1. The main idea of the first paragraph is best expressed as

   (A) The factors that make an area desirable are also those that can pose the most risk.

   (B) The Hawaiian Islands would not exist if not for powerful and explosive volcanoes.

   (C) Floods, volcanoes, and earthquakes pose threats to the natural environment.

   (D) Humans must learn to live with natural hazards such as volcanoes and tsunamis.

   (E) Natural hazards are most prevalent in areas that are sunny and warm.

2. Which of the following might the author of the passage consider an "indirect loss" associated with a disaster?

   (A) Desecration of a library due to vandalism

   (B) Damage to a school building in a fire

   (C) Loss of retail clothing sales due to a mall flood

   (D) Death of a ranch's livestock due to volcanic eruption

   (E) Destruction of a pavilion due to a hurricane

3. According to the passage, an important distinction between hazards and risks is

   (A) risks occur naturally, while hazards arise because of human actions

   (B) hazards result from risks, and risks result from vulnerability

   (C) hazards can lead to disasters, while risks cannot

   (D) hazards are not under human control, while risks usually are

   (E) risks are harder to quantify than hazards

4. The passage is primarily concerned with

   (A) describing the causes and impacts of natural disasters

   (B) assessing the impact that disasters render on the global economy

   (C) depicting the various ways human beings may endanger themselves

   (D) raising awareness of the loss of human lives due to the severity and unpredictability of natural disasters

   (E) explaining that natural disasters are not under human control

5. Which of the following best describes the purpose of the fourth paragraph in relation to the passage as a whole?

   (A) It uses numerical data and metrics to describe the economic impacts of natural disasters.

   (B) It emphasizes how little is actually known about how many lives are lost in natural disasters.

   (C) It outlines the differences between hazards and risks to set up information detailed in the remainder of the passage.

   (D) It provides sensory details about specific recent natural disasters that may be familiar to readers to evoke an emotional response.

   (E) It applies statistical data to emphasize the magnitude of damage created by natural disasters.

6. Which of the following logically follows the information given in the passage?

   (A) The number of unreported deaths in the 2010 Haitian earthquake exceeded the number of unreported deaths in the 2004 Indian Ocean tsunami.

   (B) In the years 2010 and 2004, there were more deaths due to natural disasters than average.

   (C) The number of deaths due to natural disasters along Japan's tectonic plate is greater on average than those experienced on islands such as Hawaii or Haiti.

   (D) Economic costs are more frequently unreported than numbers of deaths in any given natural disaster.

   (E) Areas of high hazard, such as Japan's Tohoku coast, may have a lower risk of natural disaster costs than areas where hazard incidents are lower.

7. Before the primary school can open to the public in time for the fall semester, the crew in charge of the project <u>must finish construction, cleaning, and safety-proofing it's interior</u>.

(A) must finish construction, cleaning, and safety-proofing it's interior

(B) must finish construction of, cleaning, and safety-proof its interior

(C) must finish constructing, cleaning and safety-proofing it's interior

(D) must finish constructing, cleaning, and safety-proofing its interior

(E) must finish construction, cleaning and safety-proofing the interior

8. So many accounts of this <u>continents' past begin with Europeans striding ashore, claiming this "newfound land" and its human inhabitants for its respective empires</u>.

(A) continents' past begin with Europeans striding ashore, claiming this "newfound land" and its human inhabitants for its respective empires

(B) continent's past begin with Europeans striding ashore, claiming this "newfound land" and its human inhabitants for their respective empires

(C) continents' past begin with Europeans striding ashore, claiming this "newfound land" and its human inhabitants for their respective empires

(D) continent's past begins with Europeans striding ashore, claiming this "newfound land" and its human inhabitants for its respective empires

(E) continent's past begins with Europeans striding ashore, claiming this "newfound land" and its human inhabitants for their respective empires

9. Injera, an East African flatbread, has been a main component of Ethiopian dishes for generations and <u>are still used by many Ethiopians today, who use it to feed themselves</u> in the same manner Americans use flatware.

(A) are still used by many Ethiopians today, who use it to feed themselves

(B) are still used by many Ethiopians today, who feed themselves with it

(C) it is still used today by many Ethiopians, who use it to feed themselves

(D) is still used today by many Ethiopians to feed themselves

(E) is still used by many Ethiopians today, who use it to feed themselves

10. The size of oceanic waves is a function of the velocity of the wind and of *fetch*, the length of the surface of the water subject to those winds. The impact of waves against a coastline is a function of the size of the waves and the shape of the sea bottom. The degree of erosion to which a coastline is subject is a function of the average impact of waves and the geologic composition of the coastline.

If these statements are true, which one of the following must also be true?

(A) The degree of erosion to which a coastline is subject is related to the shape of the sea bottom.

(B) The size of oceanic waves will not fluctuate far from an average for any given stretch of ocean.

(C) The fetch of winds is related to the shape of the sea bottom.

(D) The size of oceanic waves is related to the shape of the sea bottom.

(E) The average velocity of the wind in an area plays no role in the degree of erosion to which a coastline is subject.

GO ON TO NEXT PAGE ▶

11. Health insurers are largely immune to the factors that are limiting profit in many sectors of the healthcare economy. Consumers have shown a willingness to pay almost any price for health insurance premiums. Capital demands, which are the responsibility of doctors and hospitals, are increasing dramatically, even as cost-containment measures, largely encouraged by the insurers and their friends in government, have forced new levels of fiscal discipline upon hospitals and doctors. Patients still need MRIs and buildings to put them in, but hospitals are limited in how much they can charge patients for the use of these facilities.

Which one of the following most accurately describes the role that the statement "patients still need MRIs and buildings to put them in" plays in the argument?

(A) It is a specific example of a general condition described in the course of the argument.

(B) It is used to counter a consideration that may be taken to undermine the argument.

(C) It is used to indirectly support the claim made by the argument.

(D) It describes a social side effect of the benefit with which the argument is concerned.

(E) It introduces the conclusion that the argument intends to support.

12. The softball team tried to raise enough money to purchase new uniforms for the upcoming season, but <u>between them, the 20 players were only able to raise about 70 percent of the cost</u>.

(A) between them, the 20 players were only able to raise about 70 percent of the cost

(B) between them, the 20 players were only able to have raised about 70 percent of the cost

(C) among them, the 20 players were only able to raise about 70 percent of the cost

(D) among them, the 20 players were only able to have raised about 70 percent of the cost

(E) among them, only about 70 percent of the cost was raised by 20 players

13. Forcing businesses to furnish employees with paid leave for family concerns, such as paternity leave or leave to care for a sick child, is a terrible idea. If a business allows employees to take this time off, the workers will take advantage of the privilege and come to work as little as possible. This will destroy productivity and workplace morale.

Which one of the following, if true, most seriously weakens the argument?

(A) European countries guarantee employees generous family leave and paid vacation time, but the European standard of living is slightly below that of the United States.

(B) Most male workers refuse to take paternity leave even though it is allowed under federal law and their employers encourage it; they fear they may anger co-workers and harm their chances for promotion if they take time off for what is still seen as a frivolous reason.

(C) The FMLA requires employers to grant employees 12 weeks a year of unpaid leave for family purposes; although employers save money because the leave is unpaid, they often must spend money to find a replacement for the employee who takes time off.

(D) In some workplaces, the loss of a single employee at a busy time of year can be devastating, even if that employee plans to return after a few weeks; allowing family leave can overwhelm the employees who stay on the job.

(E) Allowing employees to take leave for family matters reduces absenteeism, improves morale, and surprisingly increases productivity because the employees who are granted leave tend to work much harder and more efficiently when they come back to work.

14. Not all of the players <u>was on board with the new uniforms for the girls' basketball team, but the team made their choices</u>.

(A) was on board with the new uniforms for the girls' basketball team, but the team made their choices

(B) was on board with the new uniforms for the girls' basketball team, but the team had made its choices

(C) were on board with the new uniforms for the girls' basketball team, but the team made their choice

(D) were on board with the new uniforms for the girls' basketball team, but the team had made its choice

(E) were on board with the new uniforms for the girls' basketball team, but the team has made its choice

15. The nation's increasing reliance on automation is reducing the number of jobs available to hardworking people, <u>forcing many families to make the unfortunate choice between having a roof over their heads or receiving healthcare</u>.

(A) forcing many families to make the unfortunate choice between having a roof over their heads or receiving healthcare

(B) forcing many families to make the unfortunate choice between having a roof over their heads and receiving healthcare

(C) forcing many families to make the unfortunate choice between having a roof over their heads or healthcare

(D) forcing many families with making the unfortunate choice between having a roof over their heads and healthcare

(E) forcing many families to make the unfortunate choice among having a roof over their heads and healthcare

16. Software engineers know that a poorly written application can consume more memory than it should and that running out of memory can cause an application to crash. However, if a crashing application causes the whole operating system to crash, the fault lies with the operating system.

Which one of the following, if true, is least helpful in establishing that this conclusion is properly drawn?

(A) Operating systems with generous amounts of memory are less susceptible to crashing, even when applications are poorly written.

(B) Operating systems can isolate the memory used by individual applications, even when an application uses a large amount of memory.

(C) An operating system can monitor an application's consumption of memory and take action when that gets too high.

(D) Techniques for programming operating systems to catch and handle memory errors are well-defined and well-known among programmers.

(E) Because many applications can run simultaneously under a single operating system, the operating system should have a well-defined method of managing memory consumption.

GO ON TO NEXT PAGE

17. This museum does not grant people the right to use images of items in its collection in online publications. We are obliged to do everything in our power to ensure the continued appeal of visiting our collection in person.

The conclusion above depends on assuming which one of the following?

(A) Taking photographs of art objects, especially using a flash, can damage the objects by accelerating the fading of paint.

(B) The museum sells pictures of its collection in its gift shop, which is an important source of income for the museum.

(C) Images placed online are easily copied and reused by other people.

(D) The quality of most electronic images, especially those online, falls short of the professional standards of the museum.

(E) If people see online images of items in the museum's collection, they will no longer be interested in seeing the collection with their own eyes.

18. The town's legislators heard arguments from the crowd about how town facilities and parks no longer properly accommodate the towns-people now that <u>the number of residents have increased so considerably</u>.

(A) the number of residents have increased so considerably

(B) the numbers of residents have so considerably increased

(C) the number of residents has increased so considerably

(D) the numbers of residents have so considerably increased

(E) the number of residents has been increasing considerably so

19. <u>Risks are effected by human actions that increase or decrease vulnerability, like where people live and how they build.</u>

(A) Risks are effected by human actions that increase or decrease vulnerability, like where people live and how they build.

(B) Risks are affected by human actions that increase or decrease vulnerability, like where people live and how they build.

(C) Risks are effected by human actions that increase or decrease vulnerability, such as where people live and how they build.

(D) Risks are affected by human actions that increase or decrease vulnerability, such as where people live and how they build.

(E) Risks are affected by human actions which increase or decrease vulnerability, such as where people live and how they build.

Questions 20–23 refer to the following passage, which is excerpted from *Handbook of Early Childhood Development Programs, Practices, and Policies* by Elizabeth Votruba-Drzal (Editor) and Eric Dearing (Editor) (Wiley 2017).

Researchers, educators, and policymakers generally agree that school readiness is a multidimensional concept that includes cognitive, executive functioning, language, socioemotional, behavioral, and health characteristics that contribute to children's ability to adapt and thrive in school settings. These performance domains are correlated but typically are assessed and studied as independent indicators of school readiness and predictors of later achievement. Importantly, the guiding definitions of school readiness typically include skills and behaviors that are related to learning processes as well as learning outcomes, as opposed to the K–12 system, which often only emphasizes student outcomes based on children's performance on academic achievement tests.

In the area of cognition, school readiness includes both acquired knowledge or skills in particular content area (such as knowing a certain number of letters) as well as learning/processing skills or how fast children acquire knowledge. In particular, there has been a growing emphasis on executive functioning skills and how these skills interact with other domains to promote learning in preschool classrooms. Executive functioning typically is defined as the set of skills and behaviors required to attain a goal, including working memory, attention control, attention shifting, and response inhibition. For young children, this means being able to resist distractions (e.g., pay attention to a teacher rather than talk with peers), inhibit dominant responses in emotional contexts (e.g., raise hand instead of talking while the teacher is reading a book), and prioritize and sequence information and hold onto it in memory (e.g., plan and carry out the series of steps required to line up for lunch).

In addition, school readiness includes children's language skills, including their receptive language (i.e., the ability to listen and understand language) and expressive language (i.e., the ability to communicate with others using verbal language). Children's socioemotional skills are also an important component of school readiness and include behaviors such as cooperation with teachers and peers and developing social relationships, as well as behavior problems, including aggression or poor regulation. There are also a set of skills referred to as approaches to learning, which reflect children's curiosity, flexibility, attention, persistence, and engagement. The physical health domain includes motor development, such as development of fine and gross motor skills, and healthy behavior practices. Collectively, all of these skills are theorized to affect children's learning opportunities and their acquisition of new skills and behaviors in the classroom setting.

20. According to the passage, being able to resist distractions is a form of

   (A) socioemotional growth
   (B) executive functioning
   (C) behavioral growth
   (D) motor development
   (E) cognitive growth

21. The author of the passage makes the distinction between the guiding principles of school readiness and those observed by the K–12 system to

   (A) emphasize that school readiness regards the process as much as the results
   (B) demonstrate the failings of the K–12 system
   (C) explain why the guiding principles of school readiness are superior to those used at K–12 settings
   (D) emphasize the author's personal opinion about the importance of student outcomes
   (E) explain how cognition factors into a child's degree of success in a school setting

22. The passage indicates that attention to which of the following school readiness skills has likely increased in recent years?

   (A) responding accurately on standardized achievement tests
   (B) using verbal language to communicate ideas to others
   (C) cooperating with peers and managing aggressive behaviors
   (D) paying attention to the teacher
   (E) ensuring that students consume a healthy breakfast

23. It can be inferred from the passage that children who interact successfully with their teachers and other students have strong

   (A) motor skills
   (B) receptive language skills
   (C) expressive language skills
   (D) executive functioning skills
   (E) socioemotional skills

GO ON TO NEXT PAGE

24. Career counselor: Many large international companies have changed their practices regarding international assignments. They are placing much more emphasis on helping spouses of expatriate employees to adjust to the foreign environment. This has reduced premature returns by 67 percent.

Which one of the following is an assumption upon which the career counselor's argument depends?

(A) Spousal and marital difficulties were formerly responsible for many premature returns from foreign assignments.

(B) When an employee is placed in a foreign assignment for a year or less, his or her family sees the assignment as an adventure.

(C) Expatriate employees work long hours and travel a great deal, and their children make new friends at school, but spouses often have no friends and no work to support them while they're abroad.

(D) The majority of international assignments today last for less than a year, but ten years ago, 70 percent of them lasted much longer than one year.

(E) Many companies now offer expatriate spouses language training, career guidance, and assistance in finding homes and schools.

25. One work of art is not more important because it was made <u>after another nor does it make its predecessor obsolete</u>.

(A) after another nor does it make its predecessor obsolete

(B) after another, it neither makes its predecessor obsolete

(C) after another; nor does it make its predecessor obsolete

(D) after another neither does it make its predecessor obsolete

(E) after another, nor does it make its predecessor obsolete

26. A most unsociable dog he proved to be, <u>resenting all their advances, refusing to let them lay hands on him, menacing them with bared fangs and bristling hair</u>.

(A) resenting all their advances, refusing to let them lay hands on him, menacing them with bared fangs and bristling hair

(B) resenting all advances, refusing to let them lay hands on him, menacing them with bared fangs, and bristling hair

(C) resenting all the advances that they made, refusing to let them lay hands on him, menaced them with bared fangs and bristling hair

(D) resenting all their advances, refusing to let them lay hands on him, menaced them with bared fangs and bristling hair

(E) resenting all the advances that they made, refusing to let them lay hands on him, and menacing them with bared fangs and bristling hair

27. Scientists have discovered a gene that controls whether an individual is monogamous. They took a gene from the monogamous prairie vole and implanted it into its more promiscuous relative, the meadow vole. Thereafter, the meadow voles with the new gene became monogamous.

Which one of the following, if true, would provide the most support for the argument's conclusion?

(A) Studies on humans and other mammals have shown that receptors for the hormone vasopressin play a role in autism, drug addiction, and the formation of romantic attachments.

(B) Prairie voles typically form lifelong partnerships, which scientists have linked to an increased number of receptors for the hormone vasopressin.

(C) Meadow voles live in a harsher environment than prairie voles and cannot afford to pass up opportunities to mate as often as possible.

(D) The scientists used a harmless virus to capture the gene and transfer it into the meadow voles.

(E) The meadow voles that had the prairie vole gene implanted in them were released into and observed in the same habitat in which they had previously lived.

28. Physician: Scottish researchers have developed a test that allows them to predict at what age a woman will experience menopause. The scientists use a model that compares a woman's ovaries to "average" ovaries to see whether her ovaries are aging faster or more slowly than average. They have discovered that the size of ovaries is directly related to the number of eggs they contain, which in turn is directly related to fertility. This discovery will significantly influence women's decisions on when to have children.

The physician's conclusion follows logically if which one of the following is assumed?

(A) Women with smaller ovaries tend to have less success with assisted reproduction techniques, such as in vitro fertilization.

(B) Most women experience menopause around the age of 50, but their fertility starts to decline at the age of 37.

(C) Women who want to have children increasingly seek to delay doing so for many varied reasons.

(D) The test cannot tell women how likely they are to conceive in the years just prior to menopause.

(E) Every woman is born with several million eggs in her ovaries, which formed while she was a fetus; the number of eggs dwindles over her lifetime, until at menopause she has 1,000 or fewer.

29. The top two students, Arthur and Abraham, excelled not only academically but in athletics too.

(A) excelled not only academically but in athletics too

(B) excelled not only academically and also athletically

(C) engaged in excellence not only academically but athletically

(D) excelled not only academically but also in athletics

(E) excelled not only academically but also athletically

30. To earn a graduate equivalency diploma, a student must pass tests on subjects taught in high schools, proving that he or she has mastered them to the degree assumed of a high-school graduate. It makes sense for a student to drop out of high school and earn a GED. A GED takes much less time to earn than a high-school diploma and provides evidence that the student has learned everything he or she would have learned in high school.

Which one of the following, if true, most seriously weakens the argument?

(A) Some GED-prep programs incorporate enrichment activities into their test preparation, such as taking students to art exhibits and theatrical performances.

(B) Most colleges and universities consider a GED equivalent to a high-school degree for admission purposes.

(C) Many successful businesspeople dropped out of high school and earned a GED.

(D) Employers assume that high-school graduates generally have a much higher level of mastery of academic subjects than those who earn GEDs.

(E) Many GED students are slightly older than high-school students, and they often hold jobs in addition to studying to pass the GED tests.

Questions 31–35 refer to the following passage, which is excerpted from *Beyond Cybersecurity: Protecting Your Digital Business*, by James M. Kaplan, Tucker Bailey, Derek O'Halloran, Alan Marcus, and Chris Rezek (Wiley 2015).

All business investments require trade-offs between risk and reward. Does the interest rate on a new bond issue adequately compensate for the risk of default? Are the potential revenues from entering a new emerging market greater than the risk that the investments will be confiscated by a new regime? Does the value of oil extracted via deep-water, offshore drilling outweigh the chance of a catastrophic accident? Tough questions must be answered by weighing up the business imperatives against a calculation of the risk — and the greater the risk, the harder it is to make the case for investment.

GO ON TO NEXT PAGE

Technology investments are no different. They, too, have always been a trade-off between risk and return. However, for enterprise technology, increased global connectivity is raising the stakes on both sides of the equation. The commercial rewards from tapping into this connectivity are enormous, but the more tightly we are connected, the more vulnerabilities exist that attackers can exploit and the more damage they can do once inside. Therefore, when a manufacturer invests in a new product life-cycle management system, it is making a bet that the system will not enable the theft of valuable intellectual property. When a retailer invests in mobile commerce, it is betting that cyber-fraud won't critically damage profitability. When a bank invests in customer analytics, it is betting that the sensitive data it analyzes won't be stolen by cyber-criminals. The odds on all those bets appear to be shifting away from the institutions and toward cyber-attackers. They could swing decisively their way in the near future given most companies' siloed and reactive approach to cybersecurity.

Our interviews with business leaders, chief information officers (CIOs), chief technology officers (CTOs), and chief information security officers (CISOs) indicate that concerns about cyber-attacks are already affecting large institutions' interest in and ability to create value from technology investment and innovation. Potential losses, both direct and indirect, reduce the expected economic benefits of technology investments, as do the high cost and lengthy time frame required to build the defense mechanisms that can protect the organization against a growing range of attackers. In short, the models companies use to protect themselves from cyber-attack are limiting their ability to extract additional value from technology.

Concern about cyber-attacks is already having a noticeable impact on business along three dimensions: lower frontline productivity, fewer resources for information technology (IT) initiatives that create value, and — critically — the slower implementation of technological innovations.

31. The primary purpose of this passage is to
    (A) identify gaps in the business world that lead to cybersecurity breaches
    (B) refute the notion that companies are failing to thwart hackers
    (C) discuss how the modern business marketplace is all about risk and reward
    (D) explain how attention to cybersecurity impacts companies' technological innovation
    (E) demonstrate how today's hackers are winning the fight against big corporations

32. According to the passage, all of the following decrease the economic benefits of technological investment EXCEPT:
    (A) experiencing stolen intellectual property
    (B) realizing indirect losses
    (C) weighing business outcomes and risks
    (D) investing in cyber-security protection technology
    (E) reacting to cyber-threats only when necessary

33. When the author asserts that companies take a "siloed and reactive" approach to cybersecurity, he is implying that companies
    (A) perform thorough research before implementing programs meant to improve cybersecurity
    (B) combat problems after they have occurred
    (C) have made strides against hackers in the ultimate battle of cybersecurity
    (D) invest too much in cybersecurity
    (E) take unnecessarily large investment risks and disregard the importance of cybersecurity

34. Which of the following is most likely an example of intellectual property as mentioned in the second paragraph?

   (A) works of art posted to social media

   (B) personal information, such as Social Security numbers or banking information

   (C) computers and related technological devices

   (D) customer and client lists and related contact information

   (E) an outline of a streamlined manufacturing process

35. It can be inferred from the passage that the author considers which of the following to be true regarding increased global connectivity?

   (A) Increased global communications mean more risk for security breaches.

   (B) Global connectivity is a primary reason for the increasingly delayed progress of modern technology.

   (C) Global connections are largely detrimental to humankind.

   (D) The commercial rewards associated with global connectivity are minimal.

   (E) The more tightly companies are connected, the more power they have against hackers.

36. I bought a pair of glasses from an optometrist. One of the lenses regularly pops out of the frame. Therefore, this optometrist doesn't know how to make a good pair of glasses.

The reasoning in the argument is most vulnerable to criticism on the grounds that the argument

   (A) does not allow the optometrist a chance to defend himself

   (B) does not consider the possibility that other optometrists also make defective frames

   (C) criticizes the optometrist's use of a particular technique when making glasses

   (D) jumps to the conclusion that the defect in the glasses must be due to the optometrist's lack of skill

   (E) accuses the optometrist of deliberately sabotaging the glasses

37. A new kind of primate, the fat-tailed lemur, has been discovered in Madagascar. These lemurs hibernate, sleeping in holes in trees for up to seven months out of the year. Winter temperatures in Madagascar rarely drop below 86 degrees, so these lemurs do not hibernate to escape the cold but perhaps to conserve energy during the dry season, when food is scarce. This is the first time anyone has found an animal that hibernates during hot weather, disproving the common belief that only animals in cold climates hibernate.

Which one of the following most accurately describes the role played in the argument by the assertion that this is the first time anyone has found an animal that hibernates during hot weather?

   (A) The statement challenges the long-held belief that primates never hibernate.

   (B) The statement accuses scientists who have studied hibernation in the past of wrongfully assuming that hibernation only occurs in cold weather.

   (C) The statement highlights the importance of this discovery because it disproves a long-held theory about hibernation.

   (D) The statement calls into question the assumption that this behavior is true hibernation and suggests that it may be something else.

   (E) The statement sets up a rival theory so that the primatologist can disprove it.

GO ON TO NEXT PAGE ➡

38. When we think about peoples of the past, <u>we intuitively try to imagine what he or she would have looked like in real life and to visualize their physical features</u>, dress, and general appearance.

(A) we intuitively try to imagine what he or she would have looked like in real life and to visualize their physical features

(B) we intuitively try to imagine what they would have looked like in real life and to visualize their physical features

(C) we intuitively try to imagine what he or she would have looked like in real life and visualize his or her physical features

(D) we intuitively try to imagine what they would have looked like in real life and to visualize what their physical features were like

(E) we intuitively try to imagine what they would look like in real life and visualize their physical features

39. Motorcyclists are told to always wear helmets when they ride their motorcycles. But helmets only protect riders when they have wrecks, and wrecks occur only once out of every 1,000 rides. Therefore, a motorcyclist would be perfectly safe if he wore his helmet only once out of every 1,000 rides.

Which one of the following employs a flawed argumentative strategy that is most closely parallel to the flawed argumentative strategy in this statement?

(A) My European client calls once a week, always in the evening, after everyone has left the office. I'll be sure to get his messages if I turn on my telephone's answering machine once a week.

(B) This sunscreen allows me to stay in the sun 15 times longer than I could without sunscreen. If I apply two coats of it, it will allow me to stay in the sun 30 times longer.

(C) The odds are 1,000 to 1 against winning the big jackpot on this slot machine. If I play the slot machine 1,000 times, I'm sure to win the big jackpot.

(D) Seat belts protect passengers in automobile accidents, but accidents only occur in one out of every 2,000 car trips. Because drivers are in the car the most, they should wear their seat belts most often.

(E) Top business schools accept one out of every 20 MBA applicants. Therefore, someone who wants to get into a top business school should apply to 20 of them.

40. Even though Carter had fewer quarters in his piggybank than did his brother Clark, Clark had less money overall.

(A) Even though Carter had fewer quarters in his piggybank than did his brother Clark, Clark had less money overall.

(B) Even though Carter had fewer quarters than his brother, Clark, in his piggybank, Clark had fewer money overall.

(C) Even though Carter had less quarters than his brother, Clark, in his piggybank, Clark had less money overall.

(D) Even though Carter had less quarters in his piggybank than did his brother Clark, Clark had less money overall.

(E) Even though Carter had fewer quarters than his brother, Clark, in his piggybank, Clark had less money overall.

41. Rugby is somewhat like American football in that both involve downs, tackles, and touchdowns, but it also combines elements from other sports, like soccer and hurling.

(A) Rugby is somewhat like American football in that both involve downs, tackles, and touchdowns, but it also combines elements from other sports, like soccer and hurling.

(B) Rugby is somewhat like American football in that all involve downs, tackles, and touchdowns but it also combines elements from other sports, like soccer and hurling.

(C) Rugby is somewhat like American football in that both involve downs, tackles, and touchdowns, but it also combines elements from other sports, such as soccer and hurling.

(D) Rugby is somewhat like American football in that all involve downs, tackles, and touchdowns, but it also combines elements from other sports, such as soccer and hurling.

(E) Rugby is somewhat like American football in that both involves downs, tackles, and touchdowns, but it also combines elements from other sports, such as soccer and hurling.

Chapter 22

Practice Test Answers and Explanations

Y**ou've finished the test, but you're not done yet.** Reading through the following explanations may be the most important part of taking the practice exam. Examine the information for the questions you missed as well as those you answered correctly. You may find tips and techniques you haven't thought of before in one of the answer explanations. If you're short on time or just want to quickly check your answers, head to the end of this chapter for an abbreviated answer key.

Section 1: Analytical Writing Assessment

Scoring the practice analytical writing task is a little different than scoring the other sections. Your job is to honestly analyze the essay you've written and assign yourself a score. You can also ask a friend or composition teacher to look over your essay and give you an opinion. Refer to the scoring considerations in Chapters 7 and 9 for guidance on what readers are looking for. To help you determine your score for this section, we've included a sample essay and an explanation of its strengths and weaknesses. Use these tools to identify your own essay's strengths and weaknesses and improve your essay response before you take the actual test.

Here's a sample response to the essay prompt:

> The author of the prompt is making the argument that American charter schools have failed to "live up to the hype," so to speak, and he or she makes some sound arguments in doing so. The argument is well-organized in that the author first discusses what charter schools are supposed to accomplish (more options as far as school choice and more opportunities for teachers) before discussing some of the ways in which they have failed to accomplish what was intended, such as the fact that many teachers leave within the first year.

> While the argument *is* well-organized, the author falters somewhat in his or her explanation of why charter schools are failing. In addition to the goal of increasing opportunities for teachers, the author notes that charter schools seek to give students and families alternatives to traditional, public schools. While the author provides an explanation for why these schools aren't achieving

their goals as far as teachers (again, teachers are leaving), he or she does not address how they fail in terms of giving students and families more options as far as school choice, and the overall strength of the argument suffers because of this obvious omission.

It might make for a stronger argument if, instead of referencing school choice in the beginning, the author just cut straight to the chase and referenced teachers and accountability. He or she does discuss how charter schools are failing in terms of accountability later in the argument (when he or she notes that many are getting taken over by private companies without local interests), so it might strengthen the argument to only call out points that can be successfully refuted later on.

It also seems a little odd that the entire argument focuses on how charter schools are failing, but yet it fails to address — at all — the academic performance of charter school students. One could argue that academic performance should be the single-biggest indicator of whether a school is succeeding, and the author's failure to even touch upon that diminishes the strength of the points he or she *does* make.

Here is a quick analysis of the sample essay:

The essay author carefully considered the strengths and weaknesses of the arguments made about charter schools before crafting the response. The essay also identifies two clear omissions that probably should have made it into the original argument — the prompt author's failure to address how charter schools are "failing" in how they offer alternative environments to traditional public school settings, and the fact that she never touched upon the academic performance of students in charter schools when arguing against them.

While the argument would benefit from these additions, it might also benefit from more clarity about the areas in which the essay author thought the original argument was strong. While the essay notes that the author of the prompt made "sound arguments" for why charter schools have failed to live up to the hype while using the plural form "arguments," the only sound argument actually referenced is the fact that many teachers leave within the first year. The essay in its entirety may have proved more convincing if its author had called out other sound arguments.

Nonetheless, the author did provide a thoughtful analysis of the argument made in the prompt, and she was largely articulate and grammatically correct in doing so. The essay is also free from spelling errors and flows well. Because the author carefully considered the subject matter and poked some valid holes in the initial argument, and because she wrote a clear, concise response that was virtually free from spelling or grammar issues, it is unlikely this essay would score below a 4. However, the author's failure to clarify her comments about sound arguments might keep it from scoring higher.

Section 2: Integrated Reasoning

Refer to "Section 2: Integrated Reasoning" of Practice Exam 1 online to check your answers for the 12 questions in this section. (*Note:* You can find instructions for accessing the online practice in the Introduction.)

Section 3: Quantitative

1. **E.** **Statements (1) and (2) *together* are *not* sufficient to answer the question asked.**

Look at the information the question provides, and evaluate whether more is needed for a solution.

1. **Find out what to solve for.**

   This question is asking you how many cases of doughnuts a machine will be able to produce in a three-hour period of time. You could find the answer to the question if you knew the number of doughnuts the machine produces per hour and the number of doughnuts in a case. Rewrite the question as an equation where the solution (x) is the number of cases produced in three hours.

   $$x = \left(\frac{\text{doughnuts produced per hour}}{\text{doughnuts per case}} \right) \times 3 \text{ hours}$$

   At this point, you have two unknowns on the right side of your equation. You don't know how many doughnuts the machine can produce in each hour, and you don't know how many doughnuts are needed to fill a case.

2. **Examine Statement (1).**

   Statement (1) tells you that the machine produces 5 doughnuts per minute (which is 300 per hour). This eliminates one of the unknowns in your equation, but still doesn't give you enough information to solve the question. Write down $1 = no$. You can eliminate Choices (A) and (D).

3. **Evaluate Statement (2).**

   Statement (2) says that the company sells cases of doughnuts in two sizes: 80 doughnuts and 240 doughnuts. This statement doesn't provide you with the information needed to solve the problem. Write down $2 = no$ and eliminate Choice (B).

4. **Check out what you've written.**

   You have double *nos,* so look at all of the information provided by both statements.

5. **Evaluate the two statements together.**

   Statement (2) told you that the doughnuts may be packaged in cases of either 80 or 240 doughnuts. While this may seem to be helpful in solving the question, it actually means that you need more information to solve the problem. You would need to know which size of case is being filled. Because this information isn't provided in either statement, you won't be able to solve this question.

2. **D.** *Each* statement *alone* is sufficient to answer the question asked.

Analyze all of the information given in the problem before looking at each statement.

1. **Find out what to solve for.**

   The problem provides you with a figure showing an overlapping rectangle and circle and asks you for the area of the circle. You can convert the question into an equation, solving for the circle's area (A). Using the standard formula, the area is equal to π multiplied by the circle's radius (r) squared. So $A = \pi r^2$.

From the information the question provides, you know that you need to figure out either the value of x or the value of y to solve the problem. Looking first at x, you know one figure is a rectangle, so the height on both sides is the same. This means the height on both sides equals x. From the information provided in the problem, you also know the center of the circle is at the same point as the corner of the rectangle. So, you can solve the problem if you can solve for x. In terms of x, then, the area of the circle is $A = \pi(x)^2$.

From the information in the question, you can also write your equation in terms of y. The question tells you that Point B bisects the length of the rectangle, so $r = \frac{y}{2}$, and therefore $A = \pi\left(\frac{y}{2}\right)^2$.

2. **Examine Statement (1).**

Statement (1) tells you that $y = 6$. You can use this value for y to solve the above equation for the area of the circle, $A = \pi\left(\frac{y}{2}\right)^2$. Statement (1) is sufficient. Write *yes* next to (1) on your noteboard and eliminate Choices (B), (C), and (E).

3. **Evaluate Statement (2).**

Statement (2) tells you that the area of the rectangle is 18. This gives you $x \times y = 18$. You previously determined from the problem statement that the radius of the circle is equal to x, and also equal to half of y. So knowing $r = x$ and $r = \frac{y}{2}$, you can substitute in values for x and y in terms of r: $r \times 2r = 18$, so $2r^2 = 18$, and therefore $r^2 = 9$. This allows you to solve for the area of the circle. Statement (2) is also sufficient. Write *yes* next to (2) and pick Choice (D).

3. **A.** $-\frac{19}{3}$

This question gives you an equation with variables of x and y, and asks you to solve for the value of y. It gives you a value of x, and says that $y \neq -1.5$. Looking at the first part of the expression, you may notice that you are able to factor the numerator. Factor out the common factor of $5x$:

$$\frac{5x(2y+3)}{2y+3} + 3y = 1$$

Since you know that $y \neq -1.5$, you know that the denominator is not equal to 0, so you are able to cancel out the common factor of $(2y+3)$. Now you have $5x + 3y = 1$.

Rearranging the equation to solve for y:

$$y = \frac{1-5x}{3}$$

When you insert 4 for x, you arrive at the conclusion that $y = -\frac{19}{3}$.

4. **D.** $21.60

In this price discount problem, you will need to apply multiple price discounts to the original price of the peaches in order to calculate the final price. The problem tells you that each peach costs $1, so a carton of 30 peaches would therefore cost $30. But the problem says that the price is discounted by 10 percent when the peaches are bought in a carton of 30. If the discount is 10 percent, then the price of the peaches will be $1 - 10\%$, which is 90 percent. So, two cartons of peaches would be 60 peaches, and the price would be $\$60 \times 90\% = \$54$.

The problem tells you that there is an additional discount of 60 percent. To apply the additional discount, simply multiply $54 by 40 percent, and you get $21.60.

5. **D.** *Each* statement *alone* is sufficient to answer the question asked.

Be sure to evaluate each statement individually.

1. **Find out what to solve for.**

   The question is asking for the value of $2x + 7y$. So, it's asking you to solve the equation $z = 2x + 7y$. But, the question already provides you with the value of y. So you just need to figure out the value of x.

2. **Examine Statement (1).**

   Statement (1) tells you that $x + 3y = 2$. Since you already know $y = 4$, you can use this equation to solve for x. Going back to the question, you can plug in your values for x and y and determine the solution. Statement (1) is sufficient. Write *yes* next to (1) on your noteboard. You can eliminate Choices (B), (C), and (E).

3. **Evaluate Statement (2).**

   Statement (2) tells you that $2x + 5y = 0$. Again, since you know the value of $y = 4$ from the question, you can use this equation to solve for x. Then you can insert your values for x and y and come up with the solution. Statement (2) is also sufficient. Write *yes* next to (2), and pick Choice (D).

6. **D. AWL**

This data–interpretation question presents you with a table showing peak prices of various stocks over the course of five years. The question is asking you to find which stock had the greatest increase in peak price from Year 1 to Year 3. Looking at the peak prices for OMK, you can see that they were $5.12 in Year 1 and $9.12 in Year 3. This is an increase of $4. Use estimation to evaluate the rest of the table.

Continuing down the table, you can see that the peak price of RRW increased by about $45.00 - \$30.00 = \$15.00$, and the peak price of LKP increased by about $30.00 - \$15.00 = \$15.00$.

If you don't find an answer with a greater increase, you'll have to evaluate these two options more carefully later. But there are still two more stocks to evaluate. Looking at AWL, its peak price increased by about $155.00 - \$130.00 = \$25.00$. AWL is now the highest increase in peak price you've seen and is definitely higher than TCK, which increased from around $62.00 to $74.00, an increase of only about $12.00.

Of all the stocks, the peak price of AWL, Choice (D), increased the most from Year 1 to Year 3.

7. **C.** Both statements *together* are sufficient, but *neither* statement *alone* is sufficient to answer the question asked.

Be sure to separate out the facts of each statements:

1. **Find out what to solve for.**

   The question is asking for the distance that a bullet train will travel to get from Tokyo to Kyoto. This is a rate question. So, to find the distance travelled (d), you will need to multiply the rate of travel (r) by the time spent travelling (t). In other words, you need to solve $d = r \times t$.

2. **Examine Statement (1).**

   Statement (1) provides the time required for the bullet train to get from Tokyo to Kyoto. This gives you $t = 2$ hours. While this gets you one step closer to a solution, you still don't know the rate at which the train travels. Statement (1) isn't sufficient. Write down $1 = $ no. Eliminate Choices (A) and (D).

3. Evaluate Statement (2).

Statement (2) says that the bullet train travels at a speed of 250 kilometers per hour from Tokyo to Kyoto. This gives you the rate of travel of the train. But, as it turns out, knowing the rate of travel alone is not enough to solve for the distance travelled. Statement (2) alone isn't sufficient. Write down 2 = no. Eliminate Choice (B).

4. Check out what you've written.

You have two *nos*. Since each statement alone is insufficient, you need to consider both statements together.

5. Evaluate the two statements together.

Statement (1) gives you the time travelled $t = 2$ hours, and Statement (2) tells you that the rate of travel is $r = 250$ kilometers/hour. Because you have the necessary pieces of the equation, you're able to solve for the distance that the bullet train travels. The two statements together provide you with enough information to solve the question.

8. C. 64

This question concerns exponents. You are given an expression and asked for the value of the expression if $y = 1$. Look for a way to make the bases of the terms the same. Because $16 = 4^2$, you can rewrite the expression as:

$$4^{y+z} \times 4^2 \times 4^{-z}$$

Since exponents with the same base can be added together, you can simplify the expression to:

$$4^{y+z+2-z}$$

The z terms cancel out and you are left with 4^{y+2}. You know that $y = 1$, so the expression becomes 4^3, or 64. The answer is Choice (C).

9. A. $1 + \dfrac{x}{6}$

The first fraction involves addition, so you'll need to find a common denominator. The easiest common denominator to find for 3 and x would be $3x$. So, multiply the first fraction by $\dfrac{3}{3}$ and the second fraction by $\dfrac{x}{x}$ to create the common denominator. Then add:

$$\frac{2}{x} + \frac{1}{3} = \frac{6}{3x} + \frac{x}{3x} = \frac{6+x}{3x}$$

Multiply this new fraction by $\dfrac{x}{2}$:

$$\left(\frac{6+x}{3x}\right)\left(\frac{x}{2}\right) = \frac{6x+x^2}{6x}$$

Simplify:

$$\frac{6x+x^2}{6x} = \frac{6x}{6x} + \frac{x^2}{6x} = 1 + \frac{x}{6}$$

And you're done!

10. C. *Both* statements *together* are sufficient, but *neither* statement *alone* is sufficient to answer the question asked.

Don't get too concerned about performing calculations or attempting to completely solve the problem. Just focus on whether the statements provide enough information to reach a solution.

1. **Find out what to solve for.**

   The question is asking for the original price of a phone charger. The statement tells you that the total discounted price (t) is $630. You don't know enough about the details of the discount yet to start solving the problem, so it's time to look at each statement.

2. **Examine Statement (1).**

   Statement (1) gives you the details of the sale that the store is offering. Since you know that the discount is going to be applied to the total purchase price, you can write an equation to help determine the original price of the phone charger alone. Use d to represent the discount percentage. The discounted price will be the original price multiplied by $(1-d)$.

   The total discounted price (t) is equal to $(1-d)$ multiplied by the sum of the original prices of the smartphone (s) and the phone charger (c). So $t = (1-d)(s+c)$. You know that $t = 630, and you can figure out whether d is 15 percent or 20 percent, but you don't know the original prices for the smartphone or the phone charger. Therefore, you still have two unknowns in your equation: s and c.

   With a single equation and two unknowns, you don't have enough information to solve the problem. Statement (1) is insufficient. Write down $1 = $ no. You can eliminate Choices (A) and (D).

3. **Evaluate Statement (2).**

   Statement (2) tells you that the original price of the smartphone alone was $720. Since this doesn't give you any information about the details of the sale that the store is offering, Statement (2) is not sufficient. Write down $2 = $ no and eliminate Choice (B).

4. **Check out what you've written.**

   You have *nos* for each statement, so now you need to look at both of them together.

5. **Evaluate the two statements together.**

   Using Statement (1), you know that the total purchase must have been at least $500 to end up with a final price of $630, so you know there is a discount of at least 15 percent. To figure out if the customer is receiving a discount of 20 percent, multiply $800 by 0.8, which equals $640. Since the final price is less than $640, you know that the total price was not high enough to get the 20 percent discount. So, the discount was 15 percent, and $d = 0.15$.

   You can substitute in values for t and d:
   $$630 = (1-0.15)(s+c)$$

Statement (2) provided you with the final piece of information that you were missing after evaluating Statement (1). Now that you have this, you can plug in $720 for s in your equation and solve for the original price of the phone charger. The combination of the two statements provides enough information to answer the question.

11. **B.** $(0, -8)$

This is a coordinate geometry question, so you'll need to work with equations of lines and slope to determine where the lines intersect.

While drawing out a sketch of the points and lines will help to visualize the problem, you shouldn't rely on your artistic skills to find the correct answer; some of the points may be close together, and graphing by hand isn't 100 percent accurate.

You know that the first line passes through the points $(-2, 2)$ and $(-1, -3)$. To find the equation of this line, first you'll need to find the slope, m. To find m, figure out rise over run by dividing the difference in y values by the difference in x values:

$$m = \frac{\Delta y}{\Delta x} = \frac{2-(-3)}{-2-(-1)} = \frac{5}{-1} = -5$$

Once you know the slope is -5, you can substitute the value for m in the equation of the line: $y = -5x + b$.

You know the point $(-2, 2)$ is on the line, so substitute these coordinates for x and y to find the value for b:

$$y = -5x + b$$
$$2 = (-5)(-2) + b$$
$$2 = 10 + b$$
$$-8 = b$$

Now you know the equation for the first line: $y = -5x - 8$.

The equation for the second line is $y = x - 8$. To find where the two lines intersect, set them equal to each other and solve for x:

$$x - 8 = -5x - 8$$
$$6x = 0$$
$$x = 0$$

When you know that $x = 0$, you can tell the correct answer is Choice (B); it's the only answer with an x value of 0. You don't have to solve for y to solve this problem, but you can if you want by substituting x into either equation:

$$y = 0 - 8$$
$$y = -8$$

12. **B.** $\dfrac{x+1}{4}$

This problem deals you an algebraic expression with two unknowns: x and y. The problem tells you that $y = \frac{x}{2}$, so you can insert that value for y in the equation to get the expression solely in terms of x. Solve by performing division in the first fraction: $\frac{x}{2} \times \frac{1}{2x} = \frac{x}{4x}$, which simplifies to $\frac{1}{4}$ when you cancel x from the numerator and denominator.

Then add to find the correct answer:

$$\frac{1}{4} + \frac{x}{4} = \frac{1+x}{4}.$$

13. **D.** *Each* statement *alone* is sufficient to answer the question asked.

For this problem, drawing a Venn diagram may help you visualize the relationships in the data.

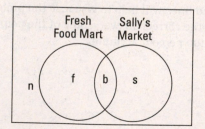

1. **Find out what to solve for.**

   The question is asking you to determine how many families have shopped at both Fresh Food Mart as well as Sally's Market.

   You are determining the number of families that have shopped at both stores (b). Based on the diagram, you know that $n + f + b + s = 20$. The problem statement tells you that 17 of the families have shopped at Fresh Food Mart, so $f + b = 17$. It also tells you that 12 of the families have shopped at Sally's Market, so $b + s = 12$. At this point, you have three equations with four unknowns. Statements that supply a value for at least one of the unknowns will allow you to solve for any of the others.

2. **Examine Statement (1).**

   Statement (1) tells you that 15 percent of the families haven't shopped at either store. Therefore, $n = 0.15 \times 20$, so $n = 3$. You can substitute n into your first equation to give you $3 + f + b + s = 20$. You now have three equations with three unknowns, so you can solve for each of the variables.

   You could stop here, but if you want to be completely sure of your answer, you can solve for b: Substituting $f + b = 17$ into your first equation, you get $3 + 17 + s = 20$. This gives you $s = 0$. When you substitute s into your final equation, you get $b + 0 = 12$, therefore $b = 12$. Statement (1) is sufficient. Write 1 = yes on your noteboard. You've eliminated Choices (B), (C), and (E).

3. **Evaluate Statement (2).**

   Statement (2) says that all the families who have shopped at Sally's Market have also shopped at Fresh Food Mart. This tells you that no families have shopped at only Sally's Market, so $s = 0$, and therefore $b = 12$. Statement (2) is also sufficient. Write 2 = yes. Both statements are sufficient.

14. D. 96,800

This is a percent change problem dealing with the number of parts produced in different years. Knowing that Anthony's business made 80,000 parts last year and 88,000 parts this year, you can calculate the percent growth using the percent change formula, which is the difference between the two values divided by the original value:

$$\frac{\text{parts produced this year} - \text{parts produced last year}}{\text{parts produced last year}} = \frac{x}{10}$$

$$\frac{88{,}000 - 80{,}000}{80{,}000} = \frac{x}{100}$$

$$\frac{8{,}000}{80{,}000} = \frac{x}{100}$$

$$\frac{1}{10} = \frac{x}{100}$$

$$10\% = x$$

To maintain 10 percent growth next year, the business will need to produce the same number of parts as last year + 10 percent more, which you can express as 110 percent or 1.1 of 88,000: $88{,}000 \times 1.1 = 96{,}800$, which is Choice (D).

Make sure you use the new year's value when calculating the percentage increase for the upcoming year. Choice (C) reflects an increase of 8,000 parts, but that amount is 10 percent of the parts made last year and only about 9.1 percent of the parts made this year. To maintain 10 percent growth, the number of additional parts made next year must be greater than this year's.

15. A. 3.5π

To find the surface area of a cylinder, you need to add up the areas of each of its components. The area of each circular base is πr^2. Multiply this formula by 2 to account for both circular ends of the cylinder: $2\pi r^2$.

You have the formula for the area of both ends, but you still have to consider the area of the curved side of the cylinder. That dimension is the circumference of the circular base $(2\pi r)$ multiplied by the height (h) of the cylinder: $2\pi rh$.

Find the total surface area by adding the two dimensions: $2\pi r^2 + 2\pi rh$.

Now plug in the values. The diameter of the cylinder is 1, and the radius is half the diameter, or 0.5. The height of the cylinder is 3. Insert 0.5 for r and 3 for h, and find the sum:

$$2\pi rh^2 + 2\pi rh = SA$$
$$2\pi(0.5)^2 + 2\pi(0.5)(3) = SA$$
$$2\pi(0.25) + 2\pi(1.5) = SA$$
$$0.5\pi + 3\pi = SA$$
$$3.5\pi = SA$$

16. A. Statement (1) *alone* **is sufficient, but Statement (2)** *alone* **is** *not* **sufficient to answer the question asked.**

Be careful not to jump ahead, even if you are able to figure out the solution with the first statement.

1. Find out what to solve for.

The question is asking whether $\frac{x}{y} > 1$. Since y is a positive integer, you can multiply both sides of the equation by y. So now you just need to figure out whether $x > y$.

2. Examine Statement (1).

Statement (1) says that $x + 3 = y$, so $x = y - 3$. Clearly, $x < y$. Therefore, x is not greater than y, and the inequality given in the question is false. Statement (1) is sufficient. Write down $1 = $ yes and eliminate Choices (B), (C), and (E).

3. Evaluate Statement (2).

Statement (2) tells you that $\frac{x+y}{y} > 1$.

Multiply both sides of the equation by y to get $x + 5 > y$, which you can also present as $x > y - 5$. While you can come up with some values for x and y that would satisfy both this equation and the equation given in the problem statement, Statement (2) really doesn't give you enough information to determine whether the statement $\frac{x}{y} > 1$ is true or false in every case. Statement (2) is not sufficient. Write down $2 = $ no on your noteboard. The answer must be Choice (A).

17. C. $64.00

This a profit question dealing with two different merchants each selling the same product.

You can eliminate Choice (A) right away. If Patrick makes more profit than Mel, he must be charging more than $60, the price Mel charges for her shirts.

A general equation for the profit of each merchant is that profit (p) is equal to selling price (s) minus cost (c). So, $p = s - c$. You can write a profit equation for each merchant to make solving the question easier. For Mel (M), $p_M = s_M - c_M$. Because Mel is selling her shirts for $60, $s_M = 60$ and $p_M = 60 - c_M$.

For Patrick (P), $p_P = s_P - c_P$. You know that Patrick's profit is $24, so $24 = s_P - c_P$.

If Patrick makes 20 percent more profit than Mel, then $p_p = 120\%\,(p_M)$. Find Mel's profit by substituting \$24 for p_p in the equation:

$$24 = (1.2)\,p_M$$
$$\frac{24}{1.2} = p_M$$
$$20 = p_M$$

Once you know Mel's profit is \$20 per shirt, you can find the cost of her shirt:

$$p_M = 60 - c_m$$
$$20 = 60 - c_m$$
$$-40 = -c_m$$
$$40 = c_m$$

Because you know Patrick and Mel have the same shirt cost, you can now find out how much Patrick sells his shirt for:

$$p_p = s_p - c_p$$
$$24 = s_p - 40$$
$$64 = s_p$$

Patrick sells his shirt for \$64.00, Choice (C).

18. **B.** $\dfrac{30}{49}$

To solve this algebra question with one unknown, begin by dividing both sides by 7:

$$7\left(\frac{x}{2} + \frac{x}{5}\right) = 3$$
$$\frac{x}{2} + \frac{x}{5} = \frac{3}{7}$$

Next, determine a common denominator for the fractions on the left side and find their sum:

$$\frac{x}{2} + \frac{x}{5} = \frac{5x}{10} + \frac{2x}{10} = \frac{7x}{10}$$

Set that sum equal to $\frac{3}{7}$ and solve for x:

$$\frac{7x}{10} = \frac{3}{7}$$
$$49x = 30$$
$$x = \frac{30}{49}$$

19. **B. Statement (2) *alone* is sufficient, but Statement (1) *alone* is *not* sufficient to answer the question asked.**

You may be tempted to start this problem by solving for variables, but wait until you're sure this activity actually helps you answer the question:

1. **Find out what to solve for.**

   The question is asking for the value of a function of x and y. The problem statement tells you that y is 1, so you just need the value of x to determine the value of the function.

2. **Examine Statement (1).**

   Statement (1) gives you the equation $\dfrac{(y+1)^2}{2} = 2$. You already know the value of y, so solving this equation isn't going to get you any closer to the solution. Statement (1) is not sufficient. Write *no* next to (1) on your noteboard and eliminate Choices (A) and (D).

3. Evaluate Statement (2).

Statement (2) tells you that $x + 4y = 5$. Substituting in $y = 1$, you can solve for x and determine that x is also equal to 1. Going back to the function, you can plug in values of 1 for x and y and determine the value of the function. Statement (2) is sufficient. Write *yes* next to (2) and pick Choice (B).

20. E. **Statements (1) and (2) *together* are *not* sufficient to answer the question asked.**

As you answer the questions, rely only on the given information and not assumptions about the properties of geometric figures.

1. Find out what to solve for.

The question is asking for the length of side m of a triangle. The figure alone doesn't really give you many clues about the angles or lengths of any of the sides of the triangle, so there's not much you can figure out up front.

2. Examine Statement (1).

Statement (1) tells you that side p has a length of 4. This alone really isn't useful. Since you don't know the angles, you can't figure anything else out. Although it may be tempting to assume that sides p and n are the same length since they look similar, resist the urge! Statement (1) is not sufficient. Write $1 = $ no on your noteboard and eliminate Choices (A) and (D).

3. Evaluate Statement (2).

Statement (2) tells you that angle A is 90 degrees, meaning that this is a right triangle. This also means that m is the hypotenuse of the triangle and can be solved for using the equation $p^2 = n^2 = m^2$. However, you still don't know what the lengths of sides n and p are, so you can't yet solve the problem. Statement (2) is also not sufficient. Write $2 = $ no. You've eliminated Choice (B).

4. Check out what you've written.

You have two *nos*, so you need to look at the information in both statements together.

5. Evaluate the two statements together.

Using the length of p from Statement (1) and the fact that the triangle is a right triangle from Statement (2), you can write the equation $4_2 + n^2 = m^2$. While each statement provides some information about the properties of the triangle, you are still missing the length of side n, so you can't quite solve for the length of side m. Even with the information from both statements combined, there is not enough to solve the problem.

21. D. $x > \dfrac{29}{17}$

This question presents you with an inequality and asks for the possible values of x to solve the inequality. The fastest way to solve this problem is to get x by itself on one side of the inequality. An easy way of getting rid of the denominators is by multiplying the entire inequality by 6.

$$6\left(\frac{3-5x}{2}\right) + 6(4) < 6\left(\frac{x+2}{3}\right)$$
$$3(3-5x) + 24 < 2(x+2)$$

Then, you can more simply solve the inequality for x:

$$3(3-5x)+24 < 2(x+2)$$
$$9-15x+24 < 2x+4$$
$$-15x+33 < 2x+4$$
$$-17x < -29$$
$$x > \frac{29}{17}$$

Remember, when dividing an inequality by a negative number, the inequality sign flips from greater than to less than or vice versa.

22. A. Statement (1) *alone* is sufficient, but Statement (2) *alone* is *not* sufficient to answer the question asked.

Rewriting the word problems as equations can help you determine whether you have enough information to solve the problem.

1. **Find out what to solve for.**

   This is a work-rate problem dealing with the rates at which Roland and Felicia can perform testing of circuit boards. The question is asking how many circuit boards Felicia can test in an hour. Let f be the number of minutes it takes for Felicia to test a circuit board alone. To find the number of circuit boards Felicia can test in an hour, you divide 60 minutes by f.

   The problem statement tells you that Roland and Felicia together can test a circuit board in eight minutes. This can be rewritten as an equation, with r being the number of minutes it takes for Roland to test a circuit board on his own: $\frac{1}{f}+\frac{1}{r}=\frac{1}{8}$.

2. **Examine Statement (1).**

   Statement (1) tells you that Felicia can test circuit boards twice as fast as Roland. This means Felicia can test a circuit board in half the time that it takes Roland. From this you can write the equation $f=\frac{r}{2}$. Using this equation in combination with the equation you wrote above, you have two equations with two variables, and can solve for f. This will allow you to find the number of circuit boards Felicia can test in an hour. Statement (1) is sufficient, so write $1 = $ yes on your noteboard. You've eliminated Choices (B), (C), and (E).

3. **Evaluate Statement (2).**

   Statement (2) throws an extra person into the mix, and tells you that with their friend Cory helping them, the three can test a circuit board in seven minutes. From this, you can write the equation $\frac{1}{f}+\frac{1}{r}+\frac{1}{c}=\frac{1}{7}$. Looking at the equation and the one you developed from the problem statement, you can see that you have two equations with three unknowns. You won't be able to solve the question with just this information. Statement (2) on its own is not sufficient, so write $2 = $ no.

23. D. 16

This question deals with the average age of cars in a parking lot. It tells you that the average age of the ten cars is seven years. The equation for averages can help for this problem:

$$\text{Average} = \frac{\text{Sum}}{\text{Quantity}}.$$

You know that the average age is seven years, and the quantity of cars is ten, so the sum of the ages is 70 years:
$$7 = \frac{\text{Sum}}{10}.$$
$$70 = \text{Sum}$$

The problem then tells you that the average age of nine of the cars is six years. Using the same average equation, you can find that the sum of the ages of those cars is 54 years:

$$6 = \frac{\text{Sum}}{9}$$
$$54 = \text{Sum}.$$

The difference in the sums is the age of the remaining car: $70 - 54 = 16$. The age of the tenth car is 16 years.

24. **C. 3**

This is a rate problem dealing with the speed and distance of a runner, Cindy. In rate problems, rate multiplied by time equals distance.

First, Cindy runs for 16 minutes at 7.5 miles per hour. Multiplying the rate by the time will get you the distance traveled. However, you need to convert the units so that you're only dealing with minutes.

$$\frac{7.5 \text{ miles}}{\text{hour}} \times \frac{1 \text{ hour}}{60 \text{ minutes}} \times 16 \text{ minutes} = 2 \text{ miles}$$

So, for the first portion of her run, Cindy traveled a distance of two miles. For the second portion, Cindy runs at six miles per hour for ten minutes.

$$\frac{6 \text{ miles}}{\text{hour}} \times \frac{1 \text{ hour}}{60 \text{ minutes}} \times 10 \text{ minutes} = 1 \text{ mile}$$

Therefore, Cindy ran for two miles at 7.5 miles per hour and then for one mile at 6 miles per hour, which results in a total of three miles.

25. **B. Statement (2) *alone* is sufficient, but Statement (1) *alone* is *not* sufficient to answer the question asked.**

Don't get tripped up dealing with decimals!

1. **Find out what to solve for.**

    The question is asking for the value of a. Since you are given an equation with two variables, a and b, you know you need to find b to solve for a. Rewriting the equation to not use scientific notation may also make it easier to handle: $a = 0.01b + 0.035$.

2. **Examine Statement (1).**

    Statement (1) gives you an additional equation, also with unknown variables of a and b. At first glance, it seems like you should be able to use this equation to solve the problem, since you have two equations and two unknowns. Solving this new equation for b gives you $b = 100a - 3.5$.

    Substituting this expression back into the original equation gives you $a = 0.01(100a - 3.5) + 0.035$. When you simplify, you get $a = a - 0.035 + 0.035$. Trying to solve for a, you realize that the equation given to you in Statement (1) is just the same equation given in the problem statement, and it doesn't help you to find the value of a. Statement (1) is not sufficient, so write $1 = $ no on your noteboard. You can eliminate Choices (A) and (D).

3. **Evaluate Statement (2).**

    Statement (2) also provides you an additional equation with unknown variables a and b. Using the same process as before, you can rearrange the equation in terms of b to get $b = 5.85 - 10a$. Substituting this expression back into the original equation, you get $a = 0.01(5.85 - 10a) + 0.035$. At this point, it's obvious you can solve for a, so Statement (2) is sufficient. Write *yes* next to (2) on your noteboard. The correct answer is Choice (B).

26. **E. Statements (1) and (2) *together* are *not* sufficient to answer the question asked.**

Use only the information the problem gives you.

1. **Find out what to solve for.**

   The question is asking you for the value of the perimeter of a four-sided shape. Since the problem statement doesn't say anything about the lengths of the sides or the angles, don't assume the shape is a square or a rectangle even if it appears so. At this point, you know that you need to add up $t + u + v + w$ to calculate the perimeter.

2. **Examine Statement (1).**

   Statement (1) says that all the angles in the figure are right angles. This tells you that the shape is a rectangle. This doesn't really get you any closer to solving the problem, because you're still stuck at $t + u + v + w =$ perimeter. Statement (1) is not sufficient, so write $1 =$ no on your noteboard. You can eliminate Choices (A) and (D).

3. **Evaluate Statement (2).**

   Statement (2) gives you a value of 2 for t. If you knew that the shape was a square, that would be enough to calculate the perimeter. But the problem statement doesn't tell you that, so Statement (2) is also not sufficient. Write $2 =$ no and eliminate Choice (B).

4. **Check out what you've written.**

   You have two *nos* on your noteboard, so you need to see if you can solve the problem with both statements together.

5. **Evaluate the two statements together.**

   Using both statements together, you know that the shape is a rectangle where one side has a length of 2. Since it's a rectangle, you know that the opposite side has the same value, so v is also 2. However, you don't have enough information to figure out the length of u and w, so you can't solve the problem. The statements together are insufficient.

27. **D. $1,500**

This problem can be translated to math equations to help visualize the information in the problem. The total amount spent is equal to the sum of buying supplies (s) plus hiring labor (l) plus truck rental (t). The equation is $2,000 = s + l + t$.

You know that Jerry spent 10 percent on supplies: $2,000 \times 10\% = 200$.

So, $s = 200$.

You also know that the truck rental cost five times as much as hiring labor: $t = 5l$.

Substitute the values for s and t into your first equation:

$$2,000 = 200 + l + 5l$$
$$1,800 = 6l$$
$$300 = l$$

When you know Jerry spent $300 on hiring labor, you know that he spent five times as much, or $1,500, on his truck rental.

28. **B. 50 percent**

This geometry problem deals with a right triangle. The question asks you to find what x would have to be if the area of the triangle were tripled and if y were doubled. Problems that concern primarily variables may be easier to solve when you give those variables simple values. For example, you could treat the triangle in the figure as a 3:4:5 right triangle. Its base and height would therefore be 3 and 4, so the area would be $\frac{1}{2}(3)(4)$, which is 6.

If you triple the area to 18 and double y to 8, the resulting value for x in the larger triangle would be $4\frac{1}{2}$:

$$\frac{1}{2}(x)(8) = 18$$
$$4x = 18$$
$$x = \frac{18}{4}$$
$$x = 4\frac{1}{2}$$

Because $4\frac{1}{2}$ is 50 percent greater than 3, the answer is Choice (B).

You can also solve by creating equations for the area of each triangle. You can use subscripts of 1 to denote the original triangle and 2 to denote the new, larger triangle:

$$A_1 = \frac{1}{2}x_1y_1$$
$$A_2 = \frac{1}{2}x_2y_2$$

Based on information in the question, you also know that $A_2 = 3A_1$ and $y_2 = 2y_1$.

Plug the value into the area expression for the larger triangle:

$$A_2 = \frac{1}{2}x_2y_2$$
$$3A_1 = \frac{1}{2}x_2(2y_1)$$
$$3\left(\frac{1}{2}x_1y_1\right) = \frac{1}{2}x_2(2y_1)$$
$$\frac{3}{2}x_1y_1 = x_2y_1$$

Simplify the equation by dividing y_1 from both sides of the equation:

$$\frac{3}{2}x_1 = x_2$$
$$1.5x_1 = x_2$$

This tells you that the larger triangle has a side length x that is 1.5 times the length of the original side x. This is an increase of 50 percent.

29. **C.** *Both* statements *together* are sufficient, but *neither* statement *alone* is sufficient to answer the question asked.

Using a chart can help you get the question information organized.

1. **Find out what to solve for.**

   The question provides some information about the types of bikes sold at a bike shop. You can tell that the shop sells mountain bikes and road bikes. The question is asking you what percentage of bikes sold are mountain bikes for kids. Since you don't have any information yet about what percentage of bikes are for kids, you need more information.

2. **Examine Statement (1).**

   Statement (1) tells you that 20 percent of the bikes sold are for kids and 80 percent are for adults. This is a key piece of information missing from the problem statement. With this new data, you can draw a table to organize the information:

	Mountain	Road	Total
Kids			20%
Adults			80%
Total	75%	25%	100%

At this point, still too many different possibilities exist for how the types of bikes could be distributed. You need more information to determine what percent of bikes sold are mountain bikes for kids. Statement (1) is not sufficient, so write $1 = no$ on your noteboard. You can eliminate Choices (A) and (D).

3. **Evaluate Statement (2).**

   Statement (2) tells you that 20 percent of the bikes sold are road bikes for adults. You can create another table, this time filling it in with the information from the question and Statement (2):

	Mountain	Road	Total
Kids		5%	
Adults		20%	
Total	75%	25%	100%

   You can determine that 5 percent of the bikes sold are road bikes for kids because you know that 25 percent of all bikes sold are road bikes and 20 percent are road bikes for adults. But once again, you don't have enough information to solve the problem. Statement (2) is not sufficient. Write $2 = no$ on your noteboard and eliminate Choice (B).

4. **Check out what you've written.**

   You've found that each statement on its own isn't sufficient, so now it's time to evaluate whether they give you enough information combined.

5. **Evaluate the two statements together.**

   You can finally fill in the table using all the information provided in both statements:

	Mountain	Road	Total
Kids	15%	5%	20%
Adults	60%	20%	80%
Total	75%	25%	100%

   Both statements combined give you what you need to determine the percentage of bikes sold that are mountain bikes for kids.

30. **D.** *Each* statement *alone* is sufficient to answer the question asked.

   Don't underestimate simple-looking questions. Be diligent and work through the steps.

   1. **Find out what to solve for.**

      The question is asking for the value of x, and gives you the expression $4x + 3y + z = 8$. At this point, all you can do is rearrange the equation to put x on one side:

      $$4x + 3y + z = 8$$
      $$4x = -3y - z + 8$$
      $$x = \frac{-3y - z + 8}{4}$$

      This information doesn't get you any closer to solving for x.

2. **Examine Statement (1).**

Statement (1) tells you that x, y, and z are all equal. Substitute x for y and z in the expression, and you get $4x + 3x + x = 8$, which you can surely solve for x. Statement (1) is sufficient. Write $1 =$ yes on your noteboard. You can eliminate Choices (B), (C), and (E).

3. **Evaluate Statement (2).**

Statement (2) gives you the equation $z = 4 - 3y$. At first glance, this may not seem too helpful, since you only have two equations and three unknowns. But when you substitute the equation into the original expression in place of z, you get $4x + 3y + 4 - 3y = 8$. The y terms end up cancelling each other, so you're left with $4x + 4 = 8$, which you can also clearly solve for x. Solution (2) is also sufficient.

31. A. Statement (1) *alone* **is sufficient, but Statement (2)** *alone* **is** *not* **sufficient to answer the question asked.**

Converting word problems into equations may help you solve them.

1. **Find out what to solve for.**

This is a mixture problem, so you know you'll need to use a mixture equation. You only know that George has 1,000 gallons of fuel in his supply tank at 11 percent ethanol, but you don't know the percentages of ethanol in the suppliers' fuel. Write the problem in equation form:

$$(\% \text{ ethanol in Supply Tank}) \times (\text{gallons in Supply Tank}) + (\% \text{ ethanol in Brian's})$$
$$\times (\text{gallons of Brian's added}) = (\text{final } \% \text{ ethanol}) \times (\text{final } \# \text{ of gallons})$$

With b designating the percent of ethanol in Brian's Biofuels and g the number of gallons of Brian's Biofuel needed to add, substitute the information you know already into the equation: $(11\%) \times (1,000) + b \times g = (12\%) \times (1,000 + g)$

You need to determine g, so you can see that what you really need is the percent of ethanol in Brian's Biofuels, or b.

2. **Examine Statement (1).**

Statement (1) tells you that Brian's Biofuels provides fuel with 80 percent ethanol. This is the value for b you were previously missing. All you have to do is plug in 80 percent for b in the equation you wrote above, and solve for g. Statement (1) is sufficient. Write $1 =$ yes on your noteboard and eliminate Choices (B), (C), and (E).

3. **Evaluate Statement (2).**

Statement (2) gives you information about the mixture currently in George's supply tank. It has 10 gallons of fuel from Brian's Biofuels and 990 gallons of fuel from Dyon. Writing this as an equation where d is the percent of ethanol in Dyon fuel, you have $11\% \times 1,000 = 10b \times 990d$.

Using this equation along with the one you developed form the problem statement, you have two equations with three unknowns, so you aren't able to reach a solution. Statement (2) is not sufficient. Write $2 =$ no on your noteboard and pick Choice (A).

32. C. $\sqrt{40.5}$

This problem shows you an isosceles right triangle and tells you that the hypotenuse has a length of 9. For a right triangle, apply the Pythagorean theorem: the sum of the legs squared equals the hypotenuse squared.

$$x^2 + x^2 = 9^2$$
$$2x^2 = 9^2$$
$$x^2 = 40.5$$
$$x = \sqrt{40.5}$$

You can also solve this problem by observing the side ratios of isosceles right triangles: $1:1:\sqrt{2}$. Because the hypotenuse is 9, the side length of each leg is $4.5\sqrt{2}$.

$$9 = x\sqrt{2}$$
$$\frac{9}{\sqrt{2}} = x$$
$$\frac{9}{\sqrt{2}} \times \frac{\sqrt{2}}{\sqrt{2}} = x$$
$$\frac{9\sqrt{2}}{2} = x$$
$$4.5\sqrt{2} = x$$

But that answer isn't available. Clearly, though, Choices (A) and (B) are wrong. To convert your answer to one that expresses the entire value as a square root, square 4.5 to get 20.25. Then take 20.25 times the 2 under the root sign to get 40.5. The answer that is the same as $4.5\sqrt{2}$ is Choice (C).

33. **C. 10**

This problem is asking how many of the 60 guests at Taco Fusion restaurant ordered both tacos and sushi for lunch. You may find it helpful to draw a diagram:

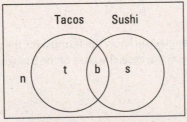

In the diagram, t is the number of guests that ordered only tacos, s is the number that ordered only sushi, b is the number that ordered both, and n is the number that ordered neither.

The problem tells you that there were 60 guests, so $n + t + b + s = 60$.

You know 20 guests ordered sushi, so $b + s = 20$. In terms of b, $s = 20 - b$.

You also know 45 of the guests ordered tacos, so $t + b = 45$. In terms of b, $t = 45 - b$.

Finally, five of the guests ordered neither item, so $n = 5$.

When you substitute these expressions for s, t, and n into your first equation, you get this:

$$5 + (45 - b) + b + (20 - b) = 60$$
$$70 - b = 60$$
$$-b = -10$$
$$b = 10$$

34. **B. Statement (2)** *alone* **is sufficient, but Statement (1)** *alone* **is** *not* **sufficient to answer the question asked.**

Even if a piece of information seems helpful, don't count it as sufficient if it isn't necessary.

1. Find out what to solve for.

The question is asking for the population of Greenvale at the end of this year. The problem statement tells you that the population grows by 10 percent each year, but doesn't give you any idea what the population is. To solve the question, you need to know the population of Greenvale.

2. Examine Statement (1).

Statement (1) tells you that the population of Greenvale grows by 21 percent over a two-year period. While this tidbit may seem useful at first, it's really just a restatement of information you already have. You know that the population grows by 10 percent each year, so this statement just tells you that over a two-year period $(1 + 10\%) \times (1 + 10\%) = 1 + 21\%$. Statement (1) is not sufficient. Write $1 = \text{no}$ on your noteboard and eliminate Choices (A) and (D).

3. Evaluate Statement (2).

Statement (2) says that there were 10,000 people living in Greenvale at the beginning of last year. This data gives you a starting point to calculate the population at the end of this year. If the population grew by 10 percent last year, then the population at the end of last year was $10,000 \times (1 + 10\%) = 11,000$. So the population at the end of this year will be $11,000 \times (1 + 10\%) = 12,100$. Statement (2) is sufficient. Write $2 = \text{yes}$ on your noteboard, and pick Choice (B).

35. A. Statement (1) *alone* is sufficient, but Statement (2) *alone* is *not* sufficient to answer the question asked.

Make sure you know your basic geometric formulas for area.

1. Find out what to solve for.

The question is asking for the area of the triangle. You know the formula for the area of a triangle is one-half the base times the height. In this case, the base of the triangle is x, and the height of the triangle is y, so $A = \dfrac{xy}{2}$.

2. Examine Statement (1).

Statement (1) tells you that $xy = 100$. This is very helpful for finding the area, because you can plug it directly into your area formula. Substituting in 100 for xy, you know you can solve for A: $A = \dfrac{100}{2}$. Statement (1) is sufficient. Write $1 = \text{yes}$ on your noteboard and eliminate Choices (B), (C), and (D).

3. Evaluate Statement (2).

Statement (2) says that $y = 10$. You can substitute this data into your area formula to get $A = \dfrac{10x}{2}$, but you still need to know the value of x to solve the problem, so Statement (2) is insufficient. Write $2 = \text{no}$ on your noteboard, and pick Choice (A).

36. C. $1.60

This question asks you to figure out the cost of production when given a profit percentage.

Be sure to set up your profit equation correctly. You can't just multiply $2.00 by 75 percent to figure out the cost. In this case, the profit percentage is based on the cost, not on the price the company charges.

Write an equation using p as the price the company is selling each gallon of liquid nitrogen for and c as the cost of production of one gallon of liquid nitrogen when it wants a profit to be 25 percent of its cost: $p - c = 0.25c$.

So $p = 1.25c$. Because you know the price is $2.00, you can solve for the cost:

$$2 = 1.25c$$
$$1.6 = c$$

The cost of production is $1.60.

37. **C. Both statements *together* are sufficient, but *neither* statement *alone* is sufficient to answer the question asked.**

Apply the steps:

1. **Find out what to solve for.**

   The question tells you that Jack has three activities that make up his morning routine. Assign a variable to each one to represent the amount of time it takes him to complete that activity. That way, you can rewrite the problem as an equation. The total time taken, 45 minutes, is equal to the time spent taking a shower (s) plus the time spent drinking coffee (c) plus the time spent walking to work (w). So, your equation is $45 = s + c + w$. The question is asking you how long it takes for Jack to drink coffee, so you're solving for c.

2. **Examine Statement (1).**

   Statement (1) says that it takes Jack four times as long to walk to work as it takes him to drink coffee. In equation form, this is $w = 4c$. Substitute this value for w in the equation: $45 = s + c + 4c$. You still have two unknown variables; you would need to know how long it takes Jack to take a shower to solve the question. Statement (1) is not sufficient. Write $1 = $ no on your noteboard and eliminate Choices (A) and (D).

3. **Evaluate Statement (2).**

   Statement (2) tells you that showering and drinking coffee take Jack a total of 25 minutes. You can write this out in equation form: $s + c = 25$. You can then substitute this value into the original equation: $45 = 25 + w$. You know $w = 20$, but you can't solve for c. Statement (2) is also not sufficient. Write $2 = $ no on your noteboard. You've eliminated Choice (B).

4. **Check out what you've written.**

   You have doubles *nos*, so you need to look at both statements together.

5. **Evaluate the two statements together.**

   When you combine the equation from Statement (1), $45 = s + c + 4c$, with the knowledge from the second statement that $s + c = 25$, you know $45 = 25 = 4c$, which clearly allows you to solve for c. The two statements together provide enough information to solve the problem.

Section 4: Verbal

1. **A. The factors that make an area desirable are also those that can pose the most risk.**

   The substantiating details in the paragraph describe situations where those factors that create desirable areas such as the Toboku coast, Florida, Hawaii, and productive farmlands are the same factors that create great destruction, so Choice (A) is the best answer. Choice (B) is too specific. Choice (C) mentions the destructive forces in the paragraph but not the concomitant desirability of the environments they also cause. Choice (D) requires too much speculation. The paragraph states that humans pay a price for living on Earth, but it doesn't state the requirement that they learn to live with the risks. The paragraph is less about humans and more about the kinds of natural risks on Earth. Choice (E) doesn't address all of the risks provided in the paragraph and is therefore too specific to be its main idea.

2. C. Loss of retail clothing sales due to a mall flood

In the final paragraph of the passage, the author discusses what he calls direct and indirect losses. Direct losses, he notes, are those that involve the destruction of physical assets; indirect losses are those that arise as a result of the direct ones. Choices (A), (B), (D) and (E) all involve the actual destruction of physical assets: a library, school building, livestock, and a pavilion, respectively. Choice (C), on the other hand, reports the loss of income due to a direct loss — a mall flood. Thus, only Choice (C) denotes an indirect loss because loss in sales isn't tangible and therefore isn't a physical asset.

3. D. hazards are not under human control, while risks usually are

Skim the answer choices to determine whether any of them can be easily eliminated. Choice (B) isn't a true statement according to the information contained in the passage. The passage notes that ". . . risk is the product of hazard," which is the opposite of stating that hazards result from risks. You can also eliminate Choice (A) because it claims that risks occur naturally while hazards result from human interaction; the passage states that the opposite is true. So, you've narrowed options down to Choices (C), (D), or (E). Choice (C) makes another false statement — nowhere in the passage does the author report that hazards, and not risks, can lead to disasters. Rather, he implies that the two together increase the risk of a disaster. Choice (D) sounds like a serious contender, and the first two lines of the third paragraph back it up. Just to be sure, however, take a look at Choice (E). The words "harder to quantify" may jump out at you because you find them in the final paragraph, but upon more scrutiny, you can determine that the author claims that "economic impacts," not risks, are hard to quantify. Choice (D) is the best answer.

4. A. describing the causes and impacts of natural disasters

Eliminate answers that contain information that appears in just a part of the passage rather than the whole. The author doesn't discuss economic impacts until the final paragraph, so Choice (B) isn't a strong contender for the passage's primary concern. The role of human beings in risk is covered early in the passage, but the passage also discusses that some hazards are simply beyond human control, so Choice (C) isn't the best expression of the primary purpose. Choice (D), too, only tells part of the story; in addition to loss of human life, the passage discusses financial costs. Choice (E) is also inaccurate; the author notes that hazards aren't under human control, but risks, at least to some degree, are. By process of elimination, Choice (A) is the best answer. This general summary statement incorporates information discussed in the entire passage.

5. E. It applies statistical data to emphasize the magnitude of damage created by natural disasters.

Choice (A) is incorrect because the numerical information in the fourth paragraph relates to human lives lost rather than economic impacts. Choice (B) mentions a specific detail in the fourth paragraph, but the detail provides supporting evidence rather than the primary purpose of the paragraph. Choice (C) provides a better description of the function of the third paragraph than the fourth. And you can eliminate Choice (D) because its statement isn't true; the paragraph gives numerical data about one event rather than sensory detail about several. Only Choice (E) offers a plausible explanation for the function of the fourth paragraph in relation to the rest of the passage. The paragraph provides statistics regarding a specific event that provides an example of the colossal destruction a natural disaster can cause.

6. E. Areas of high hazard, such as Japan's Tohoku coast, may have a lower risk of natural disaster costs than areas where hazard incidents are lower.

The third paragraph clarifies that the highest cost risk isn't always associated with the greatest hazard. Places with less hazard risk may experience greater costs because the hazard affects more people or the area is less prepared to withstand damage. Therefore, Choice (E) is correct.

The passage doesn't provide clear data regarding the number of reported and unreported deaths in the tsunami and earthquake disaster, so you can't definitively compare number of deaths in Choice (A). The passage says that the tsunami in 2004 caused many more deaths than average, but it doesn't say the same for the 2010 Haiti disaster, so Choice (B) is wrong. Because you don't have actual data for deaths due to natural disaster in Japan, Hawaii, and Haiti, you also can't pick Choice (C). The passage suggests that both economic costs and death totals are unreported for natural disasters, but it doesn't compare the two, so you can't justify Choice (D).

7. D. must finish constructing, cleaning, and safety-proofing its interior

Two primary problems exist in this sentence. The easiest to spot is likely the use of *it's* (the contraction of *it is*) instead of the possessive form *its*. Eliminate Choices (A) and (C). Then check parallel structure in the underlined list. All projects must share the same grammatical form. Choices (B) and (E) improperly mix the noun *construction* with the gerund forms of *cleaning* and *safety-proofing*, and Choice (E) improperly defines construction as cleaning and safety-proofing the interior. The only answer choice that corrects both issues is Choice (D).

8. B. continent's past begin with Europeans striding ashore, claiming this "newfound land" and its human inhabitants for their respective empires

As you compare answer choices, note that some present the plural form *continents'* and others make it singular. Because it's preceded by the singular *this* instead of the plural *these*, you know there is just one continent and Choices (A) and (C) are out of contention. Another discrepancy is whether the verb should be the plural *begin* or the singular *begins*. The subject is plural — *accounts* — so the answer needs to contain the plural form *begin* to agree with the subject. Choices (D) and (E) are wrong. Yet another issue is whether the last pronoun should be the plural *their* or the singular *its*. The respective empires belong to the Europeans, which is plural, so *their* is proper, verifying that Choice (B) is correct.

9. D. is still used today by many Ethiopians to feed themselves

Because the subject of the sentence (injera) is singular, the proper verb is the singular *is* rather than *are*. Eliminate Choices (A) and (B). Choice (C) introduces an unnecessary pronoun, *it*, that also causes the sentence to be improperly punctuated. The addition of *it* creates another independent clause, and independent clauses linked by a conjunction such as *and* must also be separated by a comma. Between Choice (D) and Choice (E), (D) is the better-constructed option. The adverb *today* describes when the bread is used and therefore should occupy a position close to the verb *used*, as presented in Choice (D). Choice (D) also eliminates the redundant inclusion of a second *use*. You already know that Ethiopians use the bread; you don't need to state the action again. Choice (D) is the properly worded answer.

10. A. The degree of erosion to which a coastline is subject is related to the shape of the sea bottom.

Choice (A) makes sense because the impact of waves is related to the shape of the sea bottom, and the coast's erosion is related to the impact of waves. Choice (B) is wrong because the statements only state the factors (wind velocity and fetch) that influence wave size; there's nothing to suggest that wave size stays close to an average. Choice (C) doesn't work; if fetch is the length of the surface of the water, it shouldn't be related to the shape of the sea bottom. Choice (D) is wrong because the size of waves comes from wind and fetch, not the shape of the bottom. Choice (E) looks wrong, too. Wind velocity creates size of waves, size of waves affects impact, and impact affects erosion, so average velocity of wind playing no role in erosion doesn't make sense. Choice (A) is the best answer.

11. **A. It is a specific example of a general condition described in the course of the argument.**

The argument is that because patients need medical care and hospitals, regardless of what those services cost, hospitals and doctors rather than insurers bear the brunt of cost-containment measures; the MRI statement provides an example. Choice (A) is a good answer; the statement is a specific example of capital demands (MRIs and buildings) of the general condition of fiscal discipline described in the argument. Choice (B) doesn't work because the MRI statement doesn't counter an attack. Choice (C) isn't as good an answer as Choice (A). The author's claim or conclusion is that health insurers are still profiting from healthcare while doctors, hospitals, and patients are being increasingly squeezed, but the MRI statement doesn't indirectly support that claim. Choice (D) doesn't work. Patients' needing treatment isn't a social side effect but a normal event that remains consistent, regardless of changing circumstances. Choice (E) is wrong; the MRI statement doesn't introduce the conclusion about the immunity of health insurers. Choice (A) is correct.

12. **C. among them, the 20 players were only able to raise about 70 percent of the cost**

Use *between* when discussing two entities, and use *among* when referring to groups of more than two. Therefore, you can easily eliminate Choices (A) and (B). Choice (D) has a verb tense problem; the present perfect tense *have raised* suggests that fundraising efforts are ongoing. Choice (E) changes to the passive voice "cost was raised by 20 players" for no apparent reason. Active voice is generally a better construction than passive voice. Choice (C) correctly changes *between* to *among* without creating new errors.

13. **E. Allowing employees to take leave for family matters reduces absenteeism, improves morale, and surprisingly increases productivity because the employees who are granted leave tend to work much harder and more efficiently when they come back to work.**

To weaken the argument, look for an answer showing that allowing family leave doesn't hurt productivity or perhaps even helps it. Choice (A) doesn't affect the argument because standard of living isn't an issue, and it doesn't mention workplace productivity. Choice (B) could arguably weaken the argument because it provides evidence that workers may not abuse the privilege of leave — fathers aren't taking family leave at all, which weakens the conclusion that workers would work less if they had leave. On the other hand, if taking paternity leave angers co-workers, that strengthens the conclusion that family leave hurts workplace morale, so this isn't the best answer. Choice (C) strengthens the argument by showing that FMLA leave costs the employer money. Choice (D) also strengthens the argument by illustrating the destruction caused by one employee leaving for a while. Choice (E) weakens the argument. If employers are worried about productivity and morale, this choice says that allowing leave actually increases productivity and morale. Choice (E) is the right answer.

14. **D. were on board with the new uniforms for the girls' basketball team, but the team had made its choice**

First, eliminate Choices (A) and (B) because they pair the singular verb *was* with the plural subject *all*. Then eliminate Choice (C) because it uses the plural pronoun *their* to refer to the singular noun *team*. Between Choices (D) and (E), (D) is the better option. Choice (E) contains the present perfect tense "has made," but the events take place in the past as indicated by the initial past-tense verb. Choice (D) is the winner.

15. **B. forcing many families to make the unfortunate choice between having a roof over their heads and receiving healthcare**

The proper conjunction is *and* for linking two elements one is choosing between. So Choices (A) and (C) are wrong because they include the conjunction *or*. Making a choice between one element *or* the other is incorrect. Choice (D) replaces "to make" with "with making," but the proper preposition to pair with *force* is *to*; one is forced *to* take action rather than forced *with* taking action. Choice (E) incorrectly swaps *between* for *among*, which doesn't work for a two-item choice.

16. **A. Operating systems with generous amounts of memory are less susceptible to crashing, even when applications are poorly written.**

Okay, you want to find the four answers indicating that operating systems are responsible for the smooth functioning of applications and are able to somehow manage their memory problems. The best way to do this is by process of elimination. If you can find four answers that show the operating system handling applications' memory issues, then the answer that's left over should be correct. Choice (B) helps the conclusion because it shows that operating systems are responsible for handling the memory used by individual applications. Choice (C) helps because it shows that operating systems can spot overuse of memory and stop it. Choice (D) helps because it tells you that programmers should know how to program an operating system that can prevent memory errors, which means all operating systems should be able to do this. Choice (E) helps the conclusion because it describes what an efficient operating system should be able to do. Choice (A) is the only answer that doesn't put responsibility for memory management on the operating system; adding memory to the computer evidently can let the operating system off the hook. Choice (A) is the right answer.

17. **E. If people see online images of items in the museum's collection, they will no longer be interested in seeing the collection with their own eyes.**

The argument seems to assume that if people see the images online, they won't have any interest in visiting in person. Choice (A) isn't the point because the author of the argument isn't worried about damaging the images. Choice (B) doesn't work because the author doesn't mention a concern for decreased revenue. Choice (C) likely isn't the author's concern. He isn't specifically worried about the extent of online distribution but rather its effect. Check the remaining answers to see whether you have a better option. Choice (D) isn't his concern, either, because he doesn't mention quality issues. Choice (E) is the best answer. The author is worried that online publication of the images will remove the incentive to visit the actual museum in person.

18. **C. the number of residents has increased so considerably**

Eliminate Choices (B) and (D) because they pluralize *numbers*. There is a number of residents rather than numbers of them. Choice (A) has the singular form *number*, but incorrectly pairs it with the plural verb *have*. That leaves you with Choices (C) and (E), and Choice (E) unnecessarily adds *been* to the verb and creates an awkward construction by moving *so* after *considerably*. Choice (C) is the best answer.

19. **D. Risks are affected by human actions that increase or decrease vulnerability, such as where people live and how they build.**

This sentence requires you to choose between *affect* and *effect*. The sentence uses the word as a verb, so you need to pick an option with *affect* rather than *effect*. Choices (A) and (C) can't be right. You can also eliminate Choice (B) because it uses *like* to mean "for example." The better option is "such as," which leaves you with Choices (D) and (E). Choice (E) switches *that* to *which*, but *which* introduces nonessential clauses and therefore should be preceded by a comma. The descriptive clause is essential, so *that* is the proper pronoun and Choice (D) is the answer.

20. **B. executive functioning**

Answering this question is pretty cut and dried. The second paragraph indicates that learning how to resist distraction is part of what it takes for a child to recognize and work toward a goal, which is defined as — you guessed it — executive functioning. Choices (A), (C), (D), and (E) are all touched upon to some extent in the passage, but the definitive answer is Choice (B).

21. **A. emphasize that school readiness regards the process as much as the results**

The author's key point is that school readiness is about assessing a child's ability to learn rather than relying on test results and the like to determine knowledge. When they're in a K–12 school setting, kids have to demonstrate "school readiness" through the results of academic testing and grades. Choice (A) expresses this point best. Choice (B) is wrong because although the author notes the difference between the guiding principles of school readiness and those used by K–12 school systems, nothing in the passage suggests that she considers those of the latter "failings." Choice (C) essentially makes the same argument as Choice (B), so you can knock that option from contention, too. Eliminate Choice (D); no evidence exists that this passage is about the author's opinion. Choice (E) is out, too. Although the author deals with cognition in the second paragraph, this factor isn't the primary reason for making the more general distinction between school readiness and K–12 guidelines. Stick with Choice (A).

22. **D. paying attention to the teacher**

In the second paragraph, the author mentions a growing emphasis on executive functioning skills in the concept of school readiness. She then defines executive functions as those pertaining to working memory, attention control, attention shifting, and response inhibition. She gives the example of paying attention to the teacher as an indication of ability to resist distractions. Because paying attention to the teacher is an indication of executive functioning, this skill has likely been one of those on which there has been a "growing emphasis," and Choice (D) is best.

Choice (A) is easy to eliminate; performance on achievement tests is associated with the K–12 system. The other answers relate to school readiness factors mentioned in the last paragraph and aren't included as part of executive functioning. Choice (B) is associated with language skills, Choice (C) is defined as a socioemotional skill, and Choice (E) is part of the physical health domain.

23. **E. socioemotional skills**

In the final paragraph of the passage, the author mentions cooperation with teachers and peers and developing social relationships as examples of socioemotional skills, which is Choice (E). Motor skills pertain to the physical health domain. As for Choices (B) and (C), the author places them into the language skills category. Strong executive functioning skills are discussed in detail in the second paragraph, where the author notes that these skills help kids work toward achieving specific goals. Choice (E) is the best bet.

24. **A. Spousal and marital difficulties were formerly responsible for many premature returns from foreign assignments.**

If helping spouses has improved expatriate retention by such a huge amount, then unhappy spouses must have previously been responsible for lots of premature returns. Choice (A) looks like a good answer. If unhappy spouses contributed to employees' leaving international assignments, helping spouses adjust would improve the situation. Choice (B) is wrong. If spouses are already thrilled with the international experience, their dissatisfaction is unlikely to contribute to employees' leaving their overseas posts. Choice (C) would support the argument, but it's too specific to be a necessary assumption on which the conclusion depends (there could well be other reasons why spouses are dissatisfied). Choice (D) doesn't explain why helping spouses has improved retention. Choice (E) provides an example of what companies are doing to help spouses but isn't the assumption that links the argument's premises to the conclusion. Choice (A) is the best answer.

25. **E. after another, nor does it make its predecessor obsolete**

The conjunction *nor* should be preceded by a comma when it joins two independent clauses, so Choices (A) and (C) improperly punctuate independent clauses joined by a conjunction. Choice (B) doesn't help; it changes the last part of the sentence to an independent clause and therefore creates a comma splice. It also uses *neither* incorrectly. The conjunction *neither* has to be followed by its partner *nor.* Choice (D) creates the same conjunction error, and it also has a punctuation problem. Joining independent clauses in the same sentence with no punctuation creates a fused sentence. Choice (E) is the only answer that uses conjunctions properly.

26. **A. resenting all their advances, refusing to let them lay hands on him, menacing them with bared fangs and bristling hair**

Check the answers for parallel structure. The list of the dog's unsociable traits is presented in *–ing* form, so eliminate Choices (C) and (D) because they break the structure with the past-tense form *menaced.* Pay attention as you examine Choice (B); it can't be correct. *Bristling* is used as an adjective to describe the dog's hair rather than a noun to end the list of traits. So the comma before the *and* is incorrect. The options are down to Choices (A) and (E). Choice (E) contains unnecessary words. The use of *their advances* is more succinct than *the advances that they made,* so Choice (A) is a better answer. Don't get caught up with the lack of a comma and conjunction before the last element of the list. The sentence takes a bit of poetic license with standard list form, and no option exists to change the format.

27. **E. The meadow voles that had the prairie vole gene implanted in them were released into and observed in the same habitat in which they had previously lived.**

Look for information that supports the assumption that the meadow voles' change in behavior was caused by the implanted gene. Choice (A) is wrong. The choice doesn't relate the effects of the hormone to the gene that makes meadow voles monogamous. Choice (B) explains what's up with prairie voles but not with meadow voles, and neither's genes are mentioned. Choice (C) explains why meadow voles are typically promiscuous but says nothing about whether a gene plays a part in that. Choice (D) says nothing about whether the transferred gene is the cause of the monogamous behavior. Choice (E) provides the most support for the assertion that the scientists' work with genes was the factor that turned the formerly promiscuous meadow voles into models of monogamy because it rules out a possible other important factor that may have explained the change (different surroundings). Choice (E) is the correct answer.

28. **C. Women who want to have children increasingly seek to delay doing so for many varied reasons.**

The conclusion is that predicting when menopause will occur will make a difference to women planning when to have children, which must mean that not knowing when menopause will occur makes it difficult to plan. Choice (A) is wrong because it doesn't explain why predicting menopause will help anyone. Choice (B) just provides general information about menopause. Choice (C) may be right — it provides a reason that women would benefit from knowing when they will experience menopause (they're delaying longer, so they need to know how long is too long to delay). Choice (D) isn't relevant because the argument is about how accurately predicting the onset of menopause affects childbearing decisions, not how likely a woman is to conceive in the years immediately prior to menopause. Choice (E) is just information about ovaries, not an explanation of how this test will help make family planning decisions. Choice (C) is the best answer.

29. **E. excelled not only academically but also athletically**

To maintain parallel structure, the two elements joined by the conjunction *but* must share the same grammatical form. So *athletically* is a better choice to pair with *academically* than is "in athletics." Eliminate Choices (A) and (D). The conjunction *not only* must be paired with either *but also* or *but*, so Choice (B) is out. Choice (C) contains the awkward phrasing "engaged in excellence," which is less precise than simply *excelled*. Choice (E) is the best answer.

30. **D. Employers assume that high-school graduates generally have a much higher level of mastery of academic subjects than those who earn GEDs.**

The argument suggests that a GED is just as good as a high-school education; look for an answer that contradicts that. Choice (A) doesn't work. You don't want evidence showing the benefits of earning GEDs. Choice (B) doesn't pose a problem. If universities accept GEDs, that's more evidence that they're as good as diplomas. Choice (C) actually strengthens the argument. Choice (D) does weaken it. If a GED might put one at a disadvantage in the job market, that's a reason to stay in school. Choice (E) doesn't strengthen or weaken the argument. Choice (D) is correct.

31. **D. explain how attention to cybersecurity impacts companies' technological innovation**

Perform a quick scan through the answer choices and see if any catch your eye. Of those available, only Choice (D) specifically references the relationship between cyber-attacks and technological innovation, which was a major part of the subject matter. Choices (A), (B), and (E) similarly suggest that the main idea regards the hackers' success, but the passage is less about hackers and more about how companies react to hacking. And Choice (E) even suggests that hacking is heroic. Choice (C) presents the primary purpose of the first paragraph but not the entire passage. Choice (D) is the only option that incorporates ideas that appear throughout the passage.

32. **C. weighing business outcomes and risks**

The third paragraph clearly states that indirect losses and the cost of defending against cyber-threats reduce the benefits of technology investments, so you can eliminate Choices (B) and (D). Likewise, in the second paragraph, you find evidence to support that theft of intellectual property is a risk of increased global connectivity created by technology investment, so Choice (A) is out. The last sentence of the second paragraph also suggests that the way that companies approach cyber-threats — reacting to them only when they occur — is costly and will likely result in more cyber-attacks. Therefore, Choice (E) likely decreases the benefit of investing in technology. The passage doesn't indicate that the mere act of weighing risk and reward in itself incurs cost, so Choice (C) is the answer that has the least chance of decreasing the potential gains of investing in technology.

33. **B. combat problems after they have occurred**

When the author references companies' "siloed and reactive approach" to cybersecurity, he does so after his discussion about how investing in technology comes with inherent cybersecurity risks. The implication is that companies take on these risks without a clear plan for protecting against them, and therefore, the hackers seem to be winning the battle against business security systems. Choice (A) incorrectly asserts that companies are performing their due diligence when it comes to trying to prevent cybersecurity, so you can likely count this one out. Choice (C) mistakenly gives the credit to companies, so you can eliminate that one for the same reason you knocked out Choice (A). The passage doesn't quantify what constitutes "too much" investment, and regardless of whether Choice (D) is true, the passage infers that this "siloed and reactive approach" is not so much about spending money but about waiting for issues to develop rather than attempting to prepare for them. Finally,

Choice (E) suggests that companies are moving full speed ahead with unnecessary techno-logical innovations and advancements, which is contradictory to the information in the rest of the passage that suggests companies are becoming slower to innovate because of cyberse-curity concerns. Choice (B) correctly indicates that companies' reactive approach waits for problems to happen before considering the potential risks of technological investment. It's the best answer.

34. **E. an outline of a streamlined manufacturing process**

The second paragraph specifically links intellectual property to a new product life-cycle management system. The answer that relates most directly to proprietary product informa-tion is Choice (E), information regarding a proprietary product producing process. Choice (A) describes intellectual property but not that which would likely be leaked in a new product life-cycle management system. The other choices aren't examples of intellectual property.

35. **A. Increased global communications mean more risk for security breaches.**

The passage reveals that increased global connectivity created rewards as well as risks; Choice (C) overstates its risks and Choice (D) understates the rewards, so eliminate Choices (C) and (D). Choice (B) is incorrect. According to the passage, global connectivity makes companies more vulnerable to hackers, but dealing with the attacks is the primary reason for delayed technological innovation, not general connectivity. The second paragraph links tight connections to greater vulnerability rather than to greater power over hackers, so Choice (E) is wrong. The best answer is Choice (A). The author mentions global connectivity to set up the paragraph about the risks associated with increased access.

36. **D. jumps to the conclusion that the defect in the glasses must be due to the optometrist's lack of skill**

The conclusion is that the optometrist is incompetent; the evidence is that one lens pops out regularly. But there's no evidence that that's because of the optometrist's lack of skill. Choice (A) is wrong. Although giving the optometrist a chance to defend himself would be nice, it's not a fault of the argument that the speaker doesn't provide one. Choice (B) is wrong because other potentially unskilled optometrists have no bearing on the skills of the one in question here. Choice (C) doesn't work. The author doesn't mention any particular techniques. Choice (D) may be the answer. The author does jump to a conclusion here with-out making a connection between the glasses and the optometrist's skill. Choice (E) is wrong because the author doesn't suggest that sabotage played a role in the bad glasses. Choice (D) is the best answer.

37. **C. The statement highlights the importance of this discovery because it disproves a long-held theory about hibernation.**

This discovery of an animal that hibernates in hot weather may be groundbreaking, espe-cially if previous scientific wisdom held that hibernation only happens in cold weather. Choice (A) is wrong because the belief being challenged isn't that primates never hibernate but that animals never hibernate in the heat. Choice (B) isn't right because the assertion isn't an accusation of any kind. Choice (C) makes the most sense because it's an important discovery. Choice (D) is wrong. The argument never disputes the conclusion that the behav-ior is in fact hibernation. Choice (E) doesn't work because the argument doesn't set up a rival theory in a deliberate ploy to attack it. Choice (C) is right.

38. **B. we intuitively try to imagine what they would have looked like in real life and to visualize their physical features**

The easiest issue to spot is the improper use of "he or she" to refer to the plural noun *peoples*. The proper plural pronoun is *they*, so Choices (A) and (C) are out. Choice (D) corrects the pronoun problem, but it replaces "their physical features" with the wordy "what their physical features were like," a phrasing that is not only awkward but also constructed differently from the rest of the nouns in the series. Choice (E) improperly changes the verb from the conditional perfect tense "would have looked" to the conditional present tense "would look," a construction that projects the appearance of past peoples in the yet-to-be-realized future rather than from a place in the past. Choice (B) applies the proper pronoun without creating additional errors, so it's the best answer.

39. **A. My European client calls once a week, always in the evening, after everyone has left the office. I'll be sure to get his messages if I turn on my telephone's answering machine once a week.**

The flaw in the argument is the mistaken belief that the odds of an event occurring can tell you how often you need to do a certain act. Odds of 1 in 1,000 don't mean that every 1,000th trip will realize a certain event. It means that an accident could happen in any trip out of 1,000, and you can't predict which one. The flawed reasoning in Choice (A) is similar; turning on the answering machine on just one particular day won't necessarily catch a weekly phone call because the call could come on any day of the week. Choice (B) is wrong. The conclusion is mistaken but in a different way from the original argument. It's about proportionality, not probability. Choice (C) isn't the same as the original argument because you're not trying to guess which one of the 1,000 games will result in the jackpot; instead you're covering them all. That's closer to wearing the helmet for all 1,000 rides on the assumption that one of them will involve a wreck. Choice (D) is totally wrong because the second sentence is nothing like the original argument's conclusion; it doesn't state how many times people in cars should wear seat belts based on seat-belt statistics. Choice (E) is flawed but not in the same way as the original argument. The flaw would be more similar to the original argument if the MBA student applied to only one of 20 business schools because the odds are 1 in 20 of being chosen. Choice (A) is the closest and is correct.

40. **A. Even though Carter had fewer quarters in his piggybank than did his brother Clark, Clark had less money overall.**

This question requires you to access your knowledge of the correct usage of *fewer* and *less*. Use *fewer* when referring to plural entities, such as M&Ms, students, sunflowers, and quarters. Use *less* to reference singular entities, such as water, damage, appreciation, and money. So the proper construction in this sentence is "fewer quarters" and "less money"; eliminate Choices (B), (C), and (D). The language in Choice (E) is potentially confusing. The descriptive phrase "in his piggybank" seems to refer to Clark rather than the quarters. Choice (A) presents clearer construction.

41. **C. Rugby is somewhat like American football in that both involve downs, tackles, and touchdowns, but it also combines elements from other sports, such as soccer and hurling.**

Because the sentence makes a comparison between only two sports, *both* is proper and *all* is improper. Eliminate Choices (B) and (D). Choice (E) contains a subject/verb agreement problem: the plural noun *both* shouldn't be paired with the singular verb *involves*. The difference between Choices (A) and (C) is the use of "like" or "such as." Generally, you use *like* to compare nouns rather than to introduce examples. So the comma before *like* in Choice (A) is a big clue that it's used incorrectly. The comma sets up examples. Therefore, Choice (C) is a better option than Choice (A).

Answers at a Glance

Section 3: Quantitative

1.	E	11.	B	21.	D	31.	A
2.	D	12.	B	22.	A	32.	C
3.	A	13.	D	23.	D	33.	C
4.	D	14.	D	24.	C	34.	B
5.	D	15.	A	25.	B	35.	A
6.	D	16.	A	26.	E	36.	C
7.	C	17.	C	27.	D	37.	C
8.	C	18.	B	28.	B		
9.	A	19.	B	29.	C		
10.	C	20.	E	30.	D		

Section 4: Verbal

1.	A	12.	C	23.	E	34.	E
2.	C	13.	E	24.	A	35.	A
3.	D	14.	D	25.	E	36.	D
4.	A	15.	B	26.	A	37.	C
5.	E	16.	A	27.	E	38.	B
6.	E	17.	E	28.	C	39.	A
7.	D	18.	C	29.	E	40.	A
8.	B	19.	D	30.	D	41.	C
9.	D	20.	B	31.	D		
10.	A	21.	A	32.	C		
11.	A	22.	D	33.	B		

7

The Part of Tens

Discover ten question types that are easiest to master.

Find out ten errors to avoid in your analytical writing essay (and to look for in the sentence-correction questions).

Go beyond just mastering the GMAT and discover ten things you can do to increase your chances of getting accepted to an MBA program.

» Revealing the kinds of questions
you've got a good chance to get
right

» Taking advantage of the easier
questions

IN THIS CHAPTER

Chapter 23

Ten Question Types You've Got a Good Shot At

With all that math, grammar, and logical reasoning, you can develop a headache just thinking about the GMAT. And knowing that you have only a half hour to write an essay doesn't help! Why can't the GMAT cut you some slack? Well, it does . . . sort of. You see, certain GMAT questions may be a little easier to answer than others. In this chapter, we lay out ten types of questions you have a greater chance of answering correctly with greater consistency so you can buy yourself a little time to use on the tougher questions in each section.

Main-Theme Reading Questions

In general, reading-comprehension questions are a little easier than critical-reasoning questions. For reading-comprehension questions, the answers are right there on the screen; you just need to find them. One reason main-theme questions in particular are easier is that 90 percent of the passages present you with one. Identifying the main theme should become automatic, so you don't even have to refer to a passage to answer a question. And usually, three of the five answer choices are clearly off topic or too specific, so all you have to do is choose the best answer of the remaining two.

Specific-Information Reading Questions

Specific-information questions appear in every reading-comprehension passage, so you'll get used to them. You have a great shot at these questions because the computer highlights the text that contains the answer. Just read the highlighted part of the passage (and maybe the text around it) to find the correct answer. As long as you stay focused, you should bat a thousand on these beauties!

Sentence Corrections

Although sentence-correction questions may not seem easy at first, they get easier with practice. The GMAT tends to focus on the same sentence errors, so taking practice tests can help you get familiar with the errors you need to know about. Answers frequently contain more than one error, providing you with more than one reason to eliminate an answer. You'll notice the same kinds of errors appearing frequently, so you'll be able to give the right answers frequently, too.

Exception Questions for Reading Passages

Exception questions ask you to choose the answer that *isn't* stated in the passage. Usually, all you have to do is eliminate each answer choice that appears in the text. The choice left standing is the correct answer.

Strengthening or Weakening Critical Arguments

Critical-reasoning questions that ask you what strengthens or weakens the argument tend to rely on cause-and-effect relationships or analogies. If an author reaches a conclusion by cause and effect, you choose an answer that either shows other causes for the effect (to weaken the argument) or that emphasizes that no other causes for the effect exist (to strengthen the argument). To weaken analogy arguments, choose an answer that shows the compared entities are dissimilar. An answer that highlights similarities strengthens the argument.

Data-Sufficiency Math Questions

Data-sufficiency questions usually take less time to answer than problem-solving math questions. You don't have to actually solve the problem to answer the question correctly. Just follow the step-by-step process outlined in Chapter 15 to stay focused.

Math Problem-Solving with Figures

One of the hardest parts of a problem-solving question is getting started. You may have trouble sifting through the information you get from word problems, but a figure presents known information clearly. Examine the information in the figure and solve the problem.

Math Problems Involving Basic Operations

Some problem-solving questions present you with an equation or a simple word problem involving arithmetic, exponents, or other basic operations. You've been applying these basics since childhood, so all you have to do is read carefully!

Substitution Math Problems

Problem-solving questions that ask you to substitute values for symbols can be simple after you understand what you're supposed to do. In most cases, you just need to exchange a value for a symbol in an otherwise simple equation.

Graph- and Table-Analysis Questions

The questions that require you to analyze graphs and tables in the integrated-reasoning section primarily test your ability to read data. Finding the correct answer is rarely based on your ability to read lengthy paragraphs or perform complex calculations. As long as you pay attention to how the chart categorizes the data, you should sail through these questions fairly smoothly. Just don't complicate matters by reading more into these questions than you have to.

Chapter 24

Ten Writing Errors to Avoid

Chapter 10 gives you what you need to know to develop a good writing style for the analytical writing assessment, but becoming a better writer takes practice. Fortunately, you can rapidly improve your writing style (and your analytical writing assessment score) if you avoid the ten common writing mistakes we share in this chapter.

Composing Complicated Sentences

The chances of making multiple grammar and punctuation errors increase with the length and complexity of your sentences. If you need to improve your writing in a hurry, concentrate on simplicity. Make your point, end your sentence, and move on. Remember that the readers have to grade many exams. Don't make your reader work too hard to understand your sentences. You can (and should) use a variety of sentence structures, but keep them simple.

Presenting Your Text in Passive Voice

Active voice is clearer and more powerful than passive voice. Passive voice uses more words than necessary and clouds the main action. You're much more likely to make errors in verb usage with a passive sentence. Remember that the passive voice is really only appropriate when the doer of the action is unknown or unimportant, such as in scientific writing. For business writing and the GMAT, use active voice. (See Chapter 4 for more about active and passive voice.)

Wasting Time with Unfamiliar Words

Trying to impress the essay readers with your advanced vocabulary is tempting. But if you aren't completely familiar with a word's meaning, don't use it on the GMAT. GMAT readers focus more on how you organize and support your thoughts than on the reading level of your essay, and they'll take points off your score if you misuse words. You have only 30 minutes to develop your argument, so don't waste time coming up with five-syllable words unless you just happen to use them in your normal conversation.

Using Unclear (Or Zero) Transitions

Tell your reader where your argument is going by including clear transitions. With just one or two words, you can tell the reader whether the next paragraph continues the current idea, refutes it, or moves in a new direction. Using transition words and phrases can really improve your assessment score.

Going Overboard with Generic Terms

To clarify your points and excite your reader, pack your sentences with lively and unambiguous descriptions rather than fuzzy generalities (like *interesting*, *great*, and *awful*). Your writing makes a greater impact and will receive a higher score when you fortify it with expressive language.

Writing in Informal English

Save slang and creative capitalization and punctuation for the text messages you send to your friends and co-workers. For the GMAT, apply the rules of standard written English you learned in grammar class.

Giving a Laundry List of Examples

Satisfy essay readers with a few clearly developed illustrations to back up your points rather than a list of undeveloped examples. Readers are more concerned with the depth of your supporting evidence than they are with its quantity. In fact, you can earn a 6 with just one example if you develop it well.

Succumbing to Sentence Fragments

Your essay shouldn't read like an outline. Fully develop your thoughts with properly punctuated, complete sentences and well-organized paragraphs.

Announcing a Position without Explanation

The essay prompt requires you to adopt a position. But merely stating your position and jumping into your argument is insufficient. Introduce your essay with a brief analysis of the argument to show the readers you understand what you're writing about.

Putting Aside Proofreading

Leave yourself enough time at the end of the 30 minutes to quickly read through your essay and correct any obvious errors. Set aside about three minutes to proofread your masterpiece and eliminate careless errors. Doing so can raise your score by a complete point.

Chapter **25**

Ten Ways to Increase Your Chances of Getting into Business School

The number of business school applications continues to increase, but quantity doesn't necessarily mean quality. And the quality of your application remains your single best bet for standing out among the crowd. A great application emphasizes your academic preparation, strong work experience, and a clear sense of what you hope to gain from your quest for an MBA. This chapter highlights what you can do to make sure your application process provides what it takes to impress the decision makers.

Accumulate a Little Work Experience

You don't have to get your MBA right after you graduate. In fact, waiting and working for a while may be to your advantage. Many admissions officers like to see at least three years of managerial work experience when you apply for an MBA program so they can be sure you're cut out for a career in business. They also look for signs of competence and career progress, such as promotions, the acquisition of new skills, and increased responsibilities in the workplace.

Ace the Interview

Some programs require an interview; others may recommend them. If a business school states that an interview is optional, grab this opportunity to demonstrate your social skills and highlight your passions. To make a good impression, heed the following advice:

» Dress in business attire.

» Smile, look your interviewer in the eye, and answer questions honestly.

>> Exude confidence without arrogance.

>> Ask questions of the interviewer that demonstrate your knowledge of the program.

>> Follow up with a thank-you note.

Apply Early

Applying early to an MBA program demonstrates strong planning skills and a significant interest in the program. Submitting your application before the rest of the crowd also increases the chances of your application getting the time and attention from admissions officers it rightfully deserves!

Apply While You're Upwardly Mobile

Business schools want go-getters, and what better time to catch someone than on the way up? Show your school of choice that you're a force to be reckoned with by highlighting any recent promotions, achievements, accolades, or anything that helps suggest that it had better snatch you up while you're in your prime before another school beats it to the punch.

Capitalize on What Makes You Unique

Don't waste too much time trying to fit into some imaginary mold of the ideal business student. Business school admissions officers are seeking students with varying life experiences and from a broad variety of backgrounds, so embrace who you are and avoid trying to present a false persona that may ultimately backfire. In fact, your non-traditional profile may make you even more desirable to a program that seeks to diversify its class.

Demonstrate Interest

Business schools want to know that if they accept you, you'll actually attend. Admissions committees equate communication with interest, so the more you reach out to them, the more interested they'll be in you. Contact your admissions representative regularly with pertinent questions. Just make sure you don't become a pest!

Focus on Fit

Just as you want to know what school is the best fit for you, admissions officers seek the students who are the best fit for them. Do your research about what a particular school is known for and what sorts of skills and personality traits it embraces, and tailor your application, essay, and interview accordingly. You can find out a lot about a particular business school's personality by researching its website, searching the Internet for articles about the program and its graduates, and visiting the campus.

Get the Right Recommendations

Business school applicants commonly fixate so much on the essay process that they diminish the importance of securing solid recommendations. Don't undervalue the crucial role of recommendations. Choose supervisors who know you well, both personally and professionally. Admissions officers focus on how well your reference knows your strengths and weaknesses. Find someone who can expound on how well you interact with others and provide evidence of your academic prowess and leadership abilities.

REMEMBER

The person who knows you best is more likely to be your direct supervisor than the company CEO.

Study for the GMAT

Your GMAT score matters. The test was designed to determine how well you'll likely do in an MBA program in comparison to a plethora of other applicants, so scoring sky-high on the GMAT can place you head and shoulders above the rest of the crowd. Use this book's step-by-step instruction for each area of the test to help you prepare, and be sure to take the practice tests to help you identify areas where you could benefit from a bit of a refresher.

Write a Memorable Admissions Essay

When crafting your admissions essay, keep in mind that the admissions committee already knows your facts and figures — what you studied, where you worked, and your scores on the GMAT. The point of the essay is to give application readers a glimpse of the *real* you — what makes you stand out from the crowd, what motivates you, what you have overcome, and what you want to achieve in life. Keep in mind that admissions committees are reading thousands of responses to the same questions, so avoid falling into the trap of writing what you *think* they want to hear and instead shift your focus to self-revelation through vivid details and thoughtful anecdotes.

Index

real numbers, 154, 157–159
reasoning, 81–84
reasoning skills, 11
reciprocal, 166
recommendations, 389
rectangle, 209
rectangular solids, 215–217
registering, 8–9
relative pronouns, 39
relaxation techniques, 26
repeated percent change, 170–171
reporting scores, 13–14
requesting essays be rescored, 126
rereading sentences, 53
restrictive clauses, 42
retaking, 15
rhetorical construction, errors in, 47–48
rhombus, 210
right angle, 200, 201
right rectangular prism, 215–217
right triangles, 202, 205–206
Roman numerals, 23–24
roots, 162–163
run-on sentences, 45–46, 128

S

sample, 243
scalene triangle, 202
scatter plots, 308–310
schedule considerations, 9
scientific notation, 172–173
scores
  analytical writing assessment (AWA), 133–134
  calculating, 13
  canceling, 14–15
  essays in analytical writing assessment, 125–126
  integrated-reasoning (IR) section, 290
  interpreting, 126
  maximizing, 17–27
  reporting, 13–14
  tips for improving for essays, 131–132
sections, completing, 19
segmented bar graphs, 306–307
selectivity, of business schools, 30
semicircle, 212
sentence fragments, 45, 129, 386

sentence-correction section
  about, 37, 104
  answer explanations to practice problems, 56–58
  common errors in, 42–51
  grammar basics, 38–42
  practice problems, 53–55
  question types, 382
  strategy for, 51–53
sentences, 40–42, 53, 130, 385
sentence-structure problems, 129
sets, 235–236
similar, 201
similar triangles, 207–208
simultaneous equations, 189–191
slang expressions, 130
slope, 220–223
slope-intercept form, 223–225
social science passages, 62–63
special programs, of business schools, 30
Special Rule of Addition, 246
Special Rule of Multiplication, 246, 247
specialties, of business schools, 30
specific-information questions, 64–65
specific-information reading questions, 381
speech, parts of, 38–40
speed reading, 25
spell check, 124, 129–130
spelling issues, 129–130
square root, 162, 209
stacking terms, 180
standard deviation, 243–245
standard expressions, 49–51
standard-issue nouns, 129
statistical arguments, 83, 87
statistics
  about, 233
  combinations, 239–241
  groups, 233–235
  mean, 241–243
  median, 241–243
  mode, 241–243
  permutations, 236–239
  range, 243
  sets, 235–236
  standard deviation, 243–245
straight angle, 200

stretching, 26
studying, 389
style, author, 66
subject, 41
subject-verb agreement, 43
subset, 235
substitution, 189–191, 383
subtraction, 155, 156, 160, 167, 177–179
supplementary angle, 201
surface area (SA), 216
symbols, for inequalities, 191
synonym finder, 124

T

table analysis, 288, 291–294, 383
tables, translating information in, 304–305
tangents, 214–215
tense, 46
terms, 176, 179–180
test banks, 3
30:60:90-degree triangle, 206
three-dimensional geometry, 215–217
time management, 12, 19–20, 25, 290–291
tone, author's, 61, 66
transitions, clarity in, 130, 386
transitive verb, 41
trapezoids, 210–211
triangles, 202–208
trinomial, 177
two-part analysis, 288, 294–297

U

union, 235
uniqueness, stressing your, 388

V

vacation, 26
variables, 175–176, 184, 188–189
variation, 243
Venn diagrams, 235–236, 311–313
verb tense, 46
verbal section, 103–119
verbal skills, 11
verbs, 38, 41
vertex, 227

About the Authors

Lisa Zimmer Hatch, M.A. and Scott A. Hatch, J.D. have prepared teens and adults since 1987 to excel on standardized tests, gain admission to colleges of their choice, and secure challenging and lucrative professional careers. For virtually 30 years, they have created and administered award-winning standardized test preparation and professional career courses worldwide for live lecture, online, and other formats through more than 500 universities worldwide.

Scott and Lisa have written the curriculum for all formats, and their books have been translated for international markets. Additionally, they wrote, produced, and appeared in the landmark weekly PBS "Law for Life" series. They continue to develop new courses for a variety of careers and extend their college admissions expertise to assist those seeking advanced degrees in law, business, and other professions. Together they have authored numerous law and standardized test prep texts, including *ACT For Dummies, 1,001 ACT Practice Problems For Dummies, LSAT For Dummies, SAT II U.S. History For Dummies, SAT II Biology For Dummies, SAT II Math For Dummies, Catholic High School Entrance Exams For Dummies,* and *Paralegal Career For Dummies* (Wiley).

Lisa is currently an independent educational consultant and the president of College Primers, where she applies her expertise to guiding high-school and college students through the under-graduate and graduate admissions and financial aid processes and prepares students for entrance exams through individualized coaching and small group courses. She prides herself in maximizing her students' financial aid packages and dedicates herself to helping them gain admission to the universities or programs that best fit their goals, personalities, and financial resources. She graduated with honors in English from the University of Puget Sound and received a master's degree in humanities with a literature emphasis from California State University. She holds a certificate in college counseling from UCLA and is for a member of the Higher Education Consultants Association (HECA) and the Rocky Mountain Association of College Admissions Counselors (RMACAC).

Scott received his undergraduate degree from the University of Colorado and his Juris Doctorate from Southwestern University School of Law. He is listed in *Who's Who in California* and *Who's Who Among Students in American Colleges and Universities* and is one of the Outstanding Young Men of America as determined by the United States Jaycees. He was also a contributing editor to McGraw-Hill's *Judicial Profiler* series and *The Colorado Law Annotated* series published *by Lawyers Cooperative Publishing.* He also served as editor of the *Freedom of Information Committee Newsletter* and functioned as editor of several national award-winning periodicals. His current law books include *A Legal Guide to Probate and Estate Planning* and *A Legal Guide to Family Law* in B & B Legal Publication's Learn the Law series.

In addition to writing law books, periodical articles, television scripts, and college curricula, Scott was editor of his law school's nationally award-winning legal periodical, winner of two first-place awards from the Columbia University School of Journalism, and another first-place award from the American Bar Association. He also contributed to Los Angeles's daily newspaper, *The Metropolitan News,* was an editorial assistant during the formation of the Los Angeles Press Club's Education Foundation, and served on the Faculty of Law at the City University of Los Angeles.

Dedication

We dedicate *GMAT For Dummies* to our children, Alison, Andrew, Zachary, and Zoe and to Dan, Paige, and Ryan Welch, Miarra Jackson, and John Gilchrist. Our family demonstrated patience, understanding, and editorial assistance while we wrote this book, and we're very blessed to have them in our lives.

Authors' Acknowledgments

This book would not be possible without the contributions of Julia Brabant, Hank Zimmer, Jackson Sutherland, Zachary Hatch, and Zoe Hatch, who provided practice test material and helpful input. We also acknowledge the input of thousands of our students who have completed our test preparation courses over the last 30 years. The classroom and online contributions offered by these dedicated and motivated learners have provided us with a significant amount of information about those subject areas that require the greatest amount of preparation for success on the GMAT.

Our project organization and attempts at wit were greatly facilitated by the editing professionals at Wiley. Our thanks go out to Chrissy Guthrie for her patience and guidance throughout the editing process and to copy editor Christy Pingleton. Thanks also to technical editor Bill Kenworthy for his attention to detail and helpful suggestions during the editing process.

Finally, we wish to thank our literary agent, Margo Maley Hutchinson, at Waterside Productions in Cardiff for her support and assistance and for introducing us to the innovative *For Dummies* series.

We thrive on feedback from our students and encourage our readers to provide comments and critiques at info@hatchedu.com.

Publisher's Acknowledgments

Executive Editor: Lindsay Sandman Lefevere

**Editorial Project Manager
and Development Editor:**
Christina N. Guthrie

Copy Editor: Christine Pingleton

Technical Editor: Bill Kenworthy

Production Editor: Antony Sami

Cover Photos: ©phototechno/iStockphoto